History of Economic Th

History of Economic Theory

Second Edition

Harry Landreth
Centre College

David C. Colander
Middlebury College

HOUGHTON MIFFLIN COMPANY   **BOSTON**
Dallas   Geneva, Illinois   Palo Alto   Princeton, New Jersey

Cover credit: © Robert Landau/West Light

Interior photo credits:

p. 36	François Quesnay, Tableau Economique
p. 47	The Scottish National Portrait Gallery
p. 81	Brown Brothers
p. 85	Culver Pictures, Inc.
p. 139	Historical Pictures Service, Chicago
p. 163	Brown Brothers
p. 210	Historical Pictures Service, Chicago
p. 220	Universite de Lausanne, Switzerland
p. 249	Historical Pictures Service, Chicago
p. 250	Historical Pictures Service, Chicago
p. 267	Brown Brothers
p. 278	Historical Pictures Service, Chicago
p. 318	Courtesy of Paul A. Samuelson
p. 341	Courtesy of Harvard University News Office
p. 355	The British Library
p. 373	UPI/Bettmann Newsphotos
p. 393	Brown Brothers
p. 396	Courtesy of Arnold Mitchell
p. 397	State Historical Society of Wisconsin
p. 405	© Jim Kalett

Excerpts from *The General Theory of Employment, Interest, and Money*, by John Maynard Keynes are reprinted by permission of Harcourt Brace Jovanovich, Inc.

Printed in the U.S.A.

Library of Congress Catalog Card Number: 88-81236

ISBN: 0-395-45691-6

ABCDEFGHIJ-WAC-9876543210/898

FOR DONNA & PAT

Contents

CHAPTER 4

CHAPTER 5
J. S. MILL AND THE DECLINE OF CLASSICAL ECONOMICS   127

CHAPTER 6
KARL MARX 162

CHAPTER 7
FROM CLASSICAL TO NEOCLASSICAL ECONOMICS:
THE EMERGENCE OF MARGINAL ANALYSIS 198

Preface

It is a sad fact that history of economic theory is often neglected in the economics curriculum. Like bosons in modern physics, this history provides the connecting threads that hold the other courses together. Without it, economics can, and has, deteriorated into the teaching of techniques, not ideas. This book attempts to reinstill ideas into economics by making the teaching of the history of thought a little bit easier and more relevant to modern economics.

In writing this book we have tried to make it as relevant as possible to individuals interested in current, not past, debates. We allocate much more space to modern economic theory than usual. We not only discuss methodology in an introductory chapter but also integrate it into each subsequent section of the book. We explicitly examine the scope of economics as it is viewed by major economists and schools, and we cover not only pre-1900 heterodox economic ideas but modern non-mainstream theory as well.

We discuss the development of the scope, method, and content of economics from about 1200 to the present, examining each writer or group of writers from several different vantage points. Particular theoretical contributions are treated in some detail so that the internal workings of given theoretical structures may be revealed. We also discuss the broad policy implications of theories and their impact on subsequent developments in theory and policy. Almost no mathematical notation is used and the number of graphs is limited, though, we trust, adequate. A bibliography of suggested readings follows each chapter.

We have written not for the scholar, but for the student. By keeping to the middle of the road we've tried to strike a balance between oversimplification and extreme complexity: to cover important issues in an intellectually satisfying manner while remaining clear and interesting to the undergraduate student. We assume the reader is familiar with introductory micro- and macroeconomics, and preferably intermediate micro- and macroeconomics as well.

The collaboration for this revision started a number of years ago when we began exchanging ideas about economic theory. It became apparent that for a number of reasons our discussions, particularly about modern economic theory, were stimulating and demonstrated gains from exchange for both parties. A friendship developed, and one day, while fishing in the Florida Keys, we decided to work together to revise Harry's history of thought book. While we both worked on all chapters, Harry concentrated on earlier writers and ideas and David on more recent issues.

Ultimately, differences of opinion had to be resolved, but we are happy to say that co-authorship has not damaged our friendship. In regard to editorial voice, we have one. Both of us are opinionated (differently opinionated, we might add), and to have masked our opinions would have been simply to foist these opinions on students unawares. We have always preferred books that drew conclusions — even if we did not fully agree with the conclusions — to those that did not. History of theory books without any assessment of the place and significance of past writers are not history of theory books. We leave it to the reader to assess our assessments; students should expect differences between their teachers' assessments and ours.

A book should have only one voice. Donna Landreth took on our divergent styles and transformed them into one. Her unending work deserves the designation "co-authorship"; only our selfishness prevented that. We are, however, not too selfish to thank her profusely.

David's chapters were written while on sabbatical at Duke University and the discussions there with Bob Coats, Neil de Marchi, Craufurd Goodwin, and Roy Weintraub were valuable in shaping those chapters. As usual he relied heavily on Helen Reiff for editorial and organizational advice. Comments from Bruce Caldwell, University of North Carolina at Greensboro, Arjo Klamer, University of Iowa, Warren Samuels, Michigan State University, and John Weeks, Middlebury College, also played an important role in shaping the book.

The chapters were revised at Middlebury where our students and colleagues helped greatly by providing an intellectually stimulating environment. Ultimately we are responsible for the ideas presented here and we gladly accept that responsibility, absolving all the previously-mentioned people of associated guilt.

H.L.
D.C.

Chapter 1
Introduction

The aim of this work is to chart the development of economics through the ages demonstrating primarily how past *mainstream* thought has contributed to the scope and content of modern economics, but also discussing *deviations* from orthodoxy that have helped to shape contemporary economic thought. This book considers major methodological issues, explains the relationships between the development of a theory and the prevailing economic conditions, and examines the internal working of theories that provide particularly useful insights. It also explains the significance of particular ideas to the development of theory and the broader implications of theory for the formulation of economic and social policy.

Since a central reason to study the history of economic thought is to better understand current economic thinking, significant portions of this text are devoted to current economic ideas. This presentation attempts, moreover, to extract the central ideas of other economics courses you may have taken and put them into perspective, showing how they relate to past economic thinking as well as to some of the most current research. The intent of this work is not to enable you to do the sort of complex analyses you might do in other courses, but rather to help you grasp the underlying principles of those courses. Chapter 1 considers the present state of economics and the economics profession, in order to convey a sense of what economists do and how they do it.

THE HISTORY OF ECONOMICS
AS A PROFESSION

Economics as an intellectual discipline is relatively young. Before 1500, no groups one can identify even in retrospect were concerned exclusively with understanding economies. Between 1500 and 1750, however, the quantity of economic literature increased significantly in Western Europe. The early writers were mostly businessmen who were interested in questions of economic policy and who wrote tracts or pamphlets on particular issues, rather than treatises that attempted to codify economic knowledge. A body of economic knowledge did begin to evolve during the last one hundred years of the period, from 1650 to 1750, when economics as an intellectual discipline emerged. Like most infants, it was at first somewhat ill-proportioned.

Adam Smith, a prodigious scholar trained in moral philosophy, took the rather inchoate economic literature generated between 1650 and 1750 and fashioned it into an intellectual discipline he named "political economy" in his *Wealth of Nations* (1776). For about the next one hundred years, there was no clear-cut profession of economics, no group concerned exclusively with analyzing economic activity. Books such as Smith's, written to codify the existing state of knowledge of political economy, appeared with increasing frequency, but their authors were often businessmen or academics who had developed an interest in economic issues. The period from 1776 to 1876 witnessed an increasing professionalization of the discipline of political economy, as its study moved more and more away from men of affairs and into academia.

By 1900 political economy had a new name, "economics," and was being offered as a course of study in both American and European universities. As economics became professionalized, those claiming to be economists had to receive graduate training, and centers for its study grew up in England as well as in Germany, where many Americans went to study graduate economics. Thereafter many public and private colleges in the United States began to expand their undergraduate offerings in economics and to start graduate programs.

The Great Depression of the 1930s and the increasing involvement of government in economic activity spurred interest in economic education. At the same time, religious persecution by the Nazis and the threatening war in Europe was bringing large numbers of academics from all disciplines to the United States. The center for graduate economic education shifted during this period from Western Europe to the United States, where many of the world's economists are now educated. By the 1930s most economists were employed by academic institutions, where their concerns were with teaching and advancing the understanding of the economy, rather than with practical business-economic affairs.

These historical events, which transferred the concerns of economics from practical policy and business affairs to the analysis of the operation of an economy, have significantly influenced the development of economic theory. The early pre-Smithian political economists, who were businessmen with considerable practical knowledge of the institutions and operation of the economy, came to be replaced by academics, who by nature and training were oriented toward more abstract, theoretical issues.

The Sociology of the Economics Profession

Economics is now a profession, and some understanding of the sociology of that profession may provide insights into the present state and direction of economic ideas. Some estimates indicate that as many as 130,000 individuals are classified as economists today, though the number varies from source to source. This figure is a rough estimate, because unlike such professions as law and medicine, economics requires no specific qualifications. Anyone who chooses is free to say, "I am an economist." Firms and institutions who hire economists, however, virtually always require some formal training, often even graduate degrees. Presently about 60,000 economists have M.A.'s and another 17,500 have doctorates in economics.[1]

About 52 percent of all economists work in business and industry, 20 percent in academia, 15 percent in the federal government, and 8 percent in other forms of government. Of those in business and industry, about 8 percent have Ph.D.'s, as compared to 75 percent in academia. The economics profession is predominantly male, especially at higher educational levels: women comprise 30 percent at the bachelor level, 23 percent at the master's level, and 14 percent of those with doctorates. The average annual salary for all economists in 1982 was

1. The data provided in this section come from various sources. The figures for the number of economists and the educational and employment breakdown are estimates rather than exact figures. The proportions within this data are fairly consistent from one source to another but there are enormous differences in the numbers. For example, estimates of the number of economists range from 88,000 to 160,000 in 1982. The data come from unpublished estimates by the National Science Foundation, *The Guide to Graduate Study in Economics*, the Census Bureau, the American Economic Association, the *U.S. Statistical Abstract*, and *A Century of Doctorates: Data Analysis of Growth and Change* by Lindsey R. Harmon (Washington, D.C.: National Academy of Sciences, 1978). Data about the undergraduate economics major come from John Siegfried and Jennie Raymond, "A Profile of Senior Economics Majors in the U.S.," pp. 19-25 in *American Economic Review*, May 1984.

Information about graduate programs comes from Colander and Klamer, "The Making of an Economist," *Journal of Economic Perspectives*, (Fall 1987), pp. 95-111; and *Guide to Graduate Study in Economics*, 7th ed., Wyn F. Owen and Larry R. Cross, editors (Boulder, Colo.: Economics Institute, 1984).

The data for salary come from the American Association of University Professors and our own estimates. Much of this information has been nicely summarized and discussed by Bob Coats, "Economics in the United States 1920 to 1970" (undated mimeograph).

about $35,000. In 1987 new Ph.D.'s in academia earned about $30,000. Economists, like mathematicians, physicists, and others in the academic world who have significant nonacademic employment opportunities, typically earn slightly higher academic salaries than professors in other social sciences and the humanities.

What economists do depends on where they work. Academic economists teach and carry on "research," which generally means they write articles. To accommodate this growing stream of articles, the number of economic journals has increased from 15 in 1920 to well over 200 in 1980.[2] The primary task of government economists is to provide statistical data, internal memoranda, studies, and reports to assist decision makers. Much of their work involves "fire-fighting," providing quick responses to immediate problems, but they also do more comprehensive studies that can help to determine the direction of government policy.

A small number of economists work for independent institutes, or "think tanks," which are like universities without students. Examples include the Brookings Institution, the Rand Corporation, and the Heritage Foundation. The research at such institutes tends to be more policy-oriented than university research but more academic than government studies. The findings of such institutes are often published as books or pamphlets that can have a significant influence on new policy initiatives in government. Business economists are usually trained in business schools rather than in graduate schools of economics and seldom have advanced degrees in economics. Their responsibilities generally include either writing memos or holding briefings for other officers in the firms that employ them. Forecasting is often their primary responsibility.

The divergent roles economists play are reflected in the low elasticity of supply among areas of employment. There is no significant flow of economists between academia and business; in 1981, for example, only 130 moved from one to the other: a lop-sided 120 of them went from academia to business. The professional association of economists is the American Economic Association (AEA), most of whose approximately 20,000 members have Ph.D.'s. In 1985 its employment service (Job Openings for Economists, or JOE) listed 2,075 openings. Nearly two-thirds were for academic positions, and 80 percent of those openings were at universities and four-year colleges. General economic theory was the area most in demand, followed by international economics, statistics, and industrial organization.

2. The figures come from the AEA *Index of Economic Journals.*

The Professionalization of Economics

Most groups tend to "professionalize" if they can; that is, they establish standards that must be met by all individuals who are to be members. Usually these are one-time standards rather than continued-testing procedures, and individuals who meet the standards are members for life. Such diverse groups as lawyers, doctors, cosmetologists, social workers, and medical technologists favor the imposition of standards on those wishing to enter their professions. They do so for two reasons: to protect the public and to restrict the supply of persons within their profession in order to keep wages up for the group.

This push toward professionalization exists in economics, too, and has become firmly established within academia. In order to secure a permanent position at a four-year college, you must have a Ph.D. or must have finished your course work, if not your dissertation, for that degree. Because of growing professionalization in the field of government economics, employment there often requires an M.A. And though an advanced degree is not presently an established requirement in business, some members of the Society of Business Economists favor requiring a Ph.D. for admission to their field.

Professionalization is significant because it can determine the direction a profession takes. The move toward professionalization has, for example, bisected the natural sciences into the pure, academic sciences and the applied, engineering sciences. Thus one can study chemistry or chemical engineering, each with its own course of study and training program. The choice will depend on what type of knowledge the student hopes to attain — practical, problem-oriented information, or theory that may or may not have useful applications.

Economics is not formally divided into engineering and pure science divisions, but some of the same forces that bifurcated the natural sciences exist in economics. The division in economics between pure science and application is manifested in the growth of business schools and M.B.A. programs independent of schools of economics. But individuals with such "applied" degrees do not consider themselves economists. Economics has, in fact, no engineering branch; economists are the social science equivalent of pure natural scientists and are trained accordingly. They study the principles and forces operating in the economy, not the practical aspects of applying those principles.

This focus on science rather than engineering is evident in the jobs economists have. Whereas the majority of engineers work as engineers, with only a small percentage teaching, most economists teach. The academic emphasis of the economics profession significantly determines the issues economists study and their approaches to them. Most of their ideas are little influenced by, and little influence, the real world economy. They choose to work with particular theoretical models as much because they are easy to teach or write about as because they are insightful. And since teaching sensitivity to economic forces is extraordinarily difficult, many instructors fall back on using formal models with definite right and wrong answers, even though economics itself rarely provides clearly distinguishable right or wrong answers.

Similarly, the research that economists do is often quite removed from the real world. Although most economists are interested in demystifying economic phenomena, often the pressures of keeping their jobs lead them to focus on less lofty goals — such as getting tenure and advancing in the profession. Developing an elegant, complicated model, even though it may have little relevance to reality, is often a good way to achieve those ends.

All this is not to say that formal modeling is not useful. It is, and long before the professionalization of economics there was a movement toward the use of formal modeling to clear up the ambiguities, inconsistencies, and the general mushiness of some nonformal analysis. But modern economics may have to decide whether this trend has gone too far and whether current work is modeling for the sake of modeling rather than for the sake of understanding. Interestingly, the more distinguished members of the profession who have made their reputations by doing formal modeling are the most critical of it. In a survey on the role of mathematics in economics, Grubel and Boland concluded that "distinguished economists...are considerably more negative on the use of mathematics than the rest of the respondents (other economists)."[3] As we consider the development of economic thought we will take up these issues further.

Education in Economics

Since the training of economists is now centered in higher education, an examination of the present educational system as it applies to the study of economics should yield some interesting insights. Most of you are already on your way to being trained as economists. That means you are likely to have a sense of undergraduate education in economics. It consists of three core areas: microeconomics, macroeconomics, and statistics. After studying these core courses, students choose among specialties, such as public finance, international trade, money and banking, corporate finance, industrial organization, or history of thought. In later chapters we will consider the content of the core courses and how they evolved into their present state.

3. Herbert Grubel and Lawrence Boland, "On the Efficient Use of Mathematics in Economics: Some Theory, Facts and Results of an Opinion Survey," *Kyklos*, 1986, p. 439.

Of the 30,000 economics majors receiving bachelor's degrees each year, only a small percentage continue to graduate school. Half of these, moreover, do not proceed directly to graduate economics studies, but work, travel, or study in another graduate field before beginning further studies in economics. The average graduate student in economics tends to be a 26-year-old, nonreligious, middle-class white male. In U.S. graduate schools, American-born economics majors are joined in their studies by foreign students and noneconomics majors. Since most of the students who begin graduate school in economics choose not to complete it, enrollment quickly dwindles. One hundred and fourteen American schools awarded one or more Ph.D.'s in 1982–1983, but only nineteen conferred ten or more; about 30 percent of the total went to foreign students. About 1,800 M.A.'s and 800 Ph.D.'s are awarded each year.

The two years of course work that inaugurate the graduate curriculum differ markedly from undergraduate courses: they are highly technical. Whereas undergraduate schools typically teach neo-Marshallian and neo-Keynesian economics using supply-and-demand geometric tools, graduate schools stress neo-Walrasian economics. These models and tools have greater precision than the simpler, geometric models but far less institutional richness and flexibility, being highly technical and mathematical. Concepts familiar to undergraduates, such as supply and demand or IS-LM, are seldom mentioned, since graduate education provides new tools by which to approach the same problems more precisely.

After two years of graduate study toward the Ph.D., students generally take comprehensive exams, and if they pass they become, informally, "A.B.D.'s" (All But Dissertation done). The third year typically includes some course work but consists primarily of seminars in which students develop ideas that will provide a basis for their dissertations, which they will write during the next two or three years, often while being employed full time.

There is a well-known hierarchy of graduate economics programs, with about twenty schools considered the elite. Conventional wisdom dictates that a student planning an academic career should choose a school from among these "elite" institutions. Although the rankings among these top schools are in dispute, Table 1.1 presents a typical ranking.

Such rankings need to be approached with care, however, because the schools that rank highly in such studies do not necessarily provide the best education for every student. We have already pointed out that academic and nonacademic economists perform very different functions, and it is quite likely that some of the less prestigious graduate schools may excel in preparing a student for a career as a nonacademic economist. Even a student planning to teach economics, however, may be wise to select a lower-ranked school, because the top schools tend to

Table 1.1   University Ranking Controlling for Age and Citation Dispersion

	Number of Citations Controlling for Age and Dispersion*	Rank Controlling Only for Age	Rank Controlling for Dispersion
1. Harvard	500	1	1
2. Princeton	366	2	5
3. Chicago	364	3	2
4. MIT	277	5	3
5. Pennsylvania	271	7	4
6. Stanford	245	4	6
7. Yale	230	6	8
8. Wisconsin-Madison	214	9	7
9. UC-Los Angeles	201	11	10
10. Columbia	180	8	12
11. Berkeley	175	13	9
12. Michigan	168	16	11
13. Northwestern	160	16	11
14. Rochester	131	18	14
15. Washington	110	21	16
16. Maryland	107	12	19
17. Minnesota	103	20	13
18. Virginia	102	30	20
19. New York University	92	15	18
20. Illinois	88	24	21
21. USC	76	14	22
22. VPI	74	17	27
23. Michigan State	68	23	23
24. Cal Tech	68	25	26
25. Duke	66	36	17
26. George Washington	64	26	25
27. Johns Hopkins	60	29	29
28. Washington	60	39	24
29. UC-San Diego	59	27	33
30. Purdue	58	22	38
31. Boston	55	28	32
32. Massachusetts-Amherst	51	19	34
33. Brown	50	37	34
34. Cornell	48	32	28
35. UC-Santa Barbara	44	35	31
36. Arizona	42	33	36
37. Ohio State	37	38	35
38. Texas-Austin	36	34	37
39. Claremont	24	31	39
40. Colorado-Boulder	10	40	40

*Where the number of citations is identical, ranking was by magnitudes after the decimal point.

Source: Paul Davis and Gustav F. Papanek, *American Economic Review*, 74 (March 1984), p. 228. Reprinted by permission of the American Economic Association.

teach students how to do academic research rather than how to teach, even though most of their graduates do teach. Another reason for selecting a lower-ranked school is that the top twenty offer only mainstream graduate programs, and as we will see in Chapter 12, many economists dispute the mainstream view, believing alternative systems provide more insight into real economic problems.

The Spread of Economic Ideas

In 1650 there were no economists, but today they seem to be everywhere — in the newspapers, on television, in government and industry. But the university is the center for much of the research activity that extends beyond the boundaries of economic knowledge. The current state and direction of economic thinking result from the process of advancement of faculty through research. Research is presented to the profession in seminars and working papers until it becomes sufficiently refined to be published, usually as an article in a journal attached to a professional organization or a graduate economics department. Many seminal ideas flow from research done as Ph.D. dissertations, and many refinements and extensions of seminal ideas are brought about by Ph.D. candidates working under giants in the profession.

Once out of graduate school, academic economists experience the market firsthand. "Publish or perish" is the cruel competitive world each potential full professor at a major graduate school must face. Since the top schools turn out many more Ph.D.'s than are required for the staffing of their own departments, the probability is high that a given graduate from these schools will find employment in the lower-ranked schools or in industry or government.

Because graduate school is so important in determining an economist's mindset, and publishing is so important to economists' success, the content of the graduate courses in economics and the decisions of editors of economics journals greatly influence the direction of economic thinking. These graduate program and editorial decisions reflect the collective judgment of prevailing orthodox professional opinion. The continuing appearance of new journals and divergent curricula reflects the lack of complete agreement in the profession on the correctness of prevailing opinion.

An open competition of thinkers and researchers in pursuit of knowledge will hopefully lead to progressive research programs and the rejection of incorrect ideas. But economics is a social science closely linked to ethical issues that have no easy answers. Each economist works within a broader social milieu permeated by normative attitudes that are difficult to expel from research and often difficult even to discern. Because of these difficulties, the choice of an appropriate methodology by economists is crucial to the advancement of economic knowledge. Before we proceed to our examination of the flow of economic ideas over time, it is therefore appropriate that we trace the development of contemporary views on methodology.

SOME METHODOLOGICAL ISSUES

In thinking about what economists do, one is naturally led to ask, what do economists know and how do they know that they know it? Such questions belong broadly to epistemology, the study of human knowledge, and in the philosophy of science they are included in the subject of "methodology." Because certain methodological terms will appear throughout this book and because methodology significantly influences what economists do, we will briefly consider the evolution of methodological thinking and its influence on economic thought.

It is sometimes said that discussions of methodology should be left to the grand old men in the profession who are ready for retirement. Quite the contrary. Before you can begin to study economic issues, you must decide what you will study and what approach you will take — you must make methodological decisions. Once you've embarked on a course of action, you often become too involved in it to change your *modus operandi*. (In economic jargon, your investment in specific human capital ties you in.) Thus methodological questions are more relevant to young than to old economists.

Enlisting young economists into methodological studies cannot, however, be undertaken without certain caveats: forays into the methodological nether world are made at one's own peril. The study of methodology is addictive; it lulls you into thinking about what you are doing rather than doing it. Methodological questions are awash with complications, and the neophyte may miss subtle points that may totally invalidate his or her insights. Nonetheless, musing over these abstract ideas with the understanding that the insights thus gained are not the final word is important. With these warnings and admitting the impossibility of going deeply into methodology, we present in the next few pages a superencapsulated survey of methodological issues that have arisen in the philosophy of science from the ancient Greeks to modern-day thinkers.

The Importance of Empirical Verification

How we go about answering the questions "What do we know?" and "How do we know that what we know is right?" depends on the answer to this question: "Is there an ultimate truth that scientists are in the process of revealing (an absolutist view), or is there no underlying truth (a relativist position)?" Methodologists past and present have failed to reach any consensus on these problems but have generated an enormous amount of material on the subject. Believing that an ultimate truth exists leaves one with the problem of deciding when one has discovered it. The means by which the growing scientific world strove to discover the truth was by trained empirical observation as exemplified in the scientific method. This entailed integrating reason with empirical observation. A subject far too complicated for us to elaborate, verification is discussed in detail in the writings of Kant, Hume, Descartes, and other seventeenth- and eighteenth-century philosophers. We will simply define two terms essential to the discussion, *inductive* and *deductive*. Inductive reasoning is empirical, proceeding from sensory perceptions to general concepts; deductive reasoning (logic) applies certain clear and distinct general ideas to particular instances. Since most philosophers believe that knowledge derives from a mix of these; the debate usually centers on the nature of the *optimal* mix.

The Rise of Logical Positivism

The methodology of science moved into the twentieth century with the development of logical positivism, which provided the scientific method with philosophical fundaments. It established a working methodology expressing the empirical and nonempirical, or rational, aspects discussed above. Logical positivism linked a positivist desire to let the facts speak for themselves with deductive reasoning. It originated with a group known as the Vienna Circle, which attempted to formalize the methods of scientists by describing the methods scientists actually followed.

The logical positivists argued that scientists develop a deductive structure (a logical theory) that leads to empirically testable propositions. A deductive theory is true, however, only after it has been empirically tested and verified. The role of the scientist, they said, is to develop these logical theories and then to test them. Although there was debate among the logical positivists as to what constituted truth, all concurred that it would be discovered by empirical observation.

Logical positivism reigned in the philosophy of science only from the 1920s through the 1930s, but its influence in economics continued much longer. It was logical positivism that led to the distinction between normative and positive economics appearing in most introductory textbooks, which describe economics as a positive science whose goal is to devise theories that can be empirically validated. Normative discussions were purged from economics as unscientific.

From Logical Positivism to Falsificationism

Logical positivism represented a culmination of the belief that the purpose of science is to establish "the truth." The methodology of science has since progressively removed itself from that view. The first departure resulted from a concern about the "verification" aspect of logical positivist theory. This concern is best expressed in the writings of Karl Popper, who argued in the 1930s that empirical tests do not establish the truth of a theory, only its falsity. It is never possible to "verify" a theory, he said, since one cannot perform all possible tests of the theory. For example, assume that a theory predicts that when the money supply increases, prices will increase by an equal percentage. Then assume that one sets up an appropriate experiment and that the predicted result does in fact occur. According to Popper, this indicates only that the theory has not yet been proved false; it may or may not be "true," since it may produce a result in the next experiment that is not consistent with the theory's prediction.

Popper asserts, therefore, that the goal of science should be to develop theories with empirically testable hypotheses and try to falsify them, discarding those that prove false. The progression of science, according to Popper, depends on the continuing falsification of theories. The reigning theory will be the one that explains the widest range of empirical observations and that has not yet been falsified.

From Falsification to Paradigms

It would be nice if methodological problems could be resolved as neatly as Popper's approach suggests, but methodological debates are anything but neat. More recent developments have moved methodology progressively away from such neat distinctions. The modern rejection of Popper's theory is not without grounds: falsificationism has several serious problems. First, empirical predictions of some theories cannot be tested because the technology to test them doesn't exist. What should one do with such theories? Second, it is difficult to determine when a theory has or has not been falsified. For example, if an empirical test does not produce the expected results, the researcher can and often does attribute the failure to shortcomings in the testing procedure or to some exogenous factor. One negative empirical test often will not, therefore, invalidate the theory.

A third problem arises from the mindset of researchers who may fail to test the implications of an established theory, assuming them to be true. Such a mindset can block the path to acceptance of new and possibly more tenable theories.

Partly in response to these problems, Thomas Kuhn, in *The Structure of Scientific Revolutions* (1962), marshaled methodology away from logical positivism by introducing the concept of the "paradigm" into the debate. A paradigm, as Kuhn uses the word, is a given approach and body of knowledge built into researchers' analyses that conforms to the accepted textbook presentation of mainstream scientific thought at any given time. Kuhn argued that most scientific work is "normal science" in which researchers try to solve puzzles posed within the framework of the existing paradigm. This work often leads to the discovery of anomalies the paradigm fails to account for, but the existence of such anomalies is not sufficient to overthrow the reigning paradigm: only an alternative paradigm better able to deal with the anomalies can do so. Once such a superior paradigm develops, a scientific revolution becomes possible. In revolutionary science first the existing paradigm is rejected by part of the scientific community, then the old and the new paradigms begin to compete and communication between researchers in the opposing camps becomes difficult. Ultimately, if the revolution is successful, new questions will be posed within the new framework and a new normal science will develop.

Thus, whereas in Popper's view "truth," or the closest we can get to truth, will win out, in Kuhn's view a superior theory might exist but not be adopted because of the inertia favoring the existing paradigm. Hence the reigning theory is not necessarily the best.

Those who disagreed with mainstream theory quickly adopted Kuhn's analysis, because it suggested that the paradigm they preferred might prove to be superior to — and thus able to supplant — the mainstream view. Kuhn's work suggested, moreover, that changes occur by revolutions, offering hope that change, when it came, would come quickly. Although Kuhn focused on the natural sciences, he significantly influenced the social sciences, such as economics. Methodological discussions throughout the 1970s and 1980s were peppered with the term "paradigm."

From Paradigms to Research Programs

The view that the existing theory might not embody the truth was extended by Imre Lakatos during the late 1960s and 1970s. He tried to grasp and articulate the procedures good scientists were actually following, observing that scientists are engaged in the development of competing research programs, each of which is analyzing and attempting to falsify a set of data but is also unquestionably accepting a set of hard-core logical postulates. Each study derives a set of peripheral implications from the hard core and attempts to falsify these. Falsification of a single peripheral implication will not require the rejection of the theory, but will occasion a reconsideration of the logical sequence and perhaps an *ad hoc* adjustment. Only if "sufficient" peripheral implications are falsified will the hard-core assumptions be reconsidered. Lakatos called research programs "progressive" if the process of falsifying the peripheral implications was proceeding, "degenerative" if it was not. Lakatos's work has two significant features: (1) it recognizes the complexity of the process whereby a theory is falsified; and (2) whereas earlier analyses required that one theory predominate, Lakatos provides for the simultaneous existence of multiple workable theories whose relative merits are not easily discernible.

From Research Programs to Sociological and Rhetorical Approaches to Method

The above developments, while they move progressively away from logical positivism, are in some ways refinements of it that chiefly add a recognition of the limitations of empirical testing. A much more radical departure from previous methodology is Paul Feyerabend's *Against Knowledge: An Outline of an Anarchistic Theory of Knowledge* (1975). Feyerabend argues that the acceptance of any method limits creativity in problem solving and that the best science is therefore to be confined to no method — anything goes. Though his radical argument at first seems crazy, he has provided some new perspectives on knowledge, which throw light on the "rhetorical" and "sociological" approaches that have influenced recent developments in the methodology of economics. Whereas earlier approaches acknowledged the difficulty of discovering truth, they did not question the Platonic vision of truth as absolute. The rhetorical and sociological approaches do just that. And since they refuse to assume the existence of an ultimate inviolable truth, they search out other reasons people believe what they believe.

The rhetorical approach to methodology emphasizes the persuasiveness of language, contending that a theory may be accepted not because it is inherently true but because its advocates succeed in convincing others of its value by their superior rhetoric. The sociological approach examines the social and institutional constraints influencing the acceptability of a theory. Funding, jobs, and control of the journals may determine which theory is accepted as much as the theory's ability to accurately explain phenomena. Those who adhere to the sociological approach contend that most researchers are less interested in whether the theories they advance are correct than in whether they are publishable. What these two theories most notably share is a skepticism about our ability to discover truth, and even whether truth exists at all. According to these approaches, a theory has not necessarily evolved because it is the closest to the truth, but for a variety of other reasons of which truth, if it exists, is only one.

Postrhetorical Methodology

So where does this leave us with respect to methodology? In a somewhat muddled state, but being muddled is not unusual for methodology. Following the progress of epistemology through the past few decades and up to the present, we have seen the answers to questions about how and what we know become progressively vaguer until methodology is all but annihilated: the most persuasive researchers win out regardless of the value of their work. Fortunately, however, we need not accept such a view as total reality. While such extreme viewpoints provide interesting insights, they clearly need to be tempered by common sense. Even admitting the social and rhetorical influences on the direction of science, one need not accept that Feyerabend's "anything goes" attitude necessarily follows. Methodology, moreover, is not going to end here. A postrhetorical methodology will probably combine insights such as Feyerabend's with more workable approaches.

Although researchers may never know for certain whether a given theory is true or false, they must accept the most promising ideas as tentatively true working hypotheses. They may revert to certain elements of logical positivist and falsificationist methodology to do this. They may even accept all the arguments of the rhetorical and sociological schools and still behave essentially as they always had toward the truth or falsity of their research. The difference will be in perspective: postrhetorical economists will be more skeptical of their knowledge, less likely to dismiss an argument as false before they have closely considered it, and more likely to "let a thousand flowers bloom." A postrhetorician will scrutinize the incentives of researchers to study particular theories and view with skepticism the results of studies that coincide with the researcher's own interests or preconceived beliefs. Finally, a postrhetorician will be much more likely to follow Bayesian, rather than classical, statistics than would a logical positivist or falsificationist.

Bayesians believe we can discover higher or lower degrees of truth in statements, but not ultimate truth. The Bayesian influence will engender a reinterpretation of classical statistical tests, rendering them less exact, less persuasive in themselves, and not independently representative of a specific confidence level. In the methodology to come, information about the researcher as well as the research will probably be a necessary component of statistical reporting.

For both the Bayesian and the rhetorician, our understanding ultimately rests on faith. But that being said, it is time to proceed with the search for understanding, and in that search too skeptical a mindset stymies creativity. Thus rhetocial methodology should provide only a metamethodology that, once accepted, little affects the day-to-day work of economists. They do what they do.

Methodological Conclusions

Methodological arguments in economics have generally lagged far behind those in epistemology and the philosophy of science. According to most economics textbooks, the reigning methodology in economics is still logical positivism, which was long ago declared dead in other fields as well as in the methodologically oriented economics journals. But occasionally the economics profession goes through a methodological spasm, looking inward and asking, "Is this what we should be doing?" After asking the question, it never fully answers it but goes on instead as before, though equipped with up-dated methodological views. We hope this brief introduction to methodological thought will help you to develop working judgments of the economic theories to come.

OUR APPROACH TO THE HISTORY OF THOUGHT

Since this book approaches the study of the history of economic thought rather differently from many others, we would like to describe some of its differences. First, it represents a new approach: unlike conventional studies that stressed the events of hundreds of years ago, this book considers what is happening today and its relation to the past. In the older history-of-thought books, three-fourths of the material dealt with pre-1870 events, but nearly half of this text treats issues after that time. Second, this book goes beyond mainstream thinking to emphasize the diversity of thought within the profession. One reason for being familiar with methodological issues, in fact, is that they underlie such diversity. The more important and interesting heterodox economists, past and present, appear in this book along with the major orthodox thinkers. Among the modern heterodox schools included are the post-Keynesians, the institutionalists, the radicals, and the Austrians, each of which shares some history with the mainstream but differs as to which previous economists deserve to be remembered and which forgotten.

Understanding these nonmainstream schools of thought contributes to a better understanding of the mainstream. The heterodox economists often ventured beyond the boundaries of mainstream economic theory into a no man's land of social science that could intermingle such diverse fields as economics, sociology, anthropology, psychology, political science, and history. While the modern mainstream economic theorist has focused on the four problems of allocation, distribution, stability, and growth, the heterodox economists have studied the forces which shape the society and the economy. The orthodox theorists have studied economic behavior in the context of specific social, political, and economic institutions; the heterodox writers have tried to explain the development of these institutions. Often what mainstream economists take as given, heterodox writers try to explain, and vice versa. The history of economic theory is filled with fierce and uncompromising controversy between mainstream and heterodox writers. This controversy has significantly contributed to the content and direction of modern theory. Even when heterodox ideas have not directly influenced orthodox theory, they have sometimes helped to shape its scope, content, and methods.

Presenting the diversity of thought included in this text poses a number of problems. The history of the economic thought that has helped to shape current economics is a multidimensional history composed of many interwoven strands, like the electrical wires in the wiring harness of a car. Separating those strands by source and effect is about as hard as finding an electrical malfunction somewhere in the harness. In order to condense the contributions of like-minded writers, we have grouped them into schools. But doing this does cause problems. We hesitate, for example, to summarize some 250 years of economic theory from 1500 to 1750 under the general term of "mercantilism"; time and space oblige us to do so. We must stress, however, that to truly know the history of economic thought one must read the original texts. We hope merely to whet your appetite for the works of the many creative minds to which this work introduces you.

Where the diversity of a school is too great to allow us to discuss all its members, we have selected one or more members as representative, realizing nevertheless that no single writer's views are likely to correspond exactly to the views imputed to the school. In selecting such representative authors, we emphasize those who most influenced subsequent thought rather than those who originated economic ideas. We do so for two reasons. First, it is very difficult to separate the original contributions of economic writers from those of their predecessors. Second, it often happens that the actual originators of ideas little influence subsequent thinking because their contemporaries ignore or reject their contributions.

Two examples will illustrate this point. Richard Cantillon's (c. 1680–1734) *Essai sur la nature du commerce en general*, written between 1730 and 1734, was not published until 1755. What little influence it had was limited almost exclusively to Western Europe and chiefly to

France, where it circulated before publication. But this book anticipates both Adam Smith's *Wealth of Nations* (1776) and the notion of
an interrelated economy developed in François Quesnay's *Tableau
économique* (1758). Though Quesnay and Smith may well have been
influenced by Cantillon, he was ignored by the majority of his contemporaries. It was not until W. S. Jevons rediscovered Cantillon's work
in 1881 that Cantillon received the recognition he deserved for his
seminal contributions. We have included Smith and Quesnay rather
than Cantillon because their works had a far greater influence on subsequent thought than did Cantillon's.

The case of H. H. Gossen provides a similar example. In the early
1870s three independently published books appeared asserting that
classical economists had erred in explaining the forces determining
relative prices by exclusively emphasizing supply. The three works, all
of which maintained that relative prices were better explained by the
forces of marginal utility, or demand, were *Theory of Political
Economy* (1871), by W. W. Jevons (1835-1921); *Grundsatze der
Volfwirtschaftslehre* (1871), by Carl Menger (1840-1921); and *Elements d'économique politique pure* (1874), by Leon Walras (1834-
1910). Jevons, in the second edition of his *Theory of Political
Economy* (1879), reports that he has become aware of a book by
H. H. Gossen published in 1854 that completely anticipated him. But
even though Gossen's work clearly antedated Jevons, Menger, and
Walras, he did not influence subsequent theory as they later did, and
therefore he is not included in our discussions of marginal utility.

Once we have chosen a representative writer, we must sometimes
further decide which of his works will provide the basis of our discussion. Thomas R. Malthus (1776-1834), for example, is best known for
his population theory, and although he was not its originator, his
presentation of the theory so influenced subsequent thinking that the
doctrine is known as the Malthusian theory. His *Essay on Population*
was so popular, in fact, that it went through seven editions. Which
should we use? Since the first and second differ significantly from each
other, whereas the rest essentially follow the second, we have chosen
to study both the first and second editions, so as to adequately cover
both the population theory and the influence of Malthus on the
development of economic methodology. Similarly, whereas J. M.
Keynes's *The General Theory* (1936) secures the author a place in the
history of theory, his views developed and changed both before and
after its publication, so that it is sometimes difficult to pin down the
"real" Keynes. Inconsistencies in the presentation of such complex
authors in this text do not necessarily indicate inaccuracies so much as
they reflect the depth and vigor of their thought, some of which is lost
in condensation. Such inconsistencies should be viewed, therefore, as
invitations to study the original works.

BENEFITS TO BE GAINED FROM A STUDY
OF THE HISTORY OF THEORY

A primary reason for studying the history of economic thought is to
become a better economist. With few exceptions, the important economists of past and present have been well acquainted with the theoretical
history of their discipline. Reading the history of theory strengthens
theoretical and logical skills by providing opportunities for the student
to relate assumptions to conclusions: one learns to work through the
logic of systems different from one's own. Social scientists also need to
be aware of their methodologies. An effective means of achieving this
awareness is to study such historical controversies as those between
deductive and inductive approaches, or between the advocates of
rigorous abstract theoretical models and of a more historical, descriptive approach, noting the gains and losses to be realized by each methodology.

The history of economic theory can also teach us humility. When we
see great minds make important theoretical errors or fail to examine
or pursue what appear from historical hindsight to be obvious paths, we
are forced to reflect that our own theoretical paradigms may be faulty
in ways that are difficult for us to perceive, because we are blinded by
our preconceptions. Ernest Hemingway said that it is counterproductive
for a writer to live in New York City, where the writers are like earth-
worms living in a jar. Our culture, with its sometimes narrow values and
preconceptions, can be like a jar in which we all live. Although it is
difficult to get outside the jar and view our society and its economy
with perfect objectivity, a study of the development of economic
theory makes us more aware of the necessity to try to do so and less
willing to accept current theory uncritically.

A final reason for studying old ideas is to foster new ideas. Study of
past economic theory is often the source of inspiration for a new idea.
Theories sometimes get lost in the past and are not carried forward to
the future, or become linked to specific applications. A good example
of this is the development around 1815 of the concept of diminishing
returns and rent. Until about 1890, when their applicability to all
factors of production was finally recognized, returns and rent were
applied only to land. Also, fruitful ideas may be discarded along with
an outworn or otherwise objectionable ideology to which they are
linked. Orthodox theory largely ignored the work of Marx until the
severe Depression of the 1930s necessitated a search through past
economic theory for an explanation of the causes of depression in a
capitalist system.

With this background, we shall proceed to a study of the history of
economic theory, tracing the emergence of modern orthodox economics while still taking into account the deviations from orthodoxy

that have helped to shape the content of present-day economics. In addition to the scope and content of theory, we shall note major methodological issues and the relationships between the development of a theory and the economic conditions at the time of its development. Where the internal workings of particular theories provide insights, we shall explain them. From time to time we shall indicate the general significance of particular ideas in the development of theory and the broader implications of theory as a basis for the formulation of economic and social policy.

SUGGESTED READINGS

Blaug, Mark. *The Methodology of Economics*. Cambridge: Cambridge University Press, 1978.

———. *Economic Theory in Retrospect*. Cambridge: Cambridge University Press, 1985.

Boland, Lawrence A. *The Foundations of Economic Method*. London: George Allen and Unwin, 1982.

Caldwell, Bruce. *Beyond Positivism: Economic Methodology in the Twentieth Century*. London: George Allen and Unwin, 1982.

Coats, A. W., ed. *Methodological Controversies in Economics: Historical Essays in Honor of T. W. Hutchison*. Greenwich, Conn.: JAI Press, 1983.

Feyerabend, Paul. *Against Method*. London: New Left Books, 1975.

Lakatos, Imre. *The Methodology of Scientific Research Programmes: Philosophical Papers*. Vol. 1. Cambridge: Cambridge University Press, 1978.

Latsis, S. J. *Method and Appraisal in Economics*. Cambridge: Cambridge University Press, 1976.

McCloskey, Donald N. *The Rhetoric of Economics*. Madison, Wisc.: The University of Wisconsin Press, 1985.

Popper, Karl R. *The Logic of Scientific Discovery* (1934). New York: Basic Books, 1959.

Chapter 2
Preclassical Economic Theory

Although economic activity has characterized human culture since the dawn of civilization, there is no record of formal analysis until merchant capitalism developed in Western Europe during the fifteenth century. At that time the chiefly agrarian European societies began increasingly to trade among themselves, setting the stage for the birth of economics as a social study. The economic studies of this time were not systematic: economic theory evolved piecemeal from individual intellectual responses to contemporary problems. No grand analytical systems appeared. It was not until the mid-eighteenth century, with the emergence of "classical economics" under Adam Smith, that economics achieved the status of a full-blown social science.

To say that the writing of preclassical theorists addressed limited aspects of the economy without articulating them into a comprehensive economic system is not to denigrate either the contributions or the mental acuity of the writers, many of whom manifest considerable insight into the economic conditions of their times. Initially, they simply were not searching for grand theories; and later, once they began to envision a more comprehensive system, they found they had to resolve complex analytical problems before they could begin to synthesize past analysis into an integral body of economic theory.

Although it was individuals, not groups, who addressed the economic problems of the preclassical period, it is convenient to group like-minded writers into schools of thought reflecting the main currents of economic thinking at the time. Preclassical writers are conventionally divided into three schools: *scholasticism*, *mercantilism*, and *physiocracy*. The changes in economic thinking that these schools represent were, in large part, responses to the changing economic organization of Europe. In England, for example, scholastic economic thought derived from feudalism, and mercantilist theory from merchant capitalism. The classical laissez faire economics that followed was associated, likewise, with producer capitalism. Similar economic developments occurred in France, but a unique set of economic ideas, called physiocracy, developed between French mercantilism and classical theory.

SCHOLASTICISM

The first writers to provide insight into the functioning of the developing economy of Western Europe were the scholastics, who wrote from the thirteenth into the sixteenth century. The most important of these writers was St. Thomas Aquinas (*c.* 1225-1274). But the theories of Aquinas and his followers owe a heavy debt to the great Greek thinker Aristotle (384-322 B.C.). Thus, in order to understand the economic tenets of scholasticism, it is necessary to know something of Aristotle's economic ideas.

Aristotle

Aristotle's main contributions to economic thinking concerned the exchange of commodities and the use of money in this exchange. Man's needs, he said, were moderate, but his desires were limitless. Hence the production of commodities to satisfy *needs* was right and natural, whereas the production of goods in an attempt to satisfy unlimited *desires* was unnatural. Aristotle concedes that when goods are produced to be sold in a market it is often difficult to determine if this activity is satisfying needs or inordinate desires, but he assumes that if a market exchange is in the form of barter it is made to satisfy natural needs and no economic gain is intended. Exchange using the medium of money, however, suggests that the objective is monetary gain, which Aristotle condemns.

   Aristotle's teacher, Plato, had argued that the ruling class of his ideal society, the soldiers and philosophers, should not possess private property but should hold their property communally, to avoid conflicts over property that might divert their attention from more important issues. Aristotle, however, believed that private property served a useful function in society and that no regulations should be made limiting the amount of property in private hands. His apparent inconsistency in condemning the pursuit of economic gain while endorsing the right to private property troubled moral philosophers until the sixteenth century.

The Feudal Foundation of Scholastic Thought

Scholastic economic doctrine is understandable only in the context of its time, extending from before the fall of the Roman Empire to the beginnings of merchant capitalism in Western Europe. We shall discuss some of the chief characteristics of medieval society that bear on the

Needs and Wants

Today's mainstream economist does not distinguish between human needs and desires, especially in a society where the household or family unit is no longer self-sufficient. Households today not only produce few of the *goods* they consume, they even buy many *services* in the market. As specialization and division of labor evolved and economic exchange began, a medium of exchange — money — became essential. According to modern orthodox theorists, distinguishing between needs and wants in a market economy is objectively impossible. They feel that Aristotle's precepts should be viewed as guidelines relevant to his times but not to ours, since they are inconsistent with present economic realities. Modern orthodox economists believe that ultimately it should be left to the individual to determine whether one is acting virtuously in producing and exchanging goods. But many heterodox groups, the institutionalists and Marxists, for example, disagree with this position. They contend that it is impossible for mainstream economists to *avoid* making value judgments. They argue, in accord with Aristotle, that needs can and must be distinguished from wants.

nature and significance of scholastic economic doctrine.[1] The kind of economic activity we see today in the industrialized areas of the world did not exist to any significant degree during the Middle Ages. In particular the production of goods for sale in a market, although it increased throughout the period, did not play a dominant role in everyday life. The feudal economy consisted of subsistence agriculture in a society bound together not by a market but by tradition, custom, and authority, in a society divided into four groups: serfs, landlords, royalty, and the church. All land was fundamentally owned by the Roman Catholic church and the king. Use of the land owned by the king was given to the lords or noblemen who, in exchange for that use, had certain obligations to the central authority. These obligations, based not on contracts as in the modern market economy, but on tradition and custom, consisted of supplying services and goods. This right of land use, with its corresponding obligations, was passed by

1. The best short historical analysis of this period is Henri Pirenne, *Economic and Social History of Medieval Europe*; trans. by I. E. Clegg (New York: Harcourt, Brace, 1937).

heredity from father to son. Since the secular central authority was never very strong during the Middle Ages, the lord was, for the most part, master of his domain. The relationship between lord and serf was also dictated by custom, tradition, and authority. The serf was tied to the land by tradition and paid the lord for the use of the land with labor, crops, and sometimes money. In return, the lord protected the serf from outsiders during times of war. Each manor or estate was a virtually complete economic and political unit. It usually had its own church, built by the lord and partly under the influence of the lord, since he nominated the pastor. The church, as the largest land holder in Western Europe, had significant secular influence. In general its estates were better managed than those of the feudal lords, partly because the churchmen were the only class proficient in reading and writing.

Most individuals accepted their place in feudal society without much question. There were scattered examples of serfs revolting against their lords, but these were unusual occurrences. All land belonged to God, who had put it in the custody of a man who was king by divine right or of the church. Not to accept the authority of your superiors was to oppose the will of God, who had given them authority, and to endanger your salvation in the next life. In such a system land, labor, and capital were not commodities bought and sold in a market as they are today, and there was very little production of any goods for sale in the market.

Although there were strong elements in the feudal society reinforcing tradition and hostile to change, other factors gradually began to erode its foundations. Most economic historians regard changing technology as the major cause of the decline of feudalism. Changes in agricultural technology had disruptive influences on the manor. Some manufacturing began, based on the replacement of man and animal power by mechanical power from water and wind. Thus in the course of the Middle Ages, and especially during the five hundred years prior to 1450, the society was transformed.

The scholastic writers were educated monks who tried to provide religious guidelines to be applied to secular activities. Their aim was not so much to analyze what little economic activity was taking place, but to prescribe rules of economic conduct compatible with religious dogma. The most important of the scholastic writers was St. Thomas Aquinas.

Thomas Aquinas

Although the scholastics, in attempting to adapt to the nascent economic changes of their times, produced a somewhat diverse body of economic ideas, they essentially addressed the same core of economic issues: the institution of private property and the concepts of just price and usury. Subject to some minor qualifications, it is reasonable to characterize and summarize this literature as a struggle to reconcile the religious teachings of the church with the slowly increasing economic activity of the time. Scholastic writing represents a gradual acceptance of certain aspects of economic activity as compatible with religious doctrine, achieved by subtle modifications of that doctrine to fit the economic conditions. The significance of St. Thomas Aquinas's ideas lies in his fusion of religious teaching with the writings of Aristotle, which provided scholastic economic doctrine with much of its content.

In attempting to reconcile religious doctrine with the institution of private property and with economic activity, Aquinas had to reckon with numerous biblical statements condemning private property, wealth, and the pursuit of economic gain. Based upon the New Testament, early Christian thought held that communal property accorded with natural law and that privately held property fell short of this ideal. Thus early Christian society, modeled on the lives of Jesus Christ and his apostles, was communal. But the early scholastic writers had long struggled to establish that some ownership of private property by laymen was not incompatible with religious teaching. In the thirteenth century, after Aristotle had been reintroduced into Western Europe, Thomas Aquinas, adapting Aristotelian thought to his own writing, was able to argue convincingly that private property is not contrary to natural law. While it is true that under natural law all property is communal, he conceded, the growth of private property is an *addition*, not a contradiction, to natural law. Aquinas argued that to be naked was in accordance with natural law and that clothing was an addition to natural law devised for the benefit of man. So too, for private property.

> We might say that for man to be naked is of the natural law, because nature did not give him clothes, but art invented them. In this sense, the *possession of all things* ...[is] said to be of the natural law, because, namely, the distinction of possession...[was] not brought in by nature, but devised by human reason for the benefit of human life.[2]

Again following Aristotle, Aquinas approved the regulation of private property by the state and accepted an unequal distribution of private property. However, in the spirit of Plato, he still advocated poverty and communal living as the ideal for those of deep religious commitment, for the common life enabled them to devote the greatest part of their energies to religious activities.

2. Quoted from *Summa Theologica*, I–II, Q. 94, Art. 5, by Richard Schlalter, *Private Property* (New Brunswick: Rutgers University Press, 1951), p. 47.

The Relevance of Scholasticism

The ethical issues raised by the medieval schoolmen remain relevant today. From the broadest perspective, we still ask ourselves what constitutes "the good life," and by what criteria we are to evaluate the quality of our experiences and activities as human beings. Relationships with family and friends, good deeds, and high ideals are all noneconomic aspects of our lives that may or may not be considered in the context of a particular religious doctrine. The medieval church was concerned that increasing economic activity would turn the minds and hearts of humans from religious and ethical concerns and toward materialism.

The post–World War II period in the United States has seen several shifts in attitudes about economic and noneconomic motivation, especially in the beliefs of young adults. During the immediate postwar period, in the aftermath of the war and the Great Depression, young adults placed high priority on economic values. By the sixties, however, many young people began to censor the older generation's concern with economic values. A society-wide "generation gap" ensued, with leaders of youth admonishing young people to trust no one over thirty. In the 1980s the pendulum swung again and young adults readopted the economic values of the postwar period. Business schools became the fastest growing divisions in many universities.

The scholastics' concern with the justice or lack of justice in the price system is another perennial part of our social and economic system. Public utility regulation represents an attempt by society, through government, to assure the fairness of such prices as telephone, electric, and water usage rates. Regulatory commissions generally try to set prices that are "just," in that they are limited to the costs of producing the services, including the costs of providing capital to the firms that provide them.

As interest rates fell during the period from 1985 to 1987, a number of consumer advocates became concerned about the fixed interest rates charged by issuers of consumer credit cards. Mortgage interest rates, business borrowing interest rates, and interest rate returns on government and business debt all declined considerably, but interest rates charged by credit card issuers remained fixed at about 18 percent. Most of the discussion of these issues was framed in ethical terms. Two other examples that illustrate how ethical considerations may outweigh economic concerns are farm programs that permit farmers to borrow at lower interest costs than other businesses, and loan programs available to minority-owned businesses.

Aquinas and other scholastics were also concerned with another aspect of the emergence of greater economic activity, the price of goods. Unlike modern economists, they were not trying to analyze the formation of prices in an economy or to understand the role that prices play in the allocation of scarce resources. They focused on the ethical aspect of prices, raising issues of equity and justice. Did religious doctrine forbid merchants to sell goods for more than they paid for them? Were making profits and taking interest sinful acts? In discussing these issues, Aquinas combined religious thinking with Aristotle's views. When exchanges take place in the market to meet the needs of the trading parties — using Aristotle's conception of need — Aquinas concludes that no ethical issues are involved. But when individuals produce for the market in anticipation of gain, they are acting virtuously only if their motives are charitable and their prices are just. If the merchant intends to use any profits for self-support, for charity, or to contribute to the public well-being, and if his prices are just, so that both the buyer and the seller benefit, the merchant has acted rightly.

Historians of economic theory differ in their interpretations of the scholastic notion of just price. Some hold that the scholastics, including Aquinas, considered a just price to be an equivalent in terms of labor cost. A second group says that it is an equivalent in terms of utility, and a third group regards it as an equivalent in terms of total cost of production. Thus the scholastic concept of just price is seen alternatively as a forerunner of the Richardian-Marxian labor theory of value, the marginal utility position, and the notion implicit in classical-neoclassical theory that competitive markets yield ideal just prices. Another widely held view regards the scholastic notion of just price as an integral part of the set of social and economic forces that maintained the hierarchy of feudalism. If all prices in the market were just prices, this view holds, no one would be able to change his or her social status by economic activity. The lack of economic analysis in scholasticism makes it difficult to judge exactly what was meant by "just price." Our interpretation is that for scholasticism in general and Aquinas in particular just price meant simply the prevailing market price. If this is correct, however, since the scholastics had no theory to explain the forces that determine market price, no useful conclusion can be reached as to the economic or even the ethical content of the concept of just price.

A corollary to the concept of just price was the scholastic notion of usury. The church's views on just price and morality in economic behavior were, for the most part, general enough to not impinge on the growing economy. But its views on usury were specific and consequential enough to create conflict between the church and the emerging business community. The meaning of the term *usury* has changed since the time of scholasticism. As used today it denotes charging an *excessive* rate of interest, but in scholastic doctrine it conveys the biblical

and Aristotelian sense of *any* taking of interest. Scholastic usury doctrine was itself derived largely from the Bible and the writings of
Aristotle. The biblical condemnation of usury rose from the danger
that the strong would take advantage of the weak. Aristotle, moreover,
had argued that the taking of interest on loans was unnatural, since
money is barren. The scholastic view gradually moderated throughout
the scholastic era, however, from a fairly strict prohibition of interest
early in the period to its acceptance — at least for business purposes —
later.

To summarize, scholastic doctrine did not attempt to analyze the
economy, but rather to set religious standards by which to judge economic conduct. In a society with very little economic activity, where
land, labor, and capital were not traded in markets, and where custom,
tradition, and authority played important roles, there seemed, at least
to the educated churchmen, to be a "higher good" than economic goods.
However, the disruptive consequences of changing technology were
slowly upsetting the feudal order, and economic life posed a greater
and greater challenge to spiritual life.

By the middle of the fifteenth century, scholastic notions of the
virtuous life were out of step with prevailing economic practice, and the
ethical judgments of the church seemed inappropriate to the developing
economies of Western Europe. Nevertheless, scholastic doctrine did
provide insights into the operation of the growing market economy and
helped form a base for the development of a more analytical approach.

MERCANTILISM

Mercantilism is the name given to some 250 years of economic literature and practice between 1500 and 1750. Although mercantilist
literature was produced in all the developing economies of Western
Europe, the most significant contributions were made by the English
and French.

The times were characterized by an increase in economic activity.
Feudalism, with its economically, socially, and politically self-sufficient
manor, was giving way to increasing trade, the growth of cities outside
the manor, and the growth of the nation state. Individual activity was
less controlled by the custom and tradition of the feudal society and by
the authority of the church. Production of goods for the market became more important, and land, labor, and capital began to be bought
and sold in markets. This laid the groundwork for the Industrial
Revolution.

Whereas the economic literature of scholasticism was written by
medieval monks, the economic theory of mercantilism was the work of
merchant businessmen. The literature they produced was closely con-

nected to questions of economic policy and usually to a particular interest the merchant-writer was trying to promote. For this reason there was often considerable skepticism as to the analytical merits of particular arguments and the validity of the conclusions reached. Few authors could claim to be sufficiently detached from the issues to render objective analysis. Yet throughout the mercantilistic period, both the quantity and the quality of economic literature grew. From 1650 to 1750, the mercantilistic literature is of distinctively higher quality, and scattered throughout it are nearly all the analytical concepts on which Adam Smith based his *Wealth of Nations*, published in 1776.

Every Man His Own Economist

The age of mercantilism has been characterized as a time when every man was his own economist. A wide diversity of views appeared from the various writers between 1500 and 1750, so it is difficult to generalize about the resulting literature. Furthermore, each writer tended to concentrate on one topic, and no single writer was able to synthesize these contributions impressively enough to influence the subsequent development of economic theory. Possibly this was because economics as an intellectual discipline had not yet found a home in the university, but was largely studied by men of affairs who wrote pamphlets about the various economic problems that concerned them.

Power and Wealth

Mercantilism can best be understood if we view it as an intellectual reaction to problems of the times. In this period of the decline of the manor and the rise of the nation state, the mercantilists tried to determine the best policies to promote the power and wealth of the nation. Just as Machiavelli, the Italian statesman, political theorist, and author of *The Prince* (1513), was advising rulers about expedient political policies, the mercantilists were advising them about the economic policies that would best consolidate and increase the power and prosperity of the developing economies.

The mercantilists proceeded on the assumption that the total wealth of the world was fixed. Using this same assumption, the scholastics had reasoned that, when trade took place between individuals, the gain of one was necessarily the loss of another. The mercantilists carried this reasoning over to trade between nations, concluding that any increase in the wealth and economic power of one nation was necessarily at the expense of others. Thus the mercantilists emphasized international trade as a means of increasing the wealth and power of a nation and, in particular, focused on the balance of trade between nations.

The goal of economic activity, according to most mercantilists, was production, not consumption, as classical economics would later have it. For the mercantilists the wealth of the nation was not defined in terms of the sum of individual wealth. They advocated increasing the nation's wealth by simultaneously encouraging production, increasing exports, and holding down domestic consumption. Thus the wealth of the nation was based on the poverty of the many. Although the mercantilists laid great stress on production, a plentiful supply of goods within a country was considered undesirable. High levels of production would permit increased exports, and through trade the nation's wealth and power could be increased. The mercantilists advocated low wages in order to give the domestic economy competitive advantages in international trade, and because they believed that wage levels above a subsistence level would result in a reduced labor effort. Higher wages would cause laborers to work fewer hours per year; thus national output would fall. Poverty for the individual, therefore, benefits the nation when the goal of economic activity is defined in terms of national output and not in terms of national consumption.

The Balance of Trade

According to mercantilistic thinking, a country should encourage exports and discourage imports by tariffs, quotas, subsidies, taxes, and like means, in order to achieve a so-called favorable balance of trade. Production should be stimulated by governmental interference in the domestic economy and by the regulation of foreign trade. Protective duties should be placed on manufactured goods from abroad, and the importation of cheap raw materials, to be used in manufacturing goods for export, should be encouraged.

Historians of economic thought disagree as to the nature and significance of the balance of trade doctrine in mercantilist literature. It is clear, however, that many early mercantilists, who defined the wealth of a nation not in terms of its production or consumption of goods, but rather in terms of its holdings of precious metals, argued for a favorable balance of trade because it would produce a flow of precious metals into the domestic economy to settle the trade balance.

The first mercantilists argued that a favorable balance of trade should be struck with each nation. A number of subsequent writers, however, argued that only the overall balance of trade with all nations was significant. Thus England might have an unfavorable balance of trade with India, but because it could import from India cheap raw materials that could be used to manufacture goods in England for export, it might well have a favorable overall trade balance when all nations were taken into account.

A related issue concerned the export of precious metals or bullion. The early mercantilists recommended that the export of bullion be strictly prohibited. Later writers suggested that exporting bullion might lead to an improvement in overall trade balances if the bullion was used to purchase raw materials for export goods. The mercantilists' persistent advocacy of a favorable balance of trade raises some perplexing questions, which are best handled by examining their views about money.

Money

Adam Smith devoted nearly two hundred pages in his *Wealth of Nations* to a harsh, and only partly justifiable, criticism of mercantilistic theory and practice, particularly its equation of the wealth of a nation with the stock of precious metals internally held. Early mercantilists were clearly much impressed with the significance of the tremendous flow of precious metals into Europe, particularly into Spain, from the New World. However, later mercantilists did not subscribe to this view and were able to develop some useful analytical insights into the role of money in an economy. For example, the relationship between the quantity of money and the general level of prices was recognized as early as 1569 by the Frenchman Jean Bodin. He offered five reasons for the rise in the general level of prices in Western Europe during the sixteenth century, the most important of which was the increase in the quantity of gold and silver in Western Europe resulting from the discovery of the New World. By the end of the seventeenth century, John Locke was able to analyze the role of money with even greater sophistication, demonstrating that the level of economic activity in an economy depends upon the quantity of money and its velocity. In the middle of the eighteenth century, David Hume presented a reasonably complete description of the interrelationships among a country's balance of trade, the quantity of money, and the general level of prices. In international trade theory this has become known as the *price specie-flow mechanism*. Hume pointed out that it would be impossible for an economy continuously to maintain a favorable balance of trade. A favorable balance of trade would lead to an increase in the quantity of gold and silver (specie) within an economy. An increase in the quantity of money would lead to a rise in the level of prices in the economy with the favorable balance of trade. If one country has a favorable balance of trade, some other country or countries must be having an unfavorable balance with a loss of gold or silver and a subsequent fall in the general level of prices. Exports will decrease and imports will increase for the economy with the initial favorable trade balance because of prices that are relatively higher than those of other economies. The opposite tendencies will prevail in an economy with the initial unfavorable balance. This process will ultimately lead to a self-correction of the trade balances.

These developments occurred later, however, since in the early 1500s there was little comprehension of the consequences of trade balances between nations and almost no understanding of the consequences of increases in the money supply. By the middle of the eighteenth century, considerable analytical progress had been made in understanding these issues. Until that time there was a fairly steady increase of analytical insight into the operation of a market economy. The period from 1660 to 1776 was marked by particularly noteworthy development.

A central feature of mercantilist literature is its conviction that money, rather than real factors, is the chief determinant of economic activity and growth. Mercantilists held that an adequate supply of money is particularly essential to the growth of trade, both domestic and international. Changes in the quantity of money, they believed, generate changes in the level of real output — in yards of cloth and bushels of grain.

All of this would change with the advent of Adam Smith and classical economics, which would contend that the level of economic activity and its rate of growth depend rather upon a number of *real* factors: the quantity of labor, natural resources, capital goods, and the institutional structure. Any changes in the quantity of money, classical economists averred, would influence neither the level of output nor growth but only the general level of prices.

Modern Analysis of Mercantilism

Evaluating past writers raises a number of difficult but interesting issues. There are always differences of opinion about what particular writers really meant by what they said. Imprecise language can make interpretation difficult. When J. M. Keynes discussed the mercantilists in a section of his *General Theory* called "Notes on Mercantilism," he credited them with clear insight into an acceptable policy by which to stimulate economic development. But Adam Smith, other classicals, and the orthodox line of economic thinkers from 1776 until the time of Keynes found little of merit in much of the mercantilist literature. This divergence of opinion is understandable, though, when we compare some aspects of classical and Keynesian thought. Since orthodox theory stressed the *real* forces that determine the level of output, it focused almost exclusively on the side of supply. Keynes, however, emphasizing the role of aggregate demand, and enlarging somewhat on actual mercantilist thought, found some common bonds between his theory and that of the mercantilists. He was sympathetic to their underconsumptionist views and declared as sound their belief that increases in the quantity of money would increase output. The mercantilists, Keynes says, held that a favorable balance of trade would increase investment spending and thus raise the level of income and employment.

Another problematical aspect of evaluating the contributions of past writers lies in the need to assess their intellectual achievement. Should this judgment be based wholly on modern standards or be kept strictly in the context of the analytical apparatus of their times? Even though most historians of ideas take a position between these polar views, a good deal of controversy as to the relative merits of past economists still results.[3]

One other attitude toward mercantilism deserves mention. Some assessments of mercantilism have scrutinized not the ideas of its proponents but their motivations. The mercantilists, in the jargon of modern economics, were "rent-seekers." They were driven by profit motives to use government to gain economic privilege for themselves. They were generally merchants who favored government granting of monopolies that would enable the merchant-monopolists to charge higher prices than would have been possible without these monopoly privileges. Thus they were rent-seekers.

The Theoretical Contributions of the Mercantilists

The study of mercantilism by historians of economic theory has made it clear that from about 1660 to 1776, the quantity and quality of economic analysis increased. The improvement in the quality of economic analysis during the later part of the mercantilistic era was so pronounced that this period has been characterized as a transitional period containing the origins of scientific economics.

Possibly the most significant accomplishment of the later mercantilists was the explicit recognition of the possibility of analyzing the economy. This development represented a transfer to the social sciences of attitudes then prevalent in the physical sciences. It reached its full fruition after the time of Isaac Newton (1642–1727), and its impact is still felt today. The substitution of cause-and-effect analysis for the moral analysis of the scholastics does not represent a clear break with the past, however, for logical analysis was used by some of the scholas-

3. For a provocative exchange on the mercantilists, see Allen, William R., "Modern Defenders of Mercantilistic Theory," *History of Political Economy*, 5 (Fall (1970); Coats, A. W., "The Interpretation of Mercantilist Economics: Some Historiographical Problems," *History of Political Economy*, 5 (Fall 1973); and Allen, William R., "Rearguard Response," *Ibid.*

tics and moralizing still exists in modern economic literature. But the view that the laws of the economy could be discovered by the same methods as the laws of physics was an important step to subsequent developments in economic theory.

Many of the mercantilists held to a highly mechanical causality in the economy, believing that if one understood the rules of causality, one could control the economy. It followed that legislation, if wisely enacted, could positively influence the course of economic events and that economic analysis would indicate what forms of government intervention would effect a given end. Mercantilists realized, however, that government interference must not be haphazard, nor complicate basic economic truths such as the law of supply and demand. Some correctly deduced, for example, that price ceilings set below equilibrium prices lead to excess demand and shortages. The later mercantilists frequently applied the concepts of the economic man and the profit motive in stimulating economic activity. Governments, they said, cannot change the basic nature of human beings, particularly their egoistic drives. The politician starts with these factors as given, in an attempt to create a set of laws and institutions that will channel these drives so as to increase the power and prosperity of the nation.

Many of the later mercantilists became aware of the serious analytical errors of their predecessors. They recognized, for example, that specie is not a measure of the wealth of a nation, that all nations could not have a favorable balance of trade, that no one country could maintain a favorable balance of trade over the long run, that trade can be mutually beneficial to nations, and that advantages will accrue to nations that practice specialization and division of labor. An increasing number of writers recommended a reduction in the amount of government intervention. Thus this literature included statements of incipient classical liberalism.

Yet none of these preclassical writers was able to present an integrated view of the operation of a market economy — the manner in which prices are formed and scarce resources are allocated. This failure of the mercantilists to reach the result eventually achieved by Adam Smith and subsequent classical economics may be attributable to one important difference between classical and mercantilistic theory. The mercantilists believed that there was a basic conflict between private interests and the public welfare. Therefore, they considered it necessary for government to channel private self-interest into public benefits. Classical economics, on the other hand, finds a basic harmony in the system and sees public good as flowing naturally from individual self-interest. Even those later mercantilists who advocated laissez faire policies lacked sufficient insight into the operation of the market to make an adequate argument to support them. Still, the writings of these later mercantilists were used by Smith to develop his analysis.

Adam Smith was also influenced during his travel in France by a group of French writers who have become known as the *physiocrats*. They perceived the interrelatedness of the sectors of the economy and analyzed the working of nonregulated markets.

PHYSIOCRACY

Although mercantilism was much in evidence in eighteenth-century France, a new but short-lived movement called physiocracy began there about 1750. Because it provided significant analytical insights into the economy, its influence on subsequent economic thought was considerable. Scholars of economic ideas often arbitrarily group men of divergent ideas into a school of thought, usually because of some single similarity. However, the writings of the physiocratic school express remarkably consistent views on all major points. There are three reasons for this: (1) Physiocracy developed exclusively in France. (2) The ideas of the physiocrats were presented over a relatively short period of time, from about 1750 to 1780. (It has been said that no one was aware of physiocratic ideas before 1750, and after 1780 only a few economists had heard of them.) (3) Physiocracy had an acknowledged intellectual leader, François Quesnay (1694-1774), whose ideas his fellow physiocrats accepted virtually without question. Their own writings were mainly designed to convince others of the merit of Quesnay's economics.

Natural Law

The physiocrats, like the later English mercantilists, developed their economic theories in order to formulate correct economic policies. Both groups held that the correct formulation of economic policy presupposed a correct understanding of the economy. Economic theory was therefore a prerequisite of economic policy. The physiocrats' unique idea was their concept of the role of natural law in the formulation of policy. They held that natural laws governed the operation of the economy and that, although these laws were independent of human will, humans could objectively discover them as they could the laws of the natural sciences. This idea contributed significantly to the development of economics and the social sciences.

The Interrelatedness of an Economy

Even though physiocratic theory was deficient in logical consistency and detail, the physiocrats did arrive at the necessity of building theo-

Francois Quesnay

retical models by isolating key economic variables for study and analysis. Using this process, they achieved significant insights into the interdependence of the various sectors of the economy, on the levels of both macro- and microeconomic analysis.

The major concern of the physiocrats, however, was with the macroeconomic process of development. They recognized that France was lagging behind England in applying new agricultural techniques. Some areas of northern France were introducing advanced techniques, but most of France was maintaining its old ways; thus the country was developing unevenly. To cope with this problem, the physiocrats, like the English and French mercantilists, wished to discover the nature and causes of the wealth of nations and the policies that would best promote economic growth. French mercantilism had been even more thoroughgoing in its regulation of domestic and foreign economic activity than its British counterpart, and physiocracy was an intellectual reaction to this regulation. The physiocrats focused not on money but on the real forces leading to economic development. In reaction to the mercantilistic notion that wealth was created by the process of exchange, they studied the creation of physical value and concluded that the origin of wealth was in agriculture, or nature.

The economy of their time obviously produced more goods than were needed to pay the real costs to society of producing these goods. This meant that a surplus was generated. Their search for the origin and size of this surplus led them to the idea of the *net product*. The agricultural production process provides a good example of a net product. After the various factors of production — seed, labor, machinery, etc. — are paid for, the annual harvest leaves an excess that the physiocrats regarded as resulting from the productivity of nature. Labor, according to them, could produce only enough goods to pay the costs of labor, and the same held true for the other factors of production with the exception of land. Production from land, therefore, created the surplus that the physiocrats termed the net product. Manufacturing and other non-agricultural economic activities were considered "sterile," because they created no net product. This belief of the physiocrats that only agricultural production was capable of returning to society an output greater than the social costs of that output may seem quaint today, but it is possibly explained by the fact that the physiocrats focused on physical productivity rather than value productivity. However, since large-scale industry had not yet developed in France in the middle of the eighteenth century, the productivity of industry was not apparent in the economy of the physiocrats. The small employer with only a few employees did not seem to be making any surplus, and his standard of living was not significantly different from that of his employees. Having established that the origin of the net product was in land, the physiocrats concluded that land rent is the measure of the society's net product.

The physiocrats considered their crowning theoretical achievement to be Quesnay's "Economic Table." Quesnay divided the economy into three sectors: farmers, landlords, and the nonfarm sector. The table was a crude representation of the flow of money incomes between the various sectors of the economy and of the creation and annual circulation of the net product throughout the economy. Quesnay's table represents a major methodological advance in the development of economics — a grand attempt to analyze raw reality by means of abstraction.

The physiocrats not only theorized about the relationships between the various sectors of the economy, but also attempted to quantify the size of the various sectors. On this level physiocracy anticipated Nobel Prize–winning Wassily Leontief's celebrated input-output table and the work of the specialized group of quantitative economists called econometricians. The economic table shows some awareness of the interdependence of the various sectors of the economy. Some of the later mercantilists also became aware of this interdependence, and their combined influence was the basis for Adam Smith's attempt at a more complete description of the working of a market economy.

Physiocratic Economic Policy

The physiocrats' contributions to micro theory were not as significant as their contributions to macro theory. They believed that the basic motivation for the economic activities of human beings was the desire to maximize gain. Prices were formed in the market by economic activity, and the formation of these prices could be studied, since it was governed by natural laws independent of human will. Although the physiocrats did not develop a coherent theory of prices, they concluded that free competition led to the best price and that society would benefit if individuals followed their self-interest. Furthermore, believing that the only source of a net product was agriculture, they concluded that the burden of taxes would ultimately rest on land. A tax on labor, for example, would be shifted to land, since competition had already assured that the wage of labor was at a subsistence level. Perhaps most important, they began to be aware of the function of prices in integrating the activities of the various factors in the economy. Like the more perceptive mercantilists, they recognized that an individual who appears to be working independently in a market economy is actually working for others and that these independent activities are integrated by the price system. Their micro analysis tended to lack detail. For example, they offered no real proof that free competition would result in an optimum allocation of resources. But they did have some notion of the nature and function of relative price, a notion subsequently used by Adam Smith.

Since the physiocrats believed that a natural order existed superior to any possible human design, they conceived the economy to be largely self-regulating and thus rejected the controls imposed by the mercantilist system. The proper role of government was to follow a policy of laissez faire — to let things alone. This idea in the hands of Adam Smith and subsequent economists was of tremendous importance in shaping the ideology of Western civilization. Certain English writers were also advocating nonintervention as a general policy at the time, and they, too, influenced Smith.

The physiocrats maintained that the primary obstacles to economic growth proceeded from the mercantilist policies regulating domestic and foreign trade. They objected particularly to the tax system of the mercantilists and advocated that a single tax be levied on land. Of course, according to their theory, all taxes would ultimately fall on land anyway, but only after causing much friction in the economic system.

But the most unfortunate of the many governmental regulations, according to the physiocrats, was prohibiting the export of French grain. This kept down the price of grain in France, they said, and was therefore an obstacle to agricultural development. Since the physiocrats did not foresee the development of manufacturing, they concluded that a laissez faire policy would produce tremendous growth in French agriculture as the small-scale agriculture of the feudal economy was replaced by large-scale capitalist agriculture. Thus the wealth and power of the French economy would be increased. The mercantilists had, in effect, found the source of the net product to be exchange — particularly exchange in the form of international trade — and had therefore advocated policies designed to foster a favorable trade balance. The physiocrats, who considered the source of the net product to be agriculture, held that laissez faire would lead to increased agriculture production and ultimately to greater economic growth.

SUMMARY

Prior to the middle of the eighteenth century, thinking and writing about the economy developed as the economy developed. The first important writers on economic questions were the scholastics, who raised ethical questions about the significance of the increasing economic activity of the medieval and Renaissance periods. Although their contribution to modern economic theory was relatively small, they raised relevant ethical issues concerning the equity and justice of the economic system. They recognized, moreover, that the process of exchange and the prices that emerge from exchange were the proper focal point in judging equity and justice. The questions they raised concerning the proper mix of economic and noneconomic activity in an individual's life are still relevant. Their view of the exchange process was flawed, however, in that it failed to recognize that exchange and specialization can lead to larger societal output and be mutually advantageous to all trading parties.

The mercantilists and the physiocrats made useful contributions to economic theory, the most important of which was to recognize that the economy could be studied. At the same time these writers developed an abstract technique by which to discover the laws that regulated the economy. They were the first model builders in economics, and since economic theory is based on this abstract, model-building process, it is reasonable to regard the mercantilists and physiocrats as the first economic theorists.

The mercantilists achieved the first tentative insights into the role of money in determining the general level of prices and into the effects of foreign trade balances on domestic economic activity. The most significant contribution of the physiocrats was their concept of the interrelatedness of the various sectors of an economy.

The mercantilists and the scholastics perceived a fundamental conflict in the economy, viewing exchange as a process in which one party gains at the expense of another. Both, therefore, advocated intervention into the economy by either government or church. The physiocrats, on the other hand, perceived the working out of the conflicts inherent in relative scarcity as basically harmonious. They called not for intervention into the economy but for laissez faire, and thus were an important influence on Adam Smith and the subsequent development of economic policy.

SUGGESTED READINGS

Allen, W. R. "Modern Defenders of Mercantilist Theory." *History of Political Economy*, 2 (Fall 1970). See also Allen's "Rearguard Response." *History of Political Economy*, 5 (Fall 1973).

Bowley, Marian. *Studies in the History of Economic Theory before 1870.* London: Macmillan, 1973.

Coats, A. W. "The Interpretation of Mercantilist Economics: Some Historiographical Problems." *History of Political Economy*, 5 (Fall 1973).

Dempsey, Bernard J. "Just Price in a Functional Economy." *American Economic Review*, 25 (1935).

De Roover, Raymond. "The Concept of Just Price: Economic Theory and Policy." *The Journal of Economic History*, 28 (December 1958).

Ekelund, Robert B. and Robert D. Tollison. *Mercantilism as a Rent-Seeking Society.* College Station: Texas A & M University Press, 1981.

Furniss, Edgar S. *The Position of the Laborer in a System of Nationalism.* New York: A. M. Kelley, 1965.

Gide, Charles, and Charles Rist. "The Physiocrats." Chapter I in *A History of Economic Doctrines.* Boston: D. C. Heath, 1948.

Grampp, William D. *Economic Liberalism*. 2 vols. New York: Random House, 1965.

Groenewegen, Peter. "Turgot's Place in the History of Economic Thought: A Bicentenary Estimate." *History of Political Economy*, 15 (Winter 1983).

Heckscher, Eli F. *Mercantilism*. 2 vols. London: George Allen and Unwin, 1935.

Hollander, Samuel. "On the Interpretation of Just Price." *Kyklos*, 18 (1965).

Langholm, Odd. *Price and Value in the Aristotelian Tradition*. Bergen, Norway: Universiteforlaget, 1979.

Letwin, William. *The Origins of Scientific Economics*. London: Methuen, 1963.

Meek, Ronald L. *The Economics of Physiocracy*. London: George Allen and Unwin, 1962.

Myers, M. L. "Philosophical Anticipations of Laissez-Faire." *History of Political Economy*, 4 (Spring 1972).

Phillips, Almarin. "The Tableau Économique as a Simple Leontief Model." *Quarterly Journal of Economics*, 69 (1955).

Pirenne, Henri. *Economic and Social History of Medieval Europe*. New York: Harcourt Brace, 1937.

Polanyi, Karl. *The Great Transformation*. New York: Farrar and Rinehart, 1944.

Spengler, Joseph J. "Mercantilistic and Physiocratic Growth Theory." In *Theories of Economic Growth*, edited by Bert F. Hoselitz. Glencoe, Ill.: Free Press, 1960.

———, and William R. Allen. *Essays in Economic Thought*. Chapters 1–9. Chicago: Rand McNally, 1960.

Taylor, Overton H. "Economics and the Idea of Natural Laws" and "Economics and the Idea of Jus Naturale." *Economics and Liberalism*. Cambridge: Harvard University Press, 1955.

Vickers, Douglas. *Studies in the Theory of Money 1690–1776*. Philadelphia: Chilton, 1959.

Viner, Jacob. "Powers versus Plenty as Objectives of Foreign Policy in the Seventeenth and Eighteenth Centuries." *The Long View and the Short*. Glencoe, Ill.: Free Press, 1958.

———. *Studies in the Theory of International Trade*. New York: Harper, 1937.

———. "Religious Thought and Economic Society." *History of Political Economy*, 10, (Spring 1978).

Worland, Stephan T. "Justium Pretium: One More Round in an Endless Series." *History of Political Economy*, 9 (Winter 1977).

———. Review of Langholm's book cited above. *History of Political Economy*, 12 (Winter 1980).

Chapter 3
Adam Smith

We have observed in the writings of the later mercantilists and the physiocrats a growing recognition of the interdependence of the elements of the economic system. Yet prior to 1776 no writer had been able to synthesize the important contributions of mercantilism and physiocracy into a single coherent system. Such was the state of economic thinking when a Scottish moral philosopher, Adam Smith (1723–1790), became interested in political economy.

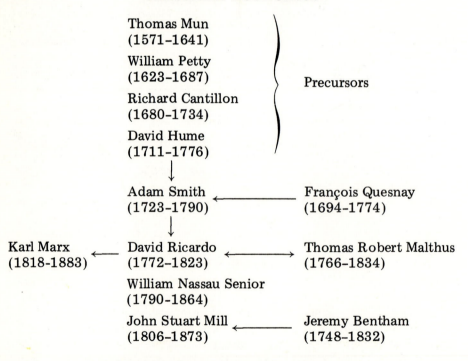

CLASSICAL ECONOMICS

Thomas Mun
(1571–1641)

William Petty
(1623–1687)   Precursors

Richard Cantillon
(1680–1734)

David Hume
(1711–1776)

Adam Smith   François Quesnay
(1723–1790)   (1694–1774)

Karl Marx   David Ricardo   Thomas Robert Malthus
(1818-1883)   (1772–1823)   (1766–1834)

William Nassau Senior
(1790–1864)

John Stuart Mill   Jeremy Bentham
(1806–1873)   (1748–1832)

Arrows indicate direction of influence

CLASSICAL ECONOMICS AND ADAM SMITH

Classical Political Economy

The economic ideas of the scholastics, physiocrats, and mercantilists contained the seeds of concepts that were eventually articulated into a more or less unified system by a group of writers historians call the *classical* economists. The classical period, extending from 1776 to the 1890s, is represented by three major writers: Adam Smith, David Ricardo, and John Stuart Mill. A number of common characteristics link these men and distinguish them from previous and subsequent economic writers. Their most significant departure from mercantilist thought was their favorable attitude toward the results that flow from the natural working of economic forces. The classical vision of a fundamentally harmonious economic system contrasts sharply with the mercantilist and scholastic beliefs that the market is characterized by disharmonies calling for restraints or intervention. This sanguine approach toward the operation of markets, with its various aspects and ramifications, is one of the chief traits of classical thought.

The view that markets automatically provide harmonious solutions to the conflicts flowing from relative scarcity was first significantly developed by the physiocrats of France. Assuming such harmony, according to the physiocrats, it followed that the government should adopt a general policy of noninterference in the economy — a policy of "laissez faire." Whereas the scholastics considered it appropriate for the church to adjudicate the morality of economic activities and the mercantilists advocated government intervention, the classicals, like the physiocrats, favored free, unregulated markets and maximum individual freedom. They felt sure that freedom and liberty were good in and of themselves and thus represented desirable goals. But freedom, and particularly economic freedom, also provided a means by which the economy might function most efficiently. Individuals and businesses, they averred, should be free to trade without government interference. The classicals, moreover, perceived political and economic freedom to be inseparably bound.

Since the development and full flowering of classical thinking in the century between 1776 and the 1870s, one can trace two broad developments relating to the concept of harmony in the economic system. On the one hand, mainstream orthodox economic thinking, while continuing to accept the basic premise of a harmoniously operating economic system, has slowly but steadily weakened its stance by increasingly advocating political rather than market responses to economic problems. On the other hand, some heterodox economic ideas have denied the harmony accepted by classical economics and find such fundamental conflicts in the system that resolution would require major changes in the institutional structure. Marxian thought provides the most significant example of economic thinking that views the economic system as replete with conflict not resolvable by market forces.

A second characteristic of the classical school is its concern for economic growth. Basically macro-oriented — though in a very different sense from that of modern macroeconomists — the classical economists sought to discover the forces that determine the rate of economic growth. Like those who study the less developed economies today, the classicals had a much broader frame of reference than modern macroeconomists. They were concerned not only with the economic forces that determined growth but also with cultural, political, sociological, and historical factors. The main focus for modern macroeconomists is on those forces determining the level of economic activity *given* these broader factors. They look at whether an economy is operating at less than full employment of its resources at a point in time. The classicals, having concluded that economies would tend to operate at a full utilization of their resources, were not interested in this question.

Their concern for growth led the classical economists to a study of markets and the price system as an allocator of resources. Neoclassical economics or modern microeconomics also examines the functioning of markets and the price system, but from a significantly different perspective. Neoclassical theory studies markets in a comparatively static framework in order to throw light on the problems of what determines relative prices, what kinds and quantities of consumer goods are produced, what kinds and scale of economic enterprises are used, and how the personal and functional distributions of income are determined. The classicals studied the formation of relative prices and markets in order to understand their impact on economic growth. For example, the classicals were very much interested in the forces *changing* the distribution of income over time and, therefore, in the causes of changes in relative prices over time. With their concern for growth, the classicals continued in the tradition of the mercantilists. It was not until the 1870s that neoclassical economic theory directed the attention of economists away from growth and almost exclusively toward microeconomic questions of allocating scarce resources among alternative uses.

A final unifying characteristic of classical economics represents another notable departure from mercantilist thinking. The mercantilists trusted absolutely in their ability to uncover the laws governing the operation of the economy. And once they believed they had uncovered these laws, they considered it appropriate to attempt to remedy any defects they discerned in the functioning of the economy, either by changing the institutional structure or by allowing government to intervene. The mercantilists liked to compare themselves to a doctor with a patient: they had *remedies* for the malfunctioning economy, which usually entailed government intervention. This absolute certainty of knowledge characteristic of the mercantilists contrasts rather starkly with the skepticism of Adam Smith, who questioned the wisdom, not to mention the expertise, of the politician who deigned to substitute his judgments for those of the market.

Classical Economists

The work of Adam Smith was a watershed in the development of economic ideas. Though Smith is the first of the group of writers termed the classical school of economists, the end of English mercantilism and the beginning of classicism occurred over a considerable period of time. The last stages of an intellectual era always produce thinkers who deviate from the accepted doctrine. Thus, anticipations of classical liberalism occur in economic literature a century before the publication of Smith's *Wealth of Nations*. Similarly, although no strong challenge was raised to the two major treatises of the classical period, the *Wealth of Nations*, published in 1776, and David Ricardo's *Principles*, published in 1817, a number of minor anticipations of neoclassical theory appeared shortly after the publication of Ricardo's book. John Stuart Mill (1806–1873) represents the end of the classical period, but we will see later that he was uncomfortable with some of the classical dogma. Smith, Ricardo, and J. S. Mill ruled economic thought from 1776 until the final part of the nineteenth century: Smith from 1776 until nearly 1820, Ricardo from roughly 1820 until the 1850s, and J. S. Mill from then until the 1890s.

Two other seminal thinkers, though in some ways classical, were in a more fundamental sense outside the classical school. The population theory of Thomas Malthus (1766–1834) accords with classical theory, but Malthus deviated significantly from the orthodox classical tradition in his analysis of certain macro aspects of the economy and in his defense of the role and significance of the landowning class. Karl Marx (1818–1883) used classical concepts to reach conclusions diametrically opposed to classical theory and policy. For these reasons we will treat Marx in a separate chapter. Malthus's population theory will be included in the discussion of classical economics, but we shall examine separately the famous debate between Malthus and Ricardo concerning the ability of the economy automatically to achieve full employment of resources.

The Changing Economy

Classical economics is fundamentally the economics of producer capitalism, which began in England and Western Europe and spread to other areas of the world. The Industrial Revolution brought important changes in economic and social structures as small-scale shops were replaced by large units of production, and animals and humans by machines. The cities grew, as did the average size of the farm. The increased productivity of agriculture simultaneously provided labor for the factories and food for the nonagricultural workers. The religious views of the Roman Catholic church were largely replaced by the Protestant ethic, and land, labor, and capital began to be traded in the market as custom and tradition gave way to the market economy. These events, together with English economic theory (mercantilism), French economic theory (physiocracy), and English political theory, contributed significantly to the development of classical political economy.

The fundamental economic problem for the classicists, as it had been for the mercantilists, was determining how they might most effectively increase the wealth of a nation. By the early part of the nineteenth century, some new economic problems concerning the distribution of income had appeared, which classical theory attempted to explain.

One aspect of the rise of the new industrial order has been the subject of frequent debate. According to R. H. Tawney, *Religion and the Rise of Capitalism* (1926), and Max Weber, *The Protestant Ethic and the Spirit of Capitalism* (translated, 1930), the Reformation and the rise of the Protestant ethic did much to promote the Industrial Revolution and the emergence of capitalism. We have already seen that Catholic teaching, with its roots in Aristotle, was basically inimical to the growth of the new industrial order. The teachings of John Calvin (1509–1564) and his followers, however, were compatible with economic activity, and the Weber-Tawney thesis is that they contributed directly to the rise of the capitalist system. Weber and Tawney have been criticized by many writers, but both were careful scholars who recognized the tremendous difficulties in assigning a sequence of causal relations among religious ideas, economic action, and economic institutions. They were aware, for instance, that causality can also run from economic institutions to religious ideas, and that the Industrial Revolution and the development of capitalism might equally well account for the development and acceptance of the Protestant ethic. On balance, however, they concluded that changing religious thought effected the profound change in the structure of the society, rather than the other way around.

Scholastic dogma had held that success in economic activity as manifested in individual wealth was a strong indication of sinful behavior — charging excessive prices, lending at high rates of interest, devoting too much attention to the pursuit of gain and too little to the search for salvation. According to the Protestant ethic, economic success bespoke predestination for eternal salvation. The Protestants

Adam Smith

also believed that hard work was good for the soul and conspicuous consumption was to be avoided. The religious views stressing the virtues of work and saving have been regarded as major factors in promoting the emergence of our modern economic society.

Smith the Man

Adam Smith is typical of early economic writers in that he was not exclusively an economist. He was an academic, which allowed him a certain detachment and objectivity lacking in the mercantilist writers, who were generally businessmen. As a professor at Glasgow giving a series of courses that encompassed what we now term the social sciences and humanities, his basic interest was moral philosophy, which colors a good part of his economics. He had read extensively in the previous literature of the social sciences and humanities and was able to synthesize it into a single work. Smith was not a seminal thinker offering new ideas, however, but a careful scholar who set down the best thinking on economics issues of his time. No previous writer had been able to integrate into a single volume an overall vision of the forces determining the wealth of nations and the appropriate policies whereby to foster economic growth and development.

Smith was largely influenced by his teacher Francis Hutcheson (1694-1746) and by David Hume (1711-1776). Smith shared Hutcheson's strong disapproval of the ideas of Bernard Mandeville (1670-1733), whose satirical style had given his presentation of the mercantilist position wide currency. Mandeville and Smith started with the same assumption as to the basically egoistical nature of humans but reached quite opposite conclusions. Mandeville felt that the pursuit of individual self-interest would generate many undesirable social and economic consequences, and therefore built a strong case for government intervention in the economy.

Smith's Conception of the Scope and Method of Economics

Smith's major book is *An Inquiry into the Nature and Causes of the Wealth of Nations*[1] (1776). Two other important sources of his ideas are his earlier book, *The Theory of Moral Sentiments*[2] (1759) and the lectures he gave at the University of Glasgow. Unfortunately Smith's own copies of his lectures were destroyed, and it was not until 1895 that a manuscript was discovered containing a copy of notes taken in 1763 by one of his students. These have been published as *Lectures on Justice, Police, Revenue, and Arms*.[3]

Smith's conception of the scope of economics followed that of the English mercantilists. He was interested in explaining the nature and causes of the wealth of nations. Modern economists would describe Smith as a macro theorist interested in the forces determining economic

1. Adam Smith, *An Inquiry into the Nature and Causes of the Wealth of Nations*, edited with an introduction, notes, marginal summary, and an enlarged index by Edwin Cannan, with an introduction by Max Lerner (New York: Modern Library, 1937).
2. Adam Smith, *The Theory of Moral Sentiments* (New York: A. M. Kelley, 1966).
3. Adam Smith, *Lectures on Justice, Police, Revenue and Arms*, reported by a student in 1763, edited with an introduction and notes by Edwin Cannan, Reprints of Economic Classics (New York: A. M. Kelley, 1964).

growth. But the forces that Smith examined were broader than those studied in modern economics, and he filled in his economic model with political, sociological, and historical material. He gave some attention to the determination of relative prices — included today in microeconomic theory — but his main interest was in economic development and policies to promote economic growth.

However, since Smith assumed that an economy would always employ its resources fully in production, he left untouched an important problem of macroeconomics: given the productive capacity of an economy, what forces determine the levels of income and employment? Smith's methodology, which entailed interweaving deductive theory with historical description, is also worth noting. His theoretical models lack elegance and rigor, but his description of the interrelationships within and the workings of the economy and his ability to weave historical examples into their analysis are unparalleled. A modern mathematical economist could condense the fundamental propositions contained in the nine hundred pages of the *Wealth of Nations* into a short pamphlet. In fact, Ricardo, who possessed some theoretical skill but did not use mathematical notation, was able to cover more theoretical ground in a book less than half the length of Smith's.

SMITH'S ANALYSIS OF MARKETS AND POLICY CONCLUSIONS

There are two possible approaches to the writings of Adam Smith. One is to examine the theoretical structure in detail to evaluate its internal consistency or lack thereof. Another is to examine the overall theoretical structure and the policy implications that are either inherent in the theoretical system or stated explicitly by Smith. We will use the second approach before examining the internal workings of the system. Our first task, therefore, will be to take a broad view of Smith's theoretical structure and examine the policy conclusions that flow from a more detailed economic analysis. Smith's great strength as an economist lay in his vision, first, of the interrelatedness of the segments of the economy and, second, of the policies to be followed to promote the wealth of a nation. On close examination his theory will be found to contain many flaws and contradictions, but his impact on subsequent economic thinking with respect to policy has been equaled by few. He was not an economist in the narrow sense of the word, but rather a philosopher pointing the way to economic development and affluence.

Contextual Economic Policy

Adam Smith's methodological approach shaped both his analysis of the economy and his determinations concerning government policy. More

abstract methodologists base their arguments on reasonably tight
theoretical structures. One such theorist might conclude, for example,
that markets without government intervention result in an optimum
allocation of resources because, in the long run under competitive
markets, firms produce at the lowest possible average cost. Another
abstract theorist may argue *against* markets and for government intervention, using theoretical contructs such as those dealing with externalities or third-party effects. In short, the more theoretical economists
judge whether markets work or fail using abstract arguments separated
from historical or institutional context. Adam Smith's argument for
laissez faire is, of course, based in part upon a theoretical model of how
markets produce certain results. But, significantly, his arguments are
more than just theoretical; they are contextual — that is, they are based
on his observations of the existing historical and institutional circumstances. Smith's laissez faire advocacy is rooted, then, in a methodological approach that asks this question: does experience show that
government intervention will produce better results than will the unimpeded working of markets? Smith realistically conceded that markets
often fail to produce ideal social results, but realism also convinced him
that the results of government intervention were less acceptable than
those flowing from free markets. Hence Smith advocates laissez faire
not because he believes markets to be perfect, but because in the context of history and the institutional structure of the England of
his time, markets usually produce better results than government
intervention.

Later economic thinkers varied in their approach. Ricardo's advocacy
of laissez faire was noncontextual in accord with his abstract, ahis-
torical methodology. J. S. Mill and Alfred Marshall returned to the
Smithian tradition of trying to blend judiciously theory, history, and
contemporary institutions in their analysis and policy conclusions.
Modern orthodox neoclassical economics, however, has reverted to the
Ricardian tradition of abstract theorizing and noncontextual policy
advocacy.

Natural Order, Harmony, and Laissez Faire

The economics of Adam Smith and the mercantilists share certain basic
elements. Influenced by developments in the physical sciences, the
mercantilists and Smith both believed it was possible to discover the
laws of the economy by hard analysis. Matter-of-fact, cause-and-effect
relationships, they believed, can be revealed by scientific investigation.
Smith also assumed the same things about human nature as the mercantilists: human beings are rational and calculating and largely driven by
economic self-interest.

One difference between Smith's system and that of most mercantilists was his assumption that, for the most part, competitive markets exist, and within these markets the factors of production move freely to advance their economic advantage. A second was the assumption that a natural process at work in the economy can resolve conflicts more effectively than any arrangements devised by human beings. Smith expresses this beneficent working of market forces in the following quotation:

As every individual, therefore, endeavors as much as he can to employ his capital in the support of domestic industry, and so to direct that industry that its produce may be of the greatest value; every individual necessarily labours to render the annual revenue of the society as great as he can. He generally, indeed, neither intends to promote the public interest, nor knows how much he is promoting it. By preferring the support of domestic to that of foreign industry, he intends only his own security; and by directing that industry in such a manner as its produce may be of the greatest value, he intends only his own gain, and he is in this, as in many other cases, led by an invisible hand to promote an end which was no part of his intention. Nor is it always the worse for the society that it was no part of it. By pursuing his own interest he frequently promotes that of society more effectually than when he really intends to promote it. I have never known much good done by those who affected to trade for the public good. It is an affectation, indeed, not very common among merchants, and very few words need be employed in dissuading them from it.[4]

The syllogism from which Smith draws his major policy conclusion is very simple. Man is rational and calculating and driven by self-interest. If left alone he will follow his own self-interest, and in promoting his own self-interest he promotes that of society. Government should not interfere in this process and should therefore follow a policy of laissez faire. Throughout his book Smith points out how private self-interest will lead to the public good in a nonregulated market economy. The key to understanding how some degree of harmony and good proceed from conflict and self-interest lies in the activities of the capitalist. Smith points out that capitalists are driven not by altruistic motives but by a desire to make profits — it is not as a result of the benevolence of the baker that we get our bread. The capitalist views the market for final goods and, in order to increase revenues, produces the commodities people desire. Competition among capitalists will result in these goods being produced at a cost of production that will

4. Smith, *Wealth of Nations*, p. 423.

return to the producer an amount just sufficient to pay the opportunity costs of the various factors. If profits above a normal rate of return exist in any sector of the economy, firms will enter these industries, forcing down prices to a cost of production where no excess profits exist. Capitalists will bid for the various factors of production, offering higher prices for the more productive factors, and thus channeling labor and land into those areas of the economy where their efficiency is greatest. Consumers direct the economy by their dollar votes in the market, and changes in their desires are shown in rising and falling prices, and thus rising and falling profits. Smith concludes, finally, that it is wonderful how the market, without planning or governmental direction, leads to the satisfaction of consumer desires at the lowest possible social cost. In the terminology of modern economics, he concludes that an optimum allocation of resources occurs in competitive markets without government intervention.

The Working of Competitive Markets

Smith's most significant contribution to economic theory was his analysis of the working of competitive markets. He was able to specify with greater accuracy than previous writers the mechanism whereby the price resulting from competition would, in the long run, equal cost of production. In his analysis of price formation and resource allocation, he calls short-run prices "market prices" and long-run prices "natural prices." His primary concern is with long-run natural price formation. He saw competition as fundamentally requiring a large number of sellers; a group of resource owners knowledgeable of profits, wages, and rents in the economy; and freedom of movement for resources among industries. Given these conditions, the self-interest of resource owners would lead to long-run natural prices, which would equalize the rate of profits, wages, and rents among the various sectors of the economy. If, for example, the price of a final good is higher than its long-run natural price, then either profits, wages, or rent in this sector of the economy must be higher than their natural return, and adjustments will take place via the movement of resources until the natural price prevails. With competitive markets and an absence of government regulation, the resulting natural prices bring about an optimum allocation of resources, in that consumers receive the goods they want at the lowest possible cost, and maximum rates of growth are assured.

Having thus established the superiority of competitive markets, Smith easily constructs his case against monopoly and government intervention. He recognizes the desire of businessmen to monopolize trade by joining forces, and although he is not able to specify what the monopoly price would be, he recognized that monopolists would extract a higher price by restricting output. Note that Smith's advocacy of laissez faire assumes the existence of competitive markets. Various groups in the economy have frequently parroted Smith's denunciation of government intervention, while ignoring his precept that a laissez faire policy presupposes the existence of competitive markets.

Smith's argument against government intervention in the economy has political, philosophical, and economic bases. He argues that, in general, any government interference is undesirable, since it infringes upon the natural rights and liberties of individuals. However, he examines the economic arguments against government intervention much more extensively. He reviews many of the mercantilist regulations of domestic and foreign trade and shows how they result in an allocation of resources less desirable than that produced by competitive market forces. Smith believed that many of the mercantilist arguments for government intervention, while purporting to promote the social good, were in fact self-serving. The regulation of domestic and foreign commerce benefited not the nation but the merchant. This was not a purely theoretical argument — it came from the context of Smith's personal observation of how governments actually operate. Maybe if governments were different, he observed, they could promote the social good, but given the way they are, they inevitably do more harm than good. In this sense, the roots of modern public choice theory extend back to Adam Smith's perception of how merchants use government to enrich themselves.

Smith's great achievement was his brilliant overview of the workings of markets. Though he did not himself fashion his analytical tools, and despite the difficulties and inaccuracies in his analysis of the formation of relative prices, his accomplishment was immense. He supplemented his broad overview of market processes with descriptive and historical material and produced a work that could be read and understood by the educated people of his time. In this manner he was able to exert an influence on economic policy and lend support to the increasingly favored view that the wealth of England would best be promoted by a government policy of laissez faire.

Smith's advocacy of laissez faire must be qualified, however, for he cites several areas where he believed government intervention, in the context of the historical, political, and institutional structure of his time, was necessary. For example, although he was generally against the regulation of international trade, he made exceptions for tariffs that protected infant industries. Trade regulation was also necessary when national defense might be weakened by a policy of perfectly free international trade. The government was to provide for the national defense, build and maintain roads and schools, administer justice, and keep vital records. Most significantly, Smith qualified his argument for laissez

How Does Adam Smith Rank?

Some historians of economic theory have attempted to rank economists according to their technical brilliance — their ability to develop new techniques of economic analysis and their virtuoso performance in applying technique. Judged by this criterion, Adam Smith ranks low. Other historians have attempted to rank past writers by originality. Judged in this way Smith ranks behind Cantillon, Quesnay, and Turgot. But viewed historically Smith's abilities and his contribution to the flow of economic ideas represent a much scarcer resource than either originality or technical competence: his role was to take up the best ideas of other men and meld them, not with technique but with judgment and wisdom, into a comprehensive system that not only revealed the essential functioning of the economy but also provided rich insights into policy questions. Smith's system was not an abstract, bare-bones analytical framework or pure economic theory; it was political economy focused almost exclusively on the question of which policies best promote what today we call economic growth and what Smith termed "the wealth of nations."

In advocating a laissez faire policy, Smith is very cautious: his invisible hand works to tie public interests to private interests only when competitive forces exist to channel self-interest to the social good. His exceptions to laissez faire — those situations in which he sees the public good as *not* flowing from competitive markets — are standard fare in modern welfare economics and are sometimes even cited in socialist calls for government intervention. No other economist, with the possible exception of J. M. Keynes, has had the impact on economic policy of Adam Smith. Modern economics has added enormous formalization to Smith's vision but little to his insights.

faire by advocating government provision of goods whose social benefits are great but which are not supplied by the private market because supplying them is not sufficiently profitable. For example, the social benefits of education are very great, but the profits to be realized from the private provision of education are so small that if the market is left alone, less education would be supplied than is socially desirable. (Much of modern welfare economics deals with externalities, third-party or spillover effects, and how these must be considered if maximum social welfare is to be achieved.) These qualifications of the laissez faire maxim are an index of Smith's scholarship and intellectual honesty. They did little, however, to diminish the vigor of his laissez faire creed.

Capital and the Capitalists

Smith contributed several important concepts concerning the role of capital in the process of producing wealth and in economic development. He points out, first, that the present wealth of a nation depends upon capital accumulation, since this is what determines the division of labor and proportion of the population engaged in productive labor. Second, Smith concludes that capital accumulation also leads to economic development.

> In the midst of all the exactions of government, this capital has been silently and gradually accumulated by private frugality and good conduct of individuals, by their universal, continual, and uninterrupted effort to better their own condition. It is this effort, protected by law and allowed by liberty to exert itself in the manner that is most advantageous, which has maintained the progress of England towards opulence and improvement in almost all former times, and which, it is to be hoped, will do so in all future times.[5]

Third, individual self-interest coupled with the accumulation of capital leads to an optimum allocation of capital among the various industries.

> Every individual is continually exerting himself to find out the most advantageous employment for whatever capital he can command. It is his own advantage, indeed, and not that of society, which he has in view. But the study of his own advantage naturally, or rather necessarily leads him to prefer that employment which is most advantageous to the society.[6]

One aspect of Smith's view of the role of the capitalist and capital accumulation needs further elaboration. It is clear that the capitalist plays the key role in the functioning of the economy. His pursuit of wealth and profits directs the economy to an efficient allocation of resources and to economic growth. The source of capital in a private property economy is saving by individuals. Smith believed that labor could not accumulate capital because the level of wages permitted only the satisfaction of immediate consumption desires. Members of the

5. *Ibid.*, pp. 328–329.
6. *Ibid.*, p. 421.

landowning class, he observed, have incomes sufficient to accumulate capital, but they spend them on unproductive labor to satisfy their immense desires for high living. It is the members of the rising industrialist class, striving for profits, striving to accumulate capital to increase their wealth by saving and investment, who are the benefactors of society, Smith concluded. An unequal distribution of income in favor of the capitalists is therefore of tremendous social importance. Without an unequal distribution of income, economic growth is not possible, for the whole of the yearly output would be consumed.

The Impact of Smith on Policy

The two major policy conclusions of Smith are that the government should follow a policy of laissez faire and that the distribution of income should be unequal. The impact of these conclusions on economic policy in the industrialized world, especially in the United States, has been immense. They have become the economic ideology of our society, and we attempt to promote these views in the underdeveloped areas of the world. Quite possibly no two ideas and no single writer have had more influence on the development of our economy and society.

Adam Smith's fundamental contribution to economic theory was not a detailed theoretical analysis but a broad overview of the way a market economy allocates scarce resources among alternative uses. We shall now examine in greater detail the theoretical aspects of Smith's work. The space we shall devote to some of the theoretical issues discussed by Smith should not lead students to believe that this was the important part of Smithian economics. Our main purpose in this extended discussion of the details of Smithian theory, particularly the labor theory of value, is to prepare the way for a discussion of the writers following Smith, particularly Ricardo and Marx. Although Smith was unable to solve correctly a number of theoretical problems, his analysis did provide a point of departure for subsequent writers.

THE NATURE AND CAUSES OF THE
WEALTH OF NATIONS

In the first sentence of the *Wealth of Nations*, Smith explains his conception of the nature of the wealth of nations and in so doing separates his views from those of the mercantilists and physiocrats.

The annual labour of every nation is the fund which originally supplies it with all the necessaries and conveniences of life which it

The Relevance of Adam Smith

The revolutions that brought into being the Soviet Union and China and the attempts by less developed countries to achieve growth by planned economies have restored the relevance of many questions Adam Smith raised concerning the appropriate mix of the private and public sectors. Smith held that the primary determinant of growth was capital accumulation. The distribution of the yearly output between capital and consumer goods, according to Smith, determines the rate of growth of national output — the slicing of today's pie determines the size of tomorrow's. Smith's conclusion has never been more assiduously applied than in the Soviet Union and, more recently, in Japan. But what Smith envisioned was that capital accumulation would take the form of private, not state-owned, property. Recent experience in the United States, which has seen falling rates of capital accumulation, or saving, and consequently slower rates of economic growth, has revived economists' interest in these issues.

Smith's less abstract, more institutional perspective on and approach to economic analysis, within its broad framework of the social sciences and history, is also increasingly attracting attention today. The term "political economy" was absent from economic jargon for nearly one hundred years, but a number of economists are now urging a return to the more Smithian breadth of economics it suggests. Public choice theory, with roots in Adam Smith, has been a growth industry in economics. It represents an attempt to understand how choices are made in the public sector, which represents a significantly larger consumer of national output today than in Adam Smith's time.

Generations continue to ask, too, how we should judge those who have the power to impinge upon our national economic destiny — those in high finance, for example, who are changing the face of corporate America through mergers and acquisitions. Should we examine the *motives* for their activities or the *consequences*? Smith, in his time, responded forcefully to such queries, asserting that *consequence* of action should be our touchstone for judging the appropriateness of economic activities.

annually consumes, and which consists always either in the immediate produce of that labour, or in what is purchased with that
produce from other nations.[7]

In a number of places throughout the *Wealth of Nations*, Smith
berates the mercantilists for their concern with the accumulation of
bullion and identification of bullion with the wealth of a nation. Smith
believed, in fact, that all the mercantilists were confused on this issue.
For him wealth is an annual flow of goods and services, not an accumulated fund of precious metals. He also reveals an understanding of the
interrelatedness of exports and imports, perceiving that a fundamental
role for exports is to pay for imports. Furthermore, in this opening
sentence he implies that the end purpose of economic activity is consumption, a position he develops more fully later in the book, and one
that further distinguishes his economics from that of the mercantilists,
who regarded production as an end in itself. Finally, in emphasizing
labor as the source of the wealth of a nation, he differs from the
physiocrats, who stressed land.

Following this introductory paragraph explaining the nature of the
wealth of nations, Smith goes on to suggest that the wealth of nations
be measured in per capita terms. Today when it is said, for example,
that England is wealthier than China, it is understood that the comparison is not based on the total output or income of the two countries,
but on the per capita income of the population. Smith's view, therefore, has been carried forward to the present. In the same paragraph in
which Smith states that consumption is "the sole end and purpose of
all production," he rebukes the mercantilists because in their system
"the interest of the consumer is almost constantly sacrificed to that of
the producer," and also for making "production, and not consumption
...the ultimate end and object of all industry and commerce."[8]

So much for the *nature* of the wealth of nations. The rest of Smith's
book is concerned with the *causes* of the wealth of nations, directly or
indirectly — sometimes very indirectly. Book I deals with value theory,
the division of labor, and the distribution of income; Book II with
capital as a cause of the wealth of nations. Book III studies the economic history of several nations in order to illustrate the theories presented earlier. Book IV is a history of economic thought and practice
examining only mercantilism and physiocracy. Book V covers what
would today be called public finance.

Causes of the Wealth of Nations

Smith holds that the wealth of a nation, what we today call the income
of a nation, depends upon (1) the productivity of labor and (2) the pro-

7. *Ibid.*, p. lvii.
8. *Ibid.*, p. 625.

portion of laborers who are usefully or productively employed. Since he assumes that the economy will automatically achieve full employment of its resources, he examines only those forces that determine the capacity of the nation to produce goods and services.

Productivity of Labor

What determines the productivity of the labor force? In Book I Smith states that the productivity of labor depends upon the division of labor. It is an observed fact that specialization and division of labor increases the productivity of labor. This had been recognized long before the publication of the *Wealth of Nations*, but no writer had emphasized this principle as Smith did. In our modern economy, and even in the academic world, division of labor is widely practiced, with notable influence on productivity. Smith illustrated the advantages of specialization and division of labor by borrowing an example from past literature, which measured output per worker in a factory producing straight pins. When each man performs every operation required to produce a pin, output per worker is very low, but if the production process is divided into a number of separate operations, each worker specializing in one of these operations, a large increase in output per worker occurs. In Smith's example, when the process is divided into eighteen distinct operations, output per worker increases from twenty pins to forty-eight hundred per day. It is interesting that while Smith recognized the economic benefits of specialization and division of labor, he perceived some serious social costs. One social disadvantage of the division of labor is that workers are given repetitious tasks that soon become monotonous. Human beings become machines tied to a production process and are dehumanized by the simple, repetitive, boring tasks they perform. But Smith has no doubt that human welfare is, on balance, increased by the division of labor.

The division of labor, in turn, depends upon what Smith termed the "extent of the market" and upon the accumulation of capital. The larger the market, the greater the volume that can be sold, and the greater the opportunity for division of labor. A limited market, on the other hand, permits only limited division of labor. The division of labor is limited by the accumulation of capital because the production process is time-consuming — there is a time lag between the beginning of production and the final sale of the finished product. In a simple economy where each household produces all of its own consumption needs and the division of labor is slight, very little capital is required to maintain (feed, clothe, house) the laborers during the production process. As the division of labor is increased, laborers no longer produce goods for their own consumption, and a stock of consumer goods must exist to maintain labor during the time-consuming production process. This stock of goods comes from saving and is, in this context, what Smith calls "capital." It is a major function of the capitalist to provide the means for bridging the gap between the time when production begins and when the final product is sold. Thus, the extent to which production processes requiring division of labor may be used is limited by the amount of capital accumulation available. Smith therefore concludes,

> As the accumulation of stock must, in the nature of things, be previous to the division of labour, so labour can be more and more subdivided in proportion only as stock is previously more and more accumulated.[9]

Productive and Unproductive Labor

The accumulation of capital, according to Smith, also determines the ratio between the number of laborers who are productively employed and those who are not so employed. Smith's attempt to distinguish between productive and unproductive labor became confused and reflected normative or value judgments on his part. However, it manifests an awareness of the problem of economic growth. Labor employed in producing a vendible commodity is productive labor, Smith held, whereas labor producing a service is unproductive. As an advocate of the changing social and economic order, he felt that the activities of the capitalists, which resulted in an increased output of real goods, were beneficial to economic growth and development while the expenditures of the landowners for servants and other intangible goods were wasteful. "A man grows rich by employing a multitude of manufacturers: he grows poor, by maintaining a multitude of menial servants."[10] According to Smith, what is true of the individual is true for the nation, so that, for the economy as a whole, the larger the share of the labor force involved in producing tangible real goods, the greater the wealth of the nation. Capital is required to support the productive labor force; therefore, the greater the capital accumulation, the larger the proportion of the total labor force involved in productive labor. "Capitals are increased by parsimony, and diminished by prodigality and misconduct."[11]

This distinction between productive and unproductive labor also affects Smith's view of the role of the government in the economy. Just

9. *Ibid.*, p. 260.
10. *Ibid.*, p. 314.
11. *Ibid.*, p. 321.

as the expenditures of the landowning class for servants and other forms of unproductive labor are detrimental to economic development, so is some part of government expenditures. "The sovereign, for example, with all the officers both of justice and war who serve under him, the whole army and navy, are unproductive labourers."[12] Smith insists that the highest rates of economic growth will be achieved by distributing large incomes to the capitalist class, who will save and invest, and low incomes to the landlords who spend for menial servants and "who leave nothing behind them in return for their consumption."[13] Furthermore, since economic growth is inhibited by government spending for unproductive labor, it is better to have less government and, consequently, lower taxes on the capitalists so that they may accumulate more capital.

Summary of the Causes of the Wealth of Nations

We began this discussion with the question: What determines the wealth of a nation? Although the opening sentence of Smith's book might suggest that it is the "annual labour of every nation" which is the cause of its wealth, a closer look at his reasoning reveals that it is the accumulation of capital. To see this, let us summarize in outline form Smith's discussion of what produces wealth.

Determinants of Wealth
I. Productivity of labor
   A. Amount of specialization and division of labor
      1. Limited by extent of the market
         a. Extent of the market is a function of capital accumulation
   B. Accumulation of capital
II. Proportion between productive and unproductive labor
   A. Accumulation of capital

Smith's own summary of this reasoning follows:

The annual produce of the land and labour of any nation can be increased in its value by no other means, but by increasing either the number of its productive labourers, or the productive powers of those labourers who had before been employed. The number of its productive labourers, it is evident, can never be much increased, but in consequence of an increase of capital, or of the funds destined for maintaining them. The productive powers of the same number of

12. *Ibid.*, p. 315.
13. *Ibid.*, p. 321.

labourers cannot be increased, but in consequence either of some addition and improvement to those machines and instruments which facilitate and abridge labour; or of a more proper division and distribution of employment. In either case an additional capital is almost always required.[14]

The result of this chain of reasoning is clear. Capital is the chief determinant of the wealth of nations. This important conclusion of Smith's has had a tremendous impact on economic policy. He stated that the rate of economic growth depends heavily on the division of the total output of the economy between consumer goods and capital goods. The larger the proportion of capital goods is to total output, the greater the rate of economic growth. This conclusion has had an important influence on economic policy in economies with widely different structures — for example, the United States and the Soviet Union.

For Adam Smith there was no question that this capital accumulation required an institutional framework of free markets and private property. Free markets operating without government direction would assure that a given level of investment spending would be allocated so as to ensure the highest rates of economic growth. In a system of private property, a further requirement for high rates of capital accumulation is an unequal distribution of income. However, the experience of the Soviet Union indicates that high rates of capital accumulation and economic growth are *not* dependent upon free markets and private property.

VALUE THEORY

Certain questions regarding value, or price, that should be kept separate were sometimes confused by early economists: (1) What determines the price of a good, or in the language of modern economics, what determines relative prices? (2) What determines the general level of prices? (3) What is the best measure of welfare? The first and third questions are part of modern microeconomics, and the second, although it defies the usually simple micro-macro dichotomy, is generally included under the broad umbrella of macroeconomics. Smith does not provide an unambiguous answer to any of these questions. His discussions of them are confusing in this regard because he intermingles his discussion of what determines relative prices with his attempt to discover a measure of changes in welfare over time.

14. *Ibid.*, p. 326.

Relative Prices

Though Adam Smith explained relative prices as determined by supply or costs of production alone, he did not completely ignore the role of demand. He believed that market, or short-run, prices are determined by both supply and demand. Natural, or long-run equilibrium, prices generally depend upon costs of production, although Smith sometimes states that natural price depends upon both demand and supply. These inconsistencies provide ample opportunity for historians of economic theory to debate Smith's real meaning.

Smith's analysis of the formation of relative prices in the economy of his time includes two time periods, the short run and the long run; and two broad sectors of the economy, agriculture and manufacturing. During the short-run, or market, period in both manufacturing and agriculture, Smith finds downward-sloping demand curves and upward-sloping supply curves: therefore, market prices depend upon demand and supply. Smith's analysis of the more complicated "natural price," occurring in the long run, contains some contradictions. For the agricultural sector, natural price depends upon supply and demand, since the long-run supply curve is upward-sloping, indicating increasing costs. But for the manufacturing sector, the long-run supply curve is at times assumed to be perfectly elastic, representing horizontal or constant costs, and in other parts of the analysis the supply curve is downward-sloping, indicating decreasing costs. In cases of manufacturing, when the long-run supply curve is perfectly elastic, price depends entirely on cost of production, but when it is downward-sloping, natural price depends upon both demand and supply.

There are a number of possible interpretations of Smith's statements with regard to the forces determining natural prices for manufactured goods. One may assume that he was merely inconsistent — possibly because of the long period of time he took to write the *Wealth of Nations* — or that he thought these issues of minor importance. Another approach is to select one of his manufacturing costs as representative of the real Adam Smith. It makes little difference which approach is employed, since Smith consistently notes the role of demand in the formation of natural prices and in the allocation of resources between the various sectors of the economy. Nevertheless, the major emphasis, regardless of the shape of the long-run supply curve in manufacturing, is on cost of production in the determination of natural prices, an emphasis characteristic of Smith and subsequent classical economists.

The scholastics became interested in the question of relative prices because they were concerned with the ethical aspects of exchange, and the mercantilists considered it because they thought wealth was created in the process of exchange. But even though Smith on occasion discussed prices in ethical terms, he had a more important reason for being interested in the factors determining relative prices. Once an economy practices specialization and division of labor, exchange becomes necessary. If exchange takes place in a market such as the one existing at the time Smith wrote, certain obvious problems arise. First, there is the question of a medium of exchange, if exchange is to be on a level higher than barter. The medium used is money, and Smith discusses the role of money as a medium of exchange in Chapter IV of Book I. Second, there is the question of value, or relative price. To use Smith's language, what principles determine the relative or exchangeable value of goods? He takes up this question in Chapters V, VI, and VII of Book I. The third question that arises as a result of the division of labor and exchange is how the output of an economy is divided among those engaged in production. Smith considers the distribution of income in the remaining chapters of Book I.

The Meaning of Value

Smith held that the word *value*

> has two different meanings, and sometimes expresses the utility of some particular object, and sometimes the power of purchasing other goods which the possession of that object conveys. The one may be called "value in use"; the other, "value in exchange." The things which have the greatest value in use have frequently little or no value in exchange; and on the contrary, those which have the greatest value in exchange have frequently little or no value in use. Nothing is more useful than water: but it will purchase scarce any thing; scarce any thing can be had in exchange for it. A diamond, on the contrary, has scarce any value in use; but a very great quantity of other goods may frequently be had in exchange for it.[15]

According to Smith value in exchange is the power of a commodity to purchase other goods — its price. This is an objective measure expressed in the market. His concept of value in use is ambiguous; it resulted in a good part of his difficulties in explaining relative prices. On the one hand, it has ethical connotations and is therefore a return to scholasticism. Smith's own puritanical standards are particularly noticeable in his statement that diamonds have hardly any value in use. On the other hand, value in use is the want-satisfying power of a commodity, the utility received by holding or consuming a good. There are several kinds of utility received when a commodity is consumed: its

15. *Ibid.*, p. 28.

total utility, its average utility, and its marginal utility. Smith's focus was on total utility, which obscured his understanding of how demand plays its role in price determination. It is clear that the total utility of water is greater than that of diamonds, and this is what Smith refers to when he points to the high use value of water as compared to diamonds. However, since a commodity's marginal utility often decreases as more of it is consumed, it is quite possible that another unit of water would give less marginal utility than another unit of diamonds. The price we are willing to pay for a commodity — the value we place on acquiring another unit — depends not on its total utility but on its marginal utility. Since Smith did not recognize this, he could neither find a satisfactory solution to the diamond-water paradox nor see the relationship between use value and exchange value. Ricardo did not share Smith's confusion, as we shall see when we examine his views on relative prices in the next chapter.

Smith's Three Theories of Relative Prices

As we have seen, Smith was somewhat confused about the factors determining relative prices, but it is worth examining some of his views in order to understand some of the important conceptual problems encountered by Ricardo and Marx in their attempts to formulate a theory of relative prices, particularly a labor theory of value. We shall confine our examination chiefly to his three major theories of relative prices, presenting only brief summaries of his explanations of wages, profits, and rents, for he had several contradictory theories for each of these income categories.

Smith develops three theories of relative prices: (1) *a labor cost theory*; (2) *a labor command theory*; and (3) *a cost of production theory*. He postulated two distinct states of the economy: the early and rude state, which is defined as an economy in which capital has not been accumulated and land is not appropriated; and an advanced economy, in which capital and land are no longer free goods (they have a price greater than zero). For the early and rude state of society, he advances two explanations of relative prices, a labor cost theory and a labor command theory.

Labor Cost Theory in a Primitive Society

In the early and rude state of society which precedes both the accumulation of stock [i.e., capital] and the appropriation of land, the proportion between the quantities of labour necessary for acquiring different objects seems to be the only circumstance which can afford any rule for exchanging them for one another. If among a nation of hunters, for example, it usually costs twice the labour to kill a beaver which it does to kill a deer, one beaver should naturally exchange for or be worth two deer.[16]

Thus, according to Smith's labor cost theory, the exchange value, or price, of a good in an economy where land and capital are nonexistent, or where these goods are free, is determined by the quantity of labor required to produce it. This brings us to the first difficulty with a labor cost theory of value. How are we to measure the quantity of labor required to produce a commodity? Suppose that two laborers are working without capital, that land is free, and that in one hour laborer Jones produces one unit of final product and Brown produces two units. Let us assume that all other things are equal, or to use the shorthand expression of theory, *ceteris paribus*, so that the only cause of the differences in productivity is the difference in the skills of the workers. Does a unit of output require one hour of labor or two? Smith recognized that the quantity of labor required to produce a good cannot be measured just by using clock hours, since in addition to time, the ingenuity or skill involved and the hardship or disagreeableness of the task must be taken into account.

At this point Smith encounters a difficulty that all labor cost theories of value have encountered and that has not been successfully solved by subsequent writers. If the quantity of labor is a function of more than one variable, then we must find a means of stating the relative importance of all the variables. Suppose we have the following information about the production of good A and good B:

	Time	Hardship	Ingenuity
Good A	1 Hour	X	2Y
Good B	2 hours	2X	Y

How does one compare the quantity of labor required for product A with that of product B? The units of measuring time are clock hours, but the units of measuring ingenuity and hardship are not given. Though it is not crucial to know these units for the problem at hand, it is essential to be able to measure the differences in the amount of hardship and ingenuity required to produce the two goods. Smith tries to solve this problem of reducing time, hardship, and ingenuity to a common denominator by holding that differences in time, hardship, and ingenuity are reflected in the wages paid to labor. If laborer Smith receives wages of $2 per hour and Jones wages of $1 per hour, these

16. *Ibid.*, p. 47.

wage payments reflect differences in their skill or ingenuity, and if they work in different industries, their wages will also reflect, in part, varying degrees of unpleasantness or hardship.

Smith's suggestion merely restates the problem rather than providing a solution. The purpose of his value theory is to explain those forces that determine relative prices, but wages themselves are one of the many prices in an economy that his theory must explain. When he concludes that the wage paid to labor is a measure of the relative amounts of time, hardship, and ingenuity required to produce a commodity, he is begging the question. He is saying that a good has value according to the wages paid to labor and not according to the quantity of labor contained in the good. This is circular reasoning. Smith is using one set of prices, namely wages, to explain another set of prices.

To gain further insight into Smith's analysis of the labor cost theory and the determination of prices in a primitive society, let us go hunting with him. If it requires two hours to capture one beaver or two deer, Smith concludes that two deer will be equal to one beaver in the market, or the price of beaver will be twice the price of deer. The reasoning necessary to reach this conclusion and the assumptions on which the model is based are worth examining carefully, for Smith, like many economists, neither gives his reasoning in full nor states explicitly all the assumptions required to reach his conclusions. The price — two deer equal one beaver — is what Smith calls the natural price and what modern theory would call the long-run equilibrium price. To explain why this is the long-run equilibrium price, let us examine other prices in order to determine if they are disequilibrium prices and to find the direction of movement away from them. Suppose that the demand for beaver increases and a new price emerges in the market: three deer equal one beaver, or 3D = 1B. This represents a rise in the price of beaver and a corresponding fall in the price of deer. This new price Smith calls a market price and modern theory terms a short-run equilibrium price.

With the rise in the price of beaver, the hunters in our primitive society would no longer hunt deer and would spend their time hunting beaver, for the following reason. Deer can be acquired in two ways, either directly, by hunting deer, or indirectly, by hunting beaver and trading it for deer in the market. With a price of 3D = 1B, the rational choice is to hunt beaver and trade beaver for deer in the market. The net gain resulting from this method can be calculated. Two deer could be acquired directly by expending two hours' labor in hunting deer. They could be acquired indirectly by hunting two hours for a beaver and trading it in the market for three deer, a net gain of one deer. Assuming that beaver and deer are divisible goods, the advantage of using the market could also be calculated in time. Rather than spend one hour directly hunting deer, the clever hunter spends two-thirds of an hour hunting beaver and trades in the market for one deer the one-third beaver acquired by hunting. The net gain is the one-third hour saved for each deer acquired through the market.

The result of this process would be to increase the supply of beaver in the market and to decrease the supply of deer. The price of beaver would then fall, and the price of deer rise. We have established that a price for beaver higher than 1B = 2D is a disequilibrium price and that at any price for beaver higher than 1B = 2D market forces will operate to lower price toward the long-run equilibrium price. At a price for beaver below this price of 1B = 2D, the supply of beaver would decrease and its price would rise toward what Smith calls the natural price.

Assumptions of the Model

There are some important insights to be gained from our examination of the Smithian model of price determination using a labor cost theory in a primitive society. First, Smith assumes that the hunters in this early state are rational and calculating and driven by motives of economic self-interest. In short, these hunters act as though they were on the floor of a stock or commodity exchange, not like members of a primitive tribe. A cultural anthropologist might take a completely different approach, considering perhaps the influence of habit and custom that might well cause a beaver hunter to follow the pursuits of his elders rather than the dictates of the market. (My father shot beaver, therefore I will shoot beaver.) Second, Smith's model assumes perfect competition: the hunters (firms) in the market are price takers and quantity adjusters who individually have no market power, and form no sort of organization to regulate supply and, consequently, market price. Third, Smith assumes that both beaver and deer can be produced in larger quantities while the average cost per unit of output remains constant; in other words, that supply curves in the long run are horizontal, or perfectly elastic. However, if more beaver are supplied, one might expect that the number of hours necessary to kill a beaver would, in fact, increase; the supply curve would slope up and to the right.

Under this assumption of constant costs, demand plays no role in determining relative prices in the long run. Changes in demand will reallocate factors of production between industries but will not influence long-run prices. Price then depends entirely on cost of production, or supply, and if labor is the only cost of production, as in Smith's model, what results is a labor theory of value. If, however, the supply curve slopes up and to the right, the industries, in the jargon of micro theory, are increasing-cost industries: price is a function of both demand and supply. Smith's model is comparatively static. His concern is with final long-run equilibrium positions rather than with the intervals between equilibria. It is a "timeless" analysis, since it starts with long-run equilibrium, then postulates some disturbance of this equilibrium, and then deduces the new equilibrium price. The time-path of the variables in the system is not considered; analytically, the process of adjustment is regarded as instantaneous.

Labor Command in a Primitive Society

Now that we have worked through the labor cost theory of relative prices for a primitive economy, the labor command theory will be smooth sailing. According to Smith, under the labor command theory, the value of a good "to those who possess it, and who want to exchange it for some new productions, is precisely equal to the quantity of labour which it can enable them to purchase or command."[17] Using Smith's example, we find that a beaver will command two hours of labor and a deer one, so that their relative price will again be 1B = 2D. Thus, in primitive societies the same prices result whether we use labor cost or labor command theory.

Labor Theory in an Advanced Economy

Smith's advanced economy model differs from his primitive economy model in two important respects: capital has been accumulated and land appropriated. They are no longer free goods and the final price of a good also must include returns to the capitalist as profits and to the landlord as rent. Final prices, then, yield an income made up of the factor payments of wages, profits, and rents. Let us assume that wages are ¾ of the final price and that profits and rents are ¼ of the final price for both beaver and deer. What are the exchange ratios using labor cost and labor command theories?

Since, under labor cost, a beaver required two hours of labor time and a deer one hour, they would exchange at a ratio of 1B = 2D. Labor command is slightly more complicated. Using X as our unknown, or the quantity of labor a beaver can command, we know that $¾X = 2$ units of labor, or that $X = 2⅔$. A beaver would therefore command 2⅔ units of labor, of which 2 units would be paid as wages and ⅔ unit would be paid as profits and rents. Thus, under the assumptions of an advanced economy, the buyer of a beaver would have to offer more units of labor than were required to produce it, since the capitalist and the landlord must be paid, as well as labor. Under these circumstances the quantity

17. *Ibid.*, pp. 30–31.

of labor the commodity beaver can command exceeds the quantity of labor required to produce it. Using the same reasoning, a deer would command $1^1/_3$ units of labor ($^3/_4 X = 1$, or $X = 1^1/_3$).

Once capital has been accumulated and land appropriated, once profits and rents must be paid, labor cost no longer equals labor command. Yet when we examine the *relative* price of beaver and deer — which is the object of any theory of relative prices — we find that the exchange ratio between beaver and deer is the same under either labor cost or labor command($1:2 = 1^1/_3 :2^2/_3$). It was at this point that Smith dimly perceived some of the real difficulties of a labor theory of relative prices and, unable to solve these problems theoretically, abandoned a labor theory for an advanced model economy in favor of a cost of production theory. Later, Ricardo, with great theoretical skill, would return to the task of trying to work out the difficulties inherent in a labor theory of value for an advanced economy. Before turning to Smith's cost of production theory, we shall examine some further implications of a labor theory.

Our conclusion that in Smith's model relative prices are the same under a labor cost or command theory depends on one crucial assumption: that wage payments are the same proportionate part of final price in both the beaver and deer industries. Is this assumption consistent with the conditions that exist in an advanced economy? If the fertility of land varies, rent is likely to be a different proportionate part of the final price for commodities produced on different grades of land. Similarly labor-capital ratios are likely to vary from one industry to another, and profit is likely to be a larger part of final prices in capital-intensive industries. Suppose we work through our example using the more reasonable assumption that labor's share of final price differs between the beaver and deer industries because of differing fertilities of land and differing labor-capital ratios. Assume that labor receives $^2/_3$ of the final price in the beaver industry and $^3/_4$ of the final price in the deer industry. A beaver now commands 3 units of labor ($^2/_3 X = 2$, or $X = 3$), and a deer commands $1^1/_3$ units of labor ($^3/_4 X = 1$, or $X = 1^1/_3$). The relative prices using labor cost and labor command are no longer the same. Using labor cost the price ratio is 1B = 2D, under labor command 1B = $2^1/_4$D. To put this another way, $1:2 \neq 1^1/_3 :3$. We will return to these and other difficulties inherent in a labor theory of value when we examine the solutions offered by Ricardo and Marx.

Cost of Production Theory of Relative Prices

Although Smith did not recognize all of the difficulties involved in applying a labor theory of value to an advanced economy, he saw enough to reject both the labor cost and command theories and to suggest that for the economy of his time the appropriate theory to explain relative prices was a cost of production theory. In a cost theory the value of a commodity depends on the payments to all the factors of production: land and capital in addition to labor. In Smith's system the term "profits" includes both profits as they are understood today and interest. The total cost of producing a beaver is then equal to wages, profits, and rent, $TC_B = W_B + P_B + R_B$; likewise for a deer, $TC_D = W_D + P_D + R_D$. The relative price for beaver and deer would then be given by the ratio of TC_B/TC_D. Where Smith assumed that average costs do not increase with increases in output, this calculation gives the same relative prices whether total costs or average costs are used. Where Smith assumed that average costs change with output, prices depend upon both demand and supply. However, in his analysis of the determination of long-run natural prices, Smith emphasized supply and cost of production, even when the supply curve was not assumed to be perfectly elastic. Where competition prevails, he maintained, the self-interest of the businessman, laborer, and landlord will result in natural prices that equal cost of production.

DISTRIBUTION THEORY

The personal distribution of income depends on the prices and quantities of factors of production sold by individuals. Labor is the only factor of production owned by most households, so a household income generally depends upon the wage rate and the number of hours worked. The amount of property income received by those households that do own property depends on the quantity of capital and land held by the household and the prices of these factors. Since wages, profits, and rents are prices in an economy, their relative values, along with the quantities of labor, capital, and land that individuals bring to the market, determine the distribution of income. Although distribution of income is not of prime concern to Smith, he does offer several different and sometimes contradictory theories of wages, profits, and rents. We shall confine ourselves to mentioning some aspects of his analysis that anticipate later writers and illustrate both his insights and his misunderstandings.

Wages

Smith offers a number of theories to explain wages. In Chapter VIII, Book I, he suggests a subsistence theory of wages, a productivity theory, a bargaining theory, a residual claimant theory, and a wages fund theory. He does not appear to be disturbed by the contradictions among these various positions, and in other parts of his book he explicitly rejects some of his own propositions. However, two aspects of his discussion of wages deserve further comment.

Smith points out that labor is at a disadvantage in the wage-bargaining process. Since there are fewer employers than employees, he says, employers can more easily group together to strengthen their position. Furthermore, the law permits these employer combinations but prohibits employees from forming unions. Parliament has many acts against raising wages, he tells us, but none against lowering them. Finally, employers have ample resources that make it possible for them to live even if they employ no labor during a strike or lockout. On the other hand, "many workmen could not subsist a week, few could subsist a month, and scarce any a year without employment."[18] In these passages Smith weakens his case for the beneficent working of market forces and appears to recognize that his assumption of perfectly competitive markets is subject to qualifications.

In his discussion of wages, Smith presents his version of the wages fund doctrine, which became an important tool of the classical economists. This doctrine supposes that there is a certain fixed fund of capital destined to pay wages. Since the production process is time-consuming, it requires previously produced goods that laborers can use for food, clothing, housing, and other things between the start of the process and the final sale. This inventory of goods or capital is termed the wages fund, and its source is the saving, or failure to consume, of the capitalists. Given the size of the labor force and the wages fund, the wage rate is determined: wage rate = wages fund/labor force. Smith does not develop all of the theoretical and policy implications of this doctrine. He does, however, suggest that an increase in wage rates will result in increased population and labor supply, so that wages will eventually fall back to the former level, thus anticipating the Malthusian theory of population. We will return in the next chapter to the implications of the wages fund doctrine and its importance in the classical system.

Profits

Surprisingly, Smith's discussion of the nature and source of profits is extremely brief. In general the classical economists made no serious attempts to explain the nature and source of profits until the 1820s, when they responded to socialist criticism of profit. Smith apparently accepts without question the legitimacy of profits as a payment to the capitalist for performing a socially useful function, namely to provide

18. *Ibid.*, p. 66.

labor with the necessities of life and with materials and machinery with which to work during the time-consuming production process. According to Smith, labor permits this deduction of profits from its output because it has no materials to work with and no independent means of support. Here, then, profit is composed of two parts: a pure interest return and a return for risk.

Smith's brief and inadequate treatment of profits opened the door to the exploitation theory of profit advanced by Marx.

> The produce of labour constitutes the natural recompence or wages of labour.
>
> In that original state of things, which precedes both the appropriation of land and the accumulation of stock, the whole produce of labour belongs to the labourer. He has neither landlord nor master to share with him.[19]

Thus in Smith's primitive economy the laborer received the whole of the product, but in his own time labor had to share the product with the capitalist and landlord. Smith never explained why profits and rents are deducted from the output of labor, and thereby exposed his system to attack by any reader who is basically critical of a private property, capitalist economy. Readers who believe, like Smith, in the basic harmony in the system would probably not even notice this omission.

Rent

Smith suggests at least four theories of rent, all of which contradict each other. The origins of rent are variously held to be (1) demands by the landlord, (2) monopoly, (3) differential advantages, and (4) the bounty of nature. Early in the *Wealth of Nations*, rent is regarded as price-determining,[20] whereas later Smith anticipates Ricardo and regards rent as price-determined.[21] Smith is usually very critical of landlords who "love to reap where they never sowed."[22] He senses the basic conflict between the interests of the landlords and the capitalists, which Ricardo expounded in full. This is another example of Smith's realization that the basic harmony in the economy is subject to some areas of discord.

19. *Ibid.*, p. 64.
20. *Ibid.*, p. 50.
21. *Ibid.*, pp. 145-146.
22. *Ibid.*, p. 49.

The Rate of Profit over Time

Smith believed that the economic growth of a nation depended on the accumulation of capital. Although he paid little attention to the nature and source of profits, he was extremely interested in changes in the rate of profit over time. He predicted that the rate of profit would fall over time for three reasons: (1) *Competition in the labor market.* The accumulation of capital will result in competition among capitalists in the labor market with the result that wages will rise. Smith concluded that the increased wages would bring about a fall in profits. (2) *Competition in the commodity market.* Smith reasoned that as output increased so would competition among producers, with the consequences that commodity prices would fall and profits decline. This implies the possibility of overproduction for the whole economy, which conflicts with his basic position that overproduction cannot occur. (3) *Competition in the investment market.* Smith apparently felt that there were a limited number of investment opportunities and that increased capital accumulation would therefore lead to falling profits. When he examined what historical information was available on the secular trend of interest rates, these data supported his theoretical conclusions. He did note that some of the colonies, for example those in North America, were characterized by both high wages and high profits.

WELFARE AND THE GENERAL LEVEL OF PRICES

We pointed out earlier that Smith's discussion of value theory fails to formulate distinct theories of welfare, relative prices, and the general price level. His examination of these three issues is interconnected and therefore confusing; he appears to have been not only confusing but confused. So it is not surprising that historians of economic ideas have argued over Smith's true opinion. One group of writers holds that Smith had three theories of relative prices (labor cost, labor command, and cost of production) and a theory explaining the general level of prices. Another group says that he had settled on a cost of production theory of relative prices, a theory measuring changes in welfare over time, and a theory of the general level of prices. This second group denies that Smith had a labor theory of relative prices. We believe that Smith experimented with all of these theories: a theory of relative prices consisting of labor cost and labor command for a primitive society, and cost of production for an advanced economy; the formulation of an index measuring changes in welfare over time; and a theory explaining the general level of prices. We shall now consider the last two of these theories.

Chapter V, Book I

Historians of economic theory have wrestled with Chapter V, Book I, of Smith's *Wealth of Nations*, entitled, "Of the Real and Nominal Price of Commodities, or of Their Price in Labour, and Their Price in Money." We believe that in this chapter Smith tried to answer several questions, which, although related, create confusion when examined simultaneously. He attempted to discover, first, the factors determining the general level of prices and, second, the best measure of changes in welfare over time. The second question is the more difficult. How are we to define welfare in an unambiguous way so that changes in welfare can be measured? Suppose that an economy produces only one final product, deer. Welfare for the economy could be defined and measured in terms of the quantity of deer consumed. Consumption of larger quantities of deer would represent increased welfare for the society, and smaller quantities decreased welfare or "illfare." The issue becomes more complex when we introduce a second final good, beaver. We can state unequivocally that more of both beaver and deer will increase welfare, and less of both will decrease it. But what if consumption of beaver increases and consumption of deer decreases? The welfare of the people in the society who place a high value on beaver would increase, while the welfare of those who value deer would decrease. Is it possible to define and measure changes in welfare for an economy of two or more products? Smith tried to answer this question.

If welfare is defined as either the total consumption or the output of society, the initial problem to be solved for a multiple-product economy is to find a way to add the output or consumption of the products, for example, beaver and deer. A possible solution to this problem is to convert all commodities to one common measure. If 1B = 2D, then an increase in output of two beaver coupled with a decrease in output of two deer represents an increase in welfare. The new level of output can be said to be one beaver better off, or two deer better off. If, however, the relative prices of beaver and deer change as their outputs change, the problem of measuring welfare becomes much more complicated. In an economy of many products, the relative prices of commodities are expressed in a common measure, usually the monetary unit of the government. In theory, and occasionally in practice, this common measure (in the jargon of economics, the *numeraire*) could be any one of the commodities of the economy, for example, cows, corn, or gold. Our economy measures output by adding up the money value of each commodity to obtain a sum we call the "gross national product." If the gross national product increases from one year to the next, can we conclude that welfare has increased?

Measuring changes in output in a multiple-product economy by this means presents difficulties, because the unit of measurement, the yardstick money, is itself variable. The general level of prices changes, and therefore the money value of output may not correctly reflect the true output. Smith considers the possibility of using gold or silver as a common measure or *numeraire* but concludes that since the prices of these commodities vary, they are unsatisfactory for this purpose. He then turns to labor, but finds that the price of labor also varies over time. In the end, the only invariant measure he can find to assess changes in welfare is the disutility of work, since "equal quantities of labour, at all times and places, may be said to be of equal value to the labourer."[23]

Given Smith's conclusion that labor disutility can be used in computing an index of welfare, the problem of measuring changes in welfare is easily solved. We first measure changes in total output in terms of the monetary unit, and then adjust for changes in the general level of prices according to changes in the price of either gold, silver, or corn. We have by this process converted money income and nominal price into real income and real price. To measure changes in welfare, we then compare the amount of labor disutility involved in producing the different outputs. For example, if the money value or output increases 10 percent, and the general level of prices as measured by the price of gold has also gone up 10 percent, the real value of output remains the same. Welfare increases if the disutility of producing this output decreases. Translated into everyday language, if we could produce the same quantity of output with less labor we would have more leisure and be better off.

Measuring changes in welfare is much more complicated than Smith thought, however, and our discussion cannot touch on all the issues involved. Smith does not discuss how to define or measure the disutility of labor. This would appear to be completely subjective. One of his assumptions that was not questioned by orthodox economists until the twentieth century was that more goods are better than fewer, or that increases in output occurring without increases in labor disutility must always result in increased welfare. The various goods making up total output is not an issue in his writing. Growth of output is an improvement in welfare even if this enlarged output includes goods of doubtful benefit to the society. Furthermore, Smith and the orthodox economists who followed did not consider the "quality of life" produced by this enlarged output. Little or no attention was given to the costs society might pay in the form of pollution or other harmful externalities for ever-larger outputs.

23. *Ibid.*, p. 33.

SUMMARY AND CONCLUSIONS

Smith's contribution to and influence on economic thought is deservedly tremendous. More than any other writer of his time he saw the central ideas and forces that govern a market economy. His work, however, is not without problems. Smith confused himself and generations of economists by failing to elaborate separate theories of, and distinguish clearly between, relative prices, the general level of prices, and changes in welfare. Historians of economic ideas have debated whether Smith propounded a labor theory of value. If this means a labor theory of relative prices, the answer is yes and no. He applied a labor theory of relative prices to a primitive economy, but for a modern economy he holds to a cost of production theory. According to Smith the general level of prices can best be measured by the price of gold, silver, or corn. To explain changes in welfare over time, he formulates a subjective labor disutility theory. We must conclude that for a modern economy Smith does not accept a labor theory of value to explain relative prices. Once land and capital become economic goods, natural prices will depend mainly on costs of production, namely wages, profits, and rents.

Smith was primarily interested in questions of economic policy affecting economic growth and development, specifically in determining those policies that would best promote the wealth of the nation. His major recommendation was that the government should follow a policy of laissez faire; this, he claimed, combined with a distribution of income in favor of the business classes, would effect a maximum rate of growth of per capita income in the economy. His analysis of the workings of markets, today what would be termed the micro aspects of the economy, must be viewed within the framework of his concern for economic development. His belief that laissez faire was the most effective policy available was based not primarily on its efficiency in allocating resources but rather on its beneficial effects on economic growth. His policy positions, both for laissez faire and government intervention, were always contextual. They were based on theoretical arguments combined with his observations of households, firms, politicians, and institutions. Nor was his methodological predilection that of a pure theorist; he also took into consideration political, historical, and institutional factors. This stance extended, moreover, from his analysis to his policy. The mercantilist regulations of domestic and foreign trade had been designed purportedly to increase the wealth of the nation, but Smith concluded that they were misguided and that economic growth was best promoted by the free operation of markets.

Although Smith was concerned chiefly with questions of economic development, it was in his investigation of the workings of competitive markets that he contributed most significantly to economic theory.

In this endeavor he drew from the later mercantilists and the physiocrats and brought together in one book much of the solid analysis of his predecessors. He was able to describe the functioning of competitive markets with greater precision than previous writers. In the details of his theoretical structure, particularly in his attempts to formulate a value theory, he was confused and confusing, but he provided a necessary point of departure for Ricardo and other theorists who followed. Smith was not a pure theorist but a political economist who was able to supplement a grand vision of the interrelatedness of the sectors of a market economy with descriptive and historical material and to influence economic policy for at least two hundred years.

With few exceptions, the methodological position of orthodox economists following Smith was one of almost exclusive focus on pure abstract theory with little attention to historical and institutional material. The pure theorist Ricardo was followed by J. S. Mill, and Mill by Alfred Marshall, who tried to return economics to Adam Smith's contextual analysis and policy. Mainstream orthodox theory has rejected the Smithian methodology, however, and modern economic theorists by training and practice use highly abstract theoretical models.

Generally speaking, the history of economic analysis and policy discloses three major developments following Smith. 1) Microeconomic theorists have tried to fill in the details of Smith's grand vision of the working market; part of this activity has been technical, aimed at giving greater precision to Smith's vision, and part has attempted to develop those areas Smith failed either to treat or to comprehend, including the development of the demand side of price analysis, the formulation of a theory of the economic forces determining the distribution of income, and the analysis of resource allocation in other than perfectly competitive markets. 2) After Smith, macroeconomic analysis received little attention from orthodox theorists until the 1930s, when Keynes returned to one of the mercantilists' concerns and attempted to explain the forces determining the level of income and employment. 3) Smithian economic policy remained virtually intact, despite the grumblings of Marx, Veblen, and others outside the orthodox camp, until the twentieth century, when theoretical developments (welfare economics and some parts of Keynesian theory) and events in the real world (revolutions that replaced some private property economies and severe depressions that shook the remaining ones) led to either rejection or reexamination of Smithian policy.

We turn now to the second great classical economist, David Ricardo. Like Smith, he was primarily interested in questions of macroeconomics, but in the course of developing a theory of distribution, he was instrumental in turning orthodox economics away from macro questions for more than a century.

SUGGESTED READINGS

Anspach, Ralph. "The Implications of the *Theory of Moral Sentiments* for Adam Smith's Economic Thought." *History of Political Economy*, 4 (Spring 1972).

Clark, John M. et. al. *Adam Smith 1776-1926*. Chicago: University of Chicago Press, 1928.

Hollander, Samuel. *The Economics of Adam Smith*. Toronto: University of Toronto Press, 1973.

Hutchison, T. W. "The Bicentenary of Adam Smith." *Economic Journal*, 86 (September 1976).

Robbins, Lionel. *The Theory of Economic Policy in English Classical Political Economy*. London: Macmillan, 1952.

Robertson, H. M., and W. L. Taylor. "Adam Smith's Approach to the Theory of Value." *Economic Journal*, 67 (June 1957).

Rosenberg, Nathan. "Adam Smith on the Division of Labor: Two Views or One?" *Economica*, 32 (May 1965).

——. "Some Institutional Aspects of the *Wealth of Nations*." *Journal of Political Economy*, 68 (December 1960).

Samuels, Warren J. *The Classical Theory of Economic Policy*. Cleveland: World, 1966.

Scott, W. R. *Adam Smith as a Student and Professor*. Glasgow: Jackson, 1937.

Skinner, A. S., and Thomas Wilson. *Essays on Adam Smith*. London: Clarendon Press, 1975.

Smith, Adam. *An Inquiry Into The Nature and Causes of the Wealth of Nations*. Edited by Edwin Cannan. New York: Modern Library, 1937.

Spengler, Joseph J. "Adam Smith's Theory of Economic Growth." *Southern Economic Journal*, 25-26 (April-July 1959).

Stephenson, Matthew A. "The Paradox of Value: A Suggested Interpretation." *History of Political Economy*, 4 (Spring 1972).

Stigler, G. J. "The Successes and Failures of Professor Smith." *Journal of Political Economy*, 84 (December 1976).

Readings in Original Sources

All readings by Adam Smith are from his *Wealth of Nations*, cited above.

Value: Introduction and Plan or Work; Book I, Chapters I-VII.

Wages: Book I, Chapters VIII and X (Part I).

Profits: Book I, Chapter IX; Book II, Chapter IV.

Rent: Book II, "Introduction" and Chapters I-III and V.

Chapter 4
Ricardo and Malthus

Until the appearance of Ricardo's *Principles of Political Economy and Taxation* in 1817, Adam Smith's *Wealth of Nations*, published in 1776, dominated English economic thought of the period. In the four decades that intervened, no major new economic theory appeared, although several significant contributions to economic analysis were made. Thomas Robert Malthus (1766–1834) published an essay in 1798 and a book in 1803 on population; and in 1815 Edward West, Robert Torrens, Malthus, and Ricardo published essays discussing the concept and economic significance of rent. Ideas on both these subjects came to be embodied into classical economics. Since the Malthusian population thesis is essential to an understanding of certain parts of Ricardian theory, we will consider it first. Then we will discuss and evaluate Ricardo's major contributions to economic thought, including his rent theory. Finally we will return to Malthus to examine certain ideas developed in his *Principles of Political Economy* (1820) concerning the ability of the economy to operate automatically at full employment. In one of the liveliest controversies in the development of economic ideas, Malthus and Ricardo hotly debated this issue.

THE MALTHUSIAN POPULATION DOCTRINE

Population Theory as an Intellectual Response to Problems of the Times

The principal thesis of Malthus, that population tends to increase faster than the food supply, was not original with him: it can be found in the writings of others, including Adam Smith and Benjamin Franklin. It was his presentation of the population problem, however, that significantly influenced existing and subsequent economic thinking.

Three circumstances appear to account for the formation of Robert Malthus's theory. First was the pressure of population on England's food supply. Until about 1790 England had been largely self-sufficient in its food supply, but beginning that year she found it necessary to import food, and prices rose noticeably. A second factor was the perceived increasing poverty of the lower-income classes. England was becoming urbanized as factory production replaced production in the home, and with the growth of the towns the misery of the lower-income class appeared to increase. The third cause, which also occasioned the writing of the first essay on population, in 1798, was an argument that developed between Malthus and his father, Daniel. Malthus's father was impressed with the views expressed by the English and French utopian

Thomas Robert Malthus

writers William Godwin and Marquis de Condorcet. The basic view of Godwin and Condorcet, which Daniel Malthus accepted, was that the character of man is not inherited but is shaped by the environment in which he lives. Godwin, in particular, was disturbed by the hardship, misery, unhappiness, and vice he perceived in the world around him. He concluded that the element primarily responsible was government, and for this reason Godwin is sometimes called the father of philosophical anarchism. Robert Malthus wanted to show that these ideas his father had accepted were incorrect. In particular, he tried to prove in the first edition of his essay on population that poverty and misery were not the result of social and political institutions and that changes in these institutions would not remove the evils of the society. Young Malthus was no match for his father in oral argument, so he decided to present his position in writing. When he showed his essay to friends, they encouraged him to publish it. He did so, anonymously, in 1798.

The Population Thesis

Malthus's basic principle, established in the first edition of his essay, was founded on two assumptions: (1) food is necessary for the existence of man; (2) passion between the sexes is necessary and will remain unchanged. He concludes from this that population tends to grow at a faster rate than the food supply. Malthus contends that human beings, in the absence of checks on population, will tend to increase their numbers geometrically, but that the food supply can only increase arithmetically. This, he says, is the cause of poverty and misery. In the first edition of his essay, he offers no statistical proof of his assertion on either population or the food supply. Nor did he use the principle of diminishing returns of agriculture to justify his claim that the economy was unable to increase the food supply significantly, although he acknowledged the limitation of the supply of land. Actually, although the principle of diminishing returns was first developed by a French economist, Turgot, in 1765, it had to be rediscovered by West, Malthus, Torrens, and Ricardo in 1815, seventeen years after this first edition of Malthus's essay. Malthus's failure to recognize the possibility of technological developments, solving the population problem also vitiated much of his theory.

He concludes that some checks will develop to keep the rate of population growth in line with the rate of growth of the food supply. He examines various checks, which differ in the first and subsequent editions. In the first edition he postulated two types, positive and negative. Positive checks are increases in the death rate as a result of wars, famines, disease, etc. A negative check is the lowering of the birth rate, which is accomplished by the postponement of marriage. In the first edition of his essay on population, Malthus concluded that the postponement of marriage could only result in vice, misery, and degradation of character, because premarital sexual relations would occur. Changing the institutional structure would therefore not remove the misery and vice from society as long as humans required food and sexual drives were strong.

This thesis caused a considerable controversy and aroused interest in the population problem. Dissatisfied with his initial offering, Malthus published a second edition of his essay (in 1803), which differed from the first in purpose, methodology, argument, and conclusions. He no longer attempted to criticize the views of his father, Godwin, and Condorcet, determining instead to articulate the population problem in as scientific a manner as available data permitted. Where the methodology of the first edition was wholly deductive, the second was more inductive, and the argument was now supported by statistical data. Thus, the second edition was scientific in method as well as purpose. Most important, the argument and conclusions were changed. In the first edition the checks on population resulted in vice and misery, but in the second edition a new check is introduced, moral restraint, or the postponement of marriage without premarital sexual activities. This new check destroyed Malthus's argument against the utopians, but he was no longer concerned with refuting them. His essay on population went through seven editions with little change after the second. The one generally available today is the seventh.

Malthus's population thesis has several obvious flaws. He never seriously discussed the feasibility of controlling population by contraception, though many so-called neo-Malthusians do advocate contraceptive measures. Malthus, moreover, confused the instinctive desire for sexual relationships with the desire to have children. Although the sexual drive is strong among people of all societies, increasing levels of affluence and education tend to introduce a distinction between sexual desires and the decision to have children. Another difficulty is Malthus's arbitrary assumption that the food supply cannot increase faster than the population. In other words, he failed to consider the possibility that developments in agricultural technology might permit increases in the supply of food sufficient to feed an increased population. But it is unfair to criticize Malthus too severely for this omission, as economists have never developed a theory explaining the rate of technological development and have, therefore, historically underestimated the impact of technology on the economy.

Present interest in the underdeveloped areas of the world and in the problems of controlling the environment in the developed economies has led to a reexamination of the Malthusian population thesis. In the period immediately following World War II, it was generally felt that controlling the rate of growth of population was of concern only in the underdeveloped economies. Beginning in the 1960s, people have expressed concern over the growth of population in developed economies, not because of an inadequate food supply, but because of the environmental damage that has been associated with increases in population density in the past. Earth has been compared to a spaceship that may already have more than an optimum number of passengers on board. During the 1980s a different sort of apprehension concerning population in the developed countries has been expressed. Some writers are alarmed at the consequences for economic growth and world power of the *declining* birthrate in the United States. Unlike the environmentalists, who continue to call for lower growth rates, some economists are advocating increasing U.S. population growth.

The population thesis of Malthus found an application in classical economic theory and policy. The wages fund doctrine, developed by Smith and extended by Ricardo and his followers, implied that an increase in the real wage of labor would result in increases in population, which would eventually bring the wage rate back to its former level. It was therefore argued that any attempt to improve the economic welfare of the lower-income groups in society would be frustrated by an increase in the size of the population. So while humanitarian feelings might call for social measures to raise the income of the laboring poor, sound economic thinking argued that such efforts would be futile. Attempts to alleviate the economic plight of low-income groups in England by legislation began around 1600; they are referred to as the "poor laws" by economic historians. Classical economists used the Malthusian population doctrine as an argument against the poor laws. The analysis of wage rates they achieved by combining the Malthusian thesis with the wages fund doctrine has been called the iron law of wages.

The Malthusian model has had far more extensive repercussions than its originator could ever have imagined. The British naturalists Charles Darwin and A. R. Wallace, who independently formulated what has become known as the Darwinian theory of evolution, both acknowledged Malthus as an important influence on their thinking.

We turn now to the great master of deductive economic theory, David Ricardo.

DAVID RICARDO

A Theorist's Theorist

David Ricardo (1772–1823), the stockbroker turned economist, is a commanding figure in the development of economic theory. The quantity of material written about Ricardo and his theories is equaled only by that on Smith, Marx, and Keynes. In 1951 *The Works and Correspondence of David Ricardo* was published in ten volumes under the capable hands of Piero Sraffa and Maurice Dobb. This edition took a good twenty years to produce and is a monument to one of the most gifted of economic theorists. That his work continues to attract attention is evidenced by the recent reexamination of Ricardo by Samuel Hollander. And this is not surprising, since in spite of his poor prose style, Ricardo made significant contributions to a number of areas of economic theory, including methodology, theories of value, inter-

David Ricardo

national trade, public finance, diminishing returns, and rent. He began his study of economics sometime around 1799, when he was twenty-eight, and in 1810 published his first pamphlet, *The High Price of Bullion*. His essays on the Corn Law controversy published around 1815 established him as one of England's most able economists. His major work, *Principles of Political Economy and Taxation*, published in 1817, soon replaced Adam Smith's *Wealth of Nations* as the accepted book on economic questions. It is the third and final edition of this work, printed as volume one in the Sraffa edition of his *Works*, that we shall use for reference.

Ricardo's Method

Adam Smith had dealt with questions of political economy in two ways: (1) by using deductive theory to analyze the particular institutional manifestations of the economy of his time, and (2) by presenting a descriptive, informal narrative of contemporary and historical institutions. Smith's method was, thus, a blend of theory with historical descriptive material. Ricardo, on the other hand, represents the pure theorist at work. He abstracted from the economy of his time and built an analysis based on the deductive method. His skill at this was so great that he is admired by pure theorists today even though his mathematical technique was somewhat clumsy. Though Ricardo's method might give the superficial observer the impression that he was a purely theoretical, nonpractical economist, Ricardian economics is strongly oriented toward policy. The burning issue of his time was the tariffs on the importation of grain into England and their effect on the distribution of income, and Ricardo was keenly aware of this question. He steadfastly maintained, nevertheless, that theory was a prerequisite to concrete analysis of the policy issues of the real world.

The Scope of Economics According to Ricardo

Ricardo represents a turning point in the conception of the basic task of economics. Whereas Adam Smith had maintained the mercantilist concern with the forces determining the wealth of nations, Ricardo held that the principal purpose of economics is to determine the laws that regulate the distribution of income between landlords, capitalists, and laborers.

> To determine the laws which regulate this distribution [of income], is the principal problem in Political Economy: much as the science has been improved by the writings of Turgot, Stuart, Smith, Say,

Sismondi, and others, they afford very little satisfactory information respecting the natural course of rent, profit, and wages.[1]

Ricardo was interested in what is now called the functional distribution of income, the relative shares of yearly output going to labor, land, and capital. In modern national income accounting, national income is defined as the payments to the factors of production at factor prices. When modern theorists analyze the functional distribution of income, they often use the concept of an aggregate production function for the economy. Though studies of the functional distribution of income do not really fit into the conventional macro-micro division of modern economics, they are generally considered to be a part of macro theory.

Ricardo was particularly interested in *changes* in the functional distribution of income over time, a part of macroeconomics in his system. He considered this problem in the context of a society made up of three classes: capitalists receiving profits and interest, landlords receiving rent, and laborers receiving wages. In order to explain changes in the shares of the capitalist, landlord, and laborer, he found it necessary to develop a theory explaining profits, interest, rent, and wages. Thus Ricardo, like Smith — although he considered many other macro questions, such as population theory, wages fund doctrine, size of the labor force, the general level of prices, and the short- and long-run stability of the economy — was obliged to formulate theories at the micro level of the economy. In particular, his interest in the forces causing a change in the distribution of income over time led him to examine the forces causing changes in relative prices over time. However, he was primarily concerned with the effects of changes in income distribution on the rate of capital accumulation and of economic growth. Thus it was contrary to his intent that he had the effect of directing subsequent economic investigation toward micro issues rather than macro ones. Nevertheless, his intensive examination of a labor theory of value became the starting point for subsequent attempts to explain the formation of relative prices. On the other hand, Ricardo's victory over Malthus concerning the macro stability of the economy closed this issue to further debate by orthodox theorists for nearly a century.

---

1. David Ricardo, *On the Principles of Political Economy and Taxation*, in *The Works and Correspondence of David Ricardo*, edited by Piero Sraffa and M. H. Dobb, I (Cambridge: Cambridge University Press, 1953), p. 5.

RICARDO'S MODEL

An Overview

As noted, there are three main groups in the Ricardian model, the capitalists, the laborers, and the landlords. The capitalists perform the essential roles in the economic play, since they are the producers, directors, and the most important actors. They perform two essential functions for the economy. First, they contribute to an efficient allocation of resources, since they move their capital to the areas of highest return, where, if perfectly competitive markets prevail, consumer demands are met at the lowest possible social cost. Second, by saving and investing they initiate economic growth.

Although Ricardo holds to a labor cost theory to explain changes in relative prices over time, labor is essentially passive in his model. He uses the wages fund doctrine and Malthusian population theory to explain the real wage of labor: real wages = wages fund/labor force. The wages fund depends upon capital accumulation, and the size of the labor force is governed by the Malthusian population principle. If the wages fund increases as a result of capital accumulation, then real wages will rise in the short run. Increasing real wages will result in an increase in population and, hence, in the labor force. Long-run equilibrium will exist when the labor force has increased sufficiently to return real wages to the cultural subsistence level.

The landlords are mere parasites in the Ricardian system. We will see this more clearly after examining his theory of land rent. For Ricardo the supply curve for land is perfectly inelastic, and the social opportunity cost of land is zero. Landlords receive an income, rent, merely for holding a factor of production without serving any socially useful function. The classical economists were particularly critical of the spending habits of the landlords. Instead of saving and accumulating capital — so as to increase the supply of capital goods in the economy — the landlords engage in consumption spending. The classical economists considered the activities of the landowning class basically harmful to the growth and development of the emerging industrial society.

Ricardo's model presents the following relationship between the growth of the wealth of the nation and the three major economic groups. The total output or gross revenue of the economy is distributed to the laborers, capitalists, and landlords. The part of total output not used to pay labor its cultural subsistence wage and to replace the capital goods worn out in the production process can be termed net revenue or economic surplus: gross revenue − (subsistence wages + depreciation) = net revenue. Net revenue will thus consist of profits, rents, and wages over the subsistence level. In long-run equilibrium, wages will be at a subsistence level and net revenue will then equal profits and rents.

The workers and landlords will always spend their entire income on consumption, so that profits are the only source of saving, or capital accumulation. Using his theory of land rent, Ricardo concluded that a redistribution of income favoring the landlord takes place over time as profits decrease and rents rise, with a consequent reduction in the rate of economic growth.

The Problem of the Times — the Corn Laws

Some of the most interesting economic questions of the early 1800s centered on the consequences of the Corn Laws, regulations placing tariffs on the importation of grain (not American Indian corn) into England. Coupled with this interest in the Corn Laws was the growing concern over the pressure of population on the food supply. Food prices, rents, and investment in land were rising steadily. The most dramatic index of the growing concern about tariffs, land rents, and food prices is the price of wheat during the period. Edwin Cannan in his *History of the Theories of Production and Distribution* reports the following average prices (shillings per quarter of a ton):

1770–79	45 shillings
1780–89	45 shillings
1790–99	55 shillings
1800–09	82 shillings
1810–13	106 shillings

The highest price was reached during 1801 when wheat was selling for 177 shillings a quarter.[2]

For a full understanding of the Corn Law controversy, it is important to remember that these were the times of the Napoleonic wars. The wars had artificially protected British agriculture from continental grain, and this, coupled with Britain's inability to be agriculturally self-sufficient after 1790, resulted in rising grain prices and rents. When the Treaty of Amiens was signed in 1802, English landlords and farmers were apprehensive about the effects of peace on grain prices, so they went to Parliament to get increased protection. The Corn Laws then in effect had been passed in 1791, and the effect of these tariffs was to place a floor on the price of grain at 50 shillings per quarter, which was raised in 1803 to 63 shillings per quarter with very little controversy or discussion of the issues. After a year of peace, the war resumed until 1813, when Napoleon was captured, and the question of the

---

2. Edwin Cannan, *A History of the Theories of Production and Distribution in English Political Economy*, 3rd ed. (London: D. S. King and Son, 1917), p. 149.

proper level of tariffs was again raised in Parliament by the agricultural interests.

The landlords were now asking for a floor of 80 shillings per quarter, and this time their request started an extensive controversy, during which Ricardo, Malthus, Torrens, and West initiated new economic ideas. There was much public discussion of these issues, and strong opposition to the agricultural interests developed inside and outside of Parliament. Study commissions were appointed by both houses of Parliament, and in 1814 a celebrated report entitled the *Parliamentary Reports Respecting Grain and the Corn Laws* was published. As a result of commission hearings, many groups were drawn into the controversy. A common method of reaching the public at this time was to publish pamphlets, and the most significant pamphlets explaining the rising prices of grain and rising rents were those of Ricardo, West, Torrens, and Malthus.

A number of the arguments disturbed Ricardo. One was that higher tariffs would result in lower grain prices. The argument was that higher tariffs would encourage greater investment in British agriculture, and when the resultant increased output or supply came to the market, the price of grain would fall. Ricardo did not agree with these conclusions. Another argument was that the high price of grain was the result of high rents. Rents, under this reasoning, were price-determining. Ricardo disagreed, arguing that rents were price-determined. The fundamental question of the Corn Laws, clearly perceived by Ricardo, concerned the distribution of income. Higher tariffs would shift the distribution of income in favor of the landlords. Since Adam Smith's discussion of the forces determining the distribution of income had not been satisfactory, Ricardo redirected economics toward this question.

Analytical Tools and Assumptions

In his attempt to deal with the many policy issues arising from the Corn Law controversy, Ricardo developed a sophisticated and extensive model, making use of a number of analytical tools and assumptions. Before examining his theories we should become familiar with these tools and assumptions. They include: (1) *Labor cost theory*. Changes in relative prices over time are explained by changes in labor cost measured in hours. (2) *Neutral money*. A change in money supply might result in changes in both the absolute level of prices and in relative prices. Ricardo, however, was interested in changes in relative prices over time other than those caused by changes in the money supply, so he assumed in his model that changes in the money supply would not cause changes in relative prices. (3) *Fixed coefficients of production for labor and capital*. One, and only one, combination of labor and capital inputs can be used to produce a given output. Three cubic yards of dirt can be dug in a day by one man and one spade. To increase output per day, as additional labor is added, additional capital (spades) must be added in a fixed proportion. Stated another way, the labor–capital ratio is fixed by technological considerations for each type of economic production and does not vary with changing output. (4) *Constant returns in manufacturing and diminishing returns in agriculture*. Supply curves in manufacturing are horizontal, or perfectly elastic (marginal costs are constant as output increases); supply curves in agriculture slope upward (marginal costs increase as output expands). (5) *Full employment*. The economy tends to operate automatically at full employment of its resources in the long run. (6) *Perfect competition*. The market contains many independent producers whose products are homogeneous, and no single seller is able to influence the market price. (7) *Economic man*. Individuals are rational and calculating in their economic activities. Capitalists strive to achieve the highest rates of profits, workers the highest wages, and landlords the highest rents. The interaction of such a society in perfectly competitive markets will lead to a uniform rate of profits for investments of comparable risk, to uniform levels of wages for laborers of the same skills and training, and to common levels of rent for land of the same fertility. (8) *Malthusian population thesis*. (9) *Wages fund doctrine*.

RICARDO'S THEORY OF LAND RENT

Diminishing Returns

In the process of analyzing the issues raised by the Corn Law controversy, Ricardo, Malthus, West, and Torrens formulated the principle of diminishing returns, which has become an important economic concept. Actually the principle of diminishing returns appears to have been first discovered by the French economist Turgot in 1765, and although a Scottish economist, Anderson, had formulated the concept for the extensive margin by 1777, it had to be rediscovered in 1815.

The principle of diminishing returns states that, if one factor of production is steadily increased while the others are held constant, the rate at which the total product increases will eventually diminish. As we have seen, Ricardo assumed that the coefficients of production for labor and capital were fixed by technological considerations, so his examples assume a fixed quantity of land to which doses of capital and labor are added. In these examples he assumes that diminishing returns begin immediately, so that the marginal product of the second dose of capital and labor is less than that of the first.

Rent Viewed from the Product Side

Ricardo was primarily interested in explaining the changing amounts of total output received by the landlord and the capitalist in the long run, so it is crucial to his theory to make a clear distinction between rent and profits. Obviously this distinction is easier to make in theory than in practice. Ricardo recognized that terms used in everyday language are not precise. A farmer pays a landlord a sum for the use of land that in commerce is called a rent; but the payment most likely contains elements of both profits and rents. If land has been improved by fencing, draining, or adding buildings, the so-called rent payment will represent, in part, a return to the landlord for these improvements.

Ricardo holds that rents exist because of (1) the scarcity of fertile land and (2) the law of diminishing returns.

> If, then, good land existed in quantity much more abundant than the production of food for an increasing population required, or if capital could be indefinitely employed without a diminished return on the old land, there could be no rise of rent; for rent invariably proceeds from the employment of an additional quantity of labour with a proportionally less return.[3]

Ricardo saw rent as a payment to the landlord that equalizes the rate of profits on land of differing fertilities. Figure 4.1 assumes that there

Figure 4.1 Ricardian Rent

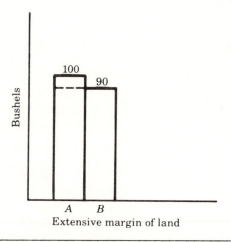

3. Ricardo, *Principles*, p. 72.

are two plots of land and that single doses of capital and labor applied to each yield a total physical output of 100 bushels of wheat on the better land and 90 bushels on the poorer. In a competitive market, forces would operate to equate the rate of profits on the two grades of land. A farmer working grade B land would be willing to pay the land-lord owning grade A land a rent for the use of the land. Any rent less than 10 bushels of wheat for grade A land would result in a higher profit from farming A than from farming B. Thus the rent on grade A land would be 10, and grade B land would yield no rent.

To understand Ricardo's concept of land rent more fully, let us extend our analysis to three grades of land and at the same time introduce the notion of an *intensive* margin and *extensive* margin. Assuming 3 doses of labor and capital are applied to grade A land, 2 doses to grade B, and 1 dose to grade C, suppose the marginal products of three separate plots of land are as shown in Table 4.1.

The intensive margin describes the effect of successive doses of capital and labor on a given plot of land. If one dose is applied to grade A land, 100 bushels of wheat are produced; if a second dose is applied, total output is 190 bushels and the marginal product of the second dose is 90 bushels; and so on. The intensive margin reflects the principle of diminishing marginal returns, which is assumed to be operative immediately in our example. As the marginal product on grade A land diminishes, it becomes economically feasible to use lands of lower fertility, and grade B land is brought into production. Moving from grade A land to grade B land represents the extensive margin, moving to the hillside after the more fertile valley is cultivated. If there were no diminishing returns in our example, plot B would never be farmed, as plot A's initial marginal product is the largest that can be produced with a single dose of labor and capital. Similarly, plot C would never be used in the absence of diminishing returns on A and B. The marginal products of the last dose of labor and capital applied to each grade of land will be

Table 4.1 The Intensive and Extensive Margin (marginal products in bushels)

Intensive margin	Extensive margin		
	Plot A	Plot B	Plot C
	100	90	80
	90	80	
	80		

equal; otherwise it would be economically feasible to shift labor and capital to the land with a higher marginal product.

We can now measure the rent on these grades of land, in order to get a notion of the Ricardian concept of rent. If rent is the payment to the landlord that will equalize the rate of profits on different grades of land, the rent on grade A land is 30 bushels, grade B is 10 bushels, and there is no rent on grade C land. Competitive market forces would result in these rents being paid in the following way. If a single dose of capital and labor were applied to three separate units of grade C land, the total product would be 240 bushels of grain. Three doses of labor and capital on one unit of grade A land yields a total product of 270 bushels (100 + 90 + 80). The price (rent) of grade A land would rise as farmers competed for it until the rent equaled 30 bushels of grain, thus making the rate of profits on the two grades equal. The same reasoning shows that the rent on grade B would equal 10 bushels (170 − 160). We also can measure rent on a given grade of land by computing the differences between the marginal product of a dose of labor and capital at the intensive margin and the marginal products of earlier, intramarginal doses. For example, rent on grade A land is 30 bushels [(100 − 80) + (90 − 80)] , and grade B receives a rent of 10 bushels (90 − 80).

Rent Viewed from the Cost Side

It is instructive to consider rent from the point of view of costs of production rather than product or output. In our example the marginal returns on grade A land diminished as successive doses of labor and capital were applied. Another way of expressing this result is to say that the marginal costs of producing grain increase as the land is more intensively farmed. Marginal cost is defined as the increase in total cost required to produce an incremental amount of final product. Suppose that a dose of capital and labor sells in the market for $100. The marginal cost of producing the one hundredth bushel of grain on grade A land is then equal to $1.00 (the change in total cost of $100 divided by the change in total product of 100 bushels). As the intensive margin on grade A land is pushed down, the marginal cost of producing grain increases, so that the marginal cost of the one-hundred-ninetieth bushel is $1.11 (100/90) and the marginal cost of the last bushel is $1.25 (100/80). The marginal cost of the last bushel of grain produced on grades B and C land is also equal to $1.25. Brief reflection will show that this must be the case if perfectly competitive markets exist. As more grain is produced on grade A land, marginal costs increase and grade B land, where the marginal cost is lower, will be used. If marginal costs differed for the last units of output on the three grades of land, it would be economically feasible to reduce the total costs of production by shifting labor and capital. In long-run equilibrium, when marginal physical products are equal on the three grades of land, marginal costs at the margin must by definition be equal.

From the cost side, rent can be measured not in bushels of wheat but in money. To compute rent in dollars, we need to find the total revenue from selling grain and the labor and capital costs of producing grain on each grade of land. For grade A land the total revenue is $337.50, which is computed by multiplying the output of 270 bushels times the price of grain of $1.25 per bushel. How did we know the price was $1.25? In competitive markets there can be only one price. If farmer Jones sells grain at a lower price than Smith, Smith will not sell any grain until he lowers his price. Competition between sellers will result in one price in the market, the price that equals the marginal cost of the most inefficiently produced grain. In competitive markets the supply curves of individual firms are their marginal cost curves, and the industry supply curve is the sum of the individual firms' supply curves. We have already concluded that the marginal cost of producing the last unit of grain on each grade of land is $1.25 per bushel, so this is the market price. Ricardo's statement of the principle that price depends upon the marginal cost of the last unit produced by the least efficient producer is as follows:

> The exchangeable value of all commodities, whether they be manufactured, or the produce of the mines, or the produce of land, is always regulated, not by the less quantity of labour that will suffice for their production under circumstances highly favorable, and exclusively enjoyed by those who have peculiar facilities of production; but by the greater quantity of labour necessarily bestowed on their production by those who have no such facilities; by those who continue to produce them under the most unfavorable circumstances; meaning — by the most unfavorable circumstance — the most unfavorable under which the quantity of produce required, renders it necessary to carry on the production.[4]

Total revenue on grade A land, then, is price times the quantity of output, or $337.50 ($1.25 × 270 bushels). Total cost of labor and capital is $300, since three doses of labor and capital were used at a cost of $100 per dose, and rent is the difference between total revenue and cost, or $37.50. Rent on grade B land is $12.50, since total revenue is $212.50 ($1.25 × 170 bushels) and labor and capital costs are $200. Rent on C grade land is zero, since the total revenue of $100 ($1.25 × 80 bushels) is just equal to the cost of one dose of labor and capital.

4. *Ibid.*, p. 73.

It was stated earlier that rent was the payment to the landlord that equalized the rate of profit on differing grades of land. Our computation of rent in dollars clarifies this point. Suppose that the $100 cost of a dose of capital and labor in our example consists of $75 of labor cost. If grades A and B land do not receive rent, the rate of profits of the three grades of land will differ. For example, let us compute the dollar return per unit of capital on grade A land assuming it receives no rent. Total revenue is $337.50, labor costs are $225 ($75 × 3 units of labor), and the residual left for profits is $112.50, or $37.50 per unit of capital. The dollar return per unit of capital on grades B and C computed in a similar manner equal $31.25 and $25. In competitive markets this would cause the farmers on grade C land to bid up the price (rent) of grades A and B land. When grade A yielded a rent to the landlord of $37.50 and grade B a rent of $12.50, the advantage of farming grades A and B as against grade C would disappear, and the rate of profit per unit of capital would be $25 on all three grades of land.

This simple agricultural model reveals several important points about the concept of rent and the workings of competitive markets. First, competition between farmers in the market will force the price of grain to the marginal cost of the highest cost unit of output; second, competition for land will result in rents being paid to the landlords owning the most fertile land; and third, competition will result in a uniform rate of profit on all grades of land. These same competitive forces play a part in determining prices, rents, and profits even in today's complex economy. Rent is thus price-determined, not price-determining, in

Figure 4.2 Land Rent

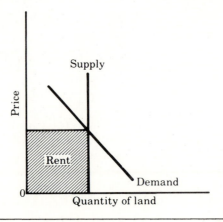

The Taxation of Land

The Ricardian analysis of rent, with its assertion that the rental income of the landlord was an unearned income, made land rents highly suitable for taxation. We have already noted the physiocrats' conclusion that because land was the only factor in the economy producing a surplus or "net product," all taxes would ultimately be shifted to the landlord. James and J. S. Mill both advocated taxes on land, but the greatest thrust to the notion of taxing land was given by the publication of *Progress and Poverty* by an American, Henry George, in 1879. This curious book has sold more than a million copies and been translated into several languages. George was an Easterner who moved to California, where he was impressed by the rising land values as the area became more densely populated. He concluded that the rising price of land and rents resulted from social and economic forces largely unconnected with the activities of the landowners. And since rent was an unearned income, he advocated a tax on land that would completely remove all rents. He held that if all land were so taxed the revenues generated would be sufficient to pay *all* the costs of government. It was for this reason that the movement he started came to be called the "single tax" movement.

Ricardo's concept of land rent helps us understand the economics of George's proposal. If the supply curve of land is perfectly inelastic, then all the return to land is rent. A tax on land would be paid wholly by the landowner, as it would not be possible to shift the burden of the tax to others in the economy. If a tax is placed on land and the net return to the landowner decreases after the tax has been paid, this has no influence, according to George, on the quantity of land supplied. The landowner then has the options of receiving lower yearly income because of the tax or of completely withdrawing his land from the market and receiving no income. He will, of course, prefer less income to no income and will therefore absorb the tax. The amount of the tax can be raised to take away all but the last penny of the landowner's rental income without affecting the quantity of land supplied. Figure 4.2 represents the supply and demand for all land in the Georgian scheme. The shaded area of rent would all become tax revenues to the government.

Ricardo's scheme. The high price of corn was not determined by high rents; high rents were determined by the high price of corn.

Import restrictions imposed by the Corn Laws would, then, result in the intensive and extensive margins being pushed down because of the scarcity of fertile land and the principle of diminishing returns. The marginal physical products of added doses of labor and capital would decrease, which is equivalent to saying that marginal costs would increase and, consequently, both grain prices and rents would rise.

A More General View of the Concept of Rent

Ricardo, in his discussion of land rents, was dealing with a very powerful tool of economic analysis. He limited his application of the notion of rent to agriculture because he thought that the amount of available land was fixed, with a perfectly inelastic (or vertical) supply curve, and that agriculture was the only sector of the economy where the principle of diminishing returns pertained. But the concepts of diminishing returns and rent actually have a much broader application, as they are the foundations of the marginal productivity theory, which explains the supply side of the forces determining the prices of all factors of production. It was not until the end of the nineteenth century, however, that economists were able to see that Ricardo's concept of land rent was a special case of a general analytical-theoretical principle. A discussion of these issues in detail will have to be postponed until we take up the economics of Alfred Marshall; but we shall now examine a more general concept of rent.

Today most economists would agree with Ricardo that, to society as a whole, land rent is not a cost of production and therefore not price-determining. The quantity of land is approximately fixed; therefore, increases in demand will result in higher prices (rents) with no increase in quantity supplied. To Ricardo, viewing rent from the level of society as a whole, the opportunity cost of land was zero. From the point of view of any individual member of society, however, land rent is a cost of production and therefore price-determining. A person who wants to use land in a production process or to use its site value must make a payment to secure and retain the services of land in the face of competition with other possible users. To farmer Brown rent is price-determining, for he must pay rent to the landlord, and the amount of rent will be equal to the opportunity cost of land — that is, to the amount of rent it could earn in alternative uses, if it was planted with a different crop, for example, or subdivided. In short, economists today distinguish between the viewpoints of society as a whole and of individual members of the society in deciding if a rental payment is price-determined or price-determining.

RICARDO'S VALUE THEORY

Ricardo's theory of value was developed in response to the Corn Law controversy. A number of writers, chiefly Malthus, argued that raising tariffs on the importation of grain would be beneficial to England. Ricardo, however, was in favor of free international trade and against tariffs, which he felt would be harmful to English economic development. He reasoned that high tariffs would reduce the rate of profits, which in turn would mean a slower rate of capital accumulation. Since the rate of economic growth depended upon the rate of capital accumulation, tariffs would lower the growth rate.

Ricardo found Adam Smith's economic theory unsatisfactory in several ways in dealing with this problem. The cost of production theory of value was being used by protectionists to argue that higher tariffs would not result in lower profits. Ricardo and the protectionists agreed that higher tariffs would result in higher money wages, but a long and bitter debate arose concerning their effect on profits and rent. Both sides agreed that increased tariffs would push down the margin as less fertile lands were utilized and land under cultivation was farmed more intensively. The resulting increase in costs of producing grain would require an increase in money wages in order for workers to maintain a subsistence standard of living, since the cost of grain was a major part of the workers' food budgets. The protectionists argued, using Smith's cost of production theory of value, that higher money wages would not necessarily reduce profits.

Some protectionists also argued that removing or lowering the tariffs on grain would produce falling food prices and money wages, followed eventually by a general fall in all prices, which would lead to depression. Ricardo, therefore, wanted to refute the prevailing cost of production theory of value to establish the benefits to England of removing the tariffs on grain. He also saw that the most important economic consequence of the Corn Laws was their impact on the distribution of income and that the prevailing economic theory had no satisfactory income-distribution theory. Thus was he led to develop an alternative theory of value.

Most theories of value attempt to explain the forces determining relative prices at a given point in time. However, according to Ricardo, the primary problem of a value theory is to explain the economic forces that cause *changes* in relative prices over time. Ricardo attacked the question of value in this way because of his interest in the income-distribution consequences of the Corn Laws. He is thus not concerned with determining why two deer exchange for one beaver at a point in time, but rather what forces cause changes in this ratio over time. If, for example, the price of beaver increased so that 3D = 1B, there is a problem of interpretation. Is it correct to say that the price of beaver increased, or that the price of deer decreased? Both these conclusions are correct, but neither tells us as much as an invariable measure of value would. With an invariable measure of value, we could ascertain whether the price of beaver had increased because beaver had become more costly to produce or because deer had become less costly to produce. If there were some commodity whose value was invariant over time, then the true causes of changes in relative prices over time could be discovered. Ricardo recognized that no such commodity existed, but finding this problem challenging, he expended some effort in trying to formulate a measure of absolute value that would be invariant over time. He considers this latter problem in the first edition of the *Principles* and discusses it thoroughly in his last paper, "Absolute Value and Exchangeable Value." (Curiously enough, this paper was lost and not rediscovered until 1943. It had passed from James Mill to John Stuart Mill and then to Mill's heirs. It can be found in Volume IV of *Ricardo's Works*, edited by P. Sraffa.) But Ricardo was never able to formulate a satisfactory measure of absolute value. We turn, therefore, to Ricardo's primary concern with respect to value: what causes changes in relative prices over time?

Ricardo's Labor Cost Theory of Value

Ricardo begins his book with a chapter on value, which starts by clearly distinguishing his views from those of Adam Smith.

> *The value of a commodity, or the quantity of any other commodity for which it will exchange, depends on the relative quantity of labour which is necessary for its production, and not on the greater or less compensation which is paid for that labour.*[5]

Ricardo italicized this opening sentence because he wanted to stress the fact that he was not caught in the confusion and circular reasoning that had trapped Smith in his formulation of a labor cost theory of relative prices. Smith had solved the problem of measuring the quantity of labor necessary to produce a commodity (the skill, hardship, ingenuity question) by concluding that the wages paid to labor were a measure of the necessary labor time. Ricardo saw that this was circular reasoning, and therefore in this first sentence he explicitly states that value depends upon the quantity of labor necessary for production, not on the wages paid to labor.

Ricardo then turns to the confusion over value in use and value in exchange that Smith had illustrated in the diamond-water paradox.

5. *Ibid.*, p. 11.

Unlike Smith, who saw little connection between use value and exchange value, Ricardo holds that use value is essential for the existence of exchange value, though not its measure. In modern terminology, he is saying that before a commodity will have a positive price in the market, a demand must exist, but demand is not the measure of price. The price of commodities that yield utility derives from two sources: their scarcity and the quantity of labor required to produce them.

Some commodities, however, have a price determined by their scarcity alone, namely, commodities that are not freely reproducible and whose supply, therefore, cannot be increased — or in modern phrasing, those that have a perfectly inelastic, or vertical, supply curve, such as rare pictures, books, coins, and wines. He says of these goods,

> their value is wholly independent of the quantity of labour originally necessary to produce them, and varies with the varying wealth and inclinations of those who are desirous to possess them.[6]

What Ricardo is saying, in effect, is that given a fixed inelastic supply curve, the position of the demand curve will determine price, and the demand curve's position is a function of an individual's preferences and income.

Competitively Produced Goods

Ricardo excludes those scarce, not freely reproducible, commodities from his labor theory of value without much concern, since they "form a very small part of the mass of commodities daily exchanged in the market."[7] His value theory therefore applies only to commodities that are freely reproducible and produced in perfectly competitive markets. He assumes that the supply curve of goods produced by the manufacturing sector of the economy is perfectly elastic, which is another way of saying that for manufacturing he assumes constant costs. For agriculture he assumes increasing costs, so supply curves slope up and to the right, exhibiting elasticities greater than zero but less than infinity.

After analyzing Smith's explanations of the determinants of relative prices, Ricardo discards the labor command and cost of production theories of value in favor of a labor cost theory of value. Whereas Adam Smith had rejected a labor cost theory as applied to an economy where capital and land received returns, Ricardo holds that this theory is appropriate to the economy of his time.

6. *Ibid.*, p. 12.
7. *Ibid.*

Difficulties of a Labor Cost Theory of Value

In literature that ranks among the most difficult to comprehend in all of economics, Ricardo next attempts to prove his labor cost theory of value. He encountered some of the problems that led Smith to abandon the labor cost theory, but he saw clearly difficulties Smith only vaguely perceived. He wrestled with these theoretical issues, trying in various ways to surmount them. A number of historians of economic ideas, with whom we tend to agree, believe that the labor theory of value received its most mature treatment in the words of Ricardo, that Ricardo developed the theory to its limit, and that Marx added little to our understanding of the theoretical difficulties of developing such a theory. Some even refer to Marx as a minor Ricardian, but since Marx's vast contributions to economics and the social sciences have little connection with his analysis of the problem of relative prices through a labor theory of value, he hardly deserves such an epithet.

Our next task is to indicate Ricardo's solutions to five fundamental problems confronting any theoretician developing a labor theory of value: (1) to measure the quantity of labor; (2) to reflect the fact that labor skills vary; (3) to account for capital goods as a factor influencing prices; (4) to account for land in price determination; and (5) to account for profits in price determination.

A Measure of the Quantity of Labor

Smith was unwilling to use clock hours, or time, as a measure of the quantity of labor necessary to produce a good because he felt that the skill of the laborer and the hardship of the job were also relevant. He argued that skill and hardship were settled by the "higgling and bargaining" in the market, and that the wage rates paid to different laborers would reflect their skills and the hardship of their jobs. Ricardo saw that Smith's logic was faulty and, as we have already observed, states explicitly in the first sentence of his *Principles* that it is the quantity of labor that determines relative prices, not the wages paid to labor. Ricardo's solution is to measure the quantity of labor by the amount of time involved in producing a good, that is, by clock hours alone.

The Differing Skills of Labor

Using clock hours as a measure of the quantity of labor embodied in a commodity creates the same problem for Ricardo that Smith was trying to avoid. We call this the skilled-labor problem; it results from the fact that labor is not a homogeneous product, so that one hour of labor time may produce different amounts of output. Assume that two laborers are working under the same conditions with the same quantities of land and capital to assist them. If one laborer produces two deer per hour and the other produces one deer per hour, what is the quantity of labor necessary to produce a deer? Ricardo solves this problem by using wages paid to laborers to measure their relative productivities. Thus, in our example above, the wage of the laborer producing two deer per hour would be twice that of the less productive laborer. Superficially it would appear that Ricardo had involved himself in the same circular reasoning as Smith, for relative wages, which are prices, are used to explain relative prices. However, Ricardo's reasoning is not circular, because he is not attempting to explain relative prices at a point in time but is devising a theory to explain changes in relative prices over time. He responds to this objection by pointing out that if differences in the wages paid to laborers because of differing skills remain constant over time, changes in the prices of final products will not be a result of the wages paid to labor. Thus if a skilled laborer receives twice the wage of an unskilled laborer today and this ratio remains the same at some future date, any changes in the relative prices of the products produced by these two laborers must be explained by factors other than the wages paid to labor. Ricardo's assumption that wages paid to laborers of differing skills remain constant over time is open to question, but, granted this assumption, his solution of measuring labor in terms of clock hours is not circular reasoning, given the problem he was trying to solve.

Capital Goods

Almost all commodities are produced by the utilization of both labor and capital. What is the influence of capital on the prices of final goods under a labor cost theory? Ricardo solves this problem by identifying capital as merely stored-up labor, labor that has been applied in a previous period. The quantity of labor in a commodity produced by both labor and capital is measured by the quantity of labor immediately applied as well as by the quantity of labor stored in the capital good that is used to produce the final product. If a capital good requires 100 hours of labor for its production and wears out, or depreciates, at the rate of one hundredth of its cost for each unit it produces, then the total labor required to produce a final good, using this capital good, is the number of hours of labor immediately applied plus 1 hour of labor used up from the capital good.

In modern terminology, when a commodity is produced with labor and capital, the capital depreciates during the production process. If the

accountant's depreciation is an accurate measure of the capital destroyed in the production process, it is equivalent to the portion of the
labor originally required to produce the capital, which becomes
embodied in final goods. Ricardo would therefore handle the capital
goods problem by summing the labor immediately or directly applied
plus the time equivalent of the depreciation of capital goods during the
manufacturing process.

Ricardo's solution to the capital goods problem is not completely
satisfactory. If labor has been applied in some past period to produce a
capital good, the price of a final good produced by using up this capital
good must include an amount necessary to pay the labor directly
applied, the indirect labor used to produce the capital good, *and* the
interest on the funds paid to the indirect labor, from the time of payment until the final good is sold. To put this in its simplest form, an
hour of labor applied to produce a capital good *two* years ago would
have a different influence on the price of a final good produced today
than would an hour of labor applied *one* year ago. A more accurate
solution would then be to sum both labor and interest costs from the
past, but this would be inconsistent with a theory of value based
exclusively on labor.

Land Rent

A labor theory of value must also deal with the question of land rent.
Adam Smith had been unable to develop a labor theory of value once
land had become an economic good, which is one reason for his turning
to cost of production theory. Suppose that there are two laborers of
equal skill working on two plots of land of different fertility. In one
year the laborer on the more fertile land will produce more than the
other laborer on the less fertile land. What, then, is the quantity of
labor necessary to produce a bushel of wheat? Ricardo solved this
problem through his theory of land rent. For him the price of a bushel
of wheat depends upon the marginal cost of the bushel of wheat produced least efficiently. Price is determined at the margin, and at the
margin there is no rent. Rent, as we have seen, is price-determined and
not price-determining. The differing rents received by lands of differing
fertilities will not, therefore, influence changes in relative prices over
time.

Profits

Another difficulty inherent in any labor theory of value is determining
the role of profits. If profits were the same proportionate part of the

final prices of all commodities, as we saw before in our discussion of Smith's value theories, finished goods would exchange at the same ratios whether a labor cost or labor command theory of value was used. If profits are a different percentage of final price for various commodities, then relative prices or changes in relative prices cannot be correctly measured by labor alone. Casual empiricism indicates that profit is not a constant percentage of the final price of commodities. The amount of profit (defined, according to the Smith-Ricardo tradition, to include what modern economics would call profits and interest) in final sales price may vary for a number of reasons. The amount of capital per unit of final output can be expected to vary from one industry to another. Profit will be a larger element in final prices in industries that are capital-intensive than in industries that are labor-intensive. The rate of turnover of capital will also vary industry by industry, depending on the proportion between fixed and circulating capital. Industries with a faster rate of capital turnover will produce goods whose ratio of profit to final price is lower than goods produced in industries with a slower rate of capital turnover.

After thoroughly examining the problems the existence of profits raises for a labor theory of value, Ricardo concludes that they do not change his fundamental proposition that changes in relative prices over time depend upon changes in the relative quantities of labor embodied in commodities. His basic conclusion is that the influence of the rate of profits or wage rates is not quantitatively important, and for this reason George Stigler has termed Ricardo's theory a 93-percent labor theory of value. Using Ricardo's own illustrative figures, 93 percent of variations in relative prices can be explained by changes in the quantity of labor required to produce commodities. Ricardo's view is that even though changes in either the rate of profit or wage rates theoretically will cause changes in relative prices over time, these various changes in prices are quantitatively insignificant. He therefore concludes, "I shall consider all the great variations which take place in the relative value of commodities to be produced by the greater or less quantity of labour which may be required from time to time to produce them."[8]

Summary of Ricardian Value Theory

After our extended treatment of Ricardo's value theory, it may prove helpful to summarize the highlights of that theory: (1) As opposed to Adam Smith, Ricardo held that use value was necessary for the existence of exchange value. (2) His labor theory of value was developed only for freely reproducible goods produced under market conditions

8. *Ibid.*, pp. 36–37.

of pure competition. (3) His main concern was to explain the economic forces causing changes in relative prices over time. (4) While changes in market, or short-run, prices may result from a number of demand and supply factors, changes in natural, or long-run equilibrium, prices are explained by changes in the quantity of labor required to produce commodities. (5) Although certain factors modify these principles, particularly the element of profits, they do not confute the essential conclusion that, for the most part, changes in relative prices are explained by the quantity of labor required to produce goods.

Did Ricardo Hold a Labor Theory of Value?

Two aspects to this question have troubled historians of economic ideas. Ricardo did not hold a theoretical labor theory of value, since he admits that changes in the quantity of labor required to produce goods are not the only forces causing changes in relative prices.

> Mr. Malthus shows that in fact the exchangeable value of commodities is not *exactly* proportional to the labour which has been employed on them, which I not only admit now, but have never denied.[9]

He did, however, feel that changes in the amount of labor necessary to produce goods were quantitatively by far the most crucial element in explaining changes in relative prices.

Prior to the Sraffa edition of Ricardo's *Works*, historians of economic thought generally held that Ricardo himself was backing away from a labor cost theory of value and moving toward a cost of production theory with costs including profits as well as labor costs. They concluded this largely on the basis of a passage from a letter Ricardo had written to his friend J. R. McCulloch in 1820, after the second edition of his *Principles* but before the third.

> I sometimes think that if I were to write the chapter on value again which is in my book, I should acknowledge that the relative value of commodities was regulated by two causes instead of by one, namely, by the relative quantity of labour necessary to produce the commodities in question, and by the rate of profit for the time that the capital remained dormant, and until the commodities were brought to market.[10]

---

9. Ricardo, *Notes on Malthus's Principles of Political Economy*, *Works*, II, p. 66.
10. Ricardo, *Letters, 1819-1821*, *Works*, VIII, p. 194.

But on the basis of all the correspondence now published in Ricardo's *Works* and on the content of the third edition of his *Principles*, the editors of Ricardo's *Works* conclude that this one letter to McCulloch represented "no more than a passing mood" and that Ricardo maintained to the end that labor was quantitatively the most important element explaining variations in prices.[11] The validity of a labor cost theory of value is certainly subject to question, but it does seem to be beyond dispute that Ricardo thought that it was valid.

RICARDIAN DISTRIBUTION THEORY

We have now reached a point where we can examine three of Ricardo's major concerns: what determines the functional distribution of income among wages, profits, and rents at a point in time; what will happen to the distribution of income over time as economic development occurs; and what are the consequences of the Corn Laws on the distribution of income and the rate of economic growth? Our examination of these questions had to be postponed until we understood Ricardo's labor theory of value, his theory of rent, and the Malthusian population doctrine. Ricardo himself could not answer these questions until he had first developed a theory of value and rent.

Distribution Theory

We can develop Ricardo's argument, with the aid of a simple graph, from the Ricardian model by which doses of capital and labor in fixed proportions are added to the fixed quantity of land available to the economy. In Figure 4.3 doses of capital and labor are plotted on the horizontal axis, and the marginal physical products of these doses are measured in bushels of wheat on the vertical axis. The curve $ABHQM$ represents these marginal physical products. Let us start with a position of equilibrium by assuming that a certain quantity of capital and labor represented by the distance $0C$ is applied to the available land. The marginal product of the last unit of capital and labor applied is represented by the distance BC, and the total agricultural output of the model is equal to the area $0ABC$, since the total product is the sum of all the marginal products. Ricardo's problem is to determine the division of the total product among wages, profits, and rent. His analysis is ingenious, for he has three variables to determine, and he solves for the various shares by subtraction. For this reason, Ricardo's theory of income distribution is often called a residual theory. First let us

11. Ricardo, *Principles*, p. xl.

determine rent. At the margin rent falls to zero and any product above the line *BD* would be paid to the landowner. Rent would therefore be equal to the area *DAB*. The subsistence level of wages is given by the Malthusian population theory, and we assume for our example that this wage is the line *EFJQN*. The wage rate is then *FC*, and total wages are the area *OEFC*. Subtracting the wage rate from the marginal product at the margin, profit is *BF* for the last dose of capital and labor, and total profit is equal to the area *EDBF*. We have therefore divided the total output into its three shares of rent (*DAB*), profits (*EDBF*), and wages (*OEFC*). Notice that the level of profits depends on the marginal product of the last dose of capital and labor, and the level of the real wage is at subsistence.

Distribution of Income over Time

A related question of great interest to Ricardo is the changing over time of the relative shares of national income received by the capitalists, landlords, and laborers. He found the analysis of Smith and other writers on this subject unsatisfactory and so developed his own theory. Smith predicted a falling rate of profit over time, as a result of competition in the labor, investment, and commodity markets. Ricardo agreed that the rate of profit would fall over time, but he rejected all of Smith's reasons.

Figure 4.3 The Stationary State

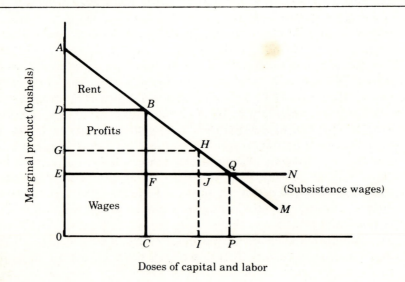

Doses of capital and labor

Smith's first reason is inconsistent with Smith's own cost of production theory of value. As competition increases in labor markets and wages rise, there is no reason, under the cost of production theory of value, to suppose profits must fall. Ricardo refuted Smith by using Malthusian population doctrine, arguing that if competition did bid real wages up, increases in population would in the long run increase the size of the labor force, and wages would fall back to the former level.

He rejected Smith's second and third reasons for falling profits, competition in the investment and commodity markets, by an argument known as *Say's Law*. Ricardo argued that Smith's second and third explanations of falling profits implied the existence of general overproduction, because competition in investment markets will result in falling profits only if it is not possible to sell at previous prices the increased output that results from new investment. Ricardo held that the increased output from new investment could be sold at previous prices, and hence the rate of profit would not fall. He used the same argument to refute Smith's third reason for falling profits, pointing out that competition in commodity markets will not result in a fall in the general level of prices. We will examine Say's Law again at the end of this chapter.

In brief, Ricardo held that Smith had the right answer — profits would fall — but for the wrong reasons. Ricardo's analysis starts with a young economy and follows it through the following sequence of economic development. The young economy is characterized by a high rate of profit and, since the source of capital accumulation is profits, a high rate of capital accumulation. This capital accumulation bids up wage rates so that real wages rise and, in accordance with the Malthusian population doctrine, the size of the population increases. These increases in population require larger quantities of agricultural food products, so the extensive and intensive margins are pushed down — lands with less and less fertility are brought into production, and land under cultivation is farmed more intensively. As the margin is pushed down, rents rise and profits fall. This is an important theoretical point: Ricardo argues that pushing down the margin causes both a rise in rents and a fall in profits. As profits fall the rate of capital accumulation decreases, and this process continues gradually until the rate of profit is close to zero and capital accumulation ceases. At this point the whole dynamic of the capitalistic system is at a standstill: the rate of profits is approaching zero; there is no capital accumulation and therefore no economic growth; population growth has stopped; wages are at a subsistence level; and rents are high.

One may argue that all Ricardo has shown is that profits must fall in agriculture. But what about industry? Assuming perfectly competitive markets, as the rate of profit falls in agriculture, capital will move to take advantage of higher rates of profit in manufacturing. In long-run

equilibrium the rate of profits must be everywhere the same throughout the economy, so as the rate of profit falls in agriculture, it must
also fall in manufacturing. Once the dynamic force in the Ricardian
model — capital accumulation — is reduced, the whole system is
affected, eventually arriving at what has been called the classical
stationary state. It was this dire prediction of classical economics that
caused economics to be called the "dismal science."

We can cover the same analytical ground by using Figure 4.3. As
capital accumulation and population growth take place in a growing
economy, more and more units of capital and labor are applied to the
fixed quantity of land. If the margin is extended so that OI represents
the last dose of capital and labor applied, we find that the new, higher
level of rent is the area GAH; profits have been reduced to the area
$EGHJ$; and the total wage bill is now $OEJI$. As the margin is pushed out
further, the level of rent increases until the total product is now comprised exclusively of wages and rents, and profits are zero. This is the
stationary state, and this point is reached when OP doses of capital and
labor are applied, rent is EAQ, wages are $OEQP$, and profits are zero.

Back to the Corn Laws

The foregoing analysis of the forces determining the distribution of
income and changes in the distribution of income over time reveal some
of the economic consequences of the Corn Laws. Protection of British
agriculture from foreign competition causes imports of grain to decline
and the output of grain in England to increase. As grain output expands
in England, the intensive and extensive margins are pushed out, and
profits decline as rents increase. Although Ricardo had already concluded that the long-run trend in the economy would bring about this
redistribution of income from the capitalists and toward the landlords,
he was against the Corn Laws because they would accelerate the
process. Since the source of economic growth was capital accumulation
by the capitalists, the Corn Laws had the undesirable consequence of
slowing down the rate of economic growth and hastening the arrival of
the stationary state.

It is interesting to note that although Ricardo bought land and presumably applied his economic analysis to the management of his own
investments, as a member of Parliament and as an individual citizen he
consistently argued against the economic interests of landlords and for
the reduction of tariffs on agricultural goods and for free international
trade. He was, in this instance, placing the welfare of the society above
his own self-interest as a landowner.

Ricardo developed a second argument against the Corn Laws, namely
that barriers to international trade diminish the welfare of *all* the world

economies. To understand this reasoning we must first examine his doctrine of comparative advantage.

COMPARATIVE ADVANTAGE

The tremendous subtlety of Ricardo's mind is evident in his doctrine of comparative advantage as applied to international trade. With this argument he strengthened the case for free trade by extending Adam Smith's analysis of the gains to be achieved by the free movement of goods across international boundaries. If nation A could produce a good at a lower cost than nation B, and nation B could produce another good at a lower cost than nation A, both nations would gain by practicing territorial specialization and trading. In the terminology of international trade theory, if one nation has an absolute advantage in the production of one commodity and another nation an absolute advantage in the production of another commodity, each can gain by specializing in the commodity that costs it the least to produce. Historians of economic thought disagree as to the originator of the doctrine of comparative advantage. The principal nominees include Ricardo and Robert Torrens (1780–1864), although it has been suggested that James Mill (1773–1836) was the first to construct a rigorous statement of the theory. In any event, it was Ricardo's presentation of it that influenced subsequent economic thinking.

Absolute Advantage

Before proceeding to Ricardo's theory of comparative advantage, let us first take a two-commodity, two-country model and examine international trade when each country has an absolute advantage in one of the commodities.

According to the data in Table 4.2, England has an absolute advantage over Portugal in the production of cloth. The data illustrate this advantage from the output side, but this advantage can also be viewed

Table 4.2 Output Per Unit of Labor

	Wine (gallons)	Cloth (yards)
England	4	2
Portugal	8	1

from the cost side. Thus the cost of producing cloth, measured in labor time, is less in England than in Portugal. Portugal has an absolute advantage in the production of wine. To demonstrate that international trade will take place, it is necessary first to show that both nations could gain by trading. If total production of wine and cloth can be increased by specialization and international prices or terms of trade for wine and cloth can be reached that benefit both nations, there will be a basis for international trade.

Now if England transfers a unit of labor from the wine to the cloth industry and Portugal transfers a unit of labor from the cloth to the wine industry, the total output of both wine and cloth is increased while the same total quantity of labor is still applied in both economies. And though the movement of a unit of labor out of the wine industry in England reduces output by 4 gallons, the application of another unit of labor in the wine industry in Portugal increases output by 8 gallons, so that the total world production of wine is now 4 gallons more. Likewise while cloth output falls by 1 yard in Portugal from the transfer of a unit of labor out of cloth production, the added unit of labor in the English cloth industry increases output by 2 yards, and the total production of cloth has thereby increased by 1 yard. Thus the total output for our two-nation world is larger as a result of transferring labor to the industries having an absolute advantage.

Our next problem is to determine if prices that would benefit both nations can be established by international trade. We shall treat prices in barter terms. In England 1 yard of cloth would trade for 2 gallons of wine; the price of cloth is twice the price of wine. The English would be willing to trade cloth for wine if they could receive more than 2 gallons of wine for 1 yard of cloth. In Portugal the internal prices for wine and cloth would be 8 gallons of wine for 1 yard of cloth. If the Portuguese could trade anything less than 8 gallons of wine and receive in exchange 1 yard of cloth, they would do so. We have therefore established that there are a series of international prices for wine and cloth that would benefit both nations, and that both would gain from trading at prices between 7.9 gallons of wine for 1 yard of cloth and 2.1 gallons of wine for 1 yard of cloth.

Comparative Advantage

Both Smith and Ricardo recognized the benefits from international specialization and trading when countries have absolute advantages, but what happens when one country is more efficient in the production of *all* commodities? Let us modify the above example by assuming that a threefold increase in productivity occurs in England, resulting in the outputs per unit of labor given in Table 4.3.

Table 4.3 Output Per Unit of Labor

	Wine (gallons)	Cloth (yards)
England	12	6
Portugal	8	1

Now England is more productive than Portugal in both industries; correspondingly, costs of production measured in labor time are less in England for both goods. The comparative advantage argument demonstrates that, with the data in Table 4.3, trade will still be advantageous to both nations. Although England has an absolute advantage in the production of both goods, it is not absolute but comparative advantage that is crucial in determining whether international trade will be beneficial. In this example England has a comparative advantage in the production of cloth, and Portugal has a comparative advantage in the production of wine. Comparative advantage is determined by examining the relative productivities *within* each economy. England's comparative advantage in cloth is demonstrated by the fact that in England each unit of added output of cloth means the loss of 2 units of wine, while for Portugal 8 gallons of wine must be given up to obtain another yard of cloth. Portugal's comparative advantage in wine is indicated by the fact that in Portugal the loss of only $1/8$ yard of cloth gains another gallon of wine, whereas England must give up $1/2$ yard of cloth to produce another gallon of wine.

To establish that total world output can be increased by specialization and trade, let us determine the gains and losses that occur if England produces more cloth and less wine, and Portugal produces less cloth and more wine. Moving a unit of labor from the wine to the cloth industry in England increases the output of cloth by 6 yards and decreases that of wine by 12 gallons. Transferring 2 units of labor in Portugal to the wine industry increases wine output by 16 gallons and decreases cloth output by 2 yards. The net gain from these transfers of labor in the two countries is 4 gallons of wine (16 − 12) and 4 yards of cloth (6 − 2).

It is easy to establish a series of mutually satisfactory prices. When we increased productivity in England in order to illustrate the principle of comparative advantage, we did not affect internal prices in England: using the data from either Table 4.2 or Table 4.3, it is clear that 2 gallons of wine are worth 1 yard of cloth in England. Both England and Portugal would gain from trading at prices between 7.9 gallons of wine for 1 yard of cloth and 2.1 gallons of wine for 1 yard of cloth.

By his comparative advantage doctrine, Ricardo proved that the determining element for gains from international trade is not absolute advantage but comparative advantage. We have shown with the data of Table 4.3 that England can benefit from trade with Portugal, even though she has an absolute advantage in every industry, as long as Portugal has a comparative advantage in one industry. Expressed another way, what is important is not the productivity of the English wine industry as compared to the Portuguese, but the opportunity cost of cloth in England as compared to the opportunity cost of cloth in Portugal. Using the data of Table 4.3 we can measure the opportunity costs of the two goods in the two nations. Using Ricardo's assumption of full employment, if we are to produce more of any good, the cost will be measured by the quantity of the goods whose output must be reduced as resources are shifted from the contracting to the expanding industry. Our simple two-commodity model allows us to measure opportunity cost in terms of the other good in the economy. The opportunity cost of cloth in England (2 gallons of wine) is less than the opportunity cost of cloth in Portugal (8 gallons of wine), and the opportunity cost of wine in Portugal ($1/8$ yard of cloth) is less than that of England ($1/2$ yard of cloth). Thus, when England produces cloth and trades for the wine that Portugal produces, total world output is larger, and both countries gain from trade.

To illustrate the importance for trade of differences in opportunity costs, let us change the data of our previous examples to that of Table 4.4. England now has an absolute advantage in the production of wine and cloth, but a comparative advantage in neither. The opportunity costs within each nation are the same — the opportunity cost of a yard of cloth is 2 gallons of wine and the opportunity cost of a gallon of wine is $1/2$ yard of cloth. Another way of stating this is to say that the relative prices of the two goods are the same in each country — 2 gallons of wine equal 1 yard of cloth (price of cloth divided by the price of wine equals 2). Where opportunity costs are the same, neither country has a comparative advantage and trade will not be beneficial to either nation.

Table 4.4 Output Per Unit of Labor

	Wine (gallons)	Cloth (yards)
England	12	6
Portugal	8	4

Although Ricardo established the benefits of trade when opportunity costs differ between nations, he failed to consider another aspect of the problem. What would be the international price of cloth and wine, and how would the gains from trade be divided between countries? In the example Ricardo used, he assumed that the price or exchange ratio between wine and cloth in international trade would settle at a point halfway between the prices most favorable to each nation, and thus the gains from trade would be evenly divided between the two countries. Torrens also considered this issue, but it was J. S. Mill who correctly solved the problem by concluding that the terms of trade or international price would depend on the relative strengths of the demand for commodities in the trading nations.

The Ricardian concept of comparative advantage has not only theoretical elegance but important policy implications as well. If we replace the simple two-commodity, two-nation model with a multi-commodity, multi-nation world, the principle of comparative advantage indicates that as long as opportunity costs differ between nations, there are gains to be achieved by international trade. The classical case against government intervention in international trade, first forcefully presented by Smith, was considerably extended by Ricardo. The English Corn Laws, by placing impediments to the free flow of goods across international boundaries, not only slowed down the rate of economic growth in England by redistributing income away from the capitalists toward the landlord, but also reduced the welfare of the citizens of all nations. The fallacy in the prevalent notion that the burden of a tariff is born by foreigners is exposed by the doctrine of comparative advantage.

STABILITY AND GROWTH IN A CAPITALISTIC ECONOMY

An argument between Ricardo and Malthus over the ability of a capitalist system to maintain full employment of its resources significantly influenced the development of economic theory. In the literature of economics this argument is called the controversy over Say's Law, after the French economist J. B. Say (1767-1832). Ricardo won the argument, and thereafter orthodox economic theory paid little attention to the issues raised by Say's Law until the 1930s, when J. M. Keynes developed his macroeconomic theory and at the same time criticized the views of Ricardo. The essence of Say's Law is that a capitalistic system will automatically provide full employment of its resources and high rates of economic growth. Ricardo, James Mill, and J. B. Say favored this position, while Malthus attacked it. Actually, the argument concerning stability and growth in a capitalist system had already developed in mercantilist literature, so we will gain perspective by starting there.

The Relevance of Ricardo

Should we have tariffs, quotas, and other devices that protect American industry and agriculture from foreign competition? Ricardo's analysis of these issues is still relevant today. He correctly perceived that measures intended to protect Americans from foreigners actually harm them in several ways. What these measures accomplish is to increase the relative share of the pie distributed to some sectors of the economy at the expense of other sectors. Quotas, tariffs, and agreements that limit the importation of Japanese automobiles, for example, effectively redistribute real income away from purchasers of cars — including purchasers of American-made cars as well as Japanese cars — and toward the labor, management, and stockholders in the automobile industry.

Ricardo's doctrine of comparative advantage demonstrates that the effect of impediments to free trade is to reduce the size of the world's economic pie. Subsidies to domestic agriculture throughout the world today are significantly reducing the well-being of most citizens of the earth.

The classical economists speculated about the long-run tendencies of capitalism. The economic future of humankind rests on the outcome of two broad forces: diminishing returns, emphasized by Ricardo, that *decrease* the incremental output of capital and labor applied in agriculture and industry; and technological development that *increases* it. Which force will prevail? Economists have historically underestimated the rate of technological development, possibly because of an imperfect understanding of this process. Can we influence the rate of technological progress through public policy that encourages research and development expenditures? But even if we do so, are expenditures to increase the rate of technological development also subject to diminishing returns, and is Ricardo's stationary state therefore inevitable? These are the questions raised by Ricardo's theory, and they remain to be answered.

Mercantilist Views of Aggregate Demand

Most of the mercantilists believed that individual thrift and saving were beneficial to the nation. Some, however, argued that saving caused unemployment and that greater consumption spending would increase economic activity and thus benefit the economy. The most forceful advocate of this view was Bernard Mandeville, who presented his views in an allegorical poem and some prose commentaries collected under the title *The Fable of the Bees* (the best edition is by F. B. Kaye, 1924). Mandeville held that prosperity and employment were furthered by spending, particularly on luxurious consumption, and that saving was detrimental to the economy because it led to lower levels of output and employment. He criticized his contemporaries because their views about saving and prosperity were inconsistent: "To wish for the Increase of Trade and Navigation, and the Decrease of Luxury at the same Time, is a Contradiction."[12]

Smith's Views of Aggregate Demand

Smith rejected these ideas of Mandeville and like-minded mercantilists. He praised frugality and saving, for according to his analysis, it was capital accumulation that was the main determinant of prosperity and growth. He argued that the underconsumptionists, who believed that an insufficiency of consumption led to depression and low rates of growth, perceived the situation incorrectly because they failed to understand the process of saving and investment and its impact on the economy. For Smith, saving does not reduce aggregate demand but merely rechannels demand from consumer goods to investment goods.

> Capitals are increased by parsimony and diminished by prodigality and misconduct....As the capital of an individual can be increased only by what he saves from his annual revenue or his annual gains, so the capital of a society, which is the same with that of all individuals who compose it, can be increased only in the same manner....What is annually saved is as regularly consumed as what is annually spent, and nearly in the same time too; but it is consumed by a different set of people.[13]

Malthusian Underconsumptionism

Those outside the field of economics usually associate Malthus only with his development of a theory of population. So did most economists until the writing of J. M. Keynes revived interest in Malthus's economic theories. In several pamphlets and particularly in his

---

12. Bernard Mandeville, *A Letter to Dion*, edited by Bonamy Dobrée (Liverpool: University Press of Liverpool, 1954), p. 49.
13. Smith, *Wealth of Nations*, p. 321.

Principles of Political Economy, first published in 1820, Malthus set forth his economic theory, which differed from Ricardo's on a number of points. Our present interest is in Malthus's views on the economic consequences of saving, or capital accumulation. These views are set forth in his *Principles*, particularly in Book II, Chapter I, "On the Progress of Wealth." (Book II, Chapter I, refers to Malthus's second edition of his *Principles*, which was published in 1836. This is the most readily available edition. This chapter is essentially the same as Chapter VII of the first edition, published in 1820.)

Smith had concluded that economic progress depends on the size and efficiency of the labor force, the quantity and quality of natural resources, the institutional structure, and the amount of capital accumulation, which he considered the crucial determinant of economic development. Ricardo also regarded capital accumulation as the chief source of growth in the wealth of a nation. This analysis is based exclusively on the aggregate supply side: growth is limited only by the degree to which a nation can increase its supply of labor, capital, and natural resources. But what happens if aggregate demand for final output falls short of aggregate supply, producing less than full employment of resources, or depression?

The few mercantilists who had raised this possibility of underconsumption or overproduction were effectively silenced by Adam Smith's refutation of their positions. Nevertheless, the issue was again raised in the early 1800s. Lord Lauderdale (1759–1839) in *An Inquiry into the Nature and Origin of Public Wealth* (1804) and Jean Charles Sismondi (1773–1842) in his *Nouveaux Principes d' économie politique* (1819) questioned the ability of an economy to produce full utilization of its resources automatically. Malthus, in 1820, also raised these questions, and a famous debate ensued between him and Ricardo. In Book II of the 1836 edition of his *Principles*, Malthus examined the alleged causes of economic growth and criticized each as being inadequate, holding that it was necessary to consider the demand side, or what he called "effectual demand." Malthus never states precisely what he means by effectual demand, and his understanding of the issues raised by Say's Law is certainly confused. Yet he perceived that there were difficulties in maintaining full employment of resources, even though he had no clear grasp of the exact nature of these difficulties.

In Malthus's discussion of the process of capital accumulation, he presents both naive and more sophisticated analyses of the problem of maintaining full employment. His more naive argument is that labor does not receive the whole of the product, and labor demand by itself is not sufficient to purchase all final goods at satisfactory prices. Labor has the will to purchase goods, he says, but lacks the purchasing power, while the capitalists have the purchasing power, but lack the will. This is certainly correct, but if the capitalists return their savings to the market in the form of demand for producer goods, there will be no deficiency of aggregate demand. Malthus accepts the notion that saving does not mean hoarding and that savings will flow back to the market as investment spending. He sometimes suggests other functions for money and questions the Ricardian view that money is only a medium of exchange and that no one withholds purchasing power, but he never explicitly develops these insights into a monetary explanation of depressions.

His more sophisticated intuitive insight into certain problems of the economy suggests that the saving-investment process cannot go on indefinitely without leading to long-run stagnation. He contends that there is an appropriate rate of capital accumulation the economy can absorb and that too much saving and investment will cause difficulties. The process of saving leads to a reduction in the demand for consumer goods, while the process of investment leads to the production of more consumer goods in the future. Malthus recognizes, moreover, that for full utilization of resources in a capitalist system to be maintained, the total level of output and consumption must keep expanding. As the Red Queen says in Lewis Carroll's *Through the Looking Glass*: "Now here, you see, it takes all the running you can to keep in the same place."

Malthus concluded that since there was insufficient effectual demand from the laborers and capitalists, the gap must be filled by those in the society who consume but do not produce. These unproductive consumers are those who provide services (teachers, servants, public officials, among others) and the landlords. One of the social functions of the landlords is, then, that they consume without producing and therefore help prevent depression and the eventual stagnation of the economy.

Say's Law

The orthodox classical economists rejected the criticisms of Lauderdale, Sismondi, and Malthus. Their position was most forcefully and explicitly developed by J. B. Say, James Mill, and Ricardo, who argued that in the process of producing goods, sufficient purchasing power was necessarily generated to take these goods off the market at satisfactory prices. They held that overproduction, or what they called "gluts," might occur in particular markets but that it was impossible to have general overproduction for the whole economy. What declines did take place in the general level of economic activity would be of short duration, since the market would automatically return the system to a full utilization of its resources. Thus the classicists insisted that in the long run there could be no excessive capital accumulation.

Admittedly, if an automobile is produced that sells for $9,000 and we deduct the payments made to the various factors of production, the residual will be zero. This is true by definition, since what is not wages, rent, or interest goes to the capitalists as profits. There is $9,000 worth of purchasing power now in the pockets of labor, landlords, and capitalists. The same holds true for the total economy; that is, the value of its yearly output is received as purchasing power by members of the economy. There can be no question, then, that sufficient purchasing power is always generated to take produced goods off the market. The classicals recognized, moreover, that demand and supply might not mesh in particular markets, and that there could be overproduction of particular goods — an excess of supply in a given industry. This glut in a particular industry is a manifestation of market forces at work, either on the demand or supply side. But an excess supply in one industry means that there must be an excess demand for the goods of another industry. And assuming a system of flexible prices and mobility of resources, factors of production will leave the industry with excess supply and flow into the industry with excess demand. Thus full employment of all resources is assured in the long run.

But although sufficient purchasing power is generated to take all goods produced off the market, what assurance is there that this purchasing power will be exercised in the market? The answer contained in Say's Law is often simply stated as follows: supply creates its own demand. There can be no question that supply creates a *potential* demand, but what is crucial is whether that potential demand is exercised in the market as *effective* demand. Ricardo, James Mill, and Say dealt with this issue by simply asserting that all potential purchasing power was returned to the market as demand for either consumer or producer goods. Essentially they returned to the Smithian position that a decision to save is necessarily a decision to invest. They denied the possibility of hoarding — no man locks his gold in a box. Money was only a medium of exchange in their system, and thus they denied any possible monetary causes of depression or stagnation. Though the classical defense of Say's Law has some weak links, Malthus never clearly perceived these difficulties. He tried to disprove the theory while accepting all the assumptions necessary for its proof. He did suspect that the theory was incorrect, but he was never able to articulate this insight into a sound criticism or an alternative theory of the determinants of the level of income and rate of economic growth.

Technological Unemployment

In the third and last edition of his *Principles*, published in 1821, Ricardo added a new chapter, "On Machinery," in which he analyzed the effect of the introduction of machinery on the economy. His previous view had been that the introduction of labor-saving machinery would not result in unemployment and would be beneficial to the entire society. There was a growing concern by labor that new machinery would create unemployment. Ricardo had not dealt directly with this issue in the first two editions of his *Principles*, but he had concluded in his *Essay on Profits* that the introduction of machinery would raise the real wages of labor. In a speech in Parliament in 1819 and in a letter to his friend McCulloch, he maintained that the introduction of machinery did not reduce the demand for labor.[14] Ricardo evidently changed his mind on this issue after reading and critically evaluating Malthus's *Principles*. In his new chapter "On Machinery" Ricardo states:

> That the opinion entertained by the labouring class, that the employment of machinery is frequently detrimental to their interests, is not founded on prejudice and error, but is conformable to the correct principles of political economy.[15]

Ricardo's discussion of the possibility of technological unemployment is not as inconsistent with his position concerning the impossibility of general gluts as the above quote would imply. He holds that if newly introduced machinery is financed by the diversion of circulating capital into fixed capital, the wages fund will be reduced and unemployment will occur. He does not discuss how long this unemployment will persist or how changes in the market might bring about a new position of full employment. If the newly introduced machinery is financed out of savings rather than circulating capital, then no unemployment will occur. It seems clear, then, that Ricardo's views on the possibilities of unemployment caused by labor-saving machinery were changing and that he never fully reconciled these views with his defense of Say's Law.

Keynes on Malthus and Ricardo

Present-day interest in the Malthus-Ricardo controversy over Say's Law and in Malthus's economic ideas, apart from his population thesis, are in large part a result of J. M. Keynes's macroeconomic theory and his praise of Malthus and criticism of Ricardo. Keynes presented his views on Malthus and Ricardo in a paper on Malthus that is most easily found in J. M. Keynes's *Essays and Sketches in Biography* and in *The General Theory*. Keynes's opinions raised three related issues: (1) the Malthus-Ricardo controversy over Say's Law; (2) the methodology appropriate

14. Ricardo, *Principles*, p. 392.
15. *Ibid.*, p. 392.

to economics; and (3) the effect of Ricardo's triumph over Malthus with regard to both these issues on the subsequent development of economics as a discipline.

In *The General Theory* Keynes states:

The idea that we can safely neglect the aggregate demand function is fundamental to the Ricardian economics, which underlie what we have been taught for more than a century. Malthus, indeed, had vehemently opposed Ricardo's doctrine that it was impossible for effective demand to be deficient; but vainly. For, since Malthus was unable to explain clearly (apart from an appeal to the facts of common observation) how and why effective demand could be deficient or excessive, he failed to furnish an alternative construction; and Ricardo conquered England as completely as the Holy Inquisition conquered Spain. Not only was his theory accepted by the city, by statesmen and by the academic world. But controversy ceased; the other point of view completely disappeared; it ceased to be discussed. The great puzzle of Effective Demand with which Malthus had wrestled vanished from economic literature. You will not find it mentioned even once in the whole works of Marshall, Edgeworth and Professor Pigou, from whose hands the classical theory has received its most mature embodiment. It could only live on furtively, below the surface, in the underworlds of Karl Marx, Silvio Gesell or Major Douglas.

The completeness of the Ricardian victory is something of a curiosity and a mystery. It must have been due to a complex of suitabilities in the doctrine to the environment into which it was projected. That it reached conclusions quite different from what the ordinary uninstructed person would expect, added, I suppose, to its intellectual prestige. That its teaching, translated into practice, was austere and often unpalatable, lent it virtue. That it was adapted to carry a vast and consistent logical superstructure, gave it beauty. That it could explain much social injustice and apparent cruelty as an inevitable incident in the scheme of progress, and the attempt to change such things as likely on the whole to do more harm than good, commended it to authority. That it afforded a measure of justification to the free activities of the individual capitalist, attracted to it the support of the dominant social force behind authority.[16]

In his essay on Malthus, Keynes praises Malthus's understanding of the difficulties of an economy maintaining full employment, quoting

16. John Maynard Keynes, *The General Theory of Employment, Interest and Money* (New York: Harcourt Brace, 1936), pp. 32-33.

letters from Malthus to Ricardo "to show Malthus's complete comprehension of the effects of excessive saving on output *via* its effects on profit."[17] Historians of economic thought agree that Keynes has read too much into Malthus's vague notions about the inability of an economy to reach full employment. While Malthus's intuition may have been correct, his criticism of Ricardo was vague and deficient, and as Keynes correctly notes, he had no alternative theoretical construction to offer in place of Say's Law.

A closely related issue raised by Keynes concerns the different methodologies used by Malthus and Ricardo. We have previously noted that Ricardo represented a turning point in economic methodology, replacing Smith's combination of theory and historical description with highly abstract theoretical models. Though the first edition of Malthus's *Essay on Population* was strictly deductive, the second and subsequent editions were much more inductive. Keynes strongly approves of Malthus's methodology and criticizes Ricardo's abstract models. In the two paragraphs from *The General Theory* quoted above, Keynes makes three references to methodology: one approving Malthus's "appeal to the facts of common observation" and two disparaging Ricardo's model, which "reached conclusions quite different from what the ordinary uninstructed person would expect" and had "a vast and consistent logical superstructure." Keynes heaps further praise on Malthus and others who in "following their intuitions, have preferred to see the truth obscurely and imperfectly rather than to maintain error, reached indeed with clearness and consistency and by easy logic, but on hypotheses inappropriate to the facts."[18] In his essay on Malthus, Keynes commends Malthus's methodology as "a method which to me is most sympathetic, and, as I think, much more likely to lead to right conclusions than the alternative approach of Ricardo."[19] Keynes's praise of Malthusian methodology is somewhat self-serving, being, as he defines it, similar to his own.

According to Keynes, "the complete domination of Ricardo's [approach] for a period of a hundred years has been a disaster to the progress of economics,"[20] and "if only Malthus, instead of Ricardo, had been the parent stem from which nineteenth-century economics had proceeded, what a much wiser and richer place the world would be today."[21] This view of Keynes contains some truth and some obvious error. Certainly economics today would have a more developed understanding of the forces that determine the level of income and employ-

17. John Maynard Keynes, *Essays and Sketches in Biography* (New York: Meridian, 1956), p. 34.
18. Keynes, *General Theory*, p. 371.
19. Keynes, *Essays*, p. 23.
20. *Ibid.*, p. 33.
21. *Ibid.*, p. 36.

ment if the questions that Malthus raised had been more thoroughly discussed. An earlier development of macro theory might have avoided the great economic and social upheavals that took place between the two world wars, and thus, conceivably, the economic and social forces which brought on World War II might never have developed. But the difficulty with Keynes's position is that it is rendered with hindsight. How are we to judge an economic proposition or theory at the time it is rendered? Should we accept the vague and intuitive feelings of a Malthus, whose position in part rationalizes the interests of the unproductive consumers, particularly the landlords, or the clear, consistent, and logical views of a Ricardo, whose position rationalizes the interests of the capitalists? It is possible that other agencies answer this question for us, that as Keynes suggests, the accepted view must have "the support of the dominant social force behind authority."[22] Hopefully, in the social sciences in general and in economics in particular, criteria for the acceptance of a theory will eventually be developed that are less politically biased.

RICARDO IN RETROSPECT

The first quarter of the nineteenth century brought many fresh contributions to economic theory. The only other short period of time of comparable significance to the development of economic theory occurred in the 1930s, when major depressions turned the attention of economists to new problems, just as the rising agricultural prices, land rents, and Corn Laws had caught the attention of Ricardo and others. David Ricardo was the right man at the right time, for his clear analytical mind was able to sort the important from the trivial and build a theoretical framework that dominated economic thinking for one hundred years. The scope of economics turned from an almost exclusive concern with questions of economic growth to include the issue of changes in the functional distribution of income over time. Ricardo's concern with the distribution of income led him to give much greater attention than previous economists had to the micro issue of formulating a theory of value, or relative prices, and thus although Ricardo's major policy interest was in macroeconomic issues, he moved the focus of economics toward micro questions. His defense of Say's Law also succeeded in precluding the examination of certain macro questions from subsequent orthodox economic literature. Ricardo represents a distinct break from the Smithian method — a loose combination of theory with historical description — to a methodology of highly abstract theoretical models. Ricardo, with brilliant analysis, was able to

22. Keynes, *General Theory*, p. 33.

demonstrate the strengths and weaknesses of a labor cost theory of value and to illuminate the pressing policy issues of the time. He strengthened the Smithian case for laissez faire with his argument showing the gains in welfare from free and open international trade. He brought together the Malthusian population doctrine and the wages fund theory to demonstrate the impossibility of improving the lot of those in the lower-income groups. His defense of Say's Law silenced one set of critics who found basic flaws in the operation of a capitalist system, where decisions concerning saving and investment are made by private individuals. His economics undermined the position of the landlords, who were beginning to lose political power to the rising capitalist class. And he cast a long shadow over the future of capitalism in his analysis of the impending stationary state. By the middle of the nineteenth century, Marx had combined the Ricardian tools with other analysis to forge his theory that capitalism was just a phase in history that contained the seeds of its own destruction.

SUGGESTED READINGS

Baumol, William J. "The Classical Dynamics." Chapter 2 in *Economic Dynamics*. New York: Macmillan, 1951.

Becker, Gary S., and William J. Baumol. "The Classical Monetary Theory: The Outcome of the Discussion." *Economica*, 19 (November 1952).

Blaug, Mark. *Ricardian Economics*. New Haven: Yale University Press, 1958.

Cannan, Edwin, *A History of the Theories of Production and Distribution in English Political Economy from 1776 to 1848*. London: Staples, 1917.

Cassels, John M. "A Re-Interpretation of Ricardo on Value." *Quarterly Journal of Economics*, 46 (May 1935).

Hollander, Samuel. "The Development of Ricardo's Position on Machinery." *History of Political Economy*, 3 (Spring 1971).

——. "On Malthus's Population Principle and Social Reform." *History of Political Economy*, 18 (Summer, 1986).

——. "David Ricardo." *Oxford Economic Papers*, 33 (1981).

——. *The Economics of David Ricardo*. Toronto: University of Toronto Press, 1979.

Hutchison, T. W. "James Mill and the Political Education of Ricardo." *Cambridge Journal*, 7 (November 1953).

Keynes, John M. "Robert Malthus." *Essays and Sketches in Biography*. New York: Meridian, 1956.

Malthus, Thomas R. *An Essay on Population*. 2 vols. London: J. M. Dent, 1914.

——. *Principles of Political Economy*. New York: A. M. Kelley, 1951.

Ricardo, David. *On the Principles of Political Economy and Taxation*. In *The Works and Correspondence of David Ricardo*, I, edited by P. Sraffa and M. Dobbs. Cambridge: The University Press, 1953.

Robbins, Lionel. "Malthus as an Economist." *Economic Journal*, 77 (June 1967).

Spengler, Joseph J. "Malthus's Total Population Theory: A Restatement and Reappraisal." *Canadian Journal of Economics and Political Science*, 11 (February–May 1945).

Sraffa, Piero, "Introduction" to *Principles of Political Economy, The Works and Correspondence of David Ricardo*, I, edited by P. Sraffa and M. Dobbs. Cambridge: The University Press, 1953.

Stigler, George J. "The Ricardian Theory of Value and Distribution," "Sraffa's 'Ricardo,'" and "Ricardo and the 93 Per Cent Labor Theory of Value." In *Essays in the History of Economics*. Chicago: University of Chicago Press, 1965.

Readings in Original Sources

Ricardo, David. *On the Principles of Political Economy and Taxation* (cited above).

Value: Chapters I, IV, XX, XXVIII, and XXX.
Rent.:   Chapters II, III, XXIV, and XXXII.
Wages: Chapter V.
Profits: Chapters VI and XXI.

Chapter 5

J. S. Mill and the Decline of Classical Economics

In his *Principles of Political Economy* (1848), John Stuart Mill attempted to rescue the essential tenets of Ricardo's *Principles* from the avalanche of criticism that had begun shortly after its publication in 1817 and continued unabated throughout three decades. Mill's work, which dominated orthodox economic thought from its publication until the 1870s, represented the culmination as well as a significant revision of classical economic theory, since saving Ricardian theory was contingent upon repairing its major flaws. Before examining Mill's contributions, therefore, it is necessary to survey some of the many criticisms of Ricardian doctrine to which Mill was responding. These stemmed from three main sources. First, there was increasing evidence of a disparity between Ricardian doctrine and the empirical evidence gathered from the operation of the English economy. Contrary to the Malthusian population theory, which was an essential premise of Ricardo's system, there was growing evidence that real per capita income was increasing, not decreasing, as population increased; and with rapidly developing technology, agriculture was experiencing increasing, not diminishing, returns. Second, the discipline of economics was becoming increasingly professionalized and consequently more critical of received doctrine. Academicians began to work through Ricardo's theoretical structure, particularly his labor theory of value, and found his treatment of demand and of the role of profits in the determination of prices to be wanting. Third, a number of humanist and socialist writers, ignoring the technical content of economic thinking, delivered broadsides attacking the foundations of the emerging capitalistic economy that Ricardo represented.

A number of subsequent developments in economic thought emerged from these criticisms of Ricardian thought. Say's Law, the theory advanced by Ricardo, Say, and James Mill which states that the economy will automatically produce full employment, came to be rejected by certain heterodox economists, notably Marx. And a growing body of socialist literature by French, Swiss, German, and English writers questioned the basic classical notion that economic harmony was best achieved by the unimpeded workings of a capitalist economy. The culmination of this heterodox thought was, of course, Marx's *Das Kapital*, but J. M. Keynes in his *General Theory* likewise rejected the classical assertion that free markets constitute the most effective approach to economic harmony.

A more technical body of criticism was advanced by men who were studying economics more as a profession than as an avocation. These writers tried to spell out more explicitly the proper scope and method of economics and to identify the chief building blocks of the classical system. Their major thrust was to reject, in part, the Malthusian population doctrine, historically diminishing returns in agriculture, and the wages fund doctrine, and to replace the labor theory of value with a value theory in which profits were a determinant of price and in which the role of demand and utility in determining relative prices was enlarged. This line of analysis finally bore fruit in the marginal utility school, which began in the 1870s, as well as in the economics of Alfred Marshall.

In this chapter we consider a number of developments occurring primarily between 1800 and 1850, including the emergence of pre-Marxian socialist writing, revisions of attitudes toward the scope and method of economics, and the rethinking of such pillars of classical economic thought as the Malthusian population doctrine, the concept of diminishing returns in agriculture, the wages fund doctrine, and the Ricardian concept of land rent. We turn then to John Stuart Mill, who would dominate orthodox theory for much of the remainder of the nineteenth century.

POST-RICARDIAN DEVELOPMENTS

Some Early Socialists

A history of economic theory concentrating exclusively on analytical contributions to orthodox economic theory would not even mention the early socialist writers, because a large part of socialist literature affected the development of political, not economic, theory. This is particularly true for the pre-Marxian socialists, whom Marx called the utopian socialists. Although these writers made no direct and lasting contribution to either orthodox or heterodox economic theories, in many cases they significantly influenced the development of these ideas. Since many of these writers have little in common other than their objection to classical economics, the use of the term "socialist" to refer to all of them may be questioned. The common thread that does bind this diverse group is their view of the functioning of capitalism in nineteenth-century Western Europe as disharmonious. Nearly all of these early pre-Marxian socialists advocated nonviolent means of eliminating the conflicts in society, although the remedies prescribed vary with each writer. These early socialists indirectly influenced the development of orthodox theory, directly influenced J. S. Mill, and had a major impact, particularly in England, on legislation and on the formation of the labor movement. One of the more careful scholars of the development of economic theory during this period believes that "in fact much of the theoretical development of the 1830s, particularly that related to the nature of profit as a source of income, was the result of a more or less conscious effort to counter the spread of socialist ideology."[1]

Robert Owen (1771-1858), the most important of the English socialists, was a successful industrialist who turned his attention to the evils of capitalism. He followed the Godwin tradition, which held that man is perfectable and that the evils in society result from environmental factors. He therefore advocated educational reform and the substitution of cooperatives for the competitive market process. Interestingly, he rejected any notion of a class conflict in the society of his time. Another group of English writers came to conclusions similar to Owen's, but because their critical analysis of the faults of society started with a labor theory of value, they have become known as Ricardian socialists. In Ricardo's system the landlord is a parasite receiving part of the social dividend while performing no essential economic function; these writers used Ricardo's labor theory of value to conclude that, since labor is the source of all value, the capitalist exploits labor by depriving it of a portion of its fruits. The most important of these writers were John Bray, John Gray, Charles Hall, Thomas Hodgskin, and William Thompson.

The most prominent of the French socialists were Henri de Saint-Simon, Charles Fourier, and Pierre-Joseph Proudhon. Saint-Simon was impressed with the possibilities of expanding economic output by state planning in which the scientist and engineer played key roles; Fourier's conception of the good society envisioned cooperatives in which a minimum income was guaranteed to all; and Proudhon, distrusting state action, recommended an anarchy in which credit would be granted to all without any interest being charged to a borrower.

Although the early German socialists had little direct or indirect influence on the development of economic theory, a Swiss writer, J. C. L. Sismondi, who is more properly classed as a social reformer than a socialist, deserves some closer attention. Sismondi was a prolific writer of history who produced a sixteen-volume history of Italy and a thirty-one-volume history of France. His major contributions to economic thought are contained in his *Nouveaux Principes d'économie*

1. Mark Blaug, *Ricardian Economics: A Historical Study* (New Haven: Yale University Press, 1958), p. 140.

politique (1819). In his early writing Sismondi followed Adam Smith in perceiving the economy as fundamentally harmonious, and believing that a governmental policy of laissez faire would most benefit society. But in his *New Principles* he concluded that Smith, Ricardo, and Say overestimated the benefits of laissez faire. He attacked Say's Law, contending that a laissez faire policy would result in unemployment and misery for a large mass of the population. Though he was convinced that the distribution of income achieved by laissez faire markets was not fair, just, and equitable, he agreed with Ricardo that the distribution of income was the most important question in economics. Sismondi was concerned about the slow but certain disappearance of the small farm owner and small shop owner, envisioning a society of class conflicts rather than harmony as society became more and more polarized between the proletariat and the capitalists. He felt that the large increases in total output resulting from increased industrialization were not being passed on to the average citizen as increased welfare. Thus the major thrust of Sismondi's criticism of orthodox doctrine was to reject the harmony of classical liberalism and find instead a discord manifested in a failure of the system to provide full employment and, consequently, in growing class conflict. Sismondi is an obvious predecessor of Marx.

Sismondi's appreciation of the failures of capitalism was more intuitive than analytical, and the remedial policies he advocated were vague and, in part, internally inconsistent. To Sismondi the primary causes of periodic fluctuation in the level of economic activity were the uncertainty of competitive markets and the elimination of the small farmer and artisan. His basic remedies were to slow down the increases in production caused by capitalism and to return to an economy where the separation of labor and capital was minimal and production would more closely mesh with the ability of the economy to consume. His advocacy of the small-scale independent industrial and agricultural economic unit led him to defend private property, a view opposed to the general tenor of socialist writing during this period. Solving the problem of overproduction by limiting, if not contracting, total output was not likely to attract much support during the nineteenth century from either the capitalist or laboring classes of France or England. Whether Sismondi should even be called a socialist is subject to question. In any event his rejection of Say's Law and his replacement of the harmony of the classical system with disharmony proceeding from a class conflict between the capitalists and laborers place his ideas in sharp contrast to the Smithian tradition Sismondi at one time had accepted.

The Scope and Method of Economics

Ricardo, as we have seen, represented a change in the methodology of economics from Smith's loose combination of theory and historical description to abstract deductive theoretical models. Ricardo seldom addressed himself directly to questions of methodology, but his followers later reached an almost complete agreement as to the proper methodology for economics. This new Ricardian methodology regarded economics as a discipline based upon certain simple assumptions. The task of the economist was therefore to correct the logic of the system — to make certain that the conclusions followed from the given assumptions. This methodological position contributed significantly to the development of economic theory during the post-Ricardian period when conflicts appeared between economic theory and the available empirical data, for it caused economists to ignore the data. Our first task is to examine this methodological position and to demonstrate that although newly gathered statistical and historical material was contradicting the theory, the majority of economists held to the major Ricardian doctrines.

The two best and most explicit statements dealing with the proper scope and method of economics made during this period were by Nassau Senior (1790–1864) and J. S. Mill (1806–1873). We will use Senior's views as representative of the times. In *An Outline of the Science of Political Economy* (1836), Senior defines political economy as treating "the Nature, the Production, and the Distribution of Wealth."[2] The basic foundations of economics as a science rest on four self-evident principles, and the task of the economist is to develop an accurate terminology and follow the rules of logic so that his or her conclusions follow from their premises. Senior believes that economists have wasted their time in trying to collect more empirical information and should orient their efforts toward improving the logical consistency of economic theory. The economist's

premises consist of a very few general propositions, the result of observation, or consciousness, and scarcely requiring proof, or even formal statement, which almost every man, as soon as he hears them, admits as familiar to his thoughts, or at least as included in his previous knowledge; and his inferences are nearly as general, and, if he has reasoned correctly, as certain, as his premises.[3]

2. Nassau William Senior, *An Outline of the Science of Political Economy* (New York: Augustus M. Kelley, 1951), p. 1.
3. *Ibid.*, pp. 2–3.

Senior's four elementary propositions on which the foundations of economics as a science rested were: (1) the principle of rationality, in that people are rational and calculating and will attempt to acquire wealth with a minimum of sacrifice; (2) the Malthusian population doctrine; (3) the principle of diminishing returns in agriculture; and (4) the principle of historically increasing returns for industry. This view that economics is a purely deductive discipline had important consequences for the development of economic theory, but before examining these consequences, we shall look at another interesting aspect of Senior's methodological position.

Senior was one of the first economists to maintain unequivocably that economics should be a positive science. Senior believed that the economist, as a scientist, should take care to distinguish between normative judgments and positive economic analysis. One example of this view in Senior's system is his distinction between the universal laws governing the nature and production of wealth as contrasted with the principles governing the distribution of income, which are relative to the particular customs and institutional structure of an economy. J. S. Mill later made this distinction between the laws of production and distribution a cornerstone of his system. Senior holds that the economist, as a scientist, can point out the consequences of various economic actions or the possible means to achieve any given end, but that he should not leave the field of positive scientific analysis and make value judgments concerning the desirability of any given line of action. Simply stated, the economist should concern himself with what is, rather than what ought to be. The economist's "conclusions, whatever be their generality and their truth, do not authorize him in adding a single syllable of advice."[4]

The acceptance of the methodology that Ricardo practiced and Senior expounded was unfortunate for post-Ricardian economics. The conflict between theory and reality, which became manifest in the 1830s and 1840s, was largely ignored, and although empirical evidence contradicted several of the basic premises of the Ricardian theoretical system, the economists doggedly adhered to the Ricardian model.

One way to judge the adequacy of a theory is to test its ability to predict. Ricardian economics, while abstract in form, was formulated to provide solutions to significant political and economic questions of the times, and therefore it made certain predictions that could be empirically tested. By comparing these predictions with the empirical evidence, we can uncover the reasons for the decline of Ricardian economics. In order to do this we will turn to the post-Ricardian treatment of certain basic tenets of orthodox theory: Malthusian population

4. *Ibid.*, p. 3.

theory, the wages fund doctrine, diminishing returns and rent, and the tendency of the rate of profits to decrease over time.

Malthusian Population Theory

In the period following the publication of Ricardo's *Principles*, economists, deeply concerned with the population problem, had begun to suggest that the only method to avoid the dire consequences of overpopulation suggested by the Malthusian theory was for families to use some form of contraception. These conclusions were always subtly stated because of the strong reaction by the church and the general public against contraception. There is ample evidence that the private views of the leading economists of this period, with the exception of McCulloch, had been in favor of some form of contraception, but their public statements supporting contraception were made with caution.

Nassau Senior was typical of the economists of his time in his simultaneous acceptance and rejection of the Malthusian population theory. Although he characterized this theory in 1836 as one of the pillars upon which the science of economics is founded, as early as 1829 he had published correspondence between himself and Malthus, together with lectures he had given the year before, that seriously questioned Malthus's basic proposition that population tends to increase faster than the food supply. Senior had concluded that historical evidence indicated instead that the food supply had increased faster than population.

In the Ricardian analytical scheme, Malthus's theory of population was, of course, an essential element. Ricardo held that the major purpose of economics should be to explain those forces that determine the distribution of income, and he had been particularly interested in the forces causing changes in the distribution of income over time. Ricardo had solved this problem by a residual theory of income distribution. The rentless margin determines rent; the remainder of output is composed of wages and profits. It is at this point that Malthusian population theory plays a crucial role. The long-run wage rate is fixed at a subsistence level by the Malthusian theory, and therefore the residual can be easily divided into wages and profits. (See Figure 4.3 and the accompanying material for a full explanation of the Ricardian theory of income distribution.) Ricardo assumed that the long-run level of real wages was fixed and known and that, at this level of real wages, the long-run supply of labor was perfectly elastic. Suppose that the long-run level of population and the size of the labor force are *not* solely dependent on the real wage rate. Under these circumstances the distribution of income at a point in time, or changes in the distribution of income over time, cannot be determined in the

Ricardian system. In the example of the Ricardian theory of distribution shown in Figure 4.3, the level of subsistence wages (*EN*) was given by Malthusian population theory. If the subsistence level of wages cannot be determined, then the curve *EN* has an infinite number of possible positions and shapes, and the calculation of profits and wages at a point in time or changes in the distribution of income over time is indeterminate. Thus Ricardian distribution theory was fundamentally dependent upon Malthusian population theory. But by the middle of the 1830s, enough historical evidence had been accumulated to completely discredit this theory, and along with it Ricardian economics, which could no longer fulfill its avowed purpose: to explain changes in the distribution of income over time.

Wages Fund Doctrine

Malthusian population theory was used to explain the level of real wages in the long run. Ricardian short-run explanations of wages were based on a supply-and-demand analysis known as the wages fund doctrine. It should be noted that "long run" in this context means a minimum of fifteen years. Under Malthusian population theory in its minimum of subsistence form, an increase in real wages in the present year would not have repercussions on the future level of wages for some time, depending upon the age of entry into the labor force. If we assume that immediate increases in population take place when real wages rise, the supply of labor will not be affected for at least fourteen years.

The wages fund doctrine as a short-run theory of wages simply suggests that the wage rate depends on the supply and demand for labor. These are not actually supply-and-demand schedules as used in modern economics. The demand for labor is fixed by the size of the wages fund, that part of capital accumulated to pay labor. Given the size of the wages fund, the short-run wage rate is determined by dividing the number of persons in the labor market into the wages fund. In the short run, then, the wages fund is fixed in amount, the quantity of labor is fixed, and the wage rate is uniquely determined.

With the demise of Malthusian population theory the wages fund doctrine had to carry the weight of being both a short-run and a long-run theory of wages. This it was unable to do, since nothing in the wages fund doctrine said anything about the long-run supply of labor. The wages fund doctrine was used, however, by many popular writers as an argument against labor's attempts to raise wages, particularly through the formation of unions. In the writings by economists of this period, there appears to be no connection between views on the wages fund doctrine and attitudes toward labor unions: many of the economists holding to the wages fund doctrine explicitly approved of the formation of labor unions. Nevertheless, in the popular literature the wages fund doctrine became known as an anti-union economic argument, and this, in part, accounts for J. S. Mill's famous rejection of the wages fund doctrine in 1869 and the importance placed on Mill's disavowal by subsequent writers.

Historically Diminishing Returns

The key element in the Ricardian model that is fundamental to his economic analysis and to the policy conclusions flowing from it is the rate at which diminishing returns occur in agriculture as compared with the rate of increase in agricultural productivity resulting from technological progress. Ricardo held that with added doses of capital and labor and a fixed quantity of land the marginal product of those doses would decrease as the margin is extended. Technological improvements in agriculture could either just offset, fail to offset, or more than offset short-run diminishing returns, and therefore it is possible in the long run to have historically either constant, decreasing, or increasing returns in agriculture. Ricardo, and most of the writers in the post-Ricardian period, believed that technological development would not offset short-run diminishing returns, and therefore predicted historically diminishing returns. The issue is not theoretical, however, but empirical.

All the available data for the British economy indicated that the Ricardian predictions based on historically diminishing returns were wrong. During the first half of the nineteenth century, empirical evidence indicated that the growth of population in England greatly exceeded the growth of labor employed in agriculture. Most economists, particularly McCulloch and J. S. Mill, interpreted these data as indicating that returns had not, in fact, diminished during their period. Yet, curiously, despite their cognizance of this evidence, the Ricardians continued to hold to their model and its prediction that returns would eventually diminish.

As Mark Blaug, probably the most astute modern scholar of this period, has said, "The divorce between theory and facts was probably never more complete than in the heyday of Ricardian economics."[5] This divorce between theory and fact was embedded in Ricardian methodology. This methodology, as practiced by Ricardo and articulated by Senior, exclusively emphasized the deductive process of reasoning from a given set of assumptions, and thus it allowed the Ricardians to ignore the contradictions between their model and fact and to busy themselves with refining the elegance of their theoretical

5. Blaug, *Ricardian Economics*, p. 187.

structure. There is some question whether the lesson to be learned from a study of economic thinking during the Ricardian period has been absorbed by present-day economists. We will see later that one common element in most non-Marxian heterodox economic thinking is the assertion that orthodox economic theory manifests precisely those faults displayed by Ricardian economics — a conflict between orthodox models and facts and an obsession with refining the deductive process and the internal consistency of its theoretical structure.

Falling Rate of Profits

The Ricardian model also predicted that the rate of profits would tend to fall over an extended period of time. The theoretical basis of this prediction was, again, historically diminishing returns. As the costs of agricultural products increase, profits on the marginal land fall as rents rise on the intramarginal land. This tendency will persist, according to Ricardo, until the rate of profit approaches zero and the stationary state results from a redistribution of income toward the landlord and away from the capitalist. But the validity of this assertion, too, can be determined only by empirical evidence and not by theory. The statistical problems of measuring changes in the rate of profit for an economy over time are, however, exceedingly difficult, and the statistical tools required for this measurement were certainly not available during the nineteenth century. Indeed, some question whether they are available today. In spite of their lack of empirical verification of historically diminishing returns in agriculture and of a falling rate of profits and the eventual coming of a stationary state, the Ricardians, and particularly J. S. Mill, persisted in these predictions.

Theory of Profits (Interest)

Two other aspects of the Ricardian theory of profits need to be examined before we turn to J. S. Mill's statement of the classical position: first, a theoretical failure of Ricardo's theory of value and, second, its use by some to criticize the prevailing distribution of income. After wrestling for a long time with the role of profits in his value theory, Ricardo concluded that changes in the rate of profits played an insignificant role in explaining changes in relative prices over time. He decided that, although relative prices depended theoretically upon the costs of both labor and capital, with the cost of capital being profits, the role played by profits in practice was so insignificant that they could be ignored. Thus Ricardo's theory of value was in effect a cost of production theory with labor being the only cost. This aspect of

Ricardo's theory of value attracted the attention of various economists who felt compelled to improve the logical consistency of value theory by including capital costs as well as labor costs of production. This concern for the theory of profits was intensified by the attacks of the Ricardian socialists, who used Ricardo's value theory to show that labor was being exploited. They argued that labor produced the entire product but did not receive all of its product as wages. Profits were a deduction from labor's rightful share, and the capitalists, like the landlords, were parasites in the system who received an income while performing no essential economic function. Their argument was simple, and for that reason it could be used effectively in popular criticism of the existing economic order. It was, then, both to correct the logical defects of Ricardo's value theory and to buttress the prevailing ideology against the attacks of the Ricardian socialists that economists turned their attention to profits.

The most significant contribution to profit and value theory in the early post-Ricardian period was by Nassau Senior, who first attempted to develop an abstinence theory of interest. In his value theory Senior gave greater emphasis to utility on the demand side than did Ricardo, and when he came to the supply side, he emphasized disutility as a real cost of production. Using the basic psychological assumptions of classical economics, he held that people were rational and calculating. Wages, he said, are the reward paid to labor for incurring the pain of working. If we are to produce capital goods, someone must abstain from consumption, and the capitalist will not abstain unless he is rewarded for this pain. Since both capital and labor are necessary to produce final goods, their price must be sufficient to pay both of these real costs of production. Thus Senior develops a cost of production theory of value with wages being the return to labor and profits being the return to the providers of capital.

In classical economics no distinction was made between profits and interest. Senior attempted to develop a theory of interest, which is a predecessor of the Austrian theory developed near the end of the nineteenth century. He actually developed only part of a theory of interest, for his discussion, in keeping with classical tradition, deals solely with the supply side. He examines only the forces that determine the supply curve of savings, whereas a theory of interest would also have to account for the demand for investment. As an argument against the socialists, Senior's abstinence theory of interest has several defects. He suggests that the supply curve of savings is perfectly elastic (horizontal), and the pain cost, or disutility, incurred in saving is the same for the wealthy as for the poor. Since he deals with interest exclusively as a payment for the pain costs or disutility of forgoing consumption, no social or economic justification is given for the receipt of interest on capital that is acquired by inheritance or by gift. Thus, in the end,

Senior's theory of interest probably raised more questions concerning the social justification for interest than it answered.

J. S. MILL: THE BACKGROUND OF HIS THOUGHT

Liberalism with Social Reform

J. S. Mill (1806-1873) was a most unusual and gifted thinker who contributed significantly not only to economics but also to political science and philosophy. His tremendous intellectual powers were complemented, moreover, by an education of unique breadth and intensity. His father, James Mill, assumed the role of instructor to his young son, restraining him from the life of a normal child. At three years of age he was studying Greek, and by eight he began Latin. After mastering mathematics, chemistry, physics, and logic, he started to study political economy at thirteen. By his fifteenth year his formal education was finished, and he spent the next four years editing a five-volume work of Bentham. The psychological costs of this unusually intense education were finally manifested in a mental breakdown at the age of twenty, but after a period of depression, Mill rallied and became one of the leading intellectuals of his and all time. His *Autobiography* contains an unusually honest and open examination of his early education and subsequent psychological difficulties.

Although J. S. Mill was an extremely capable economic theoretician, his intellectual background directed him toward much broader social issues than economists are typically concerned with. Mill was basically a social philosopher intent upon improving the role of the individual in society, and in place of the pessimism of his father and Ricardo, he advanced a guarded optimism that contemplated the development of a good society. Although he read widely, the major influences on his economic ideas were his early training in the classical economics of Smith, Ricardo, his father, and Bentham; the socialist writings of Fourier and Saint-Simon; the writings of Comte, sometimes called the father of sociology, who led Mill to view economics as only one aspect of human social activity; and, finally, his friend Harriet Taylor, who later became his wife and who taught Mill to be more receptive to the humanistic socialist ideas of his times.

J. S. Mill's position in the development of economic ideas is difficult to specify. He wrote at the end of the classical period, but his open-mindedness, one of his greatest assets, enabled him to modify classical doctrine in several ways. His economics is simultaneously the most mature statement of the classical position and the start of a new period in the development of economic thinking. His *Principles of Political*

Economy, written in less than two years, was first published in 1848 and remained, in its subsequent seven editions, the standard in the field till the end of the century. The short period it took Mill to write the book reflected his view that the discipline was so well developed that few major problems remained to be solved. He felt that his major tasks were to write a lucid exposition of Ricardian doctrine and to incorporate into it the new ideas that had appeared during the second quarter of the nineteenth century. He was, however, an original thinker and made important contributions, which he characteristically did not

John Stuart Mill

emphasize, in international trade theory as well as in supply-and-demand analysis.

Mill's Approach to Economics

Mill's views on the scope and method appropriate to economics are contained in an article published in 1836 — the same year as Senior's *Outline of Political Economy*, with its heavy emphasis on methodology — and in his *Principles*, published in 1848. Mill's article on methodology is available in his *Essays on Some Unsettled Questions of Political Economy*.[6] He regards economics as a hypothetical science using the a priori method. The economist makes certain assumptions and then deduces conclusions from these assumptions. Because the experimental method is not available to the economist, he must rely on the deductive technique and cannot use the inductive techniques that have been so fruitful in the natural sciences. Mill is, however, careful to point out that the conclusions derived by economists from their deductive models should be verified by a comparison with the facts of life. A lack of agreement between the results predicted using the deductive model and the historical facts will, in Mill's view, reveal important "disturbing causes" that have been overlooked. These causes may result in new fruitful hypotheses, which will yield new conclusions through deductive reasoning, or they may be the result of noneconomic factors the economist has failed to consider. Although Mill's statement on the proper methodology for economics is basically sound, he, like his contemporaries, did not practice what he preached. "Disturbing causes" became a rug under which orthodox economists swept any divergencies between the predictions of the Ricardian model and the empirical evidence.

Influenced by the ideas of Comte, Mill regarded economics as only a part of a much larger study of humankind. The economist assumed an abstract economic man who was motivated completely by the desire to possess wealth. Yet Mill recognized that although this abstraction yielded some useful conclusions, it ultimately had to be integrated into a more complex model of humans in their social activities. Mill's open-mindedness, breadth of knowledge, and social concerns led him to develop his own economic analysis on a much broader level than Ricardo had. The full title of his major economic work is *Principles of Political Economy with some of their Applications to Social Philoso-*

---

6. John Stuart Mill, *Essays on Some Unsettled Questions of Political Economy*, 2nd ed. (New York: Augustus M. Kelley, 1968), pp. 120–164.

phy. There are two outstanding editions of this classic. The one we will quote from was edited by W. J. Ashley.[7]

Whereas Senior had distinguished between positive and normative economics in order to eliminate normative judgments from economic inquiry, Mill drew this distinction in order to reincorporate questions of social philosophy into the Ricardian model. Mill felt that his single most important contribution to economic thinking was his distinction between the laws of production and the laws of distribution. The laws of production, according to Mill, are laws of nature, like the law of gravity, which cannot be changed by human will or institutional arrangement. But the laws of distribution are not fixed; they result chiefly from particular social and institutional arrangements. Mill was reacting strongly to the way in which classical orthodox theory was being used. In particular, many efforts to improve the quality of life of the mass of society through social legislation, the trade union movement, and income redistribution policies had been countered by conservative arguments alleging that the laws of economics invalidated these attempts. Classical economics was used to show that the distribution of income was determined by fixed, immutable laws that could not be changed any more than the law of gravity could be changed. A typical British aristocrat felt that, despite one's great sympathy for the downtrodden masses, one must not permit one's heart to rule one's head.

Mill wanted to show that most economists were wrong in believing that neither the laws of production nor the laws of distribution could be changed by the institutional structure of the society. The laws of production, for example the principle of diminishing returns in agriculture, are fixed, according to Mill, but the personal distribution of income is subject to change by social intervention.

In his *Autobiography* Mill discusses the origins of his concepts of the laws of production and laws of distribution, citing the socialist writings of the Saint-Simonians as his chief inspiration and crediting Harriet Taylor for convincing him of the importance of distinguishing between the two. Thus Ricardian theory's predictions of the stationary state at which wages would be at a subsistence level were countered by Mill's more optimistic conviction that over time society would act in a wise and humane way, so that a more equal and equitable distribution of income would result. He therefore favored high rates of taxation on inheritances but opposed progressive taxation because he feared its dis-

---

7. John Stuart Mill, *Principles of Political Economy with some of their Applications to Social Philosophy*, edited with an introduction by W. J. Ashley (London: Longmans, Green, 1929). Another excellent edition of Mill's *Principles* can be found in Volumes 2 and 3 of *Collected Works of John Stuart Mill* (Toronto: University of Toronto Press, 1965).

incentive effects. He also advocated the formation of producer coopera-tives and felt that as workers received not only wages but also profits and interest from these cooperatives, they would have greater incentives to increase their productivity. Furthermore, he believed that the results of diminishing returns in agriculture could be mitigated by the in-creased enlightenment of the people and by the reduction of the rate of population growth by later marriage and by birth control.

Some of the purely economic implications of Mill's distinction between the laws of production and of distribution require further dis-cussion. Modern orthodox economic theory discloses a close relation-ship between the laws of production and the *functional* distribution of income. The forces determining the prices of final goods and services in retail markets are closely connected to the forces determining the prices of the various factors of production. The physical relationship between inputs and outputs, what economists call production functions, deter-mines the marginal physical productivity of the various factors of pro-duction, and the price of a factor of production in the market is, in part, determined by this productivity. Modern orthodox theory has, however, very little to say concerning the forces that determine the *personal* distribution of income. The personal distribution of income depends upon a much broader set of noneconomic variables such as the laws, customs, and institutional arrangements of a society and are, therefore, in the view of the orthodox economist, outside the discipline of economics. Furthermore, the orthodox theorist hesitates to examine issues connected with the personal distribution of income, because normative issues and value judgments are necessarily involved. If Mill's distinction between the laws of production and of distribution is trans-lated into the terms of modern theory (a translation that is obviously arbitrary, since Mill made this distinction before the development of marginal productivity analysis), Mill would hold that there is only a loose connection between the marginal productivity of the various factors and the personal distribution of income. Society cannot modify production functions, but it does have the ability to effect a distribu-tion of personal income in keeping with its own value judgments.

In retrospect it appears that Mill took too rigid a view of the fixed and unchangeable nature of the laws of production. Technological development is constantly changing production relationships. Most importantly, there is no a priori reason to hold that technological improvements cannot counterbalance short-run diminishing returns in agriculture and produce historically *increasing* returns.

Mill's Eclecticism

Mill's great strength, which was also the strength of the two most important post-Millian English economists, Marshall and Keynes, was

his eclecticism, which was manifested in many ways: in his unwilling-
ness to accept uncritically the economic theory of Ricardo and his
followers, in his predominantly Smithian methodology, in his acceptance of Comte's view that economic activity must be studied in the
broader context of all human social activity, in his acknowledged
indebtedness to the French socialists and to Harriet Taylor, in his
concern with social philosophy and in his distinction between the laws
of production and of distribution. Unaccountably, he sometimes tried
to disavow this eclecticism by maintaining that in economic *theory* he
was merely modifying Ricardian economics by incorporating into it the
developments of the second quarter of the century. But in the area of
economic *policy*, as he indicated in the preface to the first edition of
his *Principles*, Mill admitted that he was breaking new ground. In his
Autobiography and his *Principles* he expressly dissociated himself from
the economists of the old school, declaring that "the design of the book
is different from that of any treatise on Political Economy which has
been produced in England since the work of Adam Smith."[8] Actually,
while Mill wanted to incorporate new theoretical developments into
Ricardian theory, his primary objective was to indicate clearly the
applications of economic theory to policy.[9] Adam Smith had done this,
but much of Smithian theory was now obsolete.

Jeremy Bentham's Influence

The most important influence on J. S. Mill's and his contemporaries'
attempts to unite theory and policy was the Englishman Jeremy Bentham (1748–1832). After Bentham's first important work was published
in 1780, he became the intellectual leader of a group of reformers
known as the philosophical radicals, or utilitarians. Historians of ideas
disagree as to the degree of influence Bentham had on various writers,
particularly on Ricardo and J. S. Mill. There is little question that
James Mill was significantly influenced by Bentham and that Bentham
and his followers had an important effect on economic, political, and
social legislation and reform during this period. Even before Malthus
had written his essay on population, Bentham had proposed birth
control, and Benthamites later advocated a long list of reforms, including adult suffrage (including women), prison reform, free speech and
free press, civil service, and legalization of unions. Bentham started
from the simple premise that people are motivated by two strong
desires: to achieve pleasure and to avoid pain. If society could measure

8. *Ibid.*, p. xxvii.
9. Pedro Schwartz. *The New Political Economy of J. S. Mill* (Durham: Duke University Press, 1972).

pleasure and pain, then laws could be created that would result in the greatest amount of happiness for the greatest number of individuals. The best way to measure pleasure and pain, according to Bentham, was by the measuring rod of money. Thus Bentham and his followers hoped to make social reform an exact science by designing laws that would lead to the greatest good for the greatest number.

Although J. S. Mill, like the philosophical radicals, was strongly interested in political, economic, and social reform, he partially rejected some aspects of Benthamism that his father accepted. Before he was twenty J. S. Mill had edited a five-volume edition of Bentham's works and had been strongly indoctrinated into the Benthamite system by James Mill. How much of the severe psychological depression that overwhelmed him as he reached adulthood is attributable to his growing dissatisfaction with his father's and Bentham's views will never be known, but for the remainder of his life he continued to emulate Bentham's concern with social reform, while eschewing certain aspects of his theoretical structure. Two parts of the Benthamite system disturbed him in particular. The first was a dogmatism in the views of the philosophical radicals, particularly evident in their insistence that the hedonistic pleasure-pain calculus could be used to analyze *all* human behavior. Mill, influenced by Comte and others, could not accept such a narrow view, which seemed to disregard many of the elements that distinguished humans from other animals. The second disturbing aspect of the philosophical radicals was that in some ways they were not radical enough. Though Mill's views, in historical perspective, may not seem particularly radical, he was nevertheless to the political left of his father and other strict adherents of the Bentham tradition. What most distinguished J. S. Mill from the utilitarians was his openness to new ideas, a trait that would have been quite foreign to a strict Benthamite.

Laissez Faire, Intervention, or Socialism?

Mill's eclecticism in economic theory carries over to his views on economic and social policy. His writing is such a strange admixture of opinions that he defies classification as an advocate of laissez faire, intervention, or even socialism. Possibly the best way to characterize such a subtle and complex thinker as Mill is to say that, in terms of public policy, he represents a midpoint between classical liberalism and socialism. His socialism was not Marxian, and Mill evidently had little contact with Marx. Yet he did distinguish between revolutionary socialists and philosophic socialists, his own views being more closely allied with the latter. The distinction usually made between left (revolutionary) and right (evolutionary) socialists is based on the strategy they consider appropriate to achieve the goals of socialism. However, Mill's preference for the right-wing evolutionary position of the philosophic socialists was based on their conception of the good society.

What then were Mill's views of the role of government in society and of the economic, political, and social framework of the good society? In his essay *On Liberty* (1859) Mill tried to state his basic view of the proper relationship between government and the people. A strong dose of classical liberalism is contained in his statement that the only rightful exercise of power by a government over an individual against his will is "to prevent harm to others. His own good, either physical or moral, is not a sufficient warrant."[10] In his discussion of practical social actions, however, Mill was forced to abandon this strong liberal position and found exception upon exception to the general rule. At one place he will make a forceful liberal statement such as "Laissez-faire, in short, should be the general practice: every departure from it, unless required by some great good, is a certain evil."[11] At another, he backs away from a strict laissez faire position and holds that "it is not admissable that the protection of persons and that of property are the sole purposes of government. The ends of government are as comprehensive as those of the social union. They consist of all the good, and all the immunity from evil, which the existence of government can be made either directly or indirectly to bestow."[12] In other words, Mill sees that the absence of government intervention does not necessarily result in maximum freedom, for there are many other restraints on freedom that only legislation or government can remove.

Although Adam Smith had considered the operation of the market to be fundamentally harmonious, he had acknowledged the existence of conflict in the fact that "landlords love to reap where they have never sowed." Mill, building on the foundation of Ricardian rent theory, similarly perceived a class conflict between landlord and the rest of society. His condemnation of the landlords was biting, and his policy recommendations would have taken all further increases in rent and land values away from landowners. Landlords "grow richer, as it were in their sleep, without working, risking, or economizing. What claim have they, on the general principle of social justice, to this accession of riches?"[13] He went on to advocate a tax on all increases in rent. Mill did not emphasize the existence of a class conflict between labor and the rest of society, particularly the capitalists, yet his whole social philosophy and the major programs he advocated, such as universal education, redistribution of income through inheritance taxes, the

10. John Stuart Mill, *On Liberty*, People's ed. (London: Longmans, Green, 1913), p. 6.
11. Mill, *Principles*, p. 950.
12. *Ibid.*, pp. 804–805.
13. *Ibid.*, p. 818.

formation of unions, the shortening of the working day, and the limitation of the rate of growth of population, all implied that there were conflicts and disharmonies in the system besides those associated with land ownership.

Mill's treatment of private property in his system reflects his blend of classical liberalism with social reform. Property rights are not absolute, and society can abrogate or alter the right of property when it judges these rights to be in conflict with the public good. Indeed, in his chapter on property, where he discusses communism as an alternative economic system, he says:

> If, therefore, the choice were to be made between Communism with all its chances, and the present (1852) state of society with all its sufferings and injustices; if the institution of private property necessarily carried with it as a consequence, that the produce of labour should be apportioned as we now see it, almost in inverse ratio to the labour — the largest portions to those who have never worked at all, the next largest to those whose work is almost nominal, and so on in a descending scale, the remuneration dwindling as the work grows harder and more disagreeable, until the most fatiguing and exhausting bodily labour cannot count with certainty on being able to earn even the necessaries of life; if this or Communism were the alternative, all the difficulties, great or small, of Communism would be but as dust in the balance.[14]

Mill then qualifies this approval of communism by pointing out that it is not appropriate to compare communism at its best with the economic order of his time, and that if the laws of private property were changed to give a more equitable distribution of income and a closer conformity between contributions of individuals to the economy and their incomes, he would prefer a system of private property, at its best, to communism. If all these changes were made "the principle of individual property would have been found to have no necessary connection with the physical and social evils which almost all Socialist writers assume to be inseparable from it."[15]

Just as he rejected the socialists' argument that private property was a major cause of the evils of society, Mill also failed to accept their argument that competition was a cause of social difficulties. In this regard Mill followed the tradition running from Adam Smith to modern orthodox theory that sees competition as beneficial and that predicts misallocation of resources in markets where monopoly power prevails. Competition is beneficial to society; "every restriction of it is an evil,

14. *Ibid.*, p. 208.
15. *Ibid.*, p. 209.

and every extension of it, even if for the time injuriously affecting some classes of labourers, is always an ultimate good."[16] The inconsistency of these views favoring competition with Mill's support of trade unions and other attempts to improve labor's position through the exercise of monopoly power causes him some difficulty. In the course of rather tortuous reasoning, Mill concludes that trade unions, "far from being a hindrance to a free market for labour, are the necessary instrumentality of that free market; the indispensable means of enabling the sellers of labour to take due care of their own interests under a system of competition."[17]

A Different Stationary State

Mill's eclecticism and the humanism he brought to economics are nowhere better reflected than in his discussion of the long-run tendencies of the economy. Even though the empirical evidence was to the contrary, Mill stayed with the basic Ricardian model that predicted falling rates of profit and the stationary state. But Mill's stationary state was not the dismal one Ricardo envisioned; in contrast to nearly all orthodox economists up to the present, Mill was not certain if a nation with a growing economy, such as the England of his times, was a desirable place in which to live. Mill finds many aspects of a prosperous, growing economy reprehensible, such as the "trampling, crushing, elbowing, and treading on each other's heels."[18] In a famous chapter on the stationary state, Mill took a critical view of his own society and outlined his hopes for the future. Individual happiness, well-being, and improvement are Mill's criteria for a good society, and he clearly indicates that these things are not necessarily measured in material goods. Nor were growth of output and growth of population good in and of themselves. According to Mill, a stationary state might be a highly desirable society, as the pace of economic activity decreases and more attention is focused on the individual and his noneconomic and economic well-being. "It is only in the backward countries of the world that increased production is still an important object: in those most advanced, what is economically needed is a better distribution."[19]

Mill wanted to see a slowing of population growth in order to increase per capita income and to reduce population density. Growing population had made it difficult for people to find solitude or to enjoy the beauty of nature. In Mill's stationary state a kinder, gentler, less

16. *Ibid.*, p. 793.
17. *Ibid.*, p. 937.
18. *Ibid.*, p. 748.
19. *Ibid.*, p. 749.

materialistic culture exists. A redistribution of income has occurred, and a reorientation of values ensures that "while no one is poor, no one desires to be richer, nor has any reason to fear being thrust back by the efforts of others to push themselves forward."[20] Finally Mill hopes that the stationary state will result in an improvement in the art of living, which, he feels, has a stronger "likelihood of its being improved, when minds ceased to be engrossed by the art of getting on."[21] He looks at the society and economy of his time and asks whether technological development has really reduced human toil and drudgery. Although increased production has improved the lot of the middle classes and made large fortunes for some, Mill finds the mass of society bypassed by the fruits of the Industrial Revolution and feels that his stationary state might bring about a good society.

Mill's Social Philosophy

The broad outline of Mill's social philosophy reflects the intellectual forces impinging upon his life. With his unique open-mindedness he was able to break away from the strict classical liberalism inculcated in his youth and to try to fuse theory and policy in an eclectic blend of liberalism and social reform. His view of the role of government in society is not dogmatic, and although his essay *On Liberty* takes a strong liberal position, when he turns to policy issues he acknowledges many exceptions to that position. Much more than Smith and Ricardo he recognized that the working of market forces did not necessarily bring about a harmonious economic and social order, and he was particularly aware of the conflict between the landlords and the society as well as the inequities of the existing order in income distribution. Although he was influenced by the utopian socialists and by his wife, he could not accept uncritically two of their major positions: that many of the faults of contemporary society were a result of the institutions of private property and of competition. Mill was concerned about the quality of life, and he found much in a materialistic growth-oriented economy that turned people from self-fulfillment and improvement to baser pursuits. He accepted the Ricardian analysis of the long-run tendency of the economy to produce a stationary state, but with his optimistic humanism he foresaw a new, better society no longer oriented toward strictly materialistic pursuits, not the gloomy world of Ricardo. With this general overview of Mill's social philosophy, we now turn to examine his modifications of and contributions to the mainstream of orthodox theory.

20. *Ibid.*
21. *Ibid.*, p. 751.

historical phenomenon and that i
custom has traditionally played a
problems surrounding the distribu
torical material describing a variet
have existed in the past and that are
market-oriented economies of his o
that the Ricardian system assumes
set of actors, businessmen, who a
make profits, and it is through their
and that market equilibrium is r
without such actors, and even mar
enterprising competitors, those w
where it is, to make less profit by i
elsewhere in his book Mill is por
importance should be given to a
institutional-historical material. Th
again by various heterodox economi

In the face of social forces suc
negate predictions based on compet
continue to use a competitive mode
says, "if we consider that only throu
political economy any pretentions
This curious conclusion makes sense
science used by Mill and his conte
nomics was "an abstract or hypo
scientific, economic theory or mode
certain conclusions. In other words,
tions be made and that the probabil
one. This view carried over then p
nomics from the natural sciences. T
scientific areas of inquiry where the
rence is less than one. Thus modern
phenomena can occur that prevent
with perfect consistency.

Value Theory

The theory of value, or relative pri
mental rejection of Ricardo's labor t
acteristically stresses not his deviatio
continuity between his theory and

23. *Ibid.*, p. 247.
24. *Ibid.*, p. 242.

Mill's Concern for Women's Rights

Of all Mill's writings on political or social causes, none was received with greater hostility than his last book, *The Subjugation of Women*, published in 1869. This would not entirely have surprised Mill, as is clear from a letter he wrote in 1850 to the editor of the *Westminster*, which reflected his misgivings about speaking out on this issue: "My opinions on the whole subject are so totally opposed to the reigning notions that it would probably be inexpedient to express all of them."*

The first paragraph of *The Subjugation of Women* succinctly states his long-held views on equality of the sexes.

> The object of this essay is to explain as clearly as I am able, the grounds of an opinion which I have held from the very earliest period when I had formed any opinions at all on social or political matters and which, instead of being weakened or modified, has been constantly growing stronger by the progress of reflection and the experience of life: That the principle which regulates the existing social relations between the two sexes — the legal subordination of one sex to the other — is wrong in itself, and now one of the chief hindrances to human improvement; and that it ought to be replaced by a principle of perfect equality, admitting no power or privilege on the one side, nor disability on the other. (*Works*, XXI, 261)

Mill's biographer records one incredulous reader as having responded, "He leads us to suppose that the relation of men and women between themselves may work on a purely voluntary basis."†

Mill completed *The Subjugation of Women* two years after the death of his wife, Harriet Taylor, but waited nine years before publishing it, no doubt because of its controversial nature. In a paper Mill and Taylor wrote jointly between 1847 and 1850, however, they had already expressed their dismay at the anomolous situation of women in English society.

> In the first place it must be observed that the disabilities of woman are exactly of the class which modern times most pride themselves on getting rid of — disabilities by birth. It is the boast of England that if some persons are privileged by birth, at least none are disqualified by it — that anyone may rise to be a peer, or a member of parliament, or a minister — that the

path of distinction is not clos
irrevocably to women. A v
cannot by any exertion get
her case an entirely peculiar
that of the negro in Amer
roturier formerly in Europe
buy a patent of nobility. Wor
indelible ones. (*Works*, XXI, ?

*Quoted in J. S. Mill, *Collected
University of Toronto Press, 198-
†Michael St. John Packe, *The Li
and Warburg, 1954), p. 495.

MILLIAN ECONOMICS

The Role of Theory

Influenced by the literature of bo
Mill approached technical econc
regarded himself as merely extenc
number of areas Mill made funda
value. Richard Jones in his *Essay*
had criticized Ricardo's theory c
position in general because thei
institutional circumstances of th
forerunner of the historical scho
tion of the Ricardian analysis to
more empirical approach in acc
structure. "Of Competition and
Mill's *Principles* implicitly recogn
Mill's recognition that abstract ecc
awareness of historically prevaili
that two forces, competition and
income, and he criticizes the ort
emphasizing the role of competiti
the role of custom. "They are
thought that competition actually
shown to be the tendency of comp

Taking a relativistic historical |
ation of competition in the mark

22. *Ibid.*, p. 242.

production theory of value in which money costs fundamentally represent the real costs or disutilities of labor and abstinence. In this regard Mill and Senior have comparable theories of value. However, Mill gave up the Ricardian search for absolute value based on some invariant measure of value, believing that the purpose of value theory is to explain relative prices. In his discussion of rent, he recognizes that the opportunity cost of land is not always zero and that rent is a social cost of production in those cases where there are alternative uses of land. Although Mill did not distinguish between short run and long run in the manner of Marshall, he does seem to have a vague idea of this distinction and regards his primary task as explaining how relative prices are determined in the long run. And though he did not explicitly formulate supply-and-demand schedules, his value theory clearly reflects a recognition that the quantities demanded and supplied are a function of price. For this reason we may present his theory of long-run prices in the familiar Marshallian form without doing an injustice to either Marshall or Mill.

For a good to have exchange value, or a price, it must be useful and difficult to obtain, but use value determines exchange value, or price, only in unusual circumstances. Mill discusses the price of a musical snuff-box using two hypothetical cases he borrowed from a contemporary writer: one set in London where, he assumes, the boxes are produced under conditions of constant costs, and the other on a boat on Lake Superior where only one such box exists. Mill's purpose in this example is to demonstrate that prices will almost always depend on cost of production rather than on utility. Where supply is absolutely limited, the supply curve is perfectly inelastic (vertical) and price depends upon supply and demand (see Figure 5.1a). This first class of commodities Mill regards as relatively unimportant, since few commodities are perfectly inelastic in supply; it includes wines, works of art,

Figure 5.1 Mill on Value

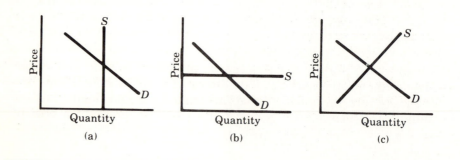

rare books, coins, the site value of land, and potentially all land as population density increases. He also uses this case to analyze monopoly situations where the monopolist can artificially limit the supply. A second group of commodities, manufactured goods, has a perfectly elastic (horizontal) supply curve, and Mill concludes that the cost of production of these goods determines their price. Mill assumes that all manufacturing industries are constant-cost situations (see Figure 5.1b), that is, their marginal costs do not change as their output increases. For Mill's third group of commodities, those produced by agriculture, he assumes that marginal costs do increase as output expands; the price of these commodities depends upon cost of production in the most unfavorable circumstances (see Figure 5.1c). Thus he applies the principle of diminishing marginal returns to agricultural production but not to manufactured goods. Although Mill was very careful to make clear that utility (demand) and difficulty of attainment (supply) must both exist before any commodity has a price, the terminology of his conclusions obscures the fundamental applicability of the laws of supply and demand to all three groups of goods.

He sees clearly how equilibrium prices are brought about in markets through the forces of demand and supply and that

> the proper mathematical analogy is that of an equation. Demand and supply, the quantity demanded and the quantity supplied, will be made equal. If unequal at any moment, competition equalizes them, and the manner in which this is done is by an adjustment of the value. If the demand increases, the value rises; if the demand diminishes, the value falls: again, if the supply falls off, the value rises; and falls if the supply is increased.[25]

Final equilibrium is reached when quantity demanded equals quantity supplied.

Even though Mill did not use mathematical equations, schedules, or supply-and-demand curves, his analysis of price determination is a notable advance over Ricardo's, particularly because Mill's conceptual apparatus was obviously set up in accord with supply-and-demand functions. The only group of commodities he fails to cover, which are certainly of minor importance, are those with decreasing costs and downward-sloping long-run supply curves.

He also made some "original" contributions to value theory in discussing noncompeting groups (he recognized that in labor markets mobility was far from perfect), pricing where a firm produces two or more products in fixed proportions (wool and mutton), rent as price-determining when land has alternative uses, and economies of scale. His

25. *Ibid.*, p. 448.

satisfaction with the development of value theory was manifested by his view that "Happily, there is nothing in the laws of value which remains (1848) for the present or any future writer to clear up; the theory of the subject is complete."[26]

A number of economists writing after Mill have been amused by this statement, and it was probably the reason Marshall suggested that his own contributions to microeconomic theory would soon be obsolete. Yet it can be argued that our general understanding of the workings of supply and demand in allocating resources under competitive markets has not been fundamentally changed since Mill. Of course many developments have occurred that permit more technical analysis and greater insights, but Mill, with cruder technical apparatus and a complete lack of mathematical notation, was able to carry out a significant analysis of markets with few analytical errors. The great gap in Mill's micro theory, which was not filled until the 1930s, was his inability to analyze less than perfectly competitive markets. Some would say that this gap still remains to be filled.

International Trade Theory

Historians of economic analysis have praised Mill for his contributions to the theory of international trade. In particular, his analysis of the division of the gains from international trade among trading countries is probably Mill's most important and lasting contribution to technical economic theory. By his comparative advantage argument, Ricardo had supported and extended Smith's analysis of the benefits of unregulated international trade. As we have seen, he argued that where comparative advantages exist, international trade will increase world output and benefit all trading economies, and that a range of international prices, or barter terms of trade, satisfactory to all the trading nations will be determined. In the simple model presented in Table 4.3, England would be willing to trade 1 yard of cloth as long as she received more than 2 gallons of wine in exchange, and Portugal would benefit by trading wine for cloth as long as she would have to give up less than 8 gallons of wine to receive 1 yard of cloth. A range of prices, or barter terms of trade, between 7.9 gallons of wine for 1 yard of cloth and 2.1 gallons of wine for 1 yard of cloth would benefit both nations. Although Ricardo was able to show the gains from trade using the comparative advantage argument, he did not indicate what the international price of wine and cloth would be, and consequently how the gains of trade would be distributed between the two countries. Obviously England would prefer to gain as much wine as possible for a yard of cloth, and

26. *Ibid.*, p. 436.

Portugal would like to give up as little wine as possible for a yard of cloth. Ricardo had simply suggested that the terms of trade, or international price, would be roughly half way between the two domestic prices. From the data in Table 4.3 the price would be 5 gallons of wine for 1 yard of cloth.

Mill considered how the gains from trade would be divided and gave a surprisingly correct answer, in view of the fact that he used no mathematical techniques and that the concept of elasticity was yet to be developed. Marshall and Edgeworth, who were later to present Mill's argument more precisely with the aid of mathematical and diagrammatic techniques, both acknowledged and praised Mill's contribution. Mill concluded that the terms of trade would depend on the demands for the imported products by the two countries. If, in the above example, the strength of England's demand for imported wine was much greater than Portugal's demand for English cloth, the barter terms and gains from trade would favor Portugal: the international price would be closer to 2 gallons of wine for 1 yard of cloth. Portugal would not have to give up much wine to get cloth. The relative strength of the demands for imports will depend on the "inclinations and circumstances of the consumers on both sides," and the international price or terms of trade will be a value such that "the quantities required by each country, of the articles which it imports from its neighbor, shall be exactly sufficient to pay for one another."[27] Mill develops what he means by "inclinations and circumstances of the consumers" indicating clearly that he is talking about the positions and elasticities of the demand curves. Although he never explicitly develops the concept of demand elasticity, he describes the cases of elastic, inelastic, and unitarily elastic demand.

Mill's other contributions to trade theory were less important, but they do indicate his analytical abilities. He introduces the cost of transportation into the analysis of foreign trade and shows how transportation costs may produce situations in which trade will not occur even with differences in comparative costs. He also analyzes the influence of tariffs on the terms of trade, indicates how both price and income changes bring about trade equilibrium between countries, and shows the adjustments in trade brought about by unilateral transfer payments between countries. It was nearly one hundred years after Mill before major changes in the classical theory of international trade were made by Ohlin and Keynes.

27. *Ibid.*, p. 587.

Excess Supply — Say's Law Reconsidered

Concerned with the attacks made on Say's Law by Malthus, Chalmers, and Sismondi, Mill refuted these criticisms in an article titled "Of the Influence of Consumption on Production," written about 1830 but not published until 1844 in *Essays on Some Unsettled Questions of Political Economy*, and in Book III, Chapter XIV, "Of Excess of Supply," of his *Principles*. An important reason Mill defended Say's Law was to counter the argument of many underconsumptionists that the economy would be better off if the wealthy saved less and spent more on unproductive consumption. His defense was not equaled until the twentieth century. Mill acknowledged that there may be an excessive supply of individual commodities as the market reacts to changing conditions of supply and demand but argued that it was illogical to carry this analysis into macroeconomics and conclude that an excess of supply could exist permanently for all commodities. In his defense of Say's Law, Mill distinguished between three possible economies: a barter economy, an economy where money is a commodity and no credit exists, and an economy where credit money exists. By overtly introducing money into the discussion of possible general overproduction, Mill considerably improves the arguments in support of Say's Law previously given by Ricardo, James Mill, and Say himself.

Mill shows very clearly that there can never be an insufficiency of aggregate demand in a barter economy, for a decision to supply commodities necessarily presupposes a demand for commodities. In a simple barter economy, an individual or firm would produce and trade goods only if it desired other goods. For example, a bootmaker will produce and trade his products because he needs clothes, food, and fuel, among other things. If money is introduced but its only function is as a medium of exchange, the conclusion is the same. If money functions in part as a store of value, then a seller may not immediately return to the market to buy, and although sufficient aggregate purchasing power is generated to give full employment, it may not be exercised in the current period and can thus lead to general oversupply. Mill shows, by developing a psychological theory of business cycles, that when credit is introduced the possibility of general oversupply of commodities may exist. An overissue of credit during a period of expansion and prosperity may be followed by contraction of credit as a result of pessimism in the business community.

At such times there is really an excess of all commodities above the money demand: in other words, there is an undersupply of money. From the sudden annihilation of a great mass of credit, every one dislikes to part with ready money, and many are anxious to procure it at any sacrifice. Almost everybody therefore is a seller, and there are scarcely any buyers....[28]

The introduction of credit money into an economy, according to Mill, thus permits the possibility of general oversupply, not because of overproduction in the Malthusian sense of general glut, but because of the changing expectations of the business community. Mill says that any such oversupply will be of short duration and will be followed by full employment, as prices change in the economy. The net effect of Mill's discussion of the issues raised by Say's Law is to defend this fundamental part of the classic system against Malthusian-like attacks and to develop a simple psychological theory of business fluctuations based on the interactions between credit money and business confidence.

The Wages Fund — Mill's Recantation

The wages fund doctrine was used by some economists and a number of popular writers as an argument against the formation of labor unions. According to the wages fund theory, the wage rate was determined by the size of the labor force and the wages fund, and any attempt by labor to raise wages, by whatever means, would be fruitless. This is an example of how orthodox economic theory was used to prove that attempts to improve the welfare of the working class by a more equal distribution of income could not be successful. We have already seen that Mill believed that his unique contribution to economic thinking was to draw a distinction between the fixed laws of production and the institutionally and culturally determined laws of distribution, and that his reason for drawing this distinction was to allow his humanism to moderate the conservative conclusions of the Ricardians.

Even though Mill had accepted the wages fund doctrine, he supported the formation of labor unions, following the reasoning of Adam Smith, who had pointed out that a single unorganized laborer was at a competitive disadvantage in bargaining over wage rates with an employer. Unions and strikes seemed to Mill to be appropriate tools for labor in its attempt to counterbalance the power of the employing firm. Quite possibly Mill's adherence to the wages fund theory can be explained by his strong concern over the consequences of unregulated population growth. After the publication of the sixth edition of Mill's *Principles*, but before the publication of the seventh, Mill reviewed a book by William Thornton that was critical of the application of supply-and-demand analysis to labor markets and that rejected the

28. *Ibid.*, p. 561.

wages fund doctrine. In his review Mill accepted nearly all of Thornton's arguments, concluding that the argument that unions cannot raise wages is invalid.

The wages fund doctrine held that the demand for labor was fixed absolutely by the size of the wages fund. Mill now retreated from this position to argue that whereas the *maximum* amount of funds that could be used to pay wages was fixed, a given labor force and wage rate might not exhaust this fixed amount. Under this reasoning the wage rate is not conclusively determined, and there is a range of possible wages. Labor unions may therefore raise wages through the bargaining process.

Although Mill rejected the wages fund doctrine in his 1869 review of Thornton's book, the seventh edition of his *Principles*, published in 1871, made no changes on this score, because Mill held that these new developments "are not yet ripe for incorporation in a general treatise on Political Economy."[29] This is quite curious, actually, for in 1862 Mill had already concluded in the fifth edition of his *Principles* that wage rates depended on the bargaining power of the employer and employee and that one important way for labor to increase its power was through unionization.[30] But this inconsistency is simply another example of Mill's attempts to stay within the general framework of classical economics, which he learned at a young age from his father, while giving vent to his humanistic feelings, which called for social reform centering around a more equal distribution of income.

THE DECLINE OF RICARDIAN ECONOMICS IN RETROSPECT

An examination of the development of orthodox economic theory in the fifty-odd years following the publication of Ricardo's *Principles* in 1817 reveals interesting contradictions and crosscurrents. The increased professionalization of economics, the growth of a socialist and humanistic literature, and the conflict between theory and fact all provoked criticism of the Ricardian analysis. Economists became more aware of their discipline and began to address themselves to the issues of the scope and method of economics and the distinction between positive and normative economic thinking. As the economy evolved and more data became available, a growing divergence between theory and fact became apparent, raising important questions about major Ricardian building blocks, such as the Malthusian population theory, the principle of historically diminishing returns, and the prediction of a fall in the rate of profits over time.

29. *Ibid.*, p. xxxi.
30. *Ibid.*, p. 937.

Malthusian population theory was an important part of the Ricardian system, because it permitted the development of a residual theory of income distribution. With its gradual abandonment, the wages fund doctrine became both a short- and long-run theory of wages. Ricardian economics had deduced that returns would diminish over time because it assumed that technological development in agriculture could not offset short-run diminishing returns. The question of long-run returns in agriculture is, however, an empirical, not a deductive issue, and the available data appeared to contradict these predictions of the theoretical model. Ricardo had also deduced a falling rate of profit over time, but although neither statistical data nor techniques were available to measure the rate of profit, the increasing returns observed in agriculture cast doubt on the validity of this conclusion. One of the most interesting and amazing aspects of the post-Ricardian period is the tenacity with which economists clung to the predictions of the Ricardian model in the face of conflicting empirical evidence. This is largely accounted for by their enthusiastic acceptance of the very abstract and deductive Ricardian model. A growing awareness of the logical difficulties inherent in a strict labor theory of value and a reaction to the criticism levied by the Ricardian socialists led to the development of an abstinence theory of interest and a cost of production theory of value of which labor and capital costs were both a part.

This was the environment into which J. S. Mill immerged, trained at an early age in the Ricardian tradition, but with strong and deep feelings about the injustices of the capitalist economy. He attempted to combine the hardheadedness of classical liberalism with the humanism of social reform to promote a society and economy less concerned with the business of business and more concerned with the art of individual improvement and self-fulfillment. He brought to economics an intellect so broad that he was able to contribute significantly to political science and philosophy as well as to economics. His original contributions to economic thought were somewhat obscured by his eclectic, open-minded incorporation of new developments into the Ricardian framework, and although he stressed the deductive character of economics as a discipline, he advocated a continuous reexamination of the relevance of theory to fact. Though his methodological position was sound, like that of most of his contemporaries, he failed to practice what he preached.

Mill's concern with social reform led him to stress insistently the distinction between the immutable laws of production and the changeable, institutionally determined laws governing the distribution of personal income. His efforts to establish a consistency between theory and policy application align him more with the tradition of Smith than of Ricardo. His eclecticism makes him difficult to classify ideologically; his writing contains strong strains of classical liberalism and laissez faire, yet he often advocates government intervention in the economy. For Mill, the clash between the interests of the landlords and those of the rest of society was a discordant element in the system. But he rejected the socialist condemnation of private property and competition, suggesting institutional adjustments that might retain their benefits and remove their glaring evils. His optimism led, moreover, to a new view of the stationary state freed of its dismal Ricardian overtones.

J. S. Mill made lasting and important contributions to economic theory. Although he did not admit it, he finally rejected the Ricardian labor theory of value and in its place developed a long-run cost of production theory of value that included both labor and capital costs. He extended the Ricardian theory of international trade to explain the terms of trade in a comparative advantage model and came close to explicitly developing the concept of price elasticity of demand. His well-reasoned defense of Say's Law ultimately saved it from the onslaughts of heterodox criticism. Toward the end of his career, he withdrew his support from the wages fund doctrine, removing an important economic argument from the arsenal of those who believed that the mass of society were forever destined to live close to the subsistence level. Orthodox thinking was ruled by Millian economics until the end of the nineteenth century, largely ignoring the grumblings of the brilliant, bushy-bearded malcontent, Karl Marx.

SUGGESTED READINGS

Anschutz, R. P. *The Philosophy of J. S. Mill.* London: Oxford University Press, 1953.

Ashley, W. J. "Introduction" to J. S. Mill's *Principles of Political Economy.* London: Longmans, Green, 1909.

Bladen V. W. "Introduction" to J. S. Mill's *Principles of Political Economy.* Vols. 2 and 3 in *Collected Works of John Stuart Mill.* Toronto: University of Toronto Press, 1965.

———. "John Stuart Mill's *Principles:* A Centenary Estimate." *American Economic Review,* 39 (May 1949).

Fetter, Frank. "The Rise and Decline of Ricardian Economics." *History of Political Economy,* 1 (Spring 1969).

Gordon, Barry. "Criticism of Ricardian Views on Value and Distribution in the British Periodicals, 1820-1850." *History of Political Economy,* 1 (Fall 1969).

———. "Say's Law, Effective Demand and the Contemporary British Periodicals, 1820-1850." *Economica* (November 1965).

Grampp, William D. "Classical Economics and Its Moral Critics." *History of Political Economy,* 5 (Fall 1973).

de Marchi, Neil B. "The Success of Mill's *Principles.*" *History of Political Economy,* 6 (Summer 1974).

Mill, John S. *Principles of Political Economy.* Edited by W. J. Ashley, London: Longmans, Green, 1909.

Packe, Michael St. John. *The Life of John Stuart Mill.* London: Martin Secker and Warburg, 1954.

Plamenatz, John. *The English Utilitarians*. Oxford: Basil Blackwell and Mott, 1958.

Schwartz, Pedro. *The New Political Economy of J. S. Mill*. Durham: Duke University Press, 1972.

Viner, Jacob. "Bentham and J. S. Mill: The Utilitarian Background," *American Economic Review*, 39 (March 1949).

Readings in Original Sources

All readings are from Mill's *Principles*.

Value: Book III, Chapters I, II, III, IV, VI, XV, and XVI.

Rent: Book II, Chapter XVI; Book III, Chapter IV, Section 6; Book III, Chapter V.

Wages: Book II, Chapters XI–XIV.

Profits: Book II, Chapter XV.

Socialism: Book II, Chapter I.

Custom and Competition: Book II, Chapter IV.

Chapter 6
Karl Marx

Possibly no economic writer is more difficult to analyze objectively than Karl Marx (1818-1883). This is particularly true for American economists trained in the orthodox tradition, which has always been openly hostile to Marxian ideas. With the general radicalization of graduate students in the United States, which gained momentum in the 1960s, and the development of a political economy of the New Left, many neophyte economists began to study Marx. Although this interest has decreased somewhat, that it continues to persist at all is an index of Marx's power and force: his ideas will not simply fade away even in a social setting unreceptive to their existence. Objectivity is also difficult to achieve when studying Marx because of the complexity of his total thought. He was more than just an economist — he was also a philosopher, sociologist, prophet, and revolutionist. To some of the converted, Marxism has become a dogma as incapable of objective analysis as any set of religious ideas. Nonbelievers are not merely stupid or misinformed, they are sinners. And Marx's revolutionary political thought has now become so intermingled with nationalism that the Soviet Marxists look with equal disdain upon the bourgeois economists of the United States and the deviationist Marxists in other parts of the world, particularly China. But one thing is clear: few writers in the social sciences have been as important as Marx.

AN OVERVIEW OF MARX

Marx's Purpose

Marx was first and foremost a philosopher who felt that his job was not merely to interpret and analyze society but also to promote the changes in society he considered desirable. As a partisan advocate of change, he does not differ from Smith, Ricardo, or J. S. Mill. In contrast to the classical economists, however, Marx advocated not small, marginal changes in the society and economy but a fundamental revolution.

Since Marx is popularly associated with the economic systems of social-ism and communism, people often assume that he wrote about these systems. Nothing could be further from the truth. Marx studied what he called capitalism — his major work is entitled *Das Kapital* or *Capital*. And in all the vast literature produced by Marx and his collaborator, Friedrich Engels, there are only a few vague references to how a social-ist or communist economy is to be organized.

Karl Marx

Marx's economic theory is an application of his theory of history to the capitalist economy. He wanted to lay bare the laws of the dynamics of capitalism. Paul M. Sweezy, possibly the most important American Marxian economist alive today, has suggested that Marxian economics is the economics of capitalism and capitalist economics is the economics of socialism. Thus Sweezy believes that to understand the capitalistic system, the proper theoretical model is the Marxian one, an opinion with which few orthodox economists would agree. But most would agree with the second half of this paradoxical statement, that an understanding of modern neoclassical orthodox theory — what Sweezy calls capitalist economics — is essential to the planning of a socialist economy. The late Oscar Lange, a Marxian who taught in the United States and later returned to Poland to become an economic planner, contends that Marxian and orthodox economic analysis should be looked upon as complementary rather than mutually exclusive. Whereas an understanding of the everyday operation of the market can be achieved by using neoclassical orthodox theory, an understanding of the evolutionary development of capitalism, Lange says, is possible only within the Marxian framework. It is only by studying Marx, moreover, that we can comprehend the Marxist view of our society and economy; and since a large part of the world is using this analytical framework, it is important for us to understand its content.

Intellectual Sources of Marx's Ideas

A study of Marx's life discloses the intellectual sources of his system. Born into a Jewish family that turned to Christianity, the young Marx began studying law but soon turned to philosophy. Early in his studies he was attracted by the intellectual framework of Hegel, another German writer, which, as we shall see, became an important element in his own system. After receiving his doctorate in philosophy, Marx was unable to find an academic appointment because of his radical views and so turned to journalism. His political views, radical for the Germany of his times but still not socialistic, resulted in his being expelled from Germany. In Paris and Brussels he began to study French socialist thought and classical political economy. Marx had tremendous intellectual powers and an almost neurotic drive to read and study. After being expelled from Paris and Brussels, he moved to London and spent the last thirty-three years of his life reading and writing in one of the world's great libraries, the British Museum.

Marx's Theory of History

Marxist thought combines Hegelian philosophy, French utopian thought, and classical political economy — particularly Ricardian.

Marx's analysis of capitalism is an application to his times of a theory of history derived from G. W. F. Hegel. Hegel maintained that history proceeds not cyclically through a series of recurring situations, as many people believe, but rather moves forward in a straight line, progressively, by the interaction of a triad of forces, which he terms thesis, antithesis, and synthesis. Since these forces are ideational, it is in the study of ideas, rather than of past events, that the laws of history can be found. At any given time, according to Hegel, an accepted idea, or thesis, exists but is soon contradicted by its opposite, or antithesis. Out of this conflict of ideas, a synthesis, representing a higher form of truth, is formed and becomes a new thesis. This new thesis is likewise opposed by its antithesis and transformed into a new synthesis, and so on and on. Thus in a never-ending chain of ideas, each one approaching closer to truth, history evolves in an endless process in which all things become gradually more perfect by means of conflict-induced change. Hegel called this process, as well as the method for investigating it, dialectic.

Marx perceived a similar process in history — and in reality in general — and used a similar method to investigate it which he also called dialectic. But the great difference between Hegel's and Marx's philosophies was that Hegel's was idealistic and Marx's materialistic. The reality in which change occurred for Hegel was ideas, but for Marx it was matter, which, he said, contained within itself the seeds of constant conflict. Marx's philosophy, therefore, is called *dialectical materialism*.

Can one develop a theory to explain the different ways societies have been organized over time, and can this theory be used to predict the possible future organization of society? These are the grand questions that engaged Marx's attention. Are the societal structures we called feudalism and capitalism part of an evolutionary development capable of analysis, or are they merely a result of random historical occurrences? Marx accused the capitalist bourgeois historians of writing as though there had been a past but would be no future, as though capitalism, a system evolved from previous systems, was somehow an ideal societal structure that would exist forever. One important ingredient in the Marxian system, then, is change: though we may not know exactly what the future will bring, Marx says, we do know it will be different from the past and the present.

In focusing on materialistic or economic forces as the primary, although not the sole, determinant of historical change, Marx revolutionized thinking in the social sciences. In the hands of the most dogmatic of Marxists, this thesis becomes completely untenable, but it has proved a fruitful hypothesis or first approximation for a good deal of important, useful work in the social sciences. Isaiah Berlin, a British critic and philosopher, applies the parable of the hedgehog and the fox to Marx's concentration on materialistic factors in explaining historical change.

The fox knows many things, Berlin says, but the hedgehog knows one main thing. The scholarly Marx was clearly an intellectual fox, but in the elaboration of his historical theory, he assumed the role of a hedgehog, ignoring many other relevant issues in order to focus on economic factors as the most important element in explaining the changing structure of society. The Marxian theory of history is most explicitly stated in the *Communist Manifesto* and in the "Preface" to *The Critique of Political Economy*, where Marx explains:

> The general conclusion at which I arrived and which, once reached, continued to serve as the leading thread in my studies, may be briefly summed up as follows: In the social production which men carry on they enter into definite relations that are indispensable and independent of their will; these relations of production correspond to a definite stage of development of their material powers of production. The sum total of these relations of production constitutes the economic structure of society — the real foundation, on which rise legal and political superstructures and to which correspond definite forms of social consciousness. The mode of production in material life determines the general character of the social, political, and spiritual processes of life. It is not the consciousness of men that determines their existence, but, on the contrary, their social existence determines their consciousness. At a certain stage of their development, the material forces of production in society come in conflict with the existing relations of production, or — what is but a legal expression for the same thing — with the property relations within which they had been at work before. From forms of development of the forces of production these relations turn into their fetters. Then comes the period of social revolution. With the change of the economic foundation the entire immense superstructure is more or less rapidly transformed.[1]

Marx holds that all societies, except classless societies, can be divided analytically into two parts: the forces of production and the relations of production. The forces of production are the technology used by the society in producing material goods, manifested in labor skills, scientific knowledge, tools, and capital goods; they are inherently dynamic. The relations of production are the rules of the game. There are relations between one person and another, or social relations; and relations between people and things, or property relations. To carry on production, the problem of economic order must be solved, and the historically determined relations of production provide the institutional

---

1. Karl Marx, *A Contribution to the Critique of Political Economy*, trans. from the 2nd German ed. by N. I. Stone (Chicago: Charles H. Kerr, 1913), pp. 11-12.

framework within which economic decisions are made. In contrast to the dynamic, changing forces of production, the relations of production are static and past-binding. The static nature of the relations of production is reinforced by what Marx terms the social superstructure, whose function is to maintain the historically determined relations of production. The social superstructure consists of the art, literature, music, philosophy, religion, and other cultural forms accepted by the society, and its purpose is to keep intact the relations of production — to maintain the status quo.

The static relations of production are the thesis in the Marxian dialectic, and the dynamic, changing forces of production are the antithesis. In the beginning of any historical period there is harmony between the forces and relations of production, but over time the changing forces of production bring about contradictions in the system as the existing relations of production (institutions) are no longer appropriate to the forces of production (technology). These contradictions will manifest themselves, Marx says, in a class struggle. Finally the contradictions become so intense that there is a period of social revolution, and a new set of relations of production is brought into being. These new relations of production are the synthesis that results from the conflict between the old thesis (relations of production) and the antithesis (the forces of production), and these relations of production become the new thesis. At this point in history there is again harmony, but the dynamic, changing forces of production ensure that new contradictions will soon develop.

A Closer Look at the Dialectic

An examination of the Marxian concept of the social superstructure will help to clarify the Marxian theory of history and the Marxist attitude toward society. Marx said that religion, a part of the social superstructure, was the opiate of the people. He believed that the function of religion in society is to maintain the status quo, to prevent change. So also for such cultural aspects of society as art, literature, music, and philosophy. Their function is to rationalize and support the existing institutional structure and to divert attention from the growing conflicts indicating that this institutional structure is no longer appropriate to the available technology. This accounts for the antireligious attitude of some Marxists as well as for their stance that the only acceptable literature, art, or music is that which promotes revolution.

The Marxian theory of history traces the development of society from feudalism to capitalism and its further development, as predicted by Marx, into socialism and finally into communism. In the early feudal period, the relations of production were appropriate to the existing forces of production, and these relations of production were supported and reinforced by the social superstructure. The changing forces of production soon destroyed this harmony, as the institutional structure of feudalism became incompatible with developing agricultural technology, increased trade, and the beginning of manufacturing. These conflicts between the forces and relations of production were manifested in a class struggle and finally produced a new set of relations of production, capitalism. In the *Communist Manifesto* Marx describes the harmony between the forces and relations of production that existed in early capitalism and the tremendous increase in output and economic activity that ensued. Capitalism, however, like feudalism, contains the seeds of its own destruction, as the inevitable conflicts develop with changes in the forces of production. With the fall of capitalism a new set of relations of production will emerge, which Marx calls socialism, and socialism, in turn, will finally give way to communism. Before turning to Marx's detailed examination of capitalism, several other issues raised by the Marxian theory of history deserve attention.

Socialism and Communism

The terms "socialism" and "communism" have no exact meaning as they are used today, but in the Marxian system they refer to stages that will occur in the historical process. Socialism, a set of relations of production following capitalism, contains some vestiges of capitalism, according to Marx. One of the chief characteristics of capitalism, he says, is that the means of production, capital, are not owned or controlled by the proletariat. The major change that occurs in the transition from capitalism to socialism is that the expropriators are expropriated — the proletariat now owns the means of production. The vestige of capitalism still remaining is that economic activity is still basically organized through the use of incentive systems: rewards must still be given in order to induce people to labor. But communism, as the concept is used by Marx, implies a society and economy quite different from that existing under socialism. People are no longer motivated to work by monetary or material incentives, and the social classes that existed under capitalism, and to a lesser extent under socialism, have disappeared. Communism is a classless society in which the state has withered away. Under socialism each person contributes to the economic process according to his ability and receives an income according to his contribution; under communism each contributes according to his ability but consumes according to his needs.

This concept of communism raises some interesting issues. Marx said that previous socialist writers were unscientific, that they were merely humanitarians of various sorts expressing their value judgments of what the good society should be like. He claimed that he was developing scientific socialism as contrasted to utopian socialism, since his theory of history was scientific and proves that the arrival of socialism and communism is inevitable. Yet the Marxian description of communism is based on debatable assumptions about the fundamental changes in basic human behavior that must occur to produce such a society. These utopian conclusions of Marx have been satirized by George Orwell in his novel *Animal Farm*, in which utopian communism finally breaks down with the emergence of the idea that "all animals are equal, except some are more equal than others." Marxians, in the lineage of Godwin, believe that humans are perfectable and that human goodness is suppressed and distorted by existing society. They hold that only by believing in a society in which all are equal and by striving to bring about that society can we have a chance of achieving it. Many non-Marxists with strong humanitarian feelings find the idea of a society of pure or ideal communism desirable, but they doubt whether such a society could ever exist. The fundamental issue dividing these views is the eternal question as to whether environmental or instinctive forces are more important in determining patterns of human behavior. In any event, one appealing facet of Marxism is the view that humans are basically good and that undesirable behavior is a result of the institutional environment.

One possible criticism of Marx's dialectic is that the whole system is not truly an ongoing dialectic but is teleological, because all conflict between the forces and relations of production cease with the emergence of communism. Marx's theory of history is directed toward an end, communism. But why would contradictions cease with the emergence of communism? Would it not be more reasonable to conclude that, as long as the forces of production remain dynamic, contradictions will always exist within any society? To avoid criticism, some modern Marxists, such as Woolfe and Resnick, have reinterpreted Marx's dialectic as overdeterminism. In an overdetermined theory, there can be many possible paths.

One other problem, of considerable contemporary interest, is to determine what Marx meant when he says that, as history moves from one set of relations of production to another, a social revolution occurs. The term "revolution" has several possible meanings. Revolution can mean a period of dramatic change as one set of institutions gives way to another. The amount of time this takes may be fairly long. The Industrial Revolution, for example, was a period of increased economic activity that took place in Western Europe. It did not occur overnight, but it was a revolution in the sense that tremendous changes took place in a relatively short period of time. Revolution, especially in the context of a class struggle, can also mean violence and armed conflict.

Does the Marxian theory of history require that bloody revolution occur as one set of relations of production is replaced by another?

Questions concerning the transition from capitalism to socialism have been much discussed. Is an evolutionary change possible, or will socialism be established only after a revolution involving violence? Historically socialists have been roughly divided into two camps: the evolutionary or right-wing socialists, who contend that a socialist society will come into being through legislation and the labor movement, among other means; and the revolutionary left-wing socialists, who hold that those in control of the capitalist society will never relinquish their power and must be brought down by force. Until recently the Fabian socialists in Britain were good examples of evolutionary right-wing socialists, and the socialists of the Soviet Union were the prototype of revolutionary left-wing socialists. In recent years, however, the official party position in the Soviet Union has moved to the right and now appears to hold that coexistence is possible until the inexorable forces of history have replaced capitalism by socialism. Some Marxists have reprimanded their comrades for deviating from orthodox Marxism, contending that capitalism's demise will come only with violent revolutions.

MARX'S ECONOMIC THEORIES

Marx's system is a mixture of philosophical, sociological, and economic analysis, and, therefore, it is somewhat of an injustice to separate out the purely economic theories from the rest. Convinced of the inevitable collapse of capitalism, he applied his theory of history to the society of his time as he searched for contradictions between the forces and relations of production. He felt that these contradictions would be made manifest in a class struggle, since, as he stated in the *Communist Manifesto*, the history of all societies is a history of class struggles. The fundamental determinant of the relations of production and thus of the institutional structure of a society will be the forces of production. With the handmill the appropriate institutional structure is feudalism, Marx asserts, and with the steam mill it is capitalism. The logic of the technological process creates the conditions and forces that enable the steam mill to evolve out of the handmill, and as the forces of production change, the old relations of production must give way to more appropriate institutional forms. Thus Marx sees the present as part of the historical unfolding of the dialectic.

Marx's Methodology

Marx's approach to the study of the economy is unconventional. Orthodox economic theory, particularly microeconomic theory, attempts to understand the whole of the economy by an examination of its parts: households, firms, prices in markets, for instance. Marx, on the other hand, starts at the level of the total society and economy and analyzes them by examining their influence on their components. Thus, in orthodox methodology, the major causation runs from the parts to the whole, whereas in the Marxian scheme the whole determines the parts. This description of the different approaches of Marxian and orthodox economic theory is an oversimplification, since both allow for an interaction between the parts and the whole, but it does clarify a basic difference in orientation.

Commodities and Classes

Marx began by examining the exchange relationship between those who own the means of production, the capitalists, and those who sell only their labor in the market, the proletariat. He held that one of the chief characteristics of capitalism was the separation of labor from the ownership of the means of production. Under capitalism labor no longer owns its workshops, tools, nor the raw materials of the production process. Capitalism is, then, essentially a society of two classes, and one of the most important aspects of this society is the exchange, the wage bargain, that takes place between the capitalist and the proletariat. For this reason Marx developed a theory explaining commodity prices, or exchange values. And since he was particularly interested in explaining the source of property incomes, he examined the forces determining the prices of the commodities produced by labor and the price labor receives as payment for its productive efforts.

Ricardian economic theory, as well as the orthodox microeconomic theory that followed, also begins its analysis of the economy with the price of commodities. People often assumed, therefore, that Marx was interested in the same basic problem, namely, to explain the forces that determine commodity prices. Marx, however, was not primarily interested in developing a theory of relative prices. His interest was in wages, which he considered to be the most crucial element in the capitalist system, since they disclosed a contradiction that would help to explain the laws of motion of the capitalist system.

In precapitalist economies human goods were produced primarily for their use value. Commodities were produced for consumption by the producer. One of the chief characteristics of capitalism is that commodities are produced by the capitalist not for their use value but for their exchange value. An understanding of capitalism, therefore, requires an understanding of the exchange relationships that develop between owners of commodities, the most important being between the capitalist and the proletariat.

This can be expressed in another way. According to Marx, the prices of commodities in a capitalist system represent two different sets of relationships: first, quantitative relationships between commodities (two beavers exchange for one deer) and second, social, or qualitative, relationships between individuals in the economy. Wages, as prices in the economy, then, represent both a quantitative relationship and a social, or qualitative, relationship between the capitalist and the proletariat. Marx is interested in prices primarily insofar as they disclose these social relationships; he was only secondarily interested in prices as they reflect a quantitative relationship between commodities.

Marx's Labor Theory of Value

In developing a theory of relative prices, or the quantitative relationship between things or commodities, Marx essentially uses Ricardo's theory of value. Since commodities manifest in their prices certain quantitative relationships, this means, according to Marx, that all commodities must contain one element in common and this element must exist in certain measurable quantities. Marx considers use value, or utility, as a common element but rejects this possibility. He then turns to labor as the common element and concludes that it is the amount of labor time necessary to produce commodities that governs their relative prices. As an advocate of a labor theory of value, Marx worked through the various problems inherent in the formulation of a labor theory of value, as Ricardo had before him, and essentially followed the Ricardian solutions. Marx was able to give a clearer presentation of the difficulties of a labor theory of value, but he was no more able to solve the problems than Ricardo.

To Marx the only social cost of producing commodities was labor. He disregarded the differing skills of labor and conceived of the total labor available to society for commodity production as a homogeneous quantity, which he called "abstract labor." The production of any commodity requires the use of a part of the total supply of abstract labor. The relative prices of commodities reflect amounts of this abstract supply of labor, measured in clock hours, necessary to produce the goods. This raises what we have called the skilled labor problem, namely, that labor of varying skills will have varying outputs. Marx meets this issue by measuring the amount of labor required to produce a commodity by the socially necessary labor time, which is defined as the time taken by a workman possessing the average degree of skill possessed by labor at the time. Labor with skill greater than the average is reduced to the average by measuring its greater productivity and making an appropriate adjustment. If, for example, a given laborer, because of greater natural ability, produced 100 percent more than a laborer with average skills, each hour of the superior labor would count as two hours of average labor. In this manner all labor time is reduced to socially necessary labor time. We saw that Smith became involved in circular reasoning by measuring differences in labor skills by wages paid to labor. Marx sidesteps the whole issue by assuming that differences in labor skills are measured not by wages but by differences in physical output.

Another problem raised by a labor theory of value is how to account for the influence of capital goods on relative prices. Marx uses Ricardo's solution to this problem, maintaining that capital is stored-up labor. The labor time required to produce a commodity is, then, the number of hours of labor immediately applied added to the number of hours required to produce the capital destroyed in the process. Marx's solution, like Ricardo's, is not completely satisfactory, since it fails to allow for the fact that, where capital is used, interest may be paid on the funds used to pay the indirect labor stored in the capital from the time of the payment of the indirect labor until the sale of the product.

A labor theory of value must also deal with the issues raised by differing fertilities of land. Equal amounts of labor time will produce varying outputs when applied to land of different fertilities. The labor theory of value that Marx develops in the first two volumes of *Capital* completely neglects this problem, but in Volume III he meets the question by adopting Ricardo's theory of differential rent: the greater productivity of labor on land of superior fertility is absorbed by the landlord as a differential rent. Competition will cause the rent on superior grades of land to rise until the rates of profit on all grades of land are equal. Rent, then, is price-determined, not price-determining.

A final difficulty inherent in a labor theory of value derives from the influence of profits on prices. In examining Smith's and Ricardo's versions of a labor theory of value, we found that when profits are a different percentage of the final price for commodities, relative prices cannot be measured correctly by labor alone. One of the crucial aspects of this problem involves labor–capital ratios in various industries. Industries that are highly capital-intensive will produce goods whose profits are a larger proportion of final price than industries of lesser capital intensity. Marx, because of his close study of Ricardo, was fully aware of this problem, but throughout the first two volumes of *Capital* he avoids this issue by assuming that all industries and firms have the same capital intensity. He drops this assumption in Volume III, however, and attempts to work out an internally consistent labor theory of value. But he failed in this, as Ricardo had before him. Before examining this failure more closely we will need to become more familiar with some other Marxian concepts.

Marxian Algebra

Marx said that the value of a commodity can be broken down into three parts:

$$\text{Value} = C + V + S$$

Constant capital (C) is defined as the expenditures of the capitalists for raw materials and depreciation charges on fixed capital. It is convenient to regard this as all nonlabor costs the capitalists incur in producing commodities. Variable capital (V) is defined as wage and salary expenditures. Surplus value (S) is a residual obtained by subtracting constant and variable capital outlays from the gross receipts of the capitalist. According to Marx constant capital outlays result in receipts to the capitalist of an amount equal to these outlays, thus the name constant capital. Variable capital outlays, where business is profitable, result in receipts greater than those outlays. By this means, Marx embeds in his system his fundamental assumption that only labor creates value.

It is important to understand clearly the nature and source of surplus value in the Marxian analysis of capitalism, because surplus value is in turn the source of property incomes. Since Marx assumes that all markets are perfectly competitive, his analysis focuses almost exclusively on long-run, competitively determined equilibrium prices. One of the first uses to which he puts his labor theory of value is to explain the nature and source of property incomes. How do property incomes, or surplus value, arise in competitive markets? According to Marx the capitalist buys various inputs, paying their long-run competitive prices, and sells the final product at its equilibrium price. Surplus value or property incomes do not, then, arise from labor being paid less than its competitive price or from final products being sold at higher than competitive prices. It appears that no one is cheated, yet surplus value exists. Marx's solution is that the capitalist purchases one commodity, labor, which when used in the production process creates more value than it is paid. Labor is the only commodity, according to Marx, with this ability to create surplus value.

The long-run competitive equilibrium price of labor is the equivalent of the socially necessary labor time required to produce the real wage of labor. If in four hours labor is able to produce enough commodities to purchase all the commodities (food, clothing, and shelter) necessary to maintain labor, then the price of labor will be equivalent to four hours of labor time. A capitalist's variable capital outlays or daily wage bill for each laborer will, then, be the equivalent of four hours of labor time. If the working day were only four hours, then no surplus value or property income could arise, since the whole of final output would be used to meet the socially necessary wage bill. A longer working day, for example, eight hours, results in surplus value, for after labor has received its competitively determined wage equal to four hours labor time, a surplus of commodities equal to four hours of labor time remains. Marx calls the ratio of surplus value to variable capital outlays the rate of surplus value, or the rate of exploitation.

$$\text{Rate of Surplus Value} = S' = \frac{S}{V}$$

In the above example the rate of surplus value would be

$$\frac{4 \text{ hrs}}{4 \text{ hrs}} = 100 \text{ percent}$$

In this example, if one laborer produced one unit of output each day, the produced commodity would in fact sell in the market at a price equivalent to eight hours of labor time, which is its long-run equilibrium price in a competitive market. Labor, however, still has a price per day equal to only four hours of labor time. Thus, although ostensibly no one is cheated in the various market transactions, since they all take place at competitive prices, there is a rate of surplus value of 100 percent. Under capitalism, with its separation of labor from ownership of the means of production, labor has an option of working eight hours each day or not at all. The capitalist, because of his ownership and control of the means of production, can require labor to work longer than is necessary to maintain itself and is thus able to realize a property income equal to the surplus value.

Surplus Value — A Digression

Marxian analysis, like other analyses, contains an objective part that throws certain aspects of the economy into perspective, but it also explicitly includes an element of ideology. Stripped of ideological overtones, Marx's message is simply that any economy will produce more goods and services than are needed to pay all the real social costs of production. It is useful to consider this phenonenon in a macroeconomic context. Subtracting from total yearly output in the United States all the real costs that must be paid to produce that output would yield a residual, which could be termed surplus value. These real costs would include both labor and capital costs. Marx's surplus value is thus similar to the physiocrat's concept of net product. The Industrial Revolution has brought about large increases in the yearly surplus value created in the world. And Marx raises a legitimate question: what is an equitable way to distribute this socially produced surplus among participants in the society?

But Marx was not content merely to raise this issue. Nor was he content to suggest that the present cutting of the social pie was inequitable, unjust, and unfair. Marx went beyond this and claimed with "scientific objectivity" that the surplus created by labor was taken from it because of its lack of ownership of the means of production. A revolution in which the means of production was taken from the capitalists would, therefore, return the surplus value to its creators, the laboring proletariat.

Back to the Marxian Algebra

The rate of surplus value can be increased by increasing the length of the working day, by increasing the productivity of labor, or by lowering the quantity of commodities that constitutes the real wage of labor. The capitalist, Marx contends, is constantly trying to increase the rate of surplus value either by increasing the length of the working day or by increasing the productivity of labor. The individual capitalist can do little to lower the real wage of labor, since this wage rate is determined by competitive market forces. Technological improvements in producing goods consumed by wage earners can, however, result in an increase in the rate of surplus value.

The rate of profit is equal to the ratio of surplus value to total capital outlays:

$$\text{Rate of Profit} = P = \frac{S}{C + V}$$

The *organic composition of capital*, Marx's term for the capital intensity of a firm or industry, is equal to the ratio of constant capital outlays to total capital outlays:

$$\text{Organic Composition of Capital} = Q = \frac{C}{C + V}$$

The greater this ratio, the more capital-intensive the firm or industry. Algebraic manipulation of the concepts of the rate of surplus value, the rate of profits, and the organic composition of capital shows that the rate of profit varies directly with the rate of surplus value and varies inversely with the organic composition of capital:[2]

$$\text{Rate of Profit} = P = S' \,(1 - Q)$$

2. See Paul M. Sweezy, *The Theory of Capitalist Development: Principles of Marxian Political Economy* (New York: Monthly Review Press, 1956), p. 68, for a proof of this derivation.

Problems with Marx's Labor Theory of Value

In examining Smith's and Ricardo's labor theories of value, we found certain inherent difficulties. One problem a labor theory must solve is the role of profits in price determination. Smith was only vaguely aware of this issue as he wrestled with his labor cost and labor command theories of value in an advanced economy. Marx, like Ricardo, was fully aware of the theoretical issues but unable to offer a satisfactory solution.

Marx assumes that competitive market forces will cause the rate of surplus value to be the same for all firms and all industries. These same competitive forces will also result in a common rate of profits for all firms and industries. A higher rate of profit, for example, in one sector of an industry or of the economy, he says, will bring about a shift of resources that will result in a uniform rate of profit in the long run. If, however, both the rate of surplus value and the rate of profit are uniform throughout the economy, the organic composition of capital must also be uniform. This can easily be demonstrated. The rate of profit is given by the formula $P = S'(1 - Q)$. If the rate of surplus value (S') is everywhere the same because of competitive forces and if the rate of profit (P) is uniform throughout the economy for the same reasons, then the organic composition of capital (Q) must be the same in every firm and industry.

It is an observable fact, however, that capital–labor ratios and the organic composition of capital differ from one industry to another; an example using this fact will illustrate the problems presented by a labor theory of value. Assume an economy with a rate of surplus value (S') equal to 100 percent; a capital-intensive industry, aluminum, where the organic composition of captial is 0.75 ($Q_A = 0.75$); and a labor-intensive industry, berries, where the organic composition of capital is 0.25 ($Q_B = 0.25$). Inserting these values into the Marxian formula, $P = S'(1 - Q)$, for determining the rate of profit gives:

Aluminum Industry

$$P_A = S'(1 - Q_A)$$
$$= 1.00(1 - 0.75)$$
$$= 0.25 \text{ or } 25 \text{ percent}$$

Berry Industry

$$P_B = S'(1 - Q_B)$$
$$= 1.00(1 - 0.25)$$
$$= 0.75, \text{ or } 75 \text{ percent}$$

This result obviously contradicts the assumption that the rate of profit is equal in all forms of economic activity. It also shows, rather curiously, that if the rate of surplus value (S') is the same between industries, the rate of profit is higher in the labor-intensive berry industry than in the capital-intensive aluminum industry.

Back to Labor Cost and Labor Command

Now that we have come a full circle, we can reexamine the difficulties encountered by Smith, Ricardo, and Marx in developing a labor theory of value. In analyzing Smith's value theory, we found that if labor-capital ratios varied between industry — in other words, if wage payments are not the same proportionate part of the final prices of all commodities — the set of relative prices given by a labor cost theory of value is different from that given by a labor command theory. Smith's intuitive perception of these difficulties led him to abandon a labor theory of value for an advanced economy where profits are paid and to opt for a cost of production theory of value. When Ricardo attacked this problem, he found that a theory of value based on labor time alone would not satisfactorily explain relative prices where industries have different labor-capital compositions. Ricardo concluded that although differing labor–capital ratios theoretically prevented a pure labor theory of value from explaining all the variations in relative prices, this disturbing factor was quantitatively of minor importance. It is, therefore, hardly surprising to find that Marx could develop an internally consistent labor theory of value only on the restrictive assumption that all industries have the same organic composition of capital.

Marx's Solution and Some Implications

Marx followed Ricardo's procedure and thoroughly examined the nuances of this problem before finally removing it by assumption. The labor theory of value used throughout the first two volumes of *Capital* assumes that the organic composition of capital is the same for all industries. But in the third volume of *Capital*, Marx dropped this restrictive assumption and attempted to develop an internally consistent labor theory of value. This he failed to do. This internal inconsistency, which has been called the great contradiction in Marxian value theory, was immediately recognized by Eugen Böhm-Bawerk in a book translated as *Karl Marx and the Close of His System*. A good deal of further work on the theoretical issues of this problem has been done by economists since Marx. The difficulties with Marx's labor theory of value have become known as the transformation problem. It came to be called this because Marx, in Volume III of *Capital*, attempted to transform his concept of the values of commodities into market prices, in order to include economies with industries of varying capital intensities. A number of later writers have also tried to solve this problem, beginning with L. Bortkiewicz in 1896. The discussion of the transformation problem was still in the journals as recently as the 1970s, when some of the best minds in the profession, such as Paul Samuelson and W. J. Baumol, added to the literature. It is an intriguing, though esoteric, theoretical problem, and debates about it are likely to continue.

What consequences does this failure of Marx's labor theory of value have for his analysis of capitalism? Value theory plays a central role in orthodox economic theory. Since one of the major tasks of orthodox theory is to explain the allocation of scarce resources among alternative uses, a failure of orthodox value theory involves a collapse of almost the entire theoretical structure. It is for this reason that most orthodox economists regard the inadequacies of Marx's theory of value as fatal to the whole of his system. It is certainly correct that the Marxian labor theory of value provides little help in understanding resource allocation and the formation of prices in a modern economy. Furthermore, planning a socialist economy by using only a labor theory of value to set relative prices would lead to undesirable results. But does the failure of the Marxian labor theory of value necessarily imply the failure of his complete system? Several answers have been given to this question.

Most orthodox economists accept the conclusion that Marx's entire system falls with the failure of his labor theory of value. Others argue that his primary purpose was to explain the laws of motion of capitalism and that he was interested to only a small degree in explaining relative prices. They therefore conclude that Marx's analysis of capitalism is only slightly damaged by the failure of his labor theory of value. Others argue that the labor theory of value in the Marxian system is designed purely to provide an ideological foundation for the revolutionary implications of the system. Admittedly, technical criticisms pointing to the internal inconsistencies of the labor theory of value do not impair the ideological use of the theory. There are also, of course, economists who reject Marx's analysis of capitalism on other grounds than the inadequacies of his value theory.

We agree that the labor theory of value fails to explain relative prices. But this failure does not vitiate Marx's complete system, for two major reasons. First, Marx was not primarily interested in questions concerning the allocation of resources and the formation of prices; he wanted to develop a theory to explain the dynamic changes taking place in the economy of his time. In this sense it is proper to regard Marx as a macroeconomist rather than a microeconomist. Second, the labor theory of value could be replaced in the Marxian system by other theories of value without changing either his essential analysis or his conclusions. Similarly, Ricardo's doctrine of comparative advantage is not dependent upon a particular value theory. Likewise, while the ideological force of Marx's system is certainly weakened by a refutation of the labor theory of value, he could raise the ethical questions that concerned him — namely, the serious inequities in the distribution of income under capitalism — without reference to this particular theory.

From the uses to which Marx put his labor theory of value, our view is that its primary role was ethical, or ideological. He wanted to show that the source of property income was exploitative, or unearned, incomes. He accomplished this by assuming that labor is the only commodity that creates surplus value. He maintains this position consistently throughout his analysis as he measures the rate of surplus value as a ratio of surplus value to variable capital outlays. One could, in principle, say that capital was the sole creator of surplus value and thus develop a capital theory of value, though it would come as no surprise to discover that a capital theory of value would contain some of the same inherent inconsistencies as a labor theory of value. As long as labor–capital ratios vary among industries, a capital theory of value cannot measure relative prices correctly. Although the ethical issues Marx raised concerning the proper distribution of income are clearly important, he was mistaken in believing that he had demonstrated objectively and scientifically, by means of a labor theory of value, that the proletariat was being exploited by the capitalists. They may indeed be exploited, but that conclusion involves an ethical judgment.

MARX'S ANALYSIS OF CAPITALISM

Marx applied his theory of history to the society and economy of his time in order to discover the laws of motion of capitalism and to point up contradictions in the system between the forces and relations of production. He was concerned with long-run trends in the economy; when he examined the present it was always in the context of the present as history. In his analysis of capitalism he formulated certain principles that have become known as Marxian laws and are treated with much the same reverence by some Marxists as the laws of supply and demand are by some orthodox economists. The Marxian laws of capitalism include the following: a reserve army of the unemployed, a falling rate of profit, business crises, increasing concentration of industry into fewer firms, and increasing misery among the proletariat.

In his analysis of the economics of capitalism, Marx uses, with a few exceptions, the basic tools of classical economics, particularly Ricardian theory. Thus, he assumes (1) a labor cost theory explaining relative prices, (2) neutral money, (3) constant returns in manufacturing and diminishing returns in agriculture, (4) perfect competition, (5) a rational, calculating economic man, and (6) a modified version of the wages fund doctrine. In most of his analysis he rejects Ricardian assumptions of fixed coefficients of production, full employment, and the Malthusian population doctrine.

It is important to realize that part of the difference between Marx and Ricardo in their analysis of the economics of capitalism does not proceed from any difference in their basic analytical framework, but comes from a difference in their respective ideologies. Since Marx was critical of capitalism, he examined it with a view of finding faults or contradictions in the system; Ricardo basically accepted it and saw it in general as a harmonious working out of the economic process. The chief actor in the Marxian model, as in the Ricardian model, is the capitalist. The capitalist's search for profits and reaction to changing rates of profits explain, in a large part, the dynamics of the capitalist system. But whereas capitalists in the Marxian system rationally and calculatingly pursue their economic advantage and sow the seeds of their own destruction, in the Ricardian system these same rational, calculating capitalists, in following their own self-interest, promote the social good. Although the classical economists' long-run prediction of a stationary state is certainly pessimistic, it is not the fault of the capitalistic system, but rather of the belief in Malthusian population doctrine and in historically diminishing returns in agriculture. For Marx, however, the capitalist system produces undesirable social consequences, and as the contradictions in capitalism become more manifest over time, he says, capitalism as a phase of history will pass away.

The Reserve Army of the Unemployed

Marx rejected Malthusian population theory. In classical analysis this theory had been essential to explain the existence of profits. The classical economists held that capital accumulation leads to an increased demand for labor and a rise in the real wage of labor. If wages continued to rise with capital accumulation, the level of profits would fall. The Malthusian population doctrine, however, explained why wages do not rise to a level where profits cease to exist: any increase in wages will lead to a larger population and labor force, and wages will then be pushed back to a subsistence level. The Malthusian population theory, therefore, not only accounts for the existence of profits in the classical system but also partly explains the forces determining wage rates.

Rejecting the Malthusian theory meant that Marx had to find some other vehicle by which to account for the existence of surplus value and profits. In the Marxian model, increased capital accumulation will increase the amount of variable capital bidding for labor. As wage rates rise, what keeps surplus value and profits from decreasing to zero? Marx's answer to this question lies in his concept of the *reserve army of the unemployed*, which plays the same role in his system as does the Malthusian population theory in the classical model. According to Marx, there is always an excess supply of labor in the market, which has the effect of depressing wages and keeping surplus value and profits positive. He sees the reserve army of the unemployed as recruited from several sources. Direct recruitment occurs when machines replace humans in production processes. The capitalists' search for profits necessarily leads them to introduce new machines, thereby increasing the organic composition of capital. The workers displaced by technology are not absorbed into other areas of the economy. Indirect recruitment results from the entry of new members into the labor force. Children finishing school and housewives who desire to enter the labor market as their family responsibilites change find that jobs are not available and enter the ranks of the unemployed. This reserve army of the unemployed keeps down wages in the competitive labor market.

The size of the reserve army and the level of profits and wages varies, in Marx's system, with the business cycle. During periods of expanding business activity and capital accumulation, wages increase and the size of the reserve army diminishes. This increase in wages leads ultimately to a reduction in profits, to which the capitalist reacts by substituting machinery for labor. The unemployment created by this substitution of capital for labor pushes down wages and leads to a rise in profits.

The concept of the reserve army of the unemployed is counter to several aspects of orthodox analysis. Ricardo had suggested the possibility of short-run technological unemployment in a new chapter, "On Machinery," in the third edition of his *Principles*. Technological unemployment, or any unemployment other than frictional unemployment, is not possible in the long run in the classical system. Marx's assumption of long-run, persistent technological unemployment amounts to a rejection of Say's Law predicting full employment of resources. Most orthodox economic theorists have never been willing to accept Marx's reserve army of the unemployed for the following reasons. The notion of the reserve army implies the existence of an excess supply of labor, of a labor market that is not cleared. But if quantity supplied exceeds quantity demanded and competitive markets exist, economic forces will push down wages until quantity supplied equals quantity demanded and the market clears. Since Marx assumes perfectly competitive markets, an orthodox theorist would argue that the logic of his own system invalidates his concept of persistent technological unemployment. A Marxist would counter this argument by pointing out that the orthodox framework is one of comparative statics — that is, it assumes that as the forces of supply and demand work to lower wages and reduce unemployment, other things are equal and that, in particular, no replacement of people by machines takes place as the labor market clears. The Marxists would admit that the orthodox analysis is theoretically correct, given the static framework of orthodox theory, but they would argue that a more dynamic analysis of the labor market would allow for permanent disequilibrium. Modern orthodox macroeconomists who focus on dynamic search theory would agree with this, although they would argue that excess labor supply suggests that an average above-competitive equilibrium wage exists in an economy.

One possible means of ascertaining the validity of Marx's concept of a reserve army of the unemployed is to examine the level of unemployment over time. This procedure will not, however, give an unequivocal answer, as the definition of unemployment used for statistical measurement contains some anomalies. In most countries unemployed persons are considered to be that part of the labor force that is seeking jobs but cannot find them. Some members of the population are not seeking jobs precisely because they have been unable to find work in the past and have therefore dropped out of the labor force. For example, a housewife who preferred to be employed might spend several months actively seeking work and then decide to drop out of the labor force. If employment opportunities should improve, she might reenter the labor force. The ratio of those actively in the labor forces to the total population, often called the *participation ratio*, varies directly with the level of business activity. A person who is working part time but would prefer full-time employment is usually considered to be employed. A Marxist would claim that both the dropout and the part-timer help to push down wage rates and should be included in the reserve army of the unemployed. A statistical rate of unemployment for the United States economy of 6 percent is not, therefore, an adequate indication of the size of the reserve army of the unemployed, as it does not take into account the proportion of the labor force willing but unable to secure full-time employment. Even if a satisfactory statistical measure of the size of the reserve army of the unemployed were available, it is not clear that it would validate or invalidate the Marxian notion that such a reserve army prevents wages from rising so that surplus value and profits are eliminated. How much unemployment is required to produce a positive rate of surplus value and profits? The issue is further clouded, perhaps hopelessly, by the fact that the Marxian model assumes competitive markets as contrasted with the oligopolistic firms and powerful labor unions of the modern economy.

Falling Rate of Profit

One of the important contradictions between the forces and relations of production that Marx said would lead ultimately to the destruction of capitalism is the falling rate of profit. Here, he followed the classical tradition of Smith, Ricardo, and Mill, who had all predicted that the rate of profit would fall over the long run. In the Marxian model the rate of profit varies directly with the rate of surplus value and inversely with the organic composition of capital.

$$P = S'(1 - Q)$$

Assuming that the rate of surplus value remains unchanged over time, any increase in the organic composition of capital will result in a falling rate of profit. Marx held that competition in commodity and labor markets will increase the organic composition of capital and thus lead to a fall in profit rates. Competition in labor markets results in a fall in profits in the following way. There is a strong drive, according to Marx, for the capitalist to accumulate capital. Capital accumulation means that more variable capital will bid for labor, forcing up wages and reducing the size of the reserve army of the unemployed. The rate of surplus value will fall as wages rise, and thus the rate of profit will fall. Capitalists will react to these rising wages and falling profits by substituting machinery for labor, that is, by increasing the organic composition of capital. If the rate of surplus value remains unchanged, this increase in the organic composition of capital will push profit rates even lower. Marx is suggesting here that each individual capitalist, in reacting to rising wages and falling profits, will take actions that will effectively reduce still further the rate of profit in the economy.

Competition in commodity markets will also result in a continuous decrease in the rate of profit, since the capitalist will keep trying to reduce the costs of production in order to sell final output at lower prices. These competitive forces lead the capitalist to search for new, lower-cost methods of production, that reduce the socially necessary labor time required to produce a given commodity. These new, more efficient production techniques almost always involve an increase in the organic composition of capital, which, given a constant rate of surplus value, will result in a falling rate of profit. Marx concludes, therefore, that competition in labor and commodity markets necessarily leads to an increase in the organic composition of capital, which in turn will result in falling rates of profit.

But it has been assumed in the above analysis that the rate of surplus value does not change with increases in the organic composition of capital, that the rate of surplus value is determined by forces independent of those determining the organic composition of capital. Marx's analysis of the forces determining the rate of surplus value, however, indicates his own awareness that these two factors are, in fact, related. Increases in the organic composition of capital will result in a substitution of machinery for labor, and consequently in a fall in wages, an increase in the rate of surplus value, and an increase in the rate of profit. Increases in the organic composition of capital, moreover, will increase the productivity of labor and, depending on how this increase in productivity is shared between capital and labor, is quite likely to lead to an increase in the rate of surplus value.

Whether the rate of profit will fall over time, then, depends on the rate of change in the organic composition of capital as compared to the rate of change in the rate of surplus value. Since $P = S'(1 - Q)$, if Q increases at a greater rate than S', P will decrease; if Q and S' increase at comparable rates, P remains unchanged; and if Q increases at a slower rate than S', P will increase in the long run. The issue can be put in broader perspective in the following way. As capital accumulation occurs, diminishing returns on capital can be expected to lower profit rates. Capital accumulation is, however, associated with technological development, which reduces costs and thus raises the rate of profit. Whether the rate of profit will decrease over time, then, depends on the rate of capital accumulation as compared to the rate of technological development. The outcome of these opposing forces cannot be determined theoretically but is empirical.

Although Marx's analysis of the falling rate of profit assumed a constant rate of surplus value, he was aware that there were many forces operating to increase the rate of surplus value over time. For example, one reaction of the capitalist to a falling rate of profit is to increase the length of the working day or to increase output per man-hour by better management. Also, increases in the organic composition of capital will enlarge the size of the reserve army of the unemployed, with a consequent fall in wages and increase in the rate of surplus value. Women and children can be hired at lower wages, which will increase the rate of surplus value. And if goods such as food, which are an important part of the real income of labor, can be purchased from foreign countries more cheaply than they are produced in the home country, the effect is again to reduce variable capital outlays in the form of money wages and to increase the rate of surplus value. Finally, Marx recognizes that technological improvements may permit replacement of manufacturing equipment by equipment with a lower money cost. A plant that produces 10,000 pairs of shoes and costs $1 million today may be replaced in the future by a plant producing the same quantity of output with only a $750,000 capital outlay. In short, increasing the output from capital equipment does not necessarily mean increasing the monetary value of that equipment. This is important, because the rate of profit and the organic composition of capital are monetary computations.

It must be concluded, therefore, even keeping within the structure of the Marxian model, that over time there are forces that will increase the rate of surplus value and the organic composition of capital. What course the rate of profits takes over time will depend upon the relative rates of increase in these two variables. Marx nevertheless posited a constantly declining rate of profit, although his model affords no theoretical grounds for doing so. Marx, Smith, Ricardo, and Mill all reached this conclusion for basically the same reason.

The crucial unknown element here, and one that is difficult to predict, is the rate of technological development. Increased investment spending or capital accumulation, other things being equal, will result in a falling rate of profit, because of the principle of diminishing returns. Technological development, other things being equal, can be expected to result in higher rates of profit. Will technological development take place in the future at a rate sufficient to offset diminishing returns from capital accumulation? This question is difficult to answer, largely because economists have no theory that satisfactorily explains the rate of technological development. In the absence of such a theory, economists have been inclined to underestimate the expected future rate of technological development. Here is the reason that Smith, Ricardo, and Mill all conclude that the rate of profit will decrease over the long run. It is also the reason that Malthus concluded that population tends to increase at a faster rate than the supply of food. The issue can be thrown into sharper focus by the aid of the simple diagram in Figure 6.1.

Diminishing returns to increased capital accumulation, or investment spending as it is known today, is represented by the downward-sloping curve M. Increased capital accumulation of ΔC ($C_2 - C_1$), other things being equal, results in a fall in the rate of profit from P_1 to P_2 because of diminishing returns. Technological development implies that, other things being equal, the rate of profit increases and thus can be graphically represented by an upward shift of the M curve to M'. Thus, increased capital accumulation is represented by movements along the horizontal axis, and technological development is represented by upward shifts

Figure 6.1 The Falling Rate of Profit

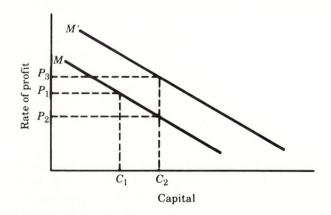

in the M curve. In the example represented in Figure 6.1, technological development has more than offset the diminishing returns associated with increased capital accumulation so that the rate of profit has increased from P_1 to P_3. It is easy to see that two other possibilities exist: M' may shift out just far enough so that the rate of profit remains unchanged, or the rate of profit may fall over time. Again, what will happen to the rate of profit over time can be determined only by reference to empirical information, not by pure theory. Unfortunately, the statistical problems of measuring changes in the rate of profit over time for an economy are very difficult.

In any event Marx held that the rate of profit would decrease over time and that this was one manifestation of a contradiction in the system between the forces and relations of production. This falling rate of profit, he claims, is brought about by the activities of the capitalists, who are therefore part of the mechanism that will bring about the ultimate collapse of the system. Thus, while a falling long-run rate of profit leads to a stationary state in the classical model, it is an ingredient in the collapse of capitalism in the Marxian model. Marx's belief in the falling rate of profit, moreover, faulty as it is, forms a part of his theories of business crises, the increasing concentration of industry, and the Marx-Lenin concept of imperialism.

The Origin of Business Crises

One curious anomaly of Marx's analysis of capitalism is that although he repeatedly refers to business crises under capitalism (what today we call depressions), he has no clearly formulated theory of a business cycle. His whole analysis of the causes of fluctuations in the general level of economic activity is combined with his more general description of the contradictions inherent in the capitalist system. It is therefore incorrect to refer to Marx's own theory of a business cycle, as opposed to the theories of his followers. He suggests a number of causes of economic fluctuations, but these suggestions are never clearly delineated in his writing. There can be no question, however, that Marx held that one of the major contradictions between the forces and relations of production under capitalism is the periodic depressions that exist in a capitalist economy. Although Marx himself did not clearly distinguish among his various insights into the source and nature of economic fluctuations, for the sake of clarity we will do so here.

Marx's view that periodic fluctuations are an integral part of the capitalist process is a definite departure from his usual adherence to the classical model and its assumptions. Classical economics accepted as a major premise Say's Law that, apart from minor fluctuations in total output, a capitalist economy tends to operate at a level of full employment. Marx attacked this classical position, alleging that it presents a distorted and unhistorical view of capitalism. Marx held that in a simple barter economy, people produced goods either for the use value they achieved by directly consuming these commodities or for the use value they obtained by bartering the produced goods. Under these circumstances production and consumption are perfectly synchronized. A household produces shoes for its own use or to trade for food it will consume. The whole motive behind economic activity or production is, then, to obtain use values. Introducing money into such an economy does not necessarily change the orientation of production from use value. In a money economy people produce commodities that they exchange for money; and money is in turn exchanged for commodities that render use value to the consumer. Money in such an economy is merely a medium of exchange facilitating the division of labor and trade. These two economies can be schematically represented as follows:

Simple Economy	$C \rightarrow C$	C = commodities
Money Economy	$C \rightarrow M \rightarrow C$	M = money

But capitalism, according to Marx, is not just a simple, or barter, economy to which money as a medium of exchange has been added. Capitalism represents a change in the orientation of economic activity from the production of use values to the production of exchange values. The capitalist, who directs the production process, wants to make profits. He enters the market with money and purchases the various factors of production and directs their activities toward the production of commodities. He then exchanges these commodities for money in the market. His success is measured by the surplus value he makes, the difference between the amount of money he begins with and the amount he ends with. A capitalist economy is represented as

$$M \rightarrow C \rightarrow M'$$

The difference, ΔM, between M' and M is the surplus value realized by the capitalist. Marx repeatedly stresses the orientation of economic activity under capitalism toward exchange value and profits. He criticizes Ricardo's acceptance of Say's Law, on the grounds that Say's Law implies that there is no basic difference between a barter economy and a capitalist economy and that money is merely a medium of exchange that facilitates the division of labor and trade.

In a barter economy or an economy where money is only a medium of exchange and where economic activity is oriented toward producing use values, there can be no problem of overproduction. People will produce goods only when they want to consume these goods or trade them and consume other commodities. Under capitalism, with its orientation toward exchange values and profit, overproduction becomes a possibility. Marx's basic approach to a study of economic fluctuations is to examine the capitalist's reactions to changes in the rate of profits, that is, to changes in the ratio of $\frac{\Delta M}{M}$ or P. Marx concluded that changes in the rate of profit will result in changes in investment spending, and he cited this volatility of investment spending as the major cause of fluctuations in the total level of economic activity. Marx's interest in investment spending is shared by many modern macroeconomic theorists.

Cyclically Recurring Fluctuations

One model of economic fluctuation suggested by Marx is a recurring cycle. Impressed by the sudden growth of the textile industry in England, he hypothesized that a burst of technological change could generate a business cycle. A technological burst will produce increased capital accumulation and an increased demand for labor. The size of the reserve army will fall, wages will rise, surplus value will fall, the rate of surplus value will fall, and the rate of profits will decrease. The falling rate of profit results in decreased capital accumulation as the economy spirals downward into depression. But depression, according to Marx, contains elements that will sooner or later generate a new expansion in economic activity. As total output falls, the size of the reserve army of the unemployed is enlarged. The competitive pressure of this unemployed labor will bring down wages and thus provide greater profit opportunities. These larger profits will stimulate more capital accumulation, and economic activity will increase as the upward stage of the cycle begins. Marx suggested that another self-corrective aspect of depressions was their destruction of capital values. Since profit is a money calculation, businesses that were not profitable because of the inflated value of their capital assets carried over from the prosperity phase of the cycle become profitable as asset values are lowered during the depression. A cycle started by a technological burst may generate further cycles in the future as capital equipment wears out. If all plants and equipment were replaced evenly over time, there would be a constant level of investment to replace worn-out capital goods. A replacement cycle can be generated, however, when the capital goods put into place during the technological burst suddenly require immediate replacement.

Disproportionality Crises

Once an economy moves from the barter stage to a high degree of labor specialization and the use of money and markets, there may be difficulty in coordinating the levels of output of its various sectors. Under capitalism the market mechanism performs this function, but Marx questioned the ability of the market to reallocate resources smoothly. Suppose there is an increase in the demand for the products of industry A and a decrease in demand for the commodities produced in industry B. In a smoothly functioning capitalist economy, prices and profits in industry A would increase and prices and profits in industry B decline. Capitalists, in reaction to these changing profits, would move resources from the contracting to the expanding industry. The excess supply or overproduction of industry B would thus be of short duration and would have no perceptible influence on the general level of economic activity. Overproduction in one industry, what Ricardo called a partial glut, would not spread to the rest of the economy and cause a general decline in economic activity, or a depression.

Marx contends that supply and demand will not always mesh this perfectly in an economy's various submarkets and that the whole process of resource reallocation will not, therefore, work as smoothly as in the classical model. His theory is that the unemployment created in industry B as demand decreased could spread to the rest of the economy and result in a general decline in economic activity, a view that directly opposes the orientation of the orthodox classical theorists. Classical theory looks to the market to solve problems of resource allocation. It stresses equilibrium, maintaining that positions of disequilibrium are of short duration and that a smooth transition occurs between equilibria. Marx assumes disharmony in the system and looks for basic contradictions in the working of market forces. Orthodox theory has not paid much attention to Marx's disproportionality crises theory, arguing that an individual industry is so small relative to the whole economy that the spread of overproduction from one industry to produce a general decline is unlikely. They also argue that the mobility of resources is much greater than Marx admits. Overproduction in a major industry such as automobiles, however, might conceivably spread to the rest of the economy.

The Falling Rate of Profit and Business Crises

The two Marxian theories of business crises we have examined so far — cyclically recurring fluctuations and disproportionality crises — explicitly reject Say's Law. Marx integrated his law of the falling rate of profit into these two theories. Thus his theories that depressions result when technology fails to develop smoothly, that disproportionality crises will occur because overproduction in one industry can adversely affect the rest of the economy, and that the rate of profit will steadily decline are all facets of a single integrated view that capitalism will fail to provide stable levels of economic activity at a full utilization of resources.

Marx has another explanation of depressions, or crises, as he calls them, which is unusual in that it accepts Say's Law. He says that even if we make all the necessary assumptions so that Say's Law holds, capitalism will still fail because of certain inherent contradictions that will bring about business crises. In the Marxian model a capitalist economy clearly depends on the behavior of the capitalist, whose reactions to changing rates of profits and changing expectations of profits form a central part in the explanation of business crises. Marx uses his law of the long-run, continual fall in the rate of profits to explain short-run fluctuations in economic activity, asserting that, in their search for greater profits, the capitalists increase the organic composition of capital, causing the rate of profit to fall. The capitalists will periodically react to this fall in profit rates by reducing investment spending, causing fluctuations in economic activity that will engender crises. Thus Marx deduces a falling rate of profit even in a model that accepts Say's Law.

Business Crises — A Summary

Marx's explanation of the source and nature of the business cycle is intertwined with his broader analysis of capitalism and is incompletely developed. He does not take any one theory and develop its full meaning and implications. This has resulted in a good deal of controversy among Marxists themselves and among historians of economic thought as to the nature and significance of Marx's contributions to business-cycle theory. Although the relative importance of Marx's various theories of crises is disputed by historians of economic thought, there is general agreement that he does offer three distinct explanations of fluctuations in business activity: the falling rate of profit, the uneven introduction of new technology, and disproportionalities that develop in one sector of the economy and spread to cause a decrease in the general level of economic activity. Marx's writing also contains some even vaguer hints of an underconsumptionist explanation of economic fluctuations, but these are never pursued. Although Marx did not fully develop his theories of business crises, he clearly held that periodic fluctuations in economic activity were a fundamental part of a capitalist economy and one more manifestation of the basic contradictions in capitalism that would lead to its ultimate destruction. It is also important to recognize that he saw these periodic fluctuations as inherent in the system, since they are based on the activities of the capitalists as they search for profits and react to changes in the rate of profits. Whatever Marx's theories of business crises may lack in internal consistency, there can be no doubt that his view of capitalism as basically unstable and subject to periodic fluctuations in economic activity because of internal contradictions represents an important insight into capitalism as an economic system. Nevertheless, the Marxian vision of capitalism as inherently unstable was largely ignored by orthodox economic theory until the 1930s.

The Concentration and Centralization of Capital

Although the basic Marxian model assumes perfectly competitive markets with a large number of small firms in each industry, Marx was aware of the growing size of the firm and the consequent weakening of competition and growth of monopoly power. He concluded that this phenomenon derives from the increasing concentration and centralization of capital. Increasing concentration of capital occurs as individual capitalists accumulate more and more capital, thus increasing the absolute amount of capital under their control. The size of the firm or economic unit of production is increased correspondingly, and the degree of competition in the market tends to be diminished.

A more important reason for the reduction of competition is the centralization of capital. Centralization occurs through a redistribution of already existing capital in a manner that places its ownership and control into fewer and fewer hands. Marx held that larger firms would be able to achieve economies of scale and produce at lower average costs than would smaller firms. Competition between the larger, lower-cost firms and the smaller firms will result in the elimination of the smaller firms and the growth of monopoly.

> The battle of competition is fought by cheapening of commodities. The cheapness of commodities depends, ceteris paribus, on the productiveness of labor, and this again on the scale of production. Therefore, the larger capitals beat the smaller.[3]

The increasing centralization of capital is furthered by the development of a credit system and of the corporate form of business organization. Although the corporation was just beginning to assume importance during Marx's time, he demonstrates a remarkable insight into some of the long-run consequences of the growth of the corporate economy. Corporate capitalism is characterized by the fact that its:

3. Karl Marx, *Capital: A Critique of Political Economy*, ed. Friedrich Engels, trans. from the 3rd German ed. by Samuel Moore and Edward Aveling, revised and amplified from the 4th German ed. by Ernest Untermann, 3 vols. (Chicago: Charles H. Kerr, 1926), I, 686.

enterprises assume the form of social enterprises as distinguished from individual enterprises. It is the abolition of capital as private property within the boundaries of capitalist production itself. Transformation of the actually functioning capitalist into a mere manager, an administrator of other people's capital, and of the owners of capital into mere owners, mere money capitalists.[4]

Marx's view, then, is that capital accumulation, economies of scale, the growth of credit markets, and the dominance of the corporation in business organization would lead to the concentration and centralization of capital into fewer and fewer hands. Competition ends by destroying itself, and the large corporation assumes monopoly power. With the large corporation comes a separation of ownership and control and a number of undesirable social consequences:

a new aristocracy of finance, a new sort of parasites in the shape of promoters, speculators, and merely nominal directors; a whole system of swindling and cheating by means of corporation juggling, stock jobbing, and stock speculation. It is private production without the control of private property.[5]

Possibly no other vision of the future of capitalism advanced by Marx has been more prophetic than his law of the concentration and centralization of capital. Yet this prediction was not backed up by any substantial reasoning, for Marx did not fully develop an explanation of the forces that would bring about the growth of the corporation and monopoly power. The growth of the large firm with its monopoly power is, according to Marx, merely another example of the contradictions in capitalism between the forces and relations of productions that will lead to the ultimate destruction of capitalism.

Increasing Misery of the Proletariat

Marx calls another contradiction of capitalism that will lead to its collapse "the increasing misery of the proletariat." Three separate, though not necessarily contradictory, interpretations of this much debated doctrine have been offered. Absolute increasing misery of the proletariat would imply that the real income of the mass of society decreases with the development of capitalism. If this is what Marx meant, history has clearly proved him wrong. Relative increasing misery of the proletariat means that the proletariat's share of the national

4. *Ibid.*, III, 516.
5. *Ibid.*, p. 519.

income declines over time. Real income could increase for each member of the proletariat, yet relative income could decrease. But historical evidence in developed countries indicates that wages have constituted a remarkably constant proportion of national income over time, so if this is what Marx meant, he was still wrong. A final interpretation of the increasing misery doctrine is that it concerns noneconomic aspects of life. With the advance of capitalism the quality of life itself declines as people become chained to the industrial process. It makes no difference, according to Marx, whether the income of the proletariat rises or falls, because "in proportion as capital accumulates, the lot of the laborer, be his payment high or low, must grow worse."[6] With the growth of capital accumulation goes the "accumulation of misery, agony of toil, slavery, ignorance, brutality, mental degradation."[7] Since there is, at present, no accepted measure of the quality of life, this prediction is not testable. It is interesting to note that a number of economists from Adam Smith to J. K. Galbraith have questioned if rising per capita income necessarily is associated with the development of a good society.

Marx actually subscribed to all three of these doctrines of increasing misery at one time or another. The doctrine of absolute increasing misery was advanced in his early writings. But sometime between the publication of the *Communist Manifesto* in 1848 and the first volume of *Capital* in 1867 he abandoned this position. It has been suggested that Marx's long period of study in the British Museum made him aware of the rising standard of living of the industrial worker and led to this recantation. He did, however, continue to hold that the relative income position of the proletariat would fall over time even though its real income would rise. Marx uses the term subsistence wage to identify the lower limit to which wages may be pushed. This refers to a cultural subsistence, not a biological subsistence; he recognized that over time the cultural subsistence level of wages would rise. Finally, and most importantly, Marx consistently held that one of the most undesirable consequences of capitalism is a deterioration of that intangible factor called the quality of life. Laboring in a capitalistic society no longer gives people the pleasure that work can give. Specialization and division of labor and all the factors resulting in increased labor productivity also beget a laborer who is "crippled by life-long repetition of one and the same trivial operation, and thus reduced to the mere fragment of a man."[8] Whatever material benefits capitalism may bring to society, Marx concludes, it brings them with great intangible costs to the individuals who constitute the masses.

6. *Ibid.*, I, 708–709.
7. *Ibid.*, p. 709.
8. *Ibid.*, p. 534.

SUMMARY AND EVALUATION

Marx the revolutionist clearly makes Marx the economist difficult to evaluate objectively. The intermingling of his economic analysis with his philosophy and sociology, moreover, makes it difficult to evaluate individual elements of his contributions to modern thinking about capitalism. Marxian analysis represents a combination of Hegelian philosophy, French socialist thought, and classical political economy. His avowed purpose was to explain the laws of motion of capitalism, and to this end he applied this theory of history, dialectical materialism. Critical of capitalism, he looked for contradictions in the system between the dynamic forces of production and the static relations of production that would lead to the collapse of capitalism and the emergence of a new economic order, socialism. Though he departed from orthodox purpose and method, he borrowed many aspects of Ricardian theory, though his different ideological position led him to conclusions quite different from those of classical analysis.

He used the labor theory of value to show that under capitalism the proletariat was being exploited, as well as to explain the forces determining relative prices. He failed in the latter task just as Ricardo had, but this failure does not of itself impair Marx's analysis of the laws of motion of capitalism, for this analysis does not depend on a labor theory of value. His critique of capitalism — clearly the most significant element of his work — must be evaluated separately from his value theory. Marx's description of the laws of motion of capitalism — the reserve army of the unemployed, the falling rate of profit, the inevitable occurrence of business crises, and the concentration and centralization of capital — lacks technical theoretical analysis and tends toward vague generalizations that have given rise to many contradictory interpretations. Yet behind all the generalization, there remains a vision, unsurpassed by his predecessors, of capitalism as a dynamic, changing economic order. Laissez faire capitalism does manifest difficulties in maintaining prosperity and preventing unemployment and depressions, and out of the competitive struggle have emerged large corporations with separation of ownership and control.

But even though some of Marx's predictions concerning the course of capitalism through history seem remarkably correct, an examination of his theoretical structure shows that he arrived at the right answers for either the wrong or no reasons. His analysis of business crises and the concentration and centralization of capital have the greatest theoretical validity of all the concepts in his system; however, macro theory, based on the work of Keynes, and micro theory, based on the work of Marshall, Chamberlin, and Robinson, in our view offer more fruitful approaches to understanding modern capitalism. His characterization of persistent unemployment resulting from the labor-saving bias of capital accumulation also appears less satisfactory than analyses derived from Keynesian-based models. His theoretical support for the law of the falling rate of profit is weak, but no weaker than that of orthodox theory as advanced by Smith, Ricardo, Mill, and Keynes. Because of statistical difficulties, the empirical validity of the law of the falling rate of profit has yet to be tested. Marx's sociological thinking concludes that a class conflict exists, but although class-consciousness is more prevalent in developed Western European countries than in the United States, the class-consciousness predicted by the Marxian model has not arisen. And whereas Marx predicted a collapse of capitalism in its advanced stages when the forces and relations of production become so contradictory that a new economic and social order would emerge, the major revolutions that have occurred and are occurring have almost all been in economies that certainly do not fit the Marxian description of capitalism. They have taken place, instead, in economies that could more properly be classified as feudal, or in non-Marxian terminology, as underdeveloped. Thus, after separating Marx's ideology from his model and discarding his inadequate theoretical structure, we are left with a methodology that may still be useful for examining certain aspects of the economy and of society. As we will discuss in Chapter 12, an eclectic merger of Marxian methodology with orthodox micro and macro theory is presently being conducted by radical political economists of the New Left and will perhaps yield fruit.

SUGGESTED READINGS

Berlin, Isaiah. *Karl Marx: His Life and Environment*. New York: Oxford University Press, 1959.

Bober, M. M. *Karl Marx's Interpretation of History*. Cambridge: Harvard University Press, 1948.

Bose, Arun. "Marx on Value, Capital, and Exploitation." *History of Political Economy*, 3 (Fall 1971).

Bronfenbrenner, M. "The Vicissitudes of Marxian Economics." *History of Political Economy*, 2 (Fall 1970).

Elliot, J. E. "Marx and Schumpeter on Capitalism's Creative Destruction: A Comparative Restatement." *Quarterly Journal of Economics* (August 1980).

King, J. E. "Marx as an Historian of Economic Thought." *History of Political Economy*, 11 (Fall 1979).

Marx, Karl. *Capital*. 3 vols. Chicago: Charles H. Kerr, 1926.

Meek, Ronald L. *Studies in the Labour Theory of Value*. London: Lawrence and Wishart, 1956.

Robinson, Joan. *An Essay on Marxian Economics*. New York: St. Martin's, 1967.

Roll, Eric. "Marx." *A History of Economic Thought*. Englewood, N.J.: Prentice-Hall, 1956.

Schumpeter, Joseph A. "The Marxian Doctrine." *Capitalism, Socialism, and Democracy*. New York: Harper, 1950.

Sherman, Howard J. "Marxist Models of Cyclical Growth." *History of Political Economy*, 3 (Spring 1971).

Sweezy, Paul M. *The Theory of Capitalistic Development.* New York: Monthly Review Press, 1956.
Wolfson, Murray. "Three Stages in Marx's Thought." *History of Political Economy*, 11 (Spring 1979).

Readings in Original Sources

Burns, Emile. *A Handbook of Marxism.* New York: International Publishers, 1935. This is a good collection of original sources on Marx.
Marx, Karl. *Capital* (cited above).
Marxian Philosophy and Interpretation of History:
Marx, Karl, and F. Engels. *The Communist Manifesto.* (Burns, pp. 21-59.)
———. *Herr Eugen Duhring's Revolution in Science.* (Burns, pp. 232-300.)
———. *Theses on Feuerbach.* (Burns, pp. 228-231.)
———. *A Contribution to the Critique of Political Economy.* Author's preface. (Burns, pp. 570-573.)
———. *Capital.* Volume I, Chapters 26, 27, 29, 30, and 31.
Marxian Economics — Value and Surplus Value:
Marx, Karl. *Capital.* Volume I, Chapters 1 and 3-8. (Also in Burns, pp. 405-475.) Volume III, Chapters 1, 3, 8, 9, and 10.
Marxian Economics — Laws of Capitalistic Development:
Marx, Karl. *Capital.* Volume II, Chapters 20 and 21. Volume III, Chapters 10, 13, 14, 15, and 51. (Both in Burns, pp. 475-537.)

Chapter 7

From Classical to Neoclassical Economics: The Emergence of Marginal Analysis

The final three decades of the nineteenth century witnessed the birth of modern microeconomic theory. During this period the forging of a new set of analytical tools helped transform classical economics to neoclassical economics. The most important of these tools was marginal analysis. In essence, marginal analysis is the application of differential calculus to the behavior of the household and the firm and to price determination in the market. Even aside from its obvious usefulness, this development was significant because it initiated an appreciable increase in the use of mathematics in economic analysis. The acceptance of marginal analysis and full realization of its importance and implications did not occur overnight, however, but developed slowly throughout the period from 1870 to 1900. Its first notable application was to the theory of demand. In the early 1870s three academicians independently applied marginal analysis to demand theory and developed the concept of marginal utility. These three, Stanley Jevons, Léon Walras, and Karl Menger, shall be the focus of this chapter.

SOME HISTORICAL LINKS

Marginal analysis is now so ingrained in economics that it is familiar to every student of introductory economics. A consideration of its origins is a key chapter in any book on the history of economic thought. The historical significance and status of economic thinking in the late nineteenth century becomes clear if we compare it to the prominent ideas of classical economics in the preceding century.

The early classicals, exemplified by Adam Smith, provide a large contrast, since they were mainly interested in analyzing the process of economic development and discovering and implementing policies that would achieve high rates of economic growth. Smith was a policy-oriented, developmental *macroeconomist* with little interest in a detailed study of microeconomic theory. Smith's method, which reflected his broad training in the humanities and social sciences, loosely intermingled theory with history and description, unlike the more mathematical methodology to come.

Early in the nineteenth century, Ricardo transformed both the scope and method of economics. First, he switched from contextual analysis to more abstract deductive analysis, emphasizing the importance of internal logical consistency in abstract models. In doing so he provided the methodological rudiments for neoclassical economics. Second, Ricardo believed that economics should not focus on developmental issues but should instead focus primarily on the forces that determine the functional distribution of income. This led him to examine what was then known as value theory or price theory but is now known simply as microeconomic theory. In analyzing the forces determinig the distribution of income, especially land, Ricardo began to use marginal analysis, which would later become a key element of micro-economic theory.

In the period immediately following Ricardo, economic theory and the capitalist system itself were subjected to a number of criticisms by humanists and socialists. Although these criticisms little affected the technical content of economic theory, they did call into question the classical assumption that laissez faire was an ideal government policy, and they initiated changes that further prepared for developments in economic thinking between 1870 and 1900. As economics became more professionalized, economists began to scrutinize the technical content of classical theory, particularly the labor theory of value. Classical economics in the hands of J. S. Mill and Nassau Senior adopted a cost of production theory of value, with capital costs as well as labor costs included.

Another contribution to the evolution of this era was the growing contradiction between Ricardian theory and the actual operation of the British economy. In particular, increases in population were occurring simultaneously with a rising real income for the masses. Empirical evidence refuted the Malthusian population doctrine, but economists of the time clung to it as a basic postulate of the classical system. When J. S. Mill finally withdrew his allegiance from the wages fund doctrine in 1869, the decline of the classical system was nearly complete. By that time, three of the basic tools and assumptions of the Ricardian system — the labor theory of value, the Malthusian population doctrine, and the wages fund doctrine — had, in effect, been abandoned. In 1874 J. E. Cairns (1823-1875), in his *Some Leading Principles of Political Economy Newly Expounded*, tried to salvage the classical system, but to no avail. Nevertheless, the century of orthodox economics in Britain from 1770 to 1870, the period of classical political economy, can be seen as a time of significant change in the scope, method, and tools of economics; it laid the foundation for the revolution in economics that came in the last three decades of the nineteenth century.

Forerunner of Marginal Analysis

Classical economics did not metamorphose into neoclassical economics overnight: the recasting of perspectives and theoretical structure occurred gradually. For example, the idea of marginal utility had existed in economic literature for a long time. Aristotle had used the concept of use value some two thousand years before, and Jeremy Bentham had used the concept of utility in utilitarian philosophy in the latter part of the eighteenth century.

In the nineteenth century, a host of minor writers had a clear conception of the principle that as an increasing quantity of a good is consumed, the good will yield diminishing marginal utility to the consumer. None of these writers, however, had been able to elaborate in full the concept of diminishing marginal utility or to apply it to the solution of economic problems. In retrospect, and with nearly perfect hindsight, one can see marginal analysis emerging as early as 1834, when Mountifort Longfield (*Lectures on Political Economy*), critical of the labor theory of value, developed a marginal productivity theory. W. F. Lloyd in his *Lectures on the Notion of Value* (1844), Jules Dupuit in an article called "On the Measurement of the Utility of Public Works" (1844), Hermann Heinrich Gossen in *Development of the Laws of Human Relationships* (1854), and Richard Jennings in *Natural Elements of Political Economy* (1855) all displayed some understanding of the usefulness of the marginal utility approach to a theory of demand. And although Augustin Cournot, in his *Researches into the Mathematical Principle of the Theory of Wealth* (1838), did not present utility theory, he was a most original and seminal thinker who used marginal tools to develop a fairly thorough analysis of the economics of the firm. He was able to define demand and determine that at lower prices quantity demanded would increase.

Another important economist was J. H. von Thünen. J. A. Schumpeter has characterized von Thünen as an economist writing before his time. In several books published collectively as *The Isolated State* (1826-1863), von Thünen applied marginal analysis through calculus, realizing important insights into a marginal productivity theory of wages, diminishing returns, and rent. He and Cournot were the first of the mathematical economists. Some of these writers would be discovered later as "neglected economists," but others, especially Cournot and von Thünen, whose influence Alfred Marshall acknowledged, contributed notably to subsequent economic theory.

George Stigler, writing about the development of utility theory, has observed that

> the principle that equal increments of utility-producing means (such as income or bread) yield diminishing increments of utility is a commonplace. The first statement in print of a commonplace is adventitious; it is of no importance in the development of economics, and it confers no intellectual stature on its author. The statement acquires interest only when it is logically developed or explicitly applied to economic problems, and it acquires importance only when a considerable number of economists are persuaded to incorporate it into their analysis. Interest and importance are of course matters of degree.[1]

Following Stigler, our criterion for determining the writers we will examine intensively is their influence on subsequent economic thinking and policy.

The Transition to Neoclassical Economics

The three academic economists mentioned at the beginning of this chapter stand out as having significant influence on the early development of marginal analysis. In the early 1870s these three independently suggested that the value, or price, of a commodity depends upon the marginal utility of the commodity to the consumer. In 1871 W. S. Jevons published his *Theory of Political Economy* in English and Carl Menger published his *Principles of Economics* in German. Three years later a French economist who taught in Switzerland, Léon Walras, published his *Elements of Pure Economics* in French. By the 1890s a number of economists, realizing this tool could be applied to the forces that determined the distribution of income, developed the concept of the marginal productivity of factors. In 1890, Alfred Marshall (1842–1924), who could justly claim to be an originator of this new analytical concept, fused all of these developments into a well-rounded and complete theory of household, firm, and markets.

The growth of marginal analysis resulted in an almost exclusive focus on problems of microeconomic theory. Thus, orthodox economic theory from 1870 to 1930 largely ignored macroeconomic questions, namely, the forces that determine the level and the rate of growth of

---

1. George Stigler, *Essays in the History of Economics* (Chicago: University of Chicago Press, 1956), p. 78.

income. And within the area of microeconomic theory, the new analysis was principally applied to the way in which competitive markets allocated scarce resources among alternative uses. Marginal analysis was fundamentally deductive in its approach, using highly abstract models of households and firms, which were assumed to be trying to maximize utility and profits. The development of these abstract models led to controversies over methodology that we will examine in the next chapter.

Since the development of marginal analysis was actually a series of several somewhat unrelated developments, we shall divide our discussion of the period from 1870 to 1900 into three parts. The present chapter deals with some of the forerunners of marginal analysis, the economists Jevons, Menger, and Walras, who applied it to the theory of demand in the early 1870s, and with the general equilibrium model first presented by Léon Walras in 1874. Chapter 8 discusses the controversy over methodology that took place during this period, the application of marginal analysis to the theory of production and the resulting notion of marginal productivity, and the contributions to capital and interest theory that followed. Chapter 9 examines the economics of Alfred Marshall, who developed the basic framework of present supply-and-demand analysis and attempted to resolve the many theoretical and methodological questions raised during this period.

JEVONS, MENGER, AND WALRAS

Between 1871 and 1874, Jevons, Menger, and Walras all published books that influenced the development of orthodox economic theory. This influence was not immediate but it developed over the last quarter of the century as the followers of these three men, the second generation of marginal utility theorists, fought for and slowly gained acceptance for some of these "new" ideas. The positions of Jevons, Menger, and Walras on the forces determining the value, or price, of final products are similar enough that we may examine them by subject rather than treating them individually. Walras's general equilibrium analysis, however, was unique because of its subsequent importance in modern micro theory, and it is important enough to deserve separate attention later in this chapter.

A Revolution in Theory?

All three of these economists, working independently of each other, were convinced that they had developed a unique, revolutionary analysis of the forces explaining the determination of relative prices. Jevons stated this most succinctly:

Repeated reflection and inquiry have led me to the somewhat novel opinion, that *value depends entirely upon utility*. Prevailing opinions make labour rather than utility the origin of value; and there are even those who distinctly assert that labour is the *cause* of value.[2]

Menger's statement was more personally modest though nationalistic.

It was a special pleasure to me that the field here treated, comprising the most general principles of our science, is in no small degree so truly the product of recent development in German political economy, and that the reform of the most important principles of our science here attempted is therefore built upon a foundation laid by previous work that was produced almost entirely by the industry of German scholars.[3]

Walras, noted for his general equilibrium analysis, also believed in the originality and uniqueness of his contribution.

I am now able to start publishing a treatise on the elements of political and social economy, conceived on a new plan, elaborated according to an original method, and reaching conclusions which, I venture to say, differ in several respects from those of current economic science.[4]

Are Jevons, Menger, and Walras justified in claiming that their work was both original and revolutionary? Original, yes, insofar as their ideas did influence the subsequent development of economic theory in a way that previous writers on the concept of marginal utility — Gossen, for example — did not. But to what extent their work is revolutionary can be determined only by an examination of their views.

Inadequacies of the Classical Theory of Value

All three of these writers found the classical theory of value inadequate to explain the forces determining prices. Their principal criticism was that the cost of production theory of value lacked generality, since there were a number of goods whose prices could not be analyzed with-

2. Jevons, *Theory*, p. 1.
3. Carl Menger, *Principles of Economics*, trans. and ed. James Dingwall and Bert F. Hoselitz, with an intro. by Frank H. Knight (Glencoe, Ill.: Free Press, 1950), p. 49.
4. Léon Walras, *Elements of Pure Economics or the Theory of Social Wealth*, trans. William Jaffé (Homewood, Ill.: Richard D. Irwin, 1954), p. 35.

in the classical framework. They criticized Ricardo's labor theory of value and Senior's and Mill's cost of production theories because those theories required a separate explanation for the prices of goods of which there was a fixed supply. The value, or price, of goods with a perfectly inelastic (vertical) supply curve — for example, land, rare coins, paintings, or wines — did not depend on their costs of production. Another difficulty with a cost of production theory of value is that it suggests that the price, or value, of a good comes from cost incurred in the past. Jevons, Menger, and Walras all held that large costs incurred in producing goods will not necessarily result in their having high prices. According to the marginal utility theory, value depends instead upon utility, or consumption, and comes not from the past but from the future. No matter what costs are incurred in producing a good, when it arrives on the market its price will depend upon the utility the buyer expects to receive. Producers who incorrectly forecast the demand for their products are painfully aware of this. The term "dead stock" was used to refer to those goods for which the demand had so declined that their prices were less than their costs of production. Jevons put this tartly.

> The fact is, that *labour once spent has no influence on the future value of any article*: it is gone and lost forever. In commerce bygones are for ever bygones.[5]

The problem these three writers were addressing was, then, whether value was produced in final goods by the factors of production, as held by the classical value theory, or whether final goods determined the values of the factors of production. The marginal utility school held that factors of production were valuable but that the extent of their value was determined by the marginal utility received from consuming the final products produced by these factors. However, factors of production, or intermediate goods, do not confer value on final goods. Richard Whately, an early critic of the Ricardian labor theory of value, had put it very neatly in the 1830s when he said that pearls are not valuable because men have dived for them, but men dive for them because they are valuable.

Another fundamental flaw in preclassical and classical economic theory, according to the marginal utility writers, was its failure to recognize that the significant element in price determination is not total or average utility, but marginal utility. Adam Smith had exhumed from earlier literature the old diamond-water paradox: diamonds have high prices but little utility, whereas water has a low price but high utility. The classical theorists had been unable to elucidate this paradox be-

5. Jevons, *Theory*, p. 164.

cause they thought in terms of the total utility diamonds and water give to consumers and did not understand the importance of their marginal utility. This paradox is easily explained in Table 7.1, which is patterned after the one used by Menger.

The Roman numerals represent classes of commodities of varying importance. The higher the number, the less essential the commodity. Thus water might be in class I and transportation in class V. The declining arabic numerals represent the diminishing marginal utility of the commodities as more of them are consumed. The marginal utility of a class I good is 10 for the first unit, but it declines as successive units are consumed. Suppose that the class I good is water and the class VIII good is diamonds. If a consumer had already consumed 8 units of water and none of diamonds, the marginal utility of another unit of water would be only 2, but it would be 3 for the first unit of diamonds. The total utility of water is clearly greater than that of diamonds, yet the value of another unit of diamonds is greater than that of another unit of water. According to the marginal utility writers, the failure of the classical writers to recognize the importance of this principle in explaining prices was one of the major reasons that they were unable to develop a correct theory of prices. The value of diamonds is greater than the value of water because it is marginal utility that determines consumer choice and hence value.

What Is Utility?

The marginal utility writers followed orthodox classical economic theory in assuming that individuals are rational and calculating. In

Table 7.1 Menger's Table

	Classes of Commodities									
	I	II	III	IV	V	VI	VII	VIII	IX	X
	10	9	8	7	6	5	4	3	2	1
	9	8	7	6	5	4	3	2	1	0
	8	7	6	5	4	3	2	1	0	
Marginal utility	7	6	5	4	3	2	1	0		
	6	5	4	3	2	1	0			
	5	4	3	2	1	0				
	4	3	2	1	0					
	3	2	1	0						
	2	1	0							
	1	0								
	0									

making buying decisions, the consumer or household considers the marginal utility they expect to enjoy from the consumption of goods. This quickly raises two questions: what is utility, and how is it measured? Jevons, Menger, and Walras are almost identical in their approach to these issues: they do not directly engage them at all. None of the three used the term marginal utilty, and Menger did not even use the word *utility*, preferring to speak of the "importance of satisfactions." All three simply assumed that utility existed and that individual introspection would disclose the varying utilities of different final goods. For them, utility is evidently a psychological phenomenon with unspecified units of measurement. Is it measured in linear space, as in an inch, or in volume, as a quart, or as weight, in an ounce? They considered utility to be a characteristic of final or consumer goods, but what about factors of production and goods not consumed directly but only indirectly? Menger gave this last problem more attention than did Jevons or Walras. And how are we to measure the utility of goods that are acquired not for consumption but to be exchanged for other commodities? Goods to be exchanged acquire their utility from the consumption goods for which they are finally exchanged. Jevons terms the utility of such goods "acquired utility."

Thus, without clearly explaining the nature of the utility concept, Jevons, Menger, and Walras all assumed what is now called the principle of diminishing marginal utility, which states that as the consumption of a good increases, its marginal utility decreases. This is based on the further assumption that whatever marginal utility is, it can be measured. Menger and Walras did not discuss measurability. Jevons said that although we are presently unable to measure utility, further developments may permit such measurement in the future. But from the examples used in their writings, it is clear that all three assumed the cardinal measurability of utility.

Jevons and Walras, using mathematical presentations of utility functions, assumed as a first approximation that both the quantity of goods consumed and the quantity of utility were continuously divisible. Both recognized the unreality of this assumption and made allowance in their presentations for nondivisibility, which would give rise to discontinuous functions. Since Menger's approach was to use no mathematics other than arithmetic tables, all his functions were discontinuous. Continuous functions when plotted have smooth curves, but discontinuous functions have steplike curves. This has some minor theoretical importance. For example, Gossen's Second Law holds that consumers will maximize their total utility by purchasing so that the last unit of money spent for any one good gives the same marginal utility as the last unit spent for any other. An algebraic statement of this proposition is:

$$\frac{MU_A}{P_A} = \frac{MU_B}{P_B} = \frac{MU_C}{P_C} \cdots$$

If the utility functions are continuous (with smooth curves), small variations in quantity and utility can occur and the above equality will still be satisfied. If, however, the utility functions are discontinuous, then the consumer may be at a maximum without the above equality being satisfied.

Comparisons of Utility

Assuming that utility can be measured, another series of questions arises. The three writers all assumed, without examining the issue, that an individual was capable of making comparisons between the utilities of different commodities. Thus the marginal utility of another glass of beer can be compared to the marginal utility of another pair of shoes. A more important issue is involved in the making of interpersonal comparisons of utility. Is it possible to compare the utility one person receives from consuming a glass of beer with the utility another one would receive from consuming another pair of shoes? Menger and Walras never addressed themselves to this question, but their analysis does not depend on the assumption that interpersonal comparisons are possible. Jevons, in a manner typical of his writing, argued that such comparisons were impossible, but he made them anyway.

We shall return later to interpersonal comparisons of utility, because of their importance for certain questions of public policy and welfare economics. In the meantime, a brief look at one of Jevons's examples will be helpful. Jevons believed that an additional amount of income given to a person with a high income will yield less marginal utility than the same amount given to someone with a low income. This clearly assumes that interpersonal comparisons of utility are possible. Jevons did no more than suggest that interpersonal comparisons of utility could be made, but let us nevertheless spell out some implications of such comparisons. If we assume that interpersonal comparisons of utility are possible, and that all individuals have the same functions relating utility to income — that, for example, the marginal utility of a 999th dollar of income is the same for everyone — some interesting conclusions follow. Given these two assumptions, an ideal distribution of income, that is, one that would maximize the total utility for a society, would be an equal distribution of income. This conclusion can be seen from Figure 7.1.

Our two assumptions permit us to represent the marginal utility functions with respect to income of both rich and poor in one curve (II'). (An implicit third assumption is that the principle of diminishing marginal utility applies to income.) Suppose that Rich's income is OR and that Poor's income is OP. A dollar in taxes taken from Rich reduces Rich's total utility by RA, and this dollar if given to Poor increases Poor's total utility by PB. This transfer of income from Rich to Poor increases the total utility of the society, since $PB > RA$. Furthermore, if this process were repeated, total utility for the society would be increased until the income of both Rich and Poor were equal.

Figure 7.1 Robin Hood Effect

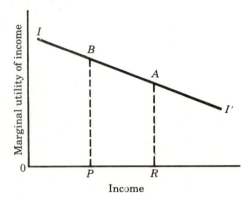

Suppose we change one of our assumptions and now assume that individuals have different functions relating utility to income and that the marginal-utility-of-income functions of upper-income receivers lie above those of lower-income receivers. This model is represented in Figure 7.2. The line rr' represents the diminishing marginal utility of income for Rich and the line pp' the marginal utility of income for Poor. The relative positions of the curves show that Rich is able to receive more marginal utility from a given amount of income than is Poor. If the initial distribution of income as represented by Poor having OP income and Rich having OR income, then an ideal distribution of income, which would maximize total utility for the society, would be achieved by taking income from Poor and giving it to Rich, since $RA > PB$. This could be called the reverse Robin Hood effect. It should be apparent that a different initial distribution of income or different positions of the curves pp' and rr' could lead to a different conclusion.

Neither Jevons, nor Menger, nor Walras investigated the implications of their theories for the distribution of income because they held that interpersonal comparisons of utility were not possible, Jevons explicitly,

Menger and Walras implicitly. We will return to some of the issues raised by interpersonal comparisons of utility and the normative issues raised by questions dealing with the distribution of income when we examine the twentieth-century development of microeconomic theory in Chapter 10.

Figure 7.2 Reverse Robin Hood Effect

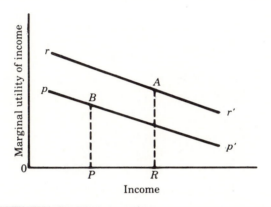

Utility Functions

Although Jevons, Menger, and Walras did not explicitly examine the exact form and nature of utility functions, Jevons and Walras did write out equations relating total utility to the quantities of goods consumed, and Menger's verbal and arithmetical examples indicate that his conception of the total utility function was the same as that of Jevons and Walras. The utility an individual receives from consuming a good depends, according to these writers, exclusively on the quantity of that good consumed. It does not depend on the quantities of other goods consumed. For example, the marginal utility received from consuming another glass of beer depends only on the quantity of beer consumed and does not depend on the quantity of wine consumed (a substitute good) or on the quantity of pretzels consumed (a complementary good). The total utility function, the utility received from consuming all goods, is therefore an additive function, which Jevons and Walras explicitly represented in the following form:

$$\text{Total Utility} = f^1(Q_a) + f^2(Q_b) + f^3(Q_c) + \cdots$$

This indicates that total utility is a function of, or depends upon, the quantity of good A consumed plus the quantity of B consumed, and so on, which denies the existence of any complementary and substitute relationships between goods. In modern micro theory these complementary and substitute relationships are not denied and the total utility function is written in a more general form such as:

$$\text{Total Utility} = f(q_A, q_B, q_C, \ldots)$$

W. S. Jevons

Utility, Demand, and Exchange

What set Jevons, Menger, and Walras apart from their predecessors, with the exception of Gossen, is that they not only postulated the principle of diminishing marginal utility but also attempted to determine the conditions that would hold when a consumer is maximizing utility, and to develop a theory of exchange. Jevons and Walras went so far as to investigate the relationship between utility and demand. Walras, because of his greater mathematical ability, was the most successful of the three in these endeavors.

Gossen's Second Law states that a consumer maximizes utility by spending a limited income so that the last unit of money spent for any particular good yields the same marginal utility as the last unit spent for any other good.

$$\frac{MU_A}{P_A} = \frac{MU_B}{P_B} = \frac{MU_C}{P_C} \cdots$$

Although both Menger and Jevons established the essence of this proposition, Menger with verbal explanations and crude arithmetic examples and Jevons with more sophisticated mathematical notation, it remained for Walras, in his justly famous Lesson 8, to derive mathematically the equations that hold when a consumer is maximizing utility.

If individual consumer utility is the underlying force explaining individual and market demand, it is necessary to show the relationship between utility functions and demand curves. Menger did not attempt this process and did not deal directly with demand curves either verbally, graphically, or arithmetically. Jevons used demand functions in his analysis but failed to establish a relationship between utility and demand. Walras *was* able to establish the relationship between utility and demand and to show that the fundamental force lying behind demand is marginal utility.

All three of these pioneers attempted to show the relationships between marginal utility, maximization of consumer satisfaction, and the exchange of goods in a market. Menger, again because of the crudeness of his arithmetical examples, was the least successful. Jevons was able to show these relationships in a simple market of two goods and two individuals. If individual A owns corn, individual B owns beef, and they barter, the final position of equilibrium can be concisely stated: "The ratio of exchange of any two commodities will be the reciprocal of the ratio of the final degrees of utility of the quantities of commodity available for consumption after the exchange is completed."[6]

Jevons's statement can be translated into the following equation:

6. Jevons, *Theory*, p. 95. The complete sentence is italicized in the original.

$$\frac{MU \text{ of corn to } A}{MU \text{ of beef to } A} = \frac{MU \text{ of corn to } B}{MU \text{ of beef to } B}$$

$$= \frac{\text{Quantity of beef traded}}{\text{Quantity of corn traded}} = \frac{\text{Price of corn}}{\text{Price of beef}}$$

Walras was able to demonstrate the relationship between marginal utility, maximization of consumer satisfaction, and exchange in a much more thorough and generalized manner than was either Jevons or Menger. He took the classical and physiocratic vision of the interrelatedness of the sectors of the economy and, with the aid of mathematics, built a general equilibrium model. This seminal contribution of Walras was so important that we will treat it separately later in this chapter.

The Value of Factors of Production

As we have seen, the early writers who emphasized the role of utility criticized the classical theory of value, which held that relative prices depend upon cost of production. This implied, they said, that value comes from the past; they argued instead that value comes from the future, from the expected utilities to be enjoyed when consuming final goods. Then how did these marginal utility writers explain the prices of the factors of production? On this issue there are important differences between Jevons and Menger, on the one hand, and Walras, on the other.

Jevons and Menger both discussed this question, and although Menger's treatment was much more complete than Jevons's, both came to essentially the same conclusion. Based on their assumption that value causation runs not from cost of production to final prices but in the opposite direction, they held that factors of production are not price-determining, but price-determined. The price of a final good depends upon its marginal utility, and the price of factors of production (otherwise known as intermediate goods, or goods of higher order) depends upon the utility of the produced final good. Walras understood this issue much more fully than did Jevons or Menger. Where Jevons and Menger were content to search for a one-way, cause-and-effect relationship among utility, prices of final goods, and prices of factors of production, Walras developed a general equilibrium model showing that all prices are interconnected. In the Walrasian explanation, all prices are mutually determined, and it is not possible to assign value causation in either direction. The prices of final goods influence and are influenced by the prices of factors of production. In a general equilibrium model, everything depends on everything.

An examination of the problems raised in determining the prices of factors of production will reveal the major difficulties and weaknesses in the marginal utility approach. By working through a simple problem in the spirit of Jevons and Menger and two disciples of Menger, Wieser and Böhm-Bawerk, we can come to an understanding of the nature of their explanation of the causal relationship between utility, prices of final goods, and prices of factors of production. Suppose we have the following information about an economy:

1. The marginal utility schedules of consumers for final goods
2. The total supply of factors of production
3. Costs of production

Given this information we can find the prices of the final goods and factors of production expressed in units of marginal utility. Assume that there are three final goods, A, B, and C, with the marginal utility schedule shown in Table 7.2. Also assume that there is a fixed stock of 100 homogeneous factors of production and the following costs of production:

Four factors of production are used to produce one A.
Six factors of production are used to produce one B.
Five factors of production are used to produce one C.

We also assume that costs of production do not change with output, in other words, that there are constant costs, or perfectly elastic (horizontal) supply curves. Our problem is to find the prices of the three final goods and the price of a single unit of the factors of production.

Table 7.2 Marginal Utility Schedule

Quantity	Good A	Good B	Good C
1	100	126	70
2	90	50	40
3	80	25	20
4	70	18	18
5	60	14	15
6	50	10	10
7	40	6	5
8	30	5	—
9	20	—	—
10	10	—	—
11	5	—	—
12	4	—	—
13	—	—	—

Let us approach the solution step by step. The first question to be answered is, what final good would be produced first? Good A would be produced first for the following reason: the marginal utility of a single factor of production is higher in the production of the first unit of good A than in any other use. Since it requires 4 factors of production to produce one A, each factor put into this use yields 25 units of marginal utility ($100 \div 4 = 25$). The first unit of good B produced yields only 21 units of marginal utility for each factor ($126 \div 6 = 21$), and the first unit of C produced yields only 14 units of marginal utility for each factor ($70 \div 5 = 14$). The rational use of the factors of production requires that they be used to produce those goods given the highest marginal utility for each unit of a factor of production. After the first unit of A is produced, 96 factors of production remain. Rational use of these remaining factors would require production of another unit of A ($90 \div 4 = 22.5$) before any units of goods B and C are produced. The factors of production would be used to produce final goods until the total stock of factors of production is exhausted. This would result in production of 10 units of A, 5 units of B, and 6 units of C.

Good	Output of Final Good	Cost	Factors Used
A	10	4	40
B	5	6	30
C	6	5	30
			100

What would be the price of the final goods and the price of the factors of production? To answer these questions we must determine the marginal utility yielded by a factor of production at the margin. The last final good produced would be the sixth unit of good C, which yields 2 units of marginal utility for each unit of factor of production ($10 \div 5 = 2$). The fifth unit of good B would be the next to last final good produced, yielding 2.33 units of marginal utility for each factor of production ($14 \div 6 = 2.33$). The price of a unit of a factor of production would be 2, or the marginal utility of the final good produced by the last unit of a factor of production. The principle of substituting at the margin can be used to explain why a factor of production would have a price of 2 units of marginal utility. Suppose that one unit of final good A is lost or destroyed. While the immediate marginal utility of the tenth, or last, unit of good A is 10, or 2.5 units of marginal utility per unit of factor of production, the loss of marginal utility from the lost or destroyed unit is actually only 8. If a unit of good A is destroyed, a rational reallocation of resources would result in 4 units of factors of production being transferred from the production of good C into the production of good A. The price of a factor of production is

2 units of utility, so the price of good A would be 8. The price of good A is not measured by the utility it actually yields, its immediate marginal utility, but by a foreign utility.

The relationships between marginal utility, the prices of factors of production, and the prices of final goods are illustrated in Table 7.3 and Figure 7.3. Column 1 of Table 7.3 contains the immediate marginal utilities of the three final goods. The prices of the three final goods are not measured by these immediate marginal utilities. The price of a unit of a factor of production is 2, since this is the marginal utility yielded by a factor at the margin. Column 3 gives the costs of production of the three final goods and is computed by multiplying the number of factors used to produce a unit of each final good times the price of a factor of production. Column 4 gives the prices of the final goods expressed in units of marginal utility. The ratios of these values are the relative prices of the final goods, for example, good B has a price 1.5 greater than good A. If good A is the unit of money, or the numeraire, then its price is 1, good B's price is 1.5, and good C's price is 1.25.

Table 7.3

Good	1 Immediate *MU* of final goods	2 Price of factors of production	3 Cost of production	4 Price of final goods
A	10	2	(2·4) 8	8
B	14	2	(2·6) 12	12
C	10	2	(2·5) 10	10

Figure 7.3 Value Causation

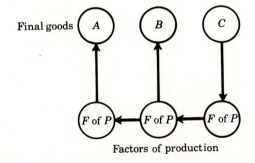

Factors of production

The marginal utility writers found the classical economists wrong in holding that prices depend upon cost of production. The above problem discloses the exact nature of this alleged misconception. The price of a factor of production is measured by the marginal utility it yields in the marginal, or last, final good produced. In the problem the last final good produced was C, which established the price of a factor of production at 2. The prices of the intramarginal final goods are determined by their costs of production, that is, the price of a factor of production multiplied by the number of factors required to produce a given final good. While it is correct to say that the prices of goods A and B depend upon their costs of production, their costs of production are determined by the value of a factor of production, and the value of a factor of production depends upon the marginal utility of the marginal final good produced. Value causation, according to Jevons and Menger, then runs from the marginal utility of the marginal final good produced (C) to the value of a factor of production (2), and finally from cost of production to the intramarginal final goods (A and B).

Criticism of Jevons and Menger

The preceding presentation of the alleged relationships between marginal utility, the prices of factors of production, and the prices of final goods was that held by Jevons and Menger and their disciples. A closer examination of this position discloses some serious theoretical misconceptions. The prices of the three final goods were shown in Table 7.3 to be $A = 8$, $B = 12$, and $C = 10$. Under the assumptions of the problem, these results could be obtained much more directly. The prices of the final goods are in the same ratios as the number of factors of production required to produce the final goods: A required 4 factors, B required 6 factors, and C required 5 factors. Assuming constant costs of production, the supply curves of the three final goods are perfectly elastic (horizontal), and their prices depend upon cost of production, or supply. The prices of the three final goods could be determined without knowing their marginal utility or demand schedules, although a knowledge of these schedules does permit one to determine the allocation of the factors among the industries producing final goods. In the problem our knowledge of the marginal utility schedules enabled us to determine that final good A used 40 factors of production, B used 30, and C used 30.

Suppose we work the problem again, dropping the assumption that the final goods are produced under constant costs and assuming increasing costs instead. Under these circumstances the prices of the final goods can be determined only if we specify the cost, or supply curves. With upward-sloping supply curves, prices depend upon supply and demand.

That Jevons's and Menger's criticisms of the classical theory of value are incorrect and inadequate in a number of ways can be seen by comparing their value theories with J. S. Mill's. Mill, as was pointed out in Chapter 5 and as illustrated with Figure 5.1, envisioned three possible cases of value: a perfectly inelastic (vertical) supply curve; a perfectly elastic (horizontal) supply representing manufacturing, which Mill assumed was composed of constant-cost industries, and an upward-sloping supply curve representing agriculture, which Mill assumed was an increasing-cost industry. Mill concluded that in constant-cost industries, cost of production alone determines price. Jevons and Menger were unable to refute this. For commodities whose supply is fixed, and that therefore have a perfectly inelastic (vertical) supply curve, Mill held that supply and demand determine price. Jevons and Menger could not refute this proposition either. Instead they said that *given* supply, demand determines price. They could just as reasonably have said that given demand, supply determines price. Mill's case of upward-sloping supply curves of increasing-cost industries was not analyzed by Jevons and Menger because they always assumed that supply was given. This is not to imply that there were no weaknesses in Millian value theory, but it does show that Jevons and Menger were not able to support their claims.

Menger stated his criticism of classical value theory succinctly:

> Among the most egregious of the fundamental errors that have had the most far-reaching consequences in the previous development of our science is the argument that goods attain value for us because goods were employed in their production that had value to us.[7]

Menger asserts that it is utility, not cost of production, that determines value. "The value of goods arises from their relationship to our needs, and is not inherent in the goods themselves."[8] Since Jevons's statement is even stronger, he is somewhat more vulnerable: "Repeated reflection and inquiry have led me to the somewhat novel opinion that *value depends entirely upon utility*."[9]

The examples used by Jevons and Menger indicate that value, or price, does not depend entirely on utility, or demand, but upon both supply *and* demand. Although these writers and their disciples claimed that value depends solely on utility, their own analysis refutes this assumption. Jevons is the best example of this. The second paragraph of his *Political Economy* opens with the sentence quoted above. After making this strong statement, Jevons proceeds in the next four sentences to refute himself.

7. Menger, *Principles*, p. 149.
8. *Ibid.*, p. 120.
9. Jevons, *Theory*, p. 1.

Prevailing opinions make labour rather than utility the origin of value, and there are even those who distinctly assert that labour is the *cause* of value. I show, on the contrary, that we have only to trace out carefully the natural laws of the variation of utility, as depending upon the quantity of commodity in our possession, in order to arrive at a satisfactory theory of exchange, of which the ordinary laws of supply and demand are a necessary consequence. This theory is in harmony with the facts; and, whenever there is any apparent reason for the belief that labor is the cause of value, we obtain an explanation of the reason. Labour is found often to determine value, but only in an indirect manner, by varying the degree of utility of the commodity through an increase or limitation of the supply.[10]

Jevons further destroys both his argument that value depends entirely upon utility and his claim to have refuted the classical theory of value, in Chapter IV of his *Political Economy*, which develops his theory of exchange. In his theory of exchange, he shows correctly that, assuming a *fixed supply* of two goods held by two individuals, the prices of these goods and the quantities exchanged will depend upon the marginal utilities of the two goods to the two individuals. Although this proposition is formally correct, it does not cover the usual economic situation where supply is not fixed but variable. When Jevons drops the assumption that supply is fixed and analyzes the relationship between cost, supply, marginal utility, and price, he arrives at the following causal relationships:

Cost of production determines supply;
Supply determines final degree of utility;
Final degree of utility determines value.[11]

This proposition can be criticized on several grounds. Jevons offers no theory of either cost or supply. Furthermore, the proposition suggests that a chain of causation runs from cost of production to value, or price. If such a chain of causation did exist, it would be possible to omit the middle part of the chain and simply conclude that cost of production determines value. Jevons and Menger erred in trying to find a simple one-way, cause-and-effect relationship between marginal utility and price. They did not perceive that cost, supply, demand, and price are interdependent and mutually determine each other.

Let us return to Mill's three cases of value and determine the strengths and weaknesses of the classical position as compared with the

10. *Ibid.*, pp. 1-2.
11. *Ibid.*, p. 165. The complete sentence is italicized in the original.

alternative theory offered by Jevons and Menger. Where supply is perfectly inelastic (vertical), as in Mill's first case, the classical cost of production theory of value does not adequately explain the determination of price. Price, under these circumstances, depends upon supply and demand, and cost of production may have no influence on supply. But the Jevons-Menger position that price depends only upon demand is also unsatisfactory, for it assumes that the supply is fixed. A few examples of situations that come under Mill's first case may make this clearer. Suppose that only one curious misprinting of a postage stamp is known to exist. The supply is fixed at one stamp and, given this fixed supply, the price will be fixed by the level of demand. That the price depends upon both supply and demand can be demonstrated by assuming that ten more of these stamps are discovered, in which case the supply curve would shift to the right and price would fall. For a second example, assume a grocer holds perishable fruits that must be marketed on a given day. As the day passes the grocer will lower the price to capture whatever demand exists, since revenue is better than failing to sell a perishable commodity before it spoils. A final example of Mill's first case would be a manufactured product fixed in supply but held at a certain price by the producer-seller. Such a price is often called a "reservation price" and might well be determined by the producer according to the cost of production. In this example the supply curve would look like a backward capital L (⌐), with the horizontal portion being the level of costs and the vertical portion representing the total existing stock of the good.

In Mill's second case, where supply is perfectly elastic (horizontal) and constant costs exist, price depends entirely on cost of production. Here classical value theory, as represented by Mill, is perfectly correct, and the Jevons-Menger position completely fails.

As in the first case, both the Jevons-Menger and classical theories fail to explain the determinants of price in Mill's third case, where the supply curve is upward-sloping (characterized by increasing costs). Under these circumstances Mill concludes that price depends upon cost of production in the most unfavorable circumstances. Translated to modern terminology, he is saying that price depends upon the marginal cost of the last good produced. What Mill is saying is that given demand, cost of production, or supply, determines price. Jevons and Menger concluded that price depends upon marginal utility. What they are saying is that given supply, demand determines price. Since price in this case depends upon both supply and demand, both these positions are erroneous. Jevons and Menger and the classicals, moreover, all made the same basic error of trying to find a simple causal chain to explain prices: the classical cause and effect runs from cost of production to price, whereas the Jevons-Menger cause and effect runs from utility to price. They all failed to see that these variables are interdependent and mutually determine each other's values. It took the brilliance of Walras and Marshall to see this interdependence. We turn now to a closer examination of Walras; Marshall will be discussed in Chapter 9.

WALRAS'S GENERAL EQUILIBRIUM SYSTEM

The interdependence of the various parts of the economic system was not a new idea in 1874. Earlier writers had had a clear vision of an economy consisting of many interconnected parts. Quesnay had given this vision form in his economic table, which traced the flow of annual production between the various sectors of the economy. Adam Smith, in his vivid descriptions of market processes, showed deep insight into

Léon Walras

the relationships among the various parts of the economy. In 1838, A. Cournot (1801–1877) achieved some insight into the interrelatedness of the economy while analyzing certain microeconomic problems. He was able to express some of the problems of the theory of the firm in mathematical form and to use calculus to prove that profits are maximized when marginal cost is equal to marginal revenue. This abstract mathematical orientation assisted him considerably in comprehending relationships within the economy. He concluded that "for a complete and rigorous solution of the problems relative to some parts of the economic system, it [is] indispensable to take the entire system into consideration."[12] Cournot felt, however, that mathematical analysis was not sufficiently developed to permit the formulation of a general equilibrium model. J. H. von Thünen (1783–1850) also applied calculus to the solution of problems in economic theory, and as in the case of Cournot, this mathematical orientation led him to see the possibility of presenting a general equilibrium model as a system of simultaneous equations. However, it was Léon Walras who was first able to give these visions clarity and precision by formulating a general equilibrium model of an economy through the use of mathematical notation. For this accomplishment, Walras is justly praised as an important predecessor of modern economic theory, with its heavy emphasis on abstract model building and the use of mathematics.

It is difficult, if not impossible, to present a brief, clear, and formally correct general equilibrium system without the use of mathematics. This is why undergraduate education in economics usually does not go deeply into general equilibrium analysis. Intermediate college micro theory courses and texts contain sections presenting the essence of Walras's general equilibrium model — usually in a chapter at the end of the book — but it is not unusual for this chapter to be passed over in class. In graduate education in economics, however, general equilibrium analysis is stressed. We shall first describe a Walrasian model in words and discuss some of the theoretical issues it raises, and then we will present a mathematical model intended to give the mathematically untrained reader some idea of the highly abstract nature of Walrasian models.

Partial and General Equilibrium Analysis

Models and theory by their very essence assume that certain elements are held constant so that those elements will not influence the behavior

12. Augustin A. Cournot, *Researches into the Mathematical Principles of the Theory of Wealth*, trans. Nathaniel T. Bacon (New York: Macmillan, 1897), p. 127.

of the variables in the model. In the physical sciences, where the laboratory method has proved so fruitful, the researcher conducts repeated experiments in which all the variables except two are held constant. One variable, for example the heat applied to a mass of water, is permitted to vary, and the effect on the other variable is observed. If, for example, the water is observed to boil at 212° Fahrenheit in repeated experiments, we conclude that with certain factors held constant — in this case constant pressure would be crucial — water boils at that temperature. The Latin phrase *ceteris paribus* is a shorthand expression used by economists to express the fact that all other factors are assumed to be held constant when statements are made about the action of an independent variable upon a dependent variable. *Ceteris paribus* means "other things being equal."

Economists distinguish between partial and general equilibrium models in terms of the degree of abstraction in the model. More factors are assumed to be held constant in partial analysis than in general equilibrium analysis. General equilibrium analysis does not allow all variables to vary and thus to influence the model, however, but only those regarded as within the scope of economics. General equilibrium models, for example, assume as given the tastes or preferences of individuals, the technology available for producing goods, and the institutional structure of the economy and society. Since the scope of economics as a social science has historically been limited by orthodox theory to variables that appear to be quantifiable, a mathematical general equilibrium model is obviously feasible.

A simple example using supply-and-demand analysis will help to distinguish between partial and general equilibrium systems. Most partial equilibrium models, following the tradition of Alfred Marshall, limit themselves to the analysis of a particular household, firm, or industry. Suppose we want to analyze the influence on beef prices of a reduction in costs in the beef industry. Using the partial equilibrium approach, we would start with the industry in assumed equilibrium, disturb this equilibrium by making the cost reduction, and then deduce the new position of equilibrium. During this analysis, all other forces in the economy are assumed to be fixed and to have no influence on the beef industry. The reduction in costs in the beef industry would result in the supply of beef increasing and the price of beef falling to a new equilibrium level. Suppose we make our model less restrictive and include in the analysis both the pork and beef industries. The immediate effect of lower costs in the beef industry is to lower beef prices as the supply of beef increases. The fall in the price of beef will, however, also influence the demand for pork. As beef prices fall relative to pork prices, the demand for pork will decrease as the quantity of beef demanded increases: consumers will substitute beef for pork. The decrease in demand for pork will result in a fall in the price of pork, which will result in a decrease in the demand for beef and a further fall in its price. And this fall in the price of beef will further decrease the demand for pork and thus again lower its price. The interaction between prices and demands for these two goods will continue, with the resulting changes in prices and outputs becoming smaller and smaller, until new equilibrium conditions are established in both industries.

Let us think through the above example using familiar supply-and-demand graphs. In our partial equilibrium model, the beef industry is assumed to be isolated from the rest of the economy, and we can plot a clear and simple graph showing the consequence of a reduction in costs in the beef industry by means of supply-and-demand curves. The supply curve of beef moves out and to the right, and a new equilibrium emerges. But if we show the interactions between the beef and pork industries, the resulting graphs become more complex. Figure 7.4 indicates the shift in the supply curve of beef from S to S_1 as a result of the decrease in costs in the beef industry. This falling price of beef results in an immediate decrease in the demand for pork from d to d_1, which lowers the price of pork. The falling price of pork brings a decrease in the demand for beef from D to D_1. The successive interactions between prices and demand for these two products is indicated by the downward shift of demand curves until a final equilibrium is reached.

Partial equilibrium analysis is an attempt to reduce a complex problem to a more manageable form by isolating one sector of the economy, for example one industry, and ignoring the interaction between that sector and the rest of the economy. It is useful for contextual argu-

Figure 7.4 The Interdependence of Industries

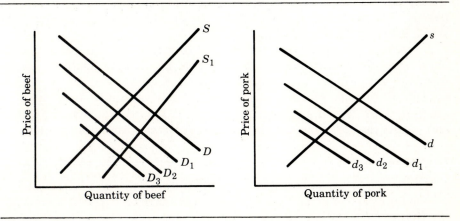

mentation. The gains in clarity and analytical neatness, however, are achieved at the expense of theoretical rigor and completeness.

If we were to move toward a more general equilibrium model by adding a third and fourth industry to the above example, the analysis would become so complex that diagrammatic representation would produce more confusion than clarity. Walras's great contribution was his recognition that the complex interdependence of industries could best be understood and communicated mathematically. His general equilibrium analysis is useful for noncontextual argumentation.

Walras in Words

Before proceeding to our study of Walras's general equilibrium model, let us think through a partial equilibrium problem in mathematical form. Suppose we are interested in price and output in the beef industry. The demand and supply for beef can be expressed as equations relating price to quantity supplied and quantity demanded. Although there are three variables in the model — price, quantity supplied, and quantity demanded — at equilibrium there are only two unknowns, since quantity demanded equals quantity supplied. The problem of finding the equilibrium price in the beef industry, then, consists of an equation for supply, an equation for demand, and two unknowns.

Let us now move from this partial equilibrium model to a more complex general equilibrium model. Since even in a general equilibrium model it is necessary to disregard certain aspects of a complex economy, we will assume an economy made up of only two sectors, firms and households, and ignore the government and foreign sectors. We will assume, moreover, that firms do not buy intermediate goods from each other, that household preferences do not change, that the level of technology is fixed, that full employment exists, and that all industries are perfectly competitive. A schematic representation of such an economy is presented in Figure 7.5.[13]

Households go into the markets for final goods with given preferences and limited incomes and express a dollar demand for these goods. Firms go into these final markets willing to supply goods, and thus a supply of final goods flows from firms to households. It is in these markets, represented by the upper part of Figure 7.5, that the prices and quantities of final goods supplied and quantities demanded are

---

13. The use of a figure such as Figure 7.5 to illustrate various aspects of an economy has a long history. For an interesting account of the uses of such a figure in the present context see Don Patinkin, "In Search of the 'Wheel of Wealth': On the Origins of Frank Knight's Circular-Flow Diagram," *American Economic Review* (December 1973).

determined. For these markets to be in equilibrium, the quantity supplied and the quantity demanded for each particular commodity must be equal. Factor markets are represented by the lower portion of Figure 7.5. In these markets, firms demand land, labor, and capital from households, and there is a dollar flow of income from firms to households. As households supply the factors of production in these markets, factor prices are determined. Equilibrium here requires that all markets be cleared so that quantities supplied equal quantities demanded for each factor. Households receive their incomes from factor markets and spend them in markets for final goods. For households to maximize the satisfaction they receive from consuming final goods, given their limited income, they distribute their expenditures so that the last dollar spent on any particular good yields the same marginal utility as the last dollar spent on any other good (Gossen's Second Law). The flow of income between firms and households represents the national income of the economy; for this to be in equilibrium, households must spend all the income they receive. The distribution of income is determined in factor markets and depends upon the prices of the various factors and the quantities of factors sold by each household.

When firms in a market economy look one way, they face the prices for final goods, and when they look the other way, they face prices for the various factors of production. Given these prices and the technology available, they combine inputs to produce outputs in a manner that will maximize their profits. This requires that they combine inputs so as to produce a given output at the lowest possible cost and that they produce at a level of output that maximizes profits. Competitive forces will result in a situation at long-run equilibrium where the price

Figure 7.5 The Interdependence of Sectors of the Economy

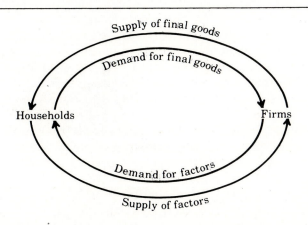

of final goods is just equal to their average cost of production. For the level of national income to be in equilibrium, firms must spend all of their receipts from final markets in factor markets.

The first and most obvious lesson from this somewhat abstract example of an economy is that the various parts of the economy are interrelated. It is misleading to think of one variable in the system as determining another variable. If equilibrium exists, all the variables are simultaneously determined. Suppose that we disturb the equilibrium by changing the price of a single final good. This will have repercussions throughout the whole system as consumers change their spending patterns and as firms change their outputs. These changes will make themselves felt also in the factor markets as firms change their demands for inputs, thereby bringing about a whole new constellation of input prices and a different distribution of income.

Smith, Quesnay, and others had recognized the interdependence of the various parts of a market economy. But to go beyond the simple statement that everything depends on everything else, it was essential to specify the relationships between the various sectors in greater detail. Walras's genius enabled him to lay the groundwork for this more exact specification by the use of mathematics. When the economy is considered in an explicitly mathematical Walrasian model with mathematical notations, questions arise that were not apparent in our loose, verbal analysis of his model.

The demands of households for final goods can be expressed as equations relating price to quantity demanded for each household. The market demand for a given final good can also be conceived of as an equation obtained by summing the household demand equations. The market supply for final goods can be obtained in a similar manner by summing the firm's equations relating price to quantity supplied. And equilibrium in the markets for final goods requires that quantity supplied equals quantity demanded for each final good. Market demand and supply equations can be derived analogously for factor markets, with the equilibrium condition being that all markets clear. For households an equation can be derived with one side indicating income (the sum of the prices of each factor sold times the quantity sold for each factor) and the other side indicating expenditures (the sum of the price of each final good bought times the quantity purchased for all goods purchased). For the household to be in equilibrium, income must equal expenditures, and expenditures be made so as to maximize utility. The equilibrium conditions for the firm to maximize profits, and for its average costs to equal price through the force of competition, can likewise be expressed in equations.

Thus we arrive at a system of simultaneous equations that indicates the interrelatedness of the sectors of the economy. The Walrasian formulation of the working of a market economy raises some new questions. For example, is a general equilibrium solution possible? Will the equilibrium conditions produced by the market in the various sectors of the economy be consistent with a general equilibrium for the whole economy? The unknowns determined by the market and given by a general equilibrium solution are: (1) the prices of final goods; (2) the prices of factors; (3) the quantities of final goods supplied and quantities demanded; and (4) the quantities of factors supplied and quantities demanded. Is there only one set of prices and quantities that will result in equilibrium for the whole economy, or are there many possible equilibria? If a solution to this problem does exist, is it a solution that is economically meaningful, or will it yield negative prices and quantities? Is the equilibrium stable or unstable? Is the system determinate? Several possibilities exist. The very process of the market working may result in shifting mathematical functions that will not result in final equilibrium. Another possibility is that a final equilibrium will be reached but that its position will depend on the path followed by the variables in the system. This suggests that different final equilibrium values are possible. Walras was aware of some of these problems, though others were not identified or solved for nearly sixty years after 1874. However, Walras did present a model that afforded greater insight into the workings of a market and could serve as a foundation for further theoretical developments.

Walras in Equations

Walras's general equilibrium model, presented in Lesson 20 of his *Elements*, assumes a market economy made up of households and firms with no government or foreign sector. Walras uses the following symbols for his analysis of this economy. There are n factors of production.

$T, T', T'', \ldots$ are different kinds of land
$P, P,' P'', \ldots$ are different kinds of labor
$K, K', K'', \ldots$ are different kinds of capital goods

There are m final goods represented by $A, B, C, \ldots$
The marginal utility function for an individual is written as $r = \phi_q$
Prices for final goods are written as $p_b, p_c, p_d, \ldots$
Prices for factors of production are written as $p_t, p_p, p_k, \ldots$
Households start with given quantities of factors of production which are written as $q_t, q_p, q_k, \ldots$
The quantities of factors of production offered by households are written as $o_t, o_p, o_k, \ldots$ These values are positive when households offer factors and are negative when households demand factors.
The demands of households for final goods are represented by $d_a, d_b, d_c, \ldots$

The first aspect of market equilibrium that Walras analyzes concerns the household or individual. Since his system does not contain money as a unit of account, what Walras terms a "numeraire" is needed. Consumer good A fills this need; its price is equal to one ($p_a = 1$). The prices of all final goods and factors of production are measured in terms of this unit. In equilibrium the flow of income to the household will be equal to the expenditures of the household. The flow of income from the sale of land is measured by the amount of land offered (o_t) times the price of land (p_t). The income from the sale of other factors is given by a similar product. The expenditure of a household for a given final product is the product of its price times the quantity consumed, or demanded, in equilibrium. Setting income equal to expenditure gives the first equilibrium condition for a household.

$$o_t p_t + o_p p_p + o_k p_k + \ldots = d_a + d_b p_b + d_c p_c + \ldots \tag{1}$$

The household or individual is faced with the prices of final goods and factors of production in the market. The first task Walras undertakes is to determine the quantities of the n factors offered by households ($o_t, o_p, o_k, \ldots$), of which there are n factors and therefore n unknowns, and the quantities of the m final goods demanded by households ($d_a, d_b, d_c, \ldots$). Since there are m final goods and n factors, the number of unknowns is $m + n$.

For households to maximize their utility, the marginal utilities of final goods purchased must be proportional to their prices, and the marginal utilities of factors of production not offered on the market but retained by households for their own use must be proportional to their prices. Since there are n factors of production, this gives n equations.

$$\begin{aligned}
\phi_t(q_t - o_t) &= p_t \phi_a(d_a) \\
\phi_p(q_p - o_p) &= p_p \phi_a(d_a) \\
\phi_k(q_k - o_k) &= p_k \phi_a(d_a)
\end{aligned} \tag{2.1}$$

There are m final goods, but since final good A is the numeraire, only $m - 1$ equations of the following type represent household equilibrium in the market for final goods.

$$\begin{aligned}
\phi_b(d_b) &= p_b \phi_a(d_a) \\
\phi_c(d_c) &= p_c \phi_a(d_a) \\
\phi_d(d_d) &= p_d \phi_a(d_a)
\end{aligned} \tag{2.2}$$

We are trying to find the household's supply functions for n factors of production and their demand functions for m final goods. The number of unknowns is $n + m$. The conditions for household maximization of utility gives us n equations of the type (2.1) and $m - 1$ equations of the type (2.2). Equation (1) can be used to determine the demand for final good A, so we have $n + m$ equations to solve for $n + m$ unknowns.

The demand functions of a household for final goods indicate that demand is a function of utility; of the household's income, which is reflected in the prices of factors of production; of the price of the final good; and of the prices of all other final goods. There are $m - 1$ of these equations. The demand for good A is given by equation (1).

$$d_b = f_b(p_t, p_p, p_k, \ldots, p_b, p_c, p_d, \ldots)$$
$$d_c = f_c(p_t, p_p, p_k, \ldots, p_b, p_c, p_d, \ldots)$$

$$(3.1)$$

The household's supply functions of factors of production indicate that supply is a function of the utility of retained factors of production, the price of the factor, the prices of all other factors, and the prices of final goods. There are n of these equations.

$$o_t = f_t(p_t, p_p, p_k, \ldots, p_b, p_c, p_d, \ldots)$$
$$o_p = f_p(p_t, p_p, p_k, \ldots, p_b, p_c, p_d, \ldots)$$

$$(3.2)$$

In considering the equilibrium of the household, we may take as given the prices of the final goods and the prices of the factors of production. It is then possible to derive the household's supply functions of factors of production (equations 3.2) and the household's demand functions for final goods (equations 3.1). In analyzing general market equilibrium, it is not permissible to assume that either final or factor prices are given; they become unknowns. In discussing general market equilibrium, Walras introduces several other concepts expressed in symbols.

The technical coefficients of production express the quantities of land, labor, and capital that must be used to produce one unit of a given final product. Thus, a_t, a_p, a_k, represent the quantities of land, labor and capital necessary to produce one unit of the final good A. Walras assumed these coefficients to be fixed in the first two editions of his *Elements*, but in the third edition, published in 1900, he drops this restrictive assumption.

Market demand and supply are represented by capital letters. For example, the market demand for final good A is written as D_a and is obtained by summing the demands of all the households for good A ($D_a = \Sigma d_a$). The market supply of factors is written and derived in a similar manner, $O_t = \Sigma o_t$.

In general market equilibrium there are $2m + 2n - 1$ unknowns. This can be ascertained by examining Table 7.4.

Four systems of equations will provide these $2m + 2n - 1$ unknowns.

The quantities of factors supplied in the market are functions of the prices of the factors and final goods. There are n equations of this type.

$$O_t = F_t(p_t, p_p, p_k, \ldots, p_b, p_c, p_d, \ldots)$$
$$O_p = F_p(p_t, p_p, p_k, \ldots, p_b, p_c, p_d, \ldots) \tag{4}$$
$$\cdots\cdots\cdots\cdots\cdots\cdots\cdots\cdots\cdots\cdots\cdots$$

The quantities of final goods demanded in the market are also functions of the prices of factors and final goods. There are $m - 1$ of these equations, and one equation expressing the demand for good A, the numeraire, for a total of m equations.

$$D_b = F_b(p_t, p_p, p_k, \ldots, p_b, p_c, p_d, \ldots)$$
$$D_c = F_c(p_t, p_p, p_k, \ldots, p_b, p_c, p_d, \ldots) \tag{5}$$
$$\cdots\cdots\cdots\cdots\cdots\cdots\cdots\cdots\cdots\cdots\cdots$$

and

$$D_a = O_t p_t + O_p p_p + \ldots - (D_b p_b + D_c p_c + \ldots) \tag{1}$$

The quantities of factors used by firms must, in equilibrium, equal the quantity offered. There are n equations of this type.

$$O_t = a_t D_a + b_t D_b + c_t D_c + \ldots$$
$$O_p = a_p D_a + b_p D_b + c_p D_c + \ldots \tag{6}$$
$$\cdots\cdots\cdots\cdots\cdots\cdots\cdots\cdots\cdots\cdots\cdots$$

Final costs of production must, in equilibrium, equal prices. There are m equations of the type.

$$1 = a_t p_t + a_p p_p + a_k p_k + \ldots$$
$$p_b = b_t p_t + b_p p_p + b_k p_k + \ldots \tag{7}$$
$$\cdots\cdots\cdots\cdots\cdots\cdots\cdots\cdots\cdots\cdots\cdots$$

These four systems of equations, (4), (5), (6), and (7), and equation (1) provide a total of $2m + 2n$ equations. One of these equations is not an independent equation, since it does not supply new information. Eliminating this equation we are left with $2m + 2n - 1$ equations to find an equal number of unknowns.

Walras in Retrospect

Walras's high place in the history of economic theory rests partly on his independent discovery of marginal utility theory, but more importantly

Table 7.4 General Market Equilibrium Unknowns

Unknowns	Number of Unknowns
Prices of final goods $(p_b, p_c, p_d, \ldots)$	$m - 1$
Prices of factors $(p_c, p_p, p_k, \ldots)$	n
Quantities of final goods demanded $(D_a, D_b, D_c, \ldots)$	m
Quantities of factors offered $(O_t, O_p, O_k, \ldots)$	n
Total	$2m + 2n - 1$

on his conceptualization of the interdependence of the sectors of a market economy. Although others before him had perceived the inter-relatedness of households, firms, prices of final goods, prices of factors of production, and of quantities supplied and quantities demanded of all final and intermediate goods, no one had been able to express this perception as precisely as Walras did by stating it as a system of simultaneous equations. Now it was possible to see that equilibrium of the household and equilibrium in the markets for final goods was consistent with equilibrium for the firm and equilibrium in factor markets. The attempts of Jevons and Menger to find a simple causal relationship between marginal utility, the prices of final goods, and the prices of factors of production seem simple-minded and unsophisticated compared to Walras's general equilibrium model. Thus Walras clearly demonstrated the power of mathematics as a tool of economic analysis, although full acceptance of his message did not come until well into the twentieth century.

Although Walras's accomplishment was immense, there are a number of areas in which his model is theoretically deficient. He was not able, for example, to demonstrate rigorously that an economically meaningful solution existed for his model. Nor was he able to prove that a single stable equilibrium solution would follow. Finally he was not able to prove that the system was determinate — in other words, that the final equilibrium reached would be independent of the path followed in reaching equilibrium. These issues occupied the attention of economists well into the 1950s. But although Walras's inability to prove that an economically meaningful solution to his model existed, that a single stable equilibrium would be reached, and that the model was determinate resulted in his formulation's being less than perfect mathematically, it does not detract from the model's economic significance. Its major economic deficiencies lie, rather, in his failure to treat in depth the economics of the firm and the relationships between cost of production and supply. He simply assumes that in equilibrium average costs for the firm will equal prices and does not demonstrate how this zero profit result is obtained. This issue, to which Alfred Marshall later devoted a good part of his theoretical attention, Walras passes by without notice. In the first two editions of his *Elements*, Walras assumed that the coefficients of production are fixed and thereby eliminated all the issues relevant to the economics of the firm and the relationships between factor prices, the optimum way to combine inputs, and the profit-maximizing level of output for a firm. And although he later dropped the assumption of fixed coefficients of production, he never accorded cost, supply, or the economics of the firm any serious attention. On this point Walras follows Jevons and Menger, with their almost exclusive emphasis on marginal utility as the major force determining relative prices.

The source of Walras's success, his use of mathematics, was also the source of some of the failures of general equilibrium theory. This highly abstract model permitted an insight into the interrelatedness of the sectors of an economy, but because it is so abstract, it is difficult to apply. And though it demonstrates the relationships existing within an economy in equilibrium, it does not explain what happens in that economy when the factors that Walras took as fixed actually change. A general equilibrium model of an economy has tremendous potential for use in answering questions concerning the consequences of alternative economic policies, but this potential has yet to be realized.

Frank Hahn, a general equilibrium theorist, writes:

> It was Adam Smith who first realized the need to explain why this kind of social arrangement does not lead to chaos. Millions of greedy, self-seeking individuals, in pursuit of their own ends and mainly uncontrolled in these pursuits by the State, seem to "common sense" a sure recipe for anarchy. Smith not only posed an obviously important question, but also started us off on the road to answering it. General Equilibrium Theory as classically stated by Arrow and Debreu (1954 and 1959) is near the end of that road. Now that we have got there we find it less enlightening than we had expected.[14]

There are empirical problems in gathering data on such a large scale, problems of specifying the equations exactly, and computational difficulties in solving large numbers of simultaneous equations. Partial equilibrium analysis, which has fewer of these problems, has therefore been much more useful up to now in dealing with questions concerning

14. Frank Hahn, "General Equilibrium Theory." *Public Interest*, Special Issue, 1980, p. 123.

economic policy. But in spite of these difficulties, modern orthodox economists have confidence in general equilibrium analysis as a means of reaching a better understanding of an economy and of building models that can be used to ascertain the consequences of various economic policies. Much of the work of present-day economists consists of attempts to provide empirical content and operational relevance to models constructed along the lines laid down by Walras in 1874.

These attempts are consistent with Walras's real aims; even though his fame rests on his work in theoretical economics, he regarded his pure economics as a tool to be used in formulating economic policy. He regarded himself as a socialist but strenuously objected to the views of Marx and the utopian socialists such as Saint-Simon. He felt that economic theory had failed to demonstrate rigorously that an optimum allocation of resources takes place under perfect competition. In Lessons 8, 22, 26, and 27 of his *Elements*, he examines these issues and concludes that "production in a market ruled by free competition... will give the greatest possible satisfaction of wants" and that "freedom procures, within certain limits, the maximum of utility."[15] He therefore advocated that the state should attempt through legislation to create systems of perfectly competitive markets. At the same time Walras was not a thoroughgoing proponent of laissez faire: he found many areas where government intervention was desirable. He might reasonably be characterized as an advocate of market socialism. He followed Mills in holding that land rents represented unearned income and should therefore accrue to the government. With perfectly competitive markets and the abolition of rents as a source of private income, Walras felt, the resulting distribution of income would not contain major inequities. In general he tried to take a policy line between the socialists of the left and the hard-line proponents of laissez faire. His attempt to prove that general equilibrium in competitive markets results in a maximum of utility for society has been, for the most part, ignored or forgotten by economists. Knut Wicksell (1851–1926) was later to prove that this conclusion of Walras would hold only if all individuals had the same utility functions and equal incomes.[16]

THE EARLY 1870S — A SUMMARY

The early 1870s represent an important period in the development of economic theory. Jevons, Menger, and Walras all published treatises

15. Walras, *Elements*, pp. 255–256. All quoted words are italicized in the original.
16. Knut Wicksell, *Lectures on Political Economy*, trans. E. Classen, ed. with an intro. by Lionel Robbins (New York: Macmillan, 1934), pp. 72–83.

criticizing the classical cost of production theory of value and offered a new theory of value that almost exclusively emphasized marginal utility. Walras succeeded in doing what no economist had done before: constructing a mathematical model correct in its essentials that demonstrated the interrelatedness of the parts of an economy. During this period, too, Alfred Marshall was improving his own theories, which he finally published in 1890.

Jevons, Menger, and Walras all felt they were revolutionizing economic theory by replacing a supply-oriented cost of production theory of value with a demand-oriented marginal utility theory of value. Their hopes were not realized, however, since their exclusive emphasis on the demand side was as deficient as the classical stress on the supply side. Jevons's and Menger's conception of the value problem was, in fact, fundamentally unsound, as they looked for a simple cause-and-effect relationship between marginal utility and price. Walras, although he too emphasized the role of marginal utility, had a much clearer understanding of the value problem, recognizing the mutual interdependence of the parts of an economy. Whereas the classical economists had in essence assumed that demand was given and concluded that supply determined prices, the early marginal utility writers assumed that supply was given and concluded that demand determined price.

Although these three writers had not revolutionized value theory as they supposed, they did make three lasting contributions to economic theory: (1) Their emphasis on marginal utility and the role of demand caused subsequent economists to pay greater attention to this part of value theory. Their use of marginal analysis in the study of demand led to the subsequent recognition of the more general applicability of this technique, a recognition that was to have important consequences for the development of economic theory. By 1890 marginal analysis had been extended to cover not only the demand side and the household, but also the supply side and the firm. (2) Jevons's and Walras's use of mathematics in economic theorizing made economists more aware of the power of this analysis and led to the present dominance of mathematical models in economic thinking. (3) Walras's general equilibrium model was seminal in the insight it provided into the interrelatedness of the sectors of a market economy and the basis it laid down for subsequent theoretical work. The spread of marginal analysis was not rapid, however, and many controversies arose concerning this new technique. We will study the growth of marginalism in the next two chapters. Chapter 8 will examine some methodological issues raised by marginalism as well as the application of marginal analysis to the firm and its demands for factors of production.

SUGGESTED READINGS

History of Political Economy, 4 (Fall 1972). This complete issue is devoted to papers on the marginal revolution in economics.

Howey, R. S. *The Rise of the Marginal Utility School, 1870–1899.* Lawrence: University of Kansas Press, 1960.

Hutchison, T. W. *A Review of Economic Doctrines 1870–1929.* Oxford: Clarendon Press, 1953.

Jaffé, William. "The Birth of Léon Walras' *Elements.*" *History of Political Economy*, 1 (Spring 1969).

——. "Léon Walras' Role in the Marginal Revolution of the 1870s." *History of Political Economy*, 4 (Fall 1972).

Jevons, W. S. *The Theory of Political Economy.* New York: Kelley and Millman, 1957.

Keynes, J. M. "William Stanley Jevons" in *Essays and Sketches In Biography.* New York: Meridian, 1956.

Menger, Carl. *Principles of Economics.* Glencoe, Ill.: Free Press, 1950.

Schabas, Margaret. "Some Reactions to Jevons' Mathematical Program: the Case of Cairnes and Mill." *History of Political Economy*, 17 (Fall 1985).

Schumpeter, Joseph A. "Carl Menger" and "Marie Esprit Léon Walras" in *Ten Great Economists.* New York: Oxford University Press, 1951.

Stigler, George J. "The Development of Utility Theory" in *Essays in the History of Economics.* Chicago: University of Chicago Press, 1965.

Viner, Jacob. "The Utility Concept in Value Theory and Its Critics" in *The Long View and The Short.* New York: Free Press, 1958.

Walker, Donald A. "Léon Walras in the Light of His Correspondence and Related Papers." *Journal of Political Economy*, 78 (July/August 1970).

Walras, Léon. *Elements of Pure Economics.* Homewood, Ill.: Richard D. Irwin, 1954.

Chapter 8

The Transition to
Neoclassical Economics:
Marginal Analysis Extended

The first generation of marginal theorists, Jevons, Menger, and Walras, transformed economic methodology by introducing marginal utility analysis. In particular, Walras's insight into the interdependence of the various sectors of the market constituted a seminal contribution to economic *theory*. Like most developments in intellectual history, the new economics of the early 1870s evinced both continuity and change, harking back to certain fundamental ideas and methods of the past but, more notably, breaking with the classical economics of J. S. Mill. These writers had discovered a tool, marginal analysis, whose usefulness they could little imagine. The full weight of their discovery eluded them: they all stressed the difference between the *content* of their theories and those of the classical school rather than their departure from classical *methods*.

Ricardo, as we have seen, was a master builder of highly abstract models based on a few rigid assumptions. J. S. Mill, however, represented a return to a methodology much closer to Adam Smith's with his attempt to weave description and history into his theoretical analysis of the English economy. The early marginalists, because they so strongly emphasized their differences with the conclusions of Ricardo's labor theory of value, failed to recognize their affinity with his abstract model building. Ricardo had also used marginal analysis in his explanation of the forces determining the rent of land. Thus, marginal analysis and abstract model building were not new to the early 1870s. What was new was the slowly developing recognition of the importance of marginal analysis and the detailed application of marginalism to all parts of microeconomic theory as the period progressed. These developments were advanced tremendously by the use of mathematical tools, particularly differential calculus. Jevons and Walras both had training in mathematics, although Menger did not. And the second generation of marginal theorists, with the exception of the Austrian disciples of Menger, all used calculus to push forward the frontiers of economic theory.

The trends set into motion by the first generation of marginal theorists have persisted to the present. Highly abstract models, developed with an impressive array of mathematical techniques, are now the order of the day. These developments have been resisted by some, notably Alfred Marshall, the German and English historical schools, the American institutionalists, neo-Austrian economists, radical economists, and a number of economists who would otherwise be classifed as mainstream.

MARGINAL ANALYSIS EXTENDED:
THE SECOND GENERATION

It is helpful to examine the weaknesses in micro theory as it was presented by Jevons, Menger, and Walras before studying the specific contributions of the second generation of marginal theorists to the theory of production, costs, prices of factors of production, and the distribution of income. The return to Ricardo's abstract model building provoked a methodological controversy, which we shall discuss before turning in the next chapter to an examination of Alfred Marshall's attempts to solve the many theoretical and methodological issues raised during this period.

Although Jevons, Menger, and Walras contributed significantly to the development of microeconomic theory by their expansion of the use of marginal analysis, the content of their theories was deficient in a number of ways. They had applied marginal analysis exclusively to the theory of demand and almost completely ignored the theory of supply. For the most part their models assumed that supply was given and that the resource allocation problem was merely one of allocating a fixed supply among alternative uses. More specifically, they had no explanation of the forces that determine the prices of the factors of production when the supply of these factors was not fixed, no explanation of the forces determining the distribution of income, no analysis of the economies of the firm, and no insight into the unique problems that must be solved in developing theories to explain wages, rents, profits, and interest.

In fact, marginal analysis had already been applied to factor pricing and the distribution of income by two earlier writers, although their efforts, like Gossen's, were ignored for the most part by contemporary economists. Mountifort Longfield (1802-1884) in his *Lectures on Political Economy* (1834) criticized the labor theory of value and presented a marginal productivity theory of distribution. Unknown to Jevons, Menger, Walras, and Marshall, his work was brought to the attention of the profession by E. R. A. Seligman in 1903. And though Johann H. von Thünen (1783-1850) had even greater insight into the issues of microeconomics, Alfred Marshall appears to be the only one of the early discoverers of marginal productivity to have been influenced by him. Von Thünen appears, in fact, to have been the first to apply calculus to economic theory. His mathematical abilities gave him insight into the interdependence of markets, which he represented in a series of simultaneous equations. He was able not only to develop the idea of the marginal products of the various factors, but also to present a reasonably correct theory of distribution based upon these principles. After wrestling for nearly twenty years with the problem of embodying in a simple statement all the economic forces determining the prices of factors, von Thünen was so pleased with his final result that he requested his formula for the wage of labor be inscribed on his tombstone. But his achievement unfortunately had almost no direct impact on subsequent economic thinking, although Marshall generously acknowledged his debt to von Thünen.

The second generation of marginalists thus came to economic theory with a new tool with broad applicability to the theories of both demand and supply. It had been used almost exclusively to analyze the demand side, however, particularly the theory of the household, and rarely to analyze the theory of supply or the firm. In the following presentation we will record the contributions of this second generation of marginalists without stressing either the originators of new concepts or the slight differences among writers.

Writers from Austria, England, Sweden, and the United States all contributed notably to this body of theory, which demonstrates not only that these developments represented the combined efforts of many scholars but also that economics as an academic endeavor was becoming increasingly professionalized. Although our discussion of some topics will extend well into the twentieth century, we will reserve the bulk of our critical evaluation of this theory until the end of the next chapter, when we will have presented the economics of Alfred Marshall, who polished his own ideas for more than twenty years before publishing his *Principles* in 1890.

MARGINAL PRODUCTIVITY THEORY

Introduction

The principle of diminishing returns plays a fundamental role in modern economic theory. In micro theory it explains the shapes of the short-run supply curves of firms and the shapes of the firm's demand curves for factors of production.

This concept was recognized early by economic theorists and applied by Ricardo to his analysis of land rent. Ricardo studied what today would be called "production functions" for agriculture, that is, the relationship between physical inputs and physical output for land. He assumed that the ratio of capital to labor in a production process was fixed by the available technology and that doses of capital and labor in these technologically fixed proportions were added to a fixed quantity of land. On the basis of these assumptions, he concluded that the resulting output would display the characteristic of diminishing marginal product for the successive doses of capital and labor. Ricardo and his followers did not grasp all the implications of this analysis, such as the difference between diminishing average product and marginal product, nor did they recognize the broader applicability of the concept of diminishing returns. One of the anomalies of the history of economic analysis is that nearly seventy-five years elapsed between Ricardo's application of marginal productivity analysis to the determination of land rent and its general application to all factors of production. A parallel anomaly is that the marginal analysis Ricardo developed for use on the supply side saw its first significant extension in the 1870s, when it came to be used to analyze not marginal productivity but marginal utility. At all events, a second generation of marginalists finally worked out the elements of what has become known as the marginal productivity theory of distribution. The most important of these writers were the Austrians Friedrich von Wieser (1851–1926) and Eugen von Böhm-Bawerk (1851-1914); an American, J. B. Clark (1847-1938); a Swede, Knut Wicksell (1851-1926); and the English writers P. H. Wicksteed (1844-1927) and F. Y. Edgeworth (1845-1926). These writers along with Jevons, Menger, Walras, and Marshall were the intellectual giants of this period of orthodox economic theory. Their first major works appeared between 1871 and 1893.

Principle of Diminishing Returns

If we hold one factor of production constant and add a variable factor to it, the resulting output will usually first increase at an increasing rate, then increase at a decreasing rate, and finally decrease. An example of this relationship between physical input and physical output is shown in Table 8.1.

The data shown in this production function would presumably be arrived at empirically in the following way: If we held the quantity of land constant at 100 acres, for example, and applied 1 man-year, we would find that total product was 10 tons of corn. We would then repeat the experiment using 2 man-years, and record an output of 21 tons of corn, and so on. Note that the total product data of column 2 in Table 8.1 are assumed to be the maximum product that can be produced given the quantities of the fixed inputs and variable inputs. In short, it is assumed that maximum engineering efficiency is achieved.

For example, it is not possible to produce more than 58 units of total product with our fixed quantity of land and 5 units of labor. Furthermore, the level of technology is assumed to continue unchanged as we record these input-output relationships.

The average and the marginal products of the variable input, labor, are shown numerically in Table 8.1 and are presented graphically in Figure 8.1. The average product of labor, computed by dividing total product by the quantity of labor, is plotted in relationship to the total product curve in the two panels of Figure 8.1. The marginal product of labor, often more precisely called the "marginal physical product of labor," is defined as

$$MPP_L = \frac{\Delta TP}{\Delta L}$$

Table 8.1 A Production Function

Labor	Total Product (tons of corn)	Average Product of Labor (tons of corn)	Marginal Product of Labor (tons of corn)
0	0	0	
			> 10
1	10	10.0	
			> 11
2	21	10.5	
			> 12
3	33	11.0	
			> 13
4	46	11.5	
			> 12
5	58	11.6	
			> 10
6	68	11.3	
			> 7
7	75	10.7	
			> 5
8	80	10.0	
			> 3
9	83	9.2	
			> 0
10	83	8.3	
			> -3
11	80	7.3	

Geometrically it is the slope of the total product curve, or the first derivative of total product with respect to labor. It is also plotted in Figure 8.1. When the quantity of labor is q_1, the marginal product of labor is at a maximum; at q_2 the average product of labor is at a maximum, and marginal and average product are equal; and at q_3 the total product is at a maximum and the marginal product of labor is zero. Quantities of labor beyond q_3 result in decreasing total product and negative marginal product of labor.

The exact properties of production functions and the implications of these properties were slowly worked out during the close of the nineteenth century. Most of the difficulties encountered are not of sufficient interest to warrant examination. The important conclusion was that diminishing returns will occur and that it is possible to represent

Figure 8.1 Total Product, Average Product, and Marginal Product

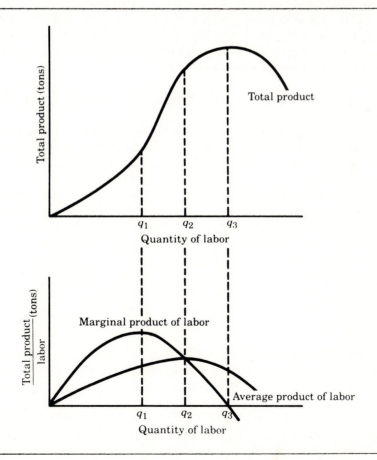

and compute the marginal product of any factor of production. We might, for example, hold the quantity of labor fixed and thus derive the marginal product curve for land.

The New and the Old

With this greater understanding of production relationships came the realization that the demand curve for factors of production could be derived from marginal product curves. Assume that a firm in a perfectly competitive industry uses only one variable factor of production, labor. The firm sells its final product in perfectly competitive markets; therefore the price of the final product does not change as the firm's sales vary. In other words, the firm faces a perfectly elastic demand curve for its final product. The firm buys the variable input in perfectly competitive markets, so the price of that input to the firm does not vary with the quantities purchased. In other words, the firm faces a perfectly elastic supply curve for the variable input. Optimally, the firm will hire the variable input up to the point where the last unit of input purchased adds as much to the total revenue of the firm as to its total cost. This condition can be stated as follows:

Price of Labor = (Marginal Physical Product of Labor) (Price of Output)

The left side of the equation measures the addition to total cost of hiring another unit of labor. The right side measures the addition to total revenue derived from the sale of the added product of labor. It is commonly referred to as the "value of the marginal product."

   Let us work through a simple arithmetical example. Given the data of Table 8.1, assume that the price of labor is $10,000 per man-year and the price of the final product is $1,000 per ton. If the firm in our example employs 5 units of labor, the equation for the optimum hiring of labor would give the following values:

$$P_L = MPP_L \cdot P_0$$
$$\$10,000 < 12 \cdot \$1,000$$
$$\$10,000 < \$12,000$$

The last unit of labor hired added $10,000 to total cost and $12,000 to total revenue; thus profits were increased by $2,000. The firm interested in maximizing profits would then increase its use of the variable input, labor. As it did, the marginal physical product of labor would decrease. The sixth unit of labor hired adds $10,000 to total costs and $10,000 to total revenue. The seventh unit of labor adds $10,000 to total cost but only $7,000 to total revenue. The optimum quantity of labor is thus 6 units, since the price of labor is then equal to the value of the marginal product of labor.

However, since most production processes involve several inputs, a more general rule for the optimum hiring of inputs is needed. Assume we have several inputs, A, B, C, ..., N. We represent their marginal physical products as MPP_A, MPP_B, MPP_C, ..., MPP_N, and their prices as P_A, P_B, P_C, ..., P_N. These inputs are being used in an optimum way when the following condition holds:

$$\frac{MPP_A}{P_A} = \frac{MPP_B}{P_B} = \frac{MPP_C}{P_C} = \cdots \frac{MPP_N}{P_N}$$

This equation states that inputs are optimally utilized when the last dollar spent in the purchase of each input yields the same marginal physical product. If this condition does not hold, it would be possible to alter the purchase of inputs and produce more final product with the same total costs, or, what is the same thing, to produce a given final output at lower total costs.

The demand for an input can now be easily derived. Demand for an input is defined as the quantities the firm would hire at various prices. Suppose we start with a firm that is hiring inputs optimally, that is, the ratios of marginal physical products to the prices of inputs are equal. If we were to lower the price of an input, the firm would use more of that input until the last dollar spent on the input would give the same marginal physical product as the last dollar spent for all other inputs. Marginal productivity theory also indicates that when firms in competitive markets are optimally hiring inputs, all inputs will receive a price equal to the value of their marginal products.

These new notions concerning marginal productivity are closely related to Ricardo's theory of land rent, as some of their originators recognized. In analyzing land rent, Ricardo reduced a three-input model to a two-input model by assuming that capital and labor are applied as if they were a single variable input to the fixed input, land, in proportions fixed by technology. To illustrate the affinity between the newly developed marginal productivity theory and Ricardo's theory of land rent, let us consider a model with only two inputs, labor and land. In such a model Ricardo would measure the rent of land in the way indicated in Figure 8.2.

In panel (a) of Figure 8.2 the quantity of land is assumed to be the fixed input, and the quantity of labor the variable input. The curve ABM represents the marginal physical product of labor. If a quantity of labor equal to $0C$ is used, total product is the area $0ABC$, the sum of the marginal products. Ricardo, however, did not focus on marginal products, although he assumed a diminishing marginal product; he focused on the determination of rent. He concluded that rent would be the area DAB. Each laborer receives a wage $0D = BC$, and the total wage bill is the area $0DBC$. Subtracting total wages from total product gives the residual DAB, which goes as rent to the fixed factor of production, land.

But suppose, now, that we hold the quantity of labor fixed and vary the quantity of land. This is done in panel (b) of Figure 8.2, with the curve FGN measuring the marginal physical product of land. The total product would be equal to the area $0FGH$, the same as the total product $0ABC$ produced in panel (a). Each unit of land would receive a rent $0I = HG$, and total rent would be $0IGH$. Wages are now measured as a residual accruing to the fixed factor, labor, and are equal to IFG.

One of the consequences of this new theory of marginal productivity was, thus, to reorient and generalize Ricardo's theory of rent. Ricardo had stressed not the marginal product of the variable input but the residual accruing to the fixed factor. The new theory, however, concentrated on the marginal product of the variable input. Whereas Ricardo applied marginal productivity analysis only to the determination of land rent, the new theorists recognized that any of the inputs could be varied and their marginal products computed. They saw, too, that the firm would hire inputs until their prices were equal to the value of the variable input's marginal product. These new ideas raised a number of issues that were much debated during this period.

Product Exhaustion

Ricardo's theory of distribution is a residual theory, in that rent is what remains after wages and profits have been deducted from total product,

Figure 8.2 Wages as Rent and Rent as Wages

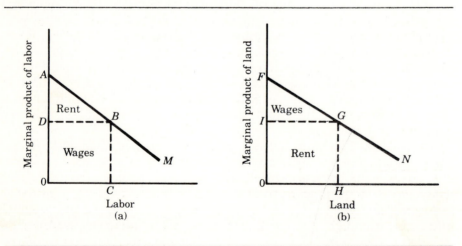

and profit is what remains after wages, determined by the Malthusian population doctrine, are deducted from wages and profits. (See Figure 4.3 and the accompanying explanation of Ricardo's procedure.) With a residual theory of distribution, there is obviously no question of whether the payments to the various factors of production are equal to the total product, since the method of determining the payments to the factors assures that the total product is distributed. Let us assume a simple economy with two inputs, labor and land. If we explain the distribution of income using Ricardian residual theory, our reasoning would be as follows: Panel (a) of Figure 8.2 shows that the total product in the economy is equal to $0ABC$, labor's share is equal to $0DBC$, and rent is the residual, or the difference between total product and total wage payments. Since rent is computed as a residual, wages plus rent must equal the total product.

A marginal productivity theory of distribution, however, does not reach this conclusion so obviously. If in competitive markets each factor receives the value of its marginal product, is there any reason to suppose that the sum of all these marginal products will be exactly equal to the total product?

The newly developed marginal productivity theory held that each factor would receive its marginal product. By referring to panel (a) of Figure 8.2, we concluded that the marginal physical product of labor is BC and that the total wage bill is quantity of labor used, $0C$, times the marginal product of labor, which yields the area $0DBC$. In panel (b) of Figure 8.2 the marginal physical product of land is GH and the total rent is the marginal product of land, GH, times the quantity of land $0H$, or the area $0IGH$. Will the sum of wages plus rent, if both are computed by the marginal product method, equal the total product? Will the area $0DBC$ (wages) plus the area $0IGH$ (rent) equal the area $0ABC$ (total product)? Another way of putting this question is: will wages computed by the marginal product ($0DBC$) equal wages computed by the residual method (IFG)? The same equation can be asked about rent: will $0IGH = DAB$? The proposition that payments to the factors of production will equal the total product can be stated in equation form.

$$Q = MPP_L \cdot L + MPP_T \cdot T$$

Here Q is the physical amount of output (total product), MPP_L and MPP_T are the marginal physical products of labor and land, and L and T are the quantities of labor and land.

J. B. Clark stated that paying each factor of production its marginal product would just exhaust the total product, but he offered no proof of this proposition. A controversy over this issue developed in the 1890s and continued into the twentieth century. The most important economists involved were Wicksteed, Wicksell, Barone, Edgeworth,

Pareto, and Walras.[1] We will confine our comments to Wicksteed and Wicksell, whose contributions significantly influenced the development of marginal productivity theory.

P. H. Wicksteed in 1894 published a small pamphlet entitled *Co-ordination of the Laws of Distribution* in which he argues that classical theory was deficient in requiring separate explanations of the payments to land, labor, and capital but that the marginal productivity theory was a better theory in that one unifying principle explains the return to any factor of production. Wicksteed concluded that in competitive markets each factor would have a price equal to the value of its marginal product, which, he recognized, raised the question of whether the total product will be exhausted if all factors receive their marginal products. He attempts to prove that this result, referred to as *product exhaustion*, will occur. Although Wicksteed failed in this attempt, he did point out that, for product exhaustion to take place, competition must exist and the production functions of firms must manifest certain properties. A. W. Flux in a review[2] of Wicksteed's *Co-ordination* also contributed to these developments. He demonstrated that product exhaustion would result only from production functions that had certain mathematical properties that have been previously examined by a Swiss mathematician, Leonhard Euler, whose name has consequently become associated with issues concerning product exhaustion.

When total product is exactly exhausted by payments to each factor for its marginal product, the production function must exhibit the property that a given proportionate increase in all inputs will increase output or total product by the same proportion. In our example, if the quantity of labor and land is doubled, then total output doubles; if both inputs are trebled, then output triples, and so forth. The mathematical term applied to these functions is that they are *homogeneous to the degree one*. These functions are also described as "linearly homogeneous," although this description may mislead the nonmathematician, since they are not necessarily linear. A production function homogeneous to a degree less than one produces a situation in which a proportionate increase in all inputs leads to a *less* than proportionate increase in output. If the production function is homogeneous to a degree greater than one, a proportionate increase in all inputs leads to a more than proportionate increase in output.

Let us examine the economic meaning of the properties of production functions. Economists use the term *returns to scale* to describe the way output or costs behave in response to proportionate increases in all

---

1. The acknowledged best summary of this issue is contained in George Stigler's *Production and Distribution Theories* (New York: Macmillan, 1941), chapter 12, "Euler's Theorem and the Marginal Productivity Theory."
2. A. W. Flux, *Economic Journal*, 4 (1894):

inputs. If all inputs are increased proportionately and total output increases by the same proportion, average costs do not change: this result is called *constant returns to scale*. Constant returns to scale are given by production functions homogeneous to the degree one. If all inputs are increased proportionately and total output increases by a smaller proportion, there are *decreasing returns to scale* and increasing average costs. Decreasing returns to scale are given by production functions homogeneous to a degree less than one.

A production function that gives constant returns to scale has a perfectly elastic (horizontal) average cost curve, and marginal cost equal to average cost. From the point of view of output, the average product curve is perfectly elastic, and marginal product equals average product. A firm selling its output and buying its inputs in perfectly competitive markets with a production function yielding constant returns to scale will find that, if all inputs are paid the value of their marginal product, the total revenues of the firm will be completely exhausted by these payments. Competition in the factor market will cause each input to receive the value of its marginal product, and competition in the final goods market will result in zero profits being earned by the firm. If zero profits are earned, then total revenue for the firm must equal total cost, and since total cost is the payments to the various inputs, product exhaustion has occurred.

A simple algebraic representation may clarify the problem. The issue as stated by Wicksteed and discussed during this period was whether paying each input its marginal product would exhaust the total output of a firm. We previously stated this in equation form for a simple labor-land production function.

$$Q = MPP_L \cdot L + MPP_T \cdot T$$

Multiplying by the price of the final good

$$PQ = P \cdot MPP_L \cdot L + P \cdot MPP_T \cdot T$$

Now $P \cdot MPP_L$ = value of the marginal product of labor (VMP_L), and $P \cdot MPP_T$ = value of the marginal product of land (VMP_T). Therefore,

$$PQ = VMP_L \cdot L + VMP_T \cdot T$$

The right side of the above equation shows the total payments to labor and the total payments to land. It therefore represents the total costs to the firm. The left side represents the total revenues of the firm. Under perfect competition all inputs receive the value of their marginal product and profits are zero, which means that total revenue of the firm will equal total cost. The payments to the factors of production, then, exhaust the total revenues of the firm.

A production function homogeneous to a degree greater than one gives *increasing returns to scale* and decreasing average costs. This means that marginal costs must be less than average costs and that the marginal physical product of an input will be greater than the average product of that input. If inputs are purchased in competitive markets, the firm must pay each input the value of its marginal product. But if all inputs receive the value of their marginal products, the total revenues of the firm will be less than the payments to all of the inputs. This result can be demonstrated by approaching the issue from either a cost or output point of view. If a firm experiencing decreasing average costs behaved competitively and sold its output at a price equal to marginal cost, it would operate at a loss; that is, total costs would exceed total revenues. Similarly, if the marginal physical products of inputs are greater than their average products, and if inputs receive payments equal to their marginal products, the payments to inputs will exceed total output, and the firm will operate at a loss.

A production function homogeneous to a degree less than one gives decreasing returns to scale, or increasing average costs. Here marginal costs are greater than average costs, and the marginal physical product of an input will be less than the average product of that input. A firm behaving competitively will equate marginal cost to price and at that output will earn profits. This implies that when all factors receive the value of their marginal product, the payments to inputs will be less than total output. Under these circumstances total revenues exceed total costs and the firm earns profits.

Wicksell on Product Exhaustion

Knut Wicksell, a Swedish economist who made a number of important contributions to both macro- and microeconomic theory, was an early independent discoverer of the marginal productivity theory. He became interested in questions relating to Euler's theorem and product exhaustion and contributed more than any other economist of his time to solving them. In his earlier writing on this subject he had thought, like most other economists, of a given firm or industry as displaying either increasing, constant, or decreasing returns to scale. These categories seemed to be mutually exclusive. In 1902 Wicksell reached a quite different conclusion, namely, that a given firm would pass through all three phases of returns to scale. A firm expanding output would first experience increasing returns to scale but would sooner or later encounter decreasing returns to scale. At the level of output where returns change from increasing to decreasing, constant returns to scale must occur. Wicksell was explicitly developing the now familiar concept of the long-run, U-shaped average cost curve for a firm, showing average costs decreasing, then reaching a minimum point, and finally increasing. Wicksell argued that it was not necessary that a firm's production function be homogeneous to the degree one for product exhaustion to occur. If firms are producing at the level of output that occurs at the minimum point of the long-run average cost curve and profits are zero, product exhaustion takes place. Wicksell reasoned that perfectly competitive markets will produce these results, since competition will result in each firm producing at minimum cost and making zero profits. Thus even though the production function of a firm would yield increasing, constant, and diminishing returns, competition will guarantee that in long-run equilibrium the firm is operating at the point on its production function where constant returns exist, where the function is homogeneous to the degree one, and where average costs are a minimum.

Knut Wicksell

Wicksell's solution to the problem of product exhaustion raised new and interesting theoretical issues, which economists pursued well into the twentieth century. Wicksell suggested some explanations for the shape of the long-run average cost curve, but these issues were not fully understood until the 1930s. Also left for later economists to grapple with was the problem of the compatibility of competition with constant returns to scale.

The Ethical Implications of Marginal Productivity Theory

John Bates Clark (1847–1938) independently discovered and developed the ideas of both marginal utility and marginal productivity. His development of marginal utility theory was not as penetrating as that of Jevons, Walras, or Menger, but his contributions to the marginal

J. B. Clark

productivity theory of distribution equaled those of the second generation of British and European economists. Clark acknowledges that his development of marginal productivity theory was in response to issues raised by the American social critic Henry George.[3] We saw in Chapter 4 that Henry George had concluded that the return to land was an unearned income, and thus he had questioned the social legitimacy of rent. These assertions of George led Clark to attempt to identify the product resulting from individual factors of production and thus to marginal productivity theory. J. B. Clark's son, J. M. Clark, also became an important economist, and in an article summarizing his father's contributions to economic theory and the intellectual and social forces that influenced the content of his father's ideas, the younger Clark holds that J. B. Clark's ethical statements on marginal productivity "are oriented at Marx, and are best construed as an earnest, and not meticulously qualified, rebuttal of Marxian exploitation theory."[4] J. B. Clark's development of marginal productivity theory, therefore, would appear to be explicable as a reaction to the economic ideas of Henry George and Karl Marx.

An interest in ethical issues is clearly manifest in Clark's early writings, which were not as theoretically oriented as his contributions to marginal productivity theory. Yet his *Distribution of Wealth*, which contains the essence of his marginal productivity theory of distribution, also contains an extensive development of the desirable ethical results that flow from competitive markets. It is not necessary to develop Clark's contributions to marginal productivity theory in detail. The relevant point here is his conclusion that, under perfectly competitive markets, each factor of production would receive a return equal to the value of its marginal product. This return measures the contribution of a factor both to the particular product being produced and to society. The return to capital is justified by the fact that capital is productive: the return is not robbery, but honest, fair, and just. The return to land is, likewise, not an unearned income, but a return to the productivity of land. So also for the return to labor. Clark's conclusion is that the distribution of income that results from perfectly competitive markets is an ethically correct distribution in that it rewards the factors of production according to their economic contributions to the social product. Theories of exploitation and unearned incomes are naive, he contends, because they fail to understand the working of market forces in an economy.

3. J. B. Clark, *The Distribution of Wealth* (1899) (New York: Kelley and Millman, 1956), pp. viii, 84-85.
4. J. M. Clark, "J. M. Clark on J. B. Clark," in *The Development of Economic Thought*, ed. H. W. Spiegel (New York: Wiley, 1952), p. 610.

J. B. Clark's contributions to marginal analysis, particularly to marginal productivity theory, have gained him worldwide recognition. It is fair to say that he was the first American economist to make important contributions to economic theory. Yet the ethical conclusions he drew from marginal productivity theory have attracted more critical attention than his contributions to positive theory. There may be some justice in this, in that Clark regarded his ethical conclusions as his most important contributions.

But how much merit is there in his argument that competitive markets result in an ethically desirable distribution of income? Subsequent economic theory has taken issue with Clark's ethical conclusions. The most important problem is its violation of Hume's Dictum: it draws an ethical implication from a nonethical analysis. What a person "should" earn may have little relation to what he or she does earn. Numerous other problems have been pointed out. For example, even given the assumption of perfectly competitive markets, there are no grounds for concluding that because each *factor* receives the value of its marginal product, each *individual* receives a return that measures his or her contribution to the economy and society. An individual's income will depend on the price of the factors he or she sells in the market and the quantity of factors sold. The only factor most individuals sell in the market is labor, so their income will be a function of the price of their labor and the number of hours worked. Individuals owning capital and land will receive incomes from these sources, but these payments represent the contribution of the factors, not the individuals. Another conspicuous flaw in Clark's ethical conclusions is that he fails to consider inheritance and the incomes that individuals receive from inherited property. Even the most precocious of children cannot choose their parents. Although it is a reasonable conclusion that capital is productive and that under perfect competition capital would receive a return equal to the value of its marginal product, it is not reasonable to suppose that this measures the contribution to society of the individual who inherited that capital. This failure of Clark's ethical conclusions is particularly devastating in view of the degree to which inequality in the personal distribution of income is accounted for by the receipt of property incomes.

Even if there were no inherited property, Clark's ethical conclusions would not be justified. Within the broad classifications of wage and salary income, there is no reason to conclude that the income of an individual is a measure of his or her contribution to the economy and society. The price of labor reflects demand and supply in the market place, but behind demand and supply are a multitude of historical and sociological factors that significantly affect the wage income of a particular individual. There is a strong correlation, for example, between an individual's income receipts for labor services and the level of that individual's educational achievement. And whereas it is certainly true that educational achievement is closely related to individual ability, it is also true that it depends in part upon environmental factors over which the individual has little control. Poverty tends to breed poverty, partly because the children of the poor do not have the same educational opportunities as the children of the rich. Although even those in lower income groups are able to complete twelve years of schooling without being forced into the market because of the low income of their parents, many are not able to pursue college education for economic reasons. A college education can be regarded as an investment in human capital that increases the value of the marginal product of the recipient. A market-oriented, private-property, free-enterprise society makes these investments in human capital largely on the basis of the economic ability of the parent, not on the ability of the student.

Another reason Clark's ethical conclusions are not valid even within the labor sector of the market is the vast amount of discrimination that occurs in present society. It is widely recognized that employers discriminate on the basis of sex, race, creed, and color and thus influence the distribution of income. Individuals frequently perform the same jobs with the same ability but receive different incomes because of race or sex. Furthermore, discrimination has prevented entry into certain occupations, usually those with higher pay. The predominance of blacks and women in lower-paying jobs in industry clearly reflects discrimination rather than lower marginal productivity on the part of those groups. A final difficulty with Clark's ethical conclusions is their reliance on perfectly competitive markets. Clark was aware of monopoly power in both firms and labor unions and tried to deal with its influence on the distribution of income and on his ethical conclusions. His particularly optimistic viewpoint led him to regard these deviations from competitive markets as quantitatively unimportant. It is curious that one of his most brilliant undergraduate students, Thorstein Veblen, was to view the same economy and society as J. B. Clark and come to quite a different conclusion about their ethical outcome.

Marginal Productivity as a Theory of Employment

Although marginal productivity analysis was originally developed to explain the forces determining the prices of factors of production and the distribution of income, it was soon believed that the theory could also be applied to the forces determining the level of employment. In a partial equilibrium analytical framework, if the price of labor is increased, a firm will hire less labor until the value of the marginal product of labor is equal to the higher price of labor. Hiring less labor will result in an increase in the marginal physical product of labor and thus in the value of the marginal product of labor. At the industry level the price of labor will depend upon the demand for labor, which is derived from the value of the marginal product of labor and the supply of labor. If the price of labor in an industry is above an equilibrium level, the quantity of labor supplied will exceed the quantity of labor demanded — there will be a surplus of labor, or unemployment.

When marginal productivity analysts extended this theory to the whole economy, they concluded that unemployment exceeding frictional unemployment of three percent was caused by prevailing wages being higher than at equilibrium. An excess supply of labor like that of any other commodity, is explained by supply-and-demand analysis. Give the analysis and flexible wage rates, a market system will automatically correct this unemployment as wages fall. Unemployment is a manifestation of disequilibrium in labor markets; when labor markets return to equilibrium, this unemployment will be eliminated. On the basis of this application of marginal productivity theory to the economy, a number of policy conclusions have been drawn at various times: that wages should be kept flexible and that any impediments to flexible wages, such as union contracts or minimum-wage legislation, are undesirable; that unions and minimum-wage legislation could cause unemployment; that if a depression produced unemployment, institutional factors that render wages inflexible could prevent the market from automatically removing the unemployment by lowering wages.

The macro policy conclusion drawn from marginal productivity theory was that depressions and unemployment could be eliminated by permitting wages to fall. Although some economists were reluctant on social grounds to advocate lowering wages to remove unemployment and depressions, there is little doubt that orthodox theory came to these conclusions. In discussing this issue Alvin Hansen cites A. C. Pigou's writings of the 1920s, which described the above relationship between employment and wages. Hansen says that although he cites "Pigou as the most eminent (and withal one of the most socially minded) representative of thinking generally current among economists in the twenties; innumerable references from a host of economists (including paragraphs from my own earlier writings) could easily be added by anyone who will take the trouble to do so."[5] These views, which flowed from marginal productivity theory, continued to be held by orthodox theorists until they were seriously criticized by J. M. Keynes in the mid-1930s. The Nobel Prize-winning economist J. R. Hicks, in his *Theory of Wages*, published in 1932, devoted two chapters to a discussion of wage regulation and unemployment. Hicks concluded that wages artificially set above competitive equilibrium wages either

5. Alvin H. Hansen, *Business Cycles and National Income* (New York: Norton, 1951), p. 518, fn. 6.

by union pressure or legislation would result in unemployment and "the unemployment must go on until the artificial wages are relaxed, or until competitive wages have risen to the artificial level."[6]

Marginal productivity theory coupled with the strong laissez faire market orientation of American economists led them to suggest that the best policy to alleviate the depression in the early 1930s was to keep the government out of the economy and let the market work to lower wages. Let us examine briefly Keynes's major criticism of marginal productivity theory as a theory of employment. The theory states that wages will equal the value of the marginal product of labor in competitive markets. The value of the marginal product of labor is the marginal physical product of labor multiplied by the price of the final good. Keynes pointed out that, while wages are a cost from the viewpoint of the firm, they are income from the viewpoint of the worker. Thus, whereas a cut in wage rates would lower costs for firms, it would also lower the income of labor. When labor incomes began to fall, the demand for and the price of final goods would fall, too. And this decrease in the price of final goods would result in a fall in the value of the marginal product of labor. The difficulty with the marginal productivity theory as a theory of employment is that it assumes that lowering wages will not lower the demand for final goods; in other words, that aggregate supply and aggregate demand are not interconnected. The theory concentrates on the cost side of wage reductions and ignores what Keynes called aggregate demand.

Marginal Productivity Theory Criticized

Almost from the time of its first formulation, marginal productivity theory was criticized, and some of this criticism has continued to the present. The early criticism included broad attacks on the general theory of marginal productivity, whether it was applied to labor, capital, or land, and specific discussions of the special problems arising when the theory was applied to the determination of profits and interest. We will discuss these special problems in the next section and look now at the most significant early criticism of marginal productivity theory, namely, that it is impossible to measure the marginal product of a factor of production.

The final output of a firm, industry, or the economy is the result of a joint effort of labor, land, and capital, and it is impossible, said the critics, to separate out the marginal products of the contributing factors. F. W. Taussig (1859-1940), a commanding figure in the early development of Harvard's economics department, held in his influential

6. J. R. Hicks, *The Theory of Wages* (London: Macmillan, 1932), p. 181.

Principles of Economics that in a process using capital and labor "there is no separate product of the tool on the one hand and of the labor using the tool on the other....We can disengage no concretely separable product of labor and capital."[7] A more popular version of this criticism is contained in George Bernard Shaw's delightful *Intelligent Woman's Guide to Socialism.* Shaw holds that whereas it might be desirable to reward labor by giving to each what he or she produces, this is impossible: "When a farmer and his laborers sow and reap a field of wheat nobody on earth can say how much of the wheat each of them has grown."[8] Suppose, for another example, that a house is being constructed by carpenters (labor) using hammers (capital). If another carpenter is added, what is his marginal physical product? In any production process the addition of labor will usually require the simultaneous addition of capital, thus creating a difficulty in separating the marginal product of the added labor from that of the added capital. Marshall's solution to this problem would be to measure the net product of labor by deducting the cost of the capital from the value of the marginal product of the additional labor and capital. J.B. Clark offered another solution, suggesting that the amount of capital be held constant but that its form be allowed to vary. Since the form of capital could only vary over time, though, Clark's solution suggests a longer-run view of the problem of computing marginal products.

PROFITS AND INTEREST

So far we have discussed only the general development of marginal productivity theory without distinguishing among its applications to various factors of production. Although labor and land have served as examples to indicate that the return to a factor can be conceived in terms of a marginal product, or a residual, we have not considered the various factors individually to discover the problems involved in analyzing the return to each one. Some of the early developers of marginal productivity theory, particularly Eugen Böhm-Bawerk (1851–1914), realized that although marginal productivity analysis was a satisfactory explanation of the return to labor and land, it failed to explain the returns called profits and interest. In retrospect, we can see that the problems associated with explaining the nature and amount of profits and interest had not even manifested themselves prior to the development of marginal productivity analysis.

7. F. W. Taussig, *Principles of Economics*, 3rd ed. (New York: Macmillan, 1924), II, 213-214.
8. G. B. Shaw, *The Intelligent Woman's Guide to Socialism and Capitalism* (New York: Brentano's, 1928), p. 21.

Classical economic theory had, for the most part, made a three-part division of the factors of production into labor, land, and capital. The return to labor is wages, to land rents, and to capital profits. The term *profits*, as used by classical economists, includes what is today called profits and interest. Even those classical writers who developed theories of interest called their theories "profit theories." This failure to distinguish between profits and interest as returns is understandable, since the typical firm of the times combined the roles of the capitalist and the entrepreneur. The supplier of capital funds and the manager were one and the same, and thus no distinction was made between profits and interest. One of the accomplishments of the period we are studying was a recognition of the need to distinguish between the two.

Can we use marginal productivity theory to explain not only the wages of labor, the rent of land, and the interest on capital, but also the profits which flow to entrepreneurs? The writers of the time realized that, whereas marginal productivity theory could satisfactorily explain wages and rents, the problems peculiar to profits and interest required more sophisticated theories.

Profit Theory

Although the classical economists had applied the term *profits* indiscriminately to all the income of the capitalist-entrepreneur, they did recognize that this income was a payment containing at least three distinct elements: a payment for the use of capital, a payment to the entrepreneur for management services rendered, and a payment that compensated for the risks of business activity. Payments to the firm for the use of capital, assuming this payment involves no risk, fall under the modern classification of interest, which is covered in the next section. Can we call entrepreneurship a fourth factor of production, defining the marginal product of the entrepreneur as the measure of his contribution to the firm for management services and assumption of risk? J. B. Clark was the most important early developer of marginal productivity theory to recognize that this solution is not satisfactory. The return to the entrepreneur as a manager is not profit, but a wage. Profit, or to be more exact *pure profit*, must be defined as a residual remaining after all the inputs used by a firm are paid a price equal to their opportunity cost. Perfectly competitive markets in long-run equilibrium result in all factors receiving the value of their marginal product, which is also equal to their opportunity cost. Assuming a homogeneous production function, these payments are costs of the firm and when subtracted from total revenues yield a zero rate of profit. The existence of profit must then be explained as a consequence either of competitive markets not being in long-run equilibrium or of actual markets not being perfectly competitive.

Long-run competitive equilibrium is, of course, a theoretical construct to which no market ever conforms. Let us keep the competitive assumption, however, while analyzing the emergence of profit in a market or an economy not in long-run equilibrium. When businesses buy inputs to produce an output, they assume risks. The final price of the output must be estimated, and the price of and payments to the inputs become contractual obligations. If the total revenues of the firm exceed the payments to the inputs, profits accrue; if revenues are less than payments, losses occur. Profits in perfectly competitive markets might, then, be explained as the result of disequilibrium occurring while the economy moves to a new position of long-run equilibrium.

An explanation of profits as temporary income resulting from dynamic changes in the economy was suggested by J. B. Clark, Alfred Marshall, and J. A. Schumpeter. Assume that an economy is in long-run equilibrium with all factors receiving a return equal to their opportunity cost and that the revenues of a typical firm are equal to its costs. A change in preferences of consumers or a change in technology will lead to profits in some industries. These profits will be eliminated, however, by competitive forces as capital moves to those markets having above-normal rates of return. Profit is thus not a return to a factor of production but a windfall associated with dynamic elements in an economy.

F. H. Knight (1885-1972) significantly integrated and extended prior theories of profit by combining in one theory the factors of risk, managerial ability, and economic change. In his *Risk, Uncertainty, and Profit*[9] Knight distinguishes between risks businesses take that can be insured against and those for which no insurance is available. A firm, for example, may lose its plant through fire, but actuarial knowledge permits this risk to be covered by insurance. The insurance premium becomes a part of the firm's costs. This kind of risk is therefore not a source of profit. Profits arise because there are uncertainties in the market that are not insurable, arising from dynamic changes in the market. However, if we drop the assumption of perfect competition, profits may arise for a number of reasons, the most important being monopoly or monopsony power.

Capital and Interest Theory

With the development of marginal productivity theory, economists began to distinguish more carefully between profits and interest. This has permitted the development of a generally accepted theory of profit; however, capital and interest theory has remained controversial

9. F. H. Knight, *Risk, Uncertainty, and Profit* (Boston: Houghton Mifflin, 1921).

to the present day. Robert M. Solow wrote that "when a theoretical question remains debatable after 80 years there is a presumption that the question is badly posed — or very deep indeed."[10] C. E. Ferguson has suggested several reasons for the unsettled nature of capital theory.

> Everyone knows, or has strongly suspected, that capital theory is difficult. There is a superficial reason for this in that so much of the literature of capital theory has been mired in polemics and semantics. There is a more fundamental reason, however. Capital theory necessarily involves time; and time involves expectations and uncertainty, although we generally abstract from them by assuming a stationary state or a golden-age growth path.[11]

We shall first survey the development of the theory of capital and interest since 1890. One set of writers, including Schumpeter, Fisher, and Knight, made a broad philosophical inquiry into the nature of capital and the reasons for the existence of interest. Another set of writers, touching only superficially on the reasons for the existence of interest, concentrated their efforts on explaining the economic forces determining the rate of interest. Theories of the forces determining the rate of interest can be classified as nonmonetary, monetary, and neo-Keynesian, the last being a synthesis of the other two approaches in a model first suggested by J. R. Hicks. The nonmonetary theories of interest concentrate on long-run real forces that fix the rate of interest and are therefore in the classical tradition. Nonmonetary theories persisted from the end of the mercantilist period until the 1930s. Monetary theories of the rate of interest include the loanable funds theory and the liquidity preference theory, which will be examined along with the Hicks synthesis of nonmonetary and monetary theories in Chapter 11. The three most important writers on interest theory from 1890 to the 1930s were Böhm-Bawerk, Knight, and Fisher, whose theories we shall examine in this chapter.

The mercantilists emphasized the role of money in the economy and consequently developed monetary theories of interest. They maintained that increases in the quantity of money would not only raise the general level of prices and lower the value of money, but also lower the general level of interest rates. Some writers on interest theory during the latter part of the mercantilist era developed more penetrating analyses. Richard Cantillon, although he presented a nonmonetary theory of interest, also pointed out that increases in the quantity of

10. Robert M. Solow, *Capital Theory and the Rate of Return* (Amsterdam: North-Holland, 1963), p. 10.
11. C. E. Ferguson, "The Current State of Capital Theory: A Tale of Two Paradigms," *Southern Economic Journal*, 39 (October 1972), 173.

money could lead to either an increase or decrease in interest rates. If the increase in the money supply went first to savers, the interest rate would fall. But if it went to spenders, the interest rate would rise, since the increased spending would cause increased investments by businessmen and a consequent increase in the demand for loanable funds.

Classical theory, with its focus on the long-run real forces that determine the wealth of nations, developed nonmonetary, or real, theories of interest. The classical economists held that the rate of interest depends on the rate of return on investment spending. Monetary forces may in the short run alter the rate of interest, but in the long run it is the productivity of capital, a real force, that fixes interest rates. Ricardo put it most succinctly when he said that the interest rate depends on

> the rate of profits which can be made by the employment of capital, and which is totally independent of the quantity, or of the value of money. Whether a Bank lent one million, ten millions, or a hundred millions, they would not permanently alter the market rate of interest, they would alter only the value of the money they had thus issued.[12]

We could quote other passages from Ricardo indicating that he did recognize that the rate of interest is not "totally independent" of the quantity of money. The point is that the classical economists' focus on long-run forces in the economy led them to deemphasize monetary forces, since these had only short-run influences on the rate of interest and could not change the productivity of capital, which was the real force fixing interest rates in the long run. In broad perspective there were some 250 years, from 1500 to 1750, when monetary theories of interest were in vogue; then 180 years, from 1750 to 1930, when nonmonetary theories were advanced by the orthodox theorists. Two new monetary theories of interest emerged during the 1930s, the liquidity preference and loanable funds theories, and with them came a realization that a theory of interest developed in a general equilibrium framework must include both monetary and real forces.

The Problem of Interest

The development of economic theory shows that a new theory that answers an old question often raises new questions. We have already seen that the development of marginal productivity analysis shattered

12. Ricardo, *Principles*, pp. 363–364.

the old classical theory of distribution. The classical theory had divided the population into workers, capitalists, and landlords, and explained the payments to these factors as wages, profits, and rents. Because the classical theory of distribution was a residual theory, the problem of product exhaustion — determining whether the payments to the factors equaled the amount of the total product — was not a theoretical issue. It was the marginal productivity theory that first raised this new issue. We have seen that the marginalists concluded that, given perfectly competitive markets, the sum of the value of the marginal products would equal the total product in long-run equilibrium. They didn't worry that this conclusion required linear homogeneous production functions. If that assumption was needed, they would simply assume it. The concept of product exhaustion raised new and complex issues that concern interest and capital. We turn now to an explanation of these issues, which we will call collectively the problem of interest, before examining the answers offered by subsequent theorists.

Under long-run equilibrium in perfectly competitive markets, all the revenues from the sale of final products will be received by the factors of production. This conclusion of marginal productivity theory raised the following question: how are we to explain the return to capital called interest? Capital is a produced good made with labor and land previously applied, whereas labor and land are original factors of production. The marginal productivity theory holds that the return to capital must exactly equal the value of the labor and land used to create the capital. If this is true, why does capital receive a further return in the form of interest? To put this another way: why is the payment to capital more than is necessary to pay for the labor and land used to produce capital? Capital appears to be unique among the factors of production in creating a surplus value that flows to its owner in perpetuity. An obvious answer would be that capital is productive, and that this accounts for the existence of interest. This answer, however, is not satisfactory. Capital is productive in that labor and land used with capital produce a greater output. The marginal productivity theory holds, however, that the productivity of capital results in a higher return to the labor and land used to produce the capital, which means that there could be no net return to capital. The return to capital in long-run equilibrium must be exactly equal to the cost of producing the capital, yet in the real world we observe that interest income is constantly flowing to the owner of capital. The issue is complicated still further by the fact that present capital is the product of past labor, land, and capital. The marginal productivity theory holds that the market will impute the value of the productivity of present capital to the factors of production used to produce it. If we go back through the production process using this procedure, we will be left with only the original factors of production, labor and land. To clarify this problem of interest, let us examine another factor of production, labor. Labor is productive, but the flow of income to labor, or wages, measures and is equal to its productivity. There is no net return to labor as there appears to be to capital. The problem of interest was recognized by Böhm-Bawerk but given its most lucid exposition by Schumpeter in Chapter 5 of his *Theory of Economic Development*, first published in German in 1911.

How can we explain the source, the basis, and the persistence of interest? In the course of examining some of the issues concerning profits, we found that, in long-run equilibrium, profits disappear and become zero. Interest, however, is observed to persist even in long-run equilibrium. Schumpeter not only succinctly posed the problem of interest but also suggested a framework to examine possible answers. Three possible solutions to the problem of interest exist. One solution is that there are not two but three original factors of production and that interest is a return to this third factor. A second possible solution is that marginal productivity theory is incorrect in holding that, in long-run competitive equilibrium, revenues from the sale of final goods will exactly equal the flow of payments to the factors of production. A third solution is that marginal productivity theory is a theory of competitive, static markets; since the real economy is neither competitive nor static, noncompetitive or dynamic elements in the economy can produce a positive rate of interest. So much for the problem of interest. Let us now examine some of the solutions offered during the period 1890 to 1930.

Böhm-Bawerk's Theory of Interest

Early in his career, Eugen Böhm-Bawerk, a follower of Menger and Wieser, was drawn to the problem of capital and interest theory. There were two reasons for this. First, he recognized the existence of the problem of interest and understood the theoretical issues involved. Second, like Menger and the conservative Austrian economists in general, Böhm-Bawerk was disturbed by the Marxist-socialist attacks that condemned profits and interest as forms of capitalistic exploitation. Menger manifested these same concerns in his *Principles*.

> One of the strangest questions ever made the subject of scientific debate is whether rent and interest are justified from an ethical point of view or whether they are "immoral."...But it seems to me that the question of the legal or moral character of these facts is beyond the sphere of our science.[13]

13. Menger, *Principles*, p. 173.

Böhm-Bawerk's *Capital and Interest, A Critical History of Economical Theory*, published in German in 1884, critically evaluated previous theories of interest. He was unmerciful in his criticism of these earlier theories and voiced particularly strong views about the exploitation theory of the socialists which, he said,

> is not only incorrect, but in theoretical value, even takes one of the lowest places among the representatives of some of the other theories, I scarcely think that anywhere else are to be found together so great a number of the worst fallacies — wanton, unproved assumption, self-contradiction, and blindness to facts.[14]

In 1888 Böhm-Bawerk offered his own ideas on capital and interest theory in *The Positive Theory of Capital*: "Present goods are, as a rule, worth more than future goods of a like kind and number. This proposition is the kernel and center of the interest theory which I have to present."[15] Given the existence of a positive rate of interest, the statement is clearly correct. Under these circumstances an individual would prefer $1 today as against $1 a year from now, since the $1 received today could be lent and thus be worth more in the future. Böhm-Bawerk's statement, however, does not immediately explain the reason for the existence of interest, although it suggests that the fundamental reason for the existence of interest is that present goods are worth more than an equal amount of future goods.

Böhm-Bawerk's examination of previous theories of interest in *Capital and Interest* led him to the conclusion that no one had yet explained the causes of interest. He maintained that the causes of interest are to be found not in the institutional structure of the society but in technological and economic considerations that are independent of social forms. In particular, he wanted to establish that the exploitation theories of interest advanced by Marx and other socialists were incorrect and that the phenomenon of interest would exist even in a socialist society, since even in such a society present goods would be worth more than an equal amount of future goods.

Böhm-Bawerk offers three reasons for the higher value of present goods. He says, "The first great cause of difference in value between present and future goods consists in the different circumstances of want and provision in the present and future."[16] In support of this first reason, he gives the following argument. Since the value of goods

14. Eugen Böhm-Bawerk, *Capital and Interest*, trans. William Smart (New York: Brentano's, 1922), pp. 390–391.
15. Eugen Böhm-Bawerk, *The Positive Theory of Capital*, trans. William Smart (London: Macmillan, 1891), p. 237.
16. *Ibid.*, p. 249.

depends upon marginal utility, and since marginal utility decreases as the quantity of goods increases, present goods are worth more than future goods for individuals who expect a larger flow of income and goods in the future. Such individuals might include those who are urgently in need of present goods because of illness, a loss from bad harvests or fire, and so forth. But the problem with these examples, which Böhm-Bawerk recognized and attempted to solve, is that many individuals might equally well prefer future to present goods because of "different circumstances of want and provision in the present and future." Many wage earners expect their income flow to be less in the future than at present and would therefore find the marginal utility of present income to be less than that of future income. Böhm-Bawerk attempts to meet this difficulty by suggesting that these individuals who expect declining income will hold money, since it is durable and nearly costless to store. If they hold money and do not spend their higher present income on goods, the marginal utility of present goods is not less than that of future goods.

The examples Böhm-Bawerk used to illustrate his first reason for the existence of interest led him into some interesting implications and contradictions of which he was not aware. If individuals want to use money as a store of value in order to transfer purchases of goods from the present to the future, then a demand for money exists that is separate from its use as a medium of exchange. This proposition contradicts the orthodox view persisting from Smith to Keynes that money was only a medium of exchange. We might conclude from Böhm-Bawerk's discussion of these issues that an economy composed largely of wage earners who expect declining future incomes and therefore prefer future to present goods would have a positive rate of interest because of the demand for money and the scarcity of its supply.

The second reason for placing a higher value on present goods is that "we systematically underestimate future wants, and the goods which are to satisfy them."[17] Böhm-Bawerk supports this statement by noting a general lack of imagination and willpower in individuals, as well as an uncertainty regarding the length of life. This second reason threatens the entire theoretical structure of orthodox economic theory. Either man is rational and calculating or he is not. Economic theory cannot assume the existence of an economic man for some purposes and disclaim it for others. Böhm-Bawerk implicitly recognizes this difficulty by choosing the activities of savages and children to illustrate the underestimation of future wants: "How many an Indian tribe, with careless greed, has sold the land of its fathers, the source of its maintenance, to the palefaces for a couple of casks of 'firewater'"![18] This is certainly a

17. *Ibid.*, p. 253.
18. *Ibid.*

curious view of American history and does not support the existence of interest. Uncertainty about the length of life is also not a strong argument for the preference of present over future goods, as few individuals would plan to consume all of their savings before death.

Böhm-Bawerk is thus arguing that for psychological reasons individuals will prefer present to future goods. Present goods command a premium, or agio, over future goods that can be measured by the interest rate individuals are willing to pay for funds that permit them to buy present goods. Observe that these first two arguments apply only to the market for consumer loans.

Böhm-Bawerk's third explanation for the existence of interest, however, deals with the market for producer loans. It states that interest exists because of the technical superiority of present goods over future goods. Böhm-Bawerk's explanation is not completely clear, and J. B. Clark and Irving Fisher were quick to point out difficulties.

In his criticisms of previous theories of interest, Böhm-Bawerk had rejected the idea that interest is a payment for the productivity of capital. He acknowledges that capital is productive but perceives that the marginal productivity theory of distribution, which holds that the higher productivity of capital would result in a higher payment to the factors of production used to produce capital, precludes the possibility of a net return to capital because of its productivity. The assertion that present goods are technically superior to future goods is an attempt to explain why capital goods earn interest. To understand what Böhm-Bawerk means by the technical superiority of present goods, we must examine his notion of the roundabout method of production.

According to Böhm-Bawerk two methods can be used to produce final goods: a direct method and a roundabout, or capitalistic, method. The direct method involves no capital goods; an example would be catching fish by hand. The roundabout method is capitalistic in that it uses capital goods and requires time. Our fisherman could spend time to make a net and then fish. The time for the production process could be further lengthened if he built a boat and made a net. The direct method takes less time, but it is less productive than a roundabout method. The roundabout method is more productive, but it requires more time. Böhm-Bawerk then asserts that the law of diminishing returns applies to roundabout production processes.

> On the whole it may be said that not only are the first steps more productive, but that every lengthening of the roundabout process is accompanied by a further increase in the technical result; as the process, however, is lengthened the amount of the product, as a rule, increases in a smaller proportion.

> This proposition is based on experience, and only on experience.[19]

19. *Ibid.*, p. 84.

He illustrates the correspondence of diminishing returns to the length of the production process with the data given in Table 8.2.[20] A unit of labor in a production process requiring one year will yield 100 units of final product. If the production process is lengthened, by making a net, the yield of final product that emerges at the end of two years is 200 units, but as the production process is lengthened and the roundaboutness increases, the flow of final product increases at a decreasing rate. The technical superiority of present over future goods is disclosed by examining columns 2 and 3 of the table. A unit of labor applied today will yield 280 units of final product three years from the present, but if that unit of labor is not applied until next year, the yield of final product three years from the present is only 200 units.

Böhm-Bawerk's concept of the technical superiority of present over future goods raised a number of issues that were extensively discussed in the literature of the time, particularly in his controversies with J. B. Clark and Irving Fisher. These issues were reexamined as late as the 1930s in a controversy involving F. H. Knight and Nicholas Kaldor. A number of the minor issues related to this topic are discussed in the suggested readings for this chapter.

Böhm-Bawerk held that this third reason for the existence of interest was independent from his first two reasons. But Irving Fisher argued correctly that the greater productivity of roundabout methods would not result in a positive rate of interest in the absence of Böhm-Bawerk's first two reasons. The first two reasons stated in essence that for psychological reasons individuals prefer present over future goods. Let us suppose that individuals do not prefer present over future goods and examine the third reason by itself. Given his assumption that capital is productive and that lengthening the productive process will increase the flow of final goods, in the absence of a time preference, a society would want to maximize the quantity of final goods emerging from the pro-

Table 8.2 Roundaboutness and Diminishing Returns

Years from Present to Final Product	Units of Product for Labor Applied	
	This Year	Next Year
1	100	—
2	200	100
3	280	200
4	350	280
5	400	350

20. *Ibid.*, p. 262.

ductive process, regardless of the date of their emergence. If society were indifferent to the time at which it consumed final goods, the technical superiority of present goods would not result in individuals being willing to pay interest to consume goods today rather than in the future. Böhm-Bawerk formulated all the necessary elements for a consistent theory of interest but incorrectly concluded that the productivity of capital separate and apart from time preference would result in a positive rate of interest. Irving Fisher took Böhm-Bawerk's seminal but confused notions, discarded some of the nonessential elements, and articulated the essential points of the currently accepted theory of interest.

Fisher on Interest

Although Irving Fisher adopted many of the basic concepts of Böhm-Bawerk's theory of interest, his approach represents a distinct break

Irving Fisher

with Böhm-Bawerk. Classical theory had proceeded on the basis that reasonably sharp distinctions could be made between the various factors of production and that the returns to these factors could be distinguished as wages, rent, interest, and profits. Böhm-Bawerk continued in this tradition; his discussion of interest theory is therefore predicated on the belief that the return to capital is interest and that a special theory is needed to explain interest as contrasted to wages and rent. Fisher presented his views first in his 1907 work, *The Theory of the Rate of Interest*, and later in a considerably revised and polished version called *The Theory of Interest*, published in 1930.

Fisher objected to the prevailing manner of classifying incomes into wages, rent, profits, and interest. He saw interest not as a share of income received by capital but as a manner of examining income flows of every kind. All productive agents yield flows of income over time. If these flows of income are discounted at the current rate of interest, their capitalized value is obtained. An owner of a productive agent computes the interest return on that agent by comparing its capitalized value with the flow of income. Some examples will clarify Fisher's viewpoint. Land is said to receive a return called rent, yet if we compare the flow of income called rent to the capitalized value of the land, the return is interest. As Fisher said, "Rent and interest are merely two ways of measuring the same income."[21] Frank Knight agreed with this perspective on interest theory and expounded on it throughout his writings on the subject. Knight claimed that "only historical accident or 'psychology' can explain the fact that 'interest' and 'rent' have been viewed as coming from different sources, specifically natural agents and capital goods."[22] The return to labor that has historically been called wages can also be looked upon as interest. An investment in vocational training will increase a worker's future income flow. Thus the productive agent that is usually called labor can be viewed as capital, with interest being the rate at which the income stream must be discounted to equate it to the cost of training. From this perspective Fisher concluded that "interest is not a part, but the whole, of income."[23]

Fisher discards Böhm-Bawerk's classification of factors and his entire concept of the period of production contending that interest is produced by individuals adjusting their income flows in the market place. The rate of interest measures the price individuals will pay to receive income now rather than in the future. The owner of any productive

21. Irving Fisher, *The Theory of Interest* (1930) (New York: Kelley and Millman, 1954), p. 331.
22. Frank Knight, "Capital and Interest," in *Readings in the Theory of Income Distribution* (Philadelphia: Blakiston, 1949), pp. 391–392.
23. Fisher, *Theory*, p. 332.

agent always has the options to alter the flow of income. Present consumption expenditures may be reduced in order to buy or build machinery that will increase future income flows or to invest in the training required for a future high-paying job.

Two kinds of forces will determine interest rates in a market economy: subjective forces reflecting the preferences of individuals for present over future goods or income, and objective forces depending upon the available investment opportunities and the productivity of the factors used to produce final goods. Individuals can change their income flows by borrowing, lending, investing, or disinvesting. Their actions will depend upon their time preferences, the rates of return available on different investments, and the rate of interest in the market. Böhm-Bawerk had believed that the productivity of capital alone, what he called the technical superiority of present goods, could account for the existence of interest. Fisher says that both the productivity of capital and individual time preferences are necessary to explain the existence of interest. In other words the productivity of capital will result in a demand for income to be deferred from current consumption to future consumption, but unless individuals prefer present to future goods, no positive rate of interest will prevail.

Although Fisher's exposition of his interest theory introduces indifference curve analysis when dealing with simple cases, and mathematics when dealing with a number of individuals and a number of time periods, we can understand the essence of his approach by using the more conventional supply-and-demand analysis. Individuals can alter their income flows by saving or by disinvestment. The supply of savings is a function of the interest rate: at higher rates of interest the quantity of savings will increase. An individual will have a preference between present and future income and will save or disinvest until his or her marginal rate of time preference between future and present income is equal to the rate of interest. The demand curve for investment is also a function of the interest rate, and at lower rates of interest, the quantity demanded will increase. The expected rate of profit on investment Fisher calls the "marginal rate of return over cost"; this is analogous to Keynes's concept of the marginal efficiency of capital. By investing and dissaving, individuals can alter their income flows, and the equilibrium, or optimum, position for an individual would require the marginal rate of return over cost to equal the rate of interest. Market equilibrium is achieved when the quantity of funds borrowers want to borrow equals the quantity of funds lenders want to lend. Interest rates will change until this occurs. For example, if at the existing rate of interest, desires to lend exceed desires to borrow, the rate will fall. In long-run equilibrium the action of individuals in altering their income flows will result in the rate of interest equaling the marginal rate of time preference and the marginal rate of return over cost.

Fisher's position, which is actually more sophisticated than we have shown in our summary, represented an important advance over previously existing notions concerning the nature of interest and the forces determining the rate of interest. His presentation starts with partial equilibrium analysis and then moves into a general equilibrium framework. He first presents his ideas in words, then moves to geometric representations, and finally employs mathematics.

The Problem of Interest: A Summary

Around the turn of the century, orthodox economists began to apply marginal analysis to the pricing of the factors of production and to a theory of distribution. The marginal productivity theory raised the issue of product exhaustion in concluding that, under perfectly competitive markets, the sum of the marginal products of the factors would just exhaust the total product. This raised serious theoretical questions with respect to the return on capital. Capital appeared to receive a return in the form of interest in perpetuity; but if the value of the final product was completely absorbed by the factors of production, there would be nothing left to provide an interest return on capital. The value of the product of a capital good would flow backward into higher values paid to the factors of production used to produce the capital good.

Böhm-Bawerk's and Fisher's theories of interest resolve this apparent contradiction, accounting for the existence of interest in long-run competitive equilibrium by the fact that individuals prefer present goods to an equal amount of future goods. Because of this time preference, the payment made today to a factor of production will be less than the value of the final goods produced tomorrow. Factors of production will receive the discounted values of their marginal products; the difference between these discounted values and the value of the marginal product when the final goods are produced will be interest.

METHODOLOGICAL CONTROVERSY

Introduction

Even before Menger, Jevons, Walras, and Marshall had begun to apply marginal analysis to the theory of value and distribution, orthodox classical theory was being criticized by certain nonsocialist German writers. Although there were some notable differences between the views of these writers, they had enough in common to be referred to collectively as the German historical school. The influence of this school began in Germany during the 1840s and extended into the present century. Many historians divide it into an older and a younger historical school, noting some differences of opinion — largely resulting from changing problems in Germany and reactions to orthodox theory — between the earlier and later writers. Criticism of orthodox classical theory and advocacy of the so-called historical method also appeared in England in the 1870s independently of the German historical school. These English advocates of the historical method, however, formed no cohesive group, and it would therefore be improper to speak of an English historical school. These German and English writers deserve our attention because of the influence they had on Alfred Marshall. The Germans also influenced economic theory and policy in the United States.

The Older Historical School

The important writers of the older historical school are Friedrich List (1789-1846), Wilhelm Rosher (1817-1894), Bruno Hildebrand (1812–1878), and Karl Knies (1821-1898). They contended that classical economic theory did not apply to all times and cultures and that the conclusions of Smith, Ricardo, and J. S. Mill, though valid for an industrializing economy such as England, did not apply to agricultural Germany. There was much nationalistic feeling in the economic analysis of these writers. Furthermore, they held that economics and the social sciences must use a historically based methodology and that classical theory, particularly in the hands of Ricardo and his followers, was mistaken in attempting to ape the methodology of the physical sciences. Some of the more moderate members of the school acknowledged that theoretical-deductive methods and historical-inductive methods were compatible, but others, particularly Knies, objected to any use of abstract theory. List expressed particularly strong nationalist views and refused to admit that the laissez faire conclusions of classical theory were applicable to countries less developed than England. Where classical theory held that national well-being would result from the pursuit of individual self-interest in an environment of laissez faire, List held that state guidance was necessary, particularly for Germany and the United States. He argued that whereas free trade would be beneficial to England, given the advanced state of her industry, tariffs and protection were necessary for Germany and the United States. He spent five years in the United States, from 1825 to 1830, and some ten years later published *The National System of Political Economy* (1841), which drew on his experience here. His protectionist views were so warmly received in the United States that he is often called the father of American protectionism.

What was the historical method advocated by these writers? Their works reflect a belief that the chief task of economics is to discover the laws governing the stages of economic growth and development. For example, List states that economies in the temperate zone will go through five stages: nomadic life, pastoral life; agriculture; agriculture and manufacturing; and manufacturing, agriculture, and commerce. Hildebrand felt the key to understanding the stages of economic growth was to be found in the conditions of exchange, and thus he posits three economic stages, based on barter, money, and credit. These descriptions of growth by stages obviously contain a certain amount of theory, and they are highly abstract. However, these writers did collect large quantities of historical and statistical information to support their analyses of economic development. W. W. Rostow has advanced a theory of economic development by stages, which is in the tradition of the older historical school.[24] As might be expected, his book was much better accepted by those in the social sciences other than economics than by economists themselves.

The Younger Historical School

The second generation of the German historical school was represented by one outstanding leader, Gustav Schmoller (1838-1917). Like the older historical school, these writers attacked classical economic theory, particularly the view that it was applicable to all times and places. Generally much less ambitious than the older school in the application of the historical method, they were content to write monographs on various aspects of the economy and society rather than to formulate grand theories of the stages of economic development. In this endeavor they preferred to use inductive methods and seemed to feel that after enough empirical evidence had been gathered, theories might emerge. They also were very much interested in social reform through state action, which led to their being called "socialists of the chair," an epithet they happily accepted, feeling that their critics who would not accept proposals such as income taxation were reactionaries.

The application of marginal analysis and the construction of abstract deductive models by Menger, Jevons, and Walras in the early 1870s had little or no influence in Germany. Although Menger, an Austrian, wrote his *Principles* in German, it was not studied in the German universities, since they subscribed exclusively to the historical method. Though

---

24. W. W. Rostow, *The Stages of Economic Growth* (Cambridge: Cambridge University Press, 1960).

Schmoller, in his earlier writings, did not recommend the construction of abstract theoretical models, he was willing to admit that both methodologies had a place in economic investigation. In 1883 Menger published a book on methodology, *Inquiries into the Method of the Social Sciences and Particularly Political Economy*, which began a long, dreary, and ultimately fruitless controversy that extended into the twentieth century. This *Methodenstreit* (controversy over method) was one of the most intense methodological controversies ever to occur in the development of economic theory; it was equaled only by the later controversy in the United States between the institutionalists and the orthodox theorists. Menger's book included a general survey of the methodological issues in economics and the social sciences, but he also launched a polemic against the errors of the historical approach. Schmoller responded to the bait, and the battle commenced. Menger published a refutation of Schmoller's response, and others joined in the fun. Both sides put their backs to the wall and argued for the virtually exclusive use of their own methodological approach. As Schumpeter has pointed out, both used honorific terms to describe their own methodology — empirical, realistic, modern, and exact — while referring to the competing methodology as speculative, futile, and subordinate.

From one point of view, this controversy could be regarded as a mere wasteland of economic literature and a detriment to the development of economics as a discipline, since capable minds occupied their time in pointless argument. On the other hand, it may be that this controversy did help economists to recognize that theory and history, deduction and induction, abstract model building and statistical data gathering are not mutually exclusive within their discipline. Although individual economists may be inclined to devote the majority of their efforts exclusively to one of these methods, a healthy, developing discipline requires a variety of methodological approaches. Since neither methodology can be accepted to the complete exclusion of the other, the real issue is the priority to be given to each one. Possibly, however, the development of the discipline will determine this issue, so that it is pointless to debate it. One other lesson to be learned from this controversy is that if practitioners of a particular methodological approach become so convinced of its correctness that they will not permit other points of view to be represented at the universities where research and the training of graduate students occur, the development of economics will suffer. This happened in Germany, where the self-righteous and rigid intellectual leadership of Schmoller was so influential that abstract theoreticians who pursued the lines laid down by Menger, Jevons, Walras, and Marshall were unable to find academic employment. The result was that the mainstream of economic thinking passed by German economists and that economics as an intellectual discipline suffered in Germany for several decades.

The Historical Method in England

During the last quarter of the nineteenth century, a number of English writers criticized orthodox classical theory and advocated the historical approach to the study of economics. These writers did not form a cohesive group as in Germany, nor were they influenced directly by the German writers. The English tradition in economic thought was no stranger to the historical inductive approach. Adam Smith's *Wealth of Nations* was a blend of historical and descriptive material tied together with a loose theoretical structure. Ricardo represented a major shift in the methodology of economics toward the building of abstract deductive models almost completely devoid of any historical or institutional content. Senior supported and extended Ricardo's use of deductive reasoning. J. S. Mill, however, moved back in the direction of Smith's methodology, using his great scholarship and knowledge of historical and institutional material to give substance to his theoretical structure.

The leading English advocate of the historical method was T. E. Cliffe Leslie (1825-1882), who directed his criticism of the methodology of classical economics largely toward Ricardo and his followers. Leslie felt that Smith's economic theory was not applicable to the contemporary English situation but that on balance Smith's methodology was reasonably sound, since Smith made extensive use of historical material in arriving at his conclusions. Although Arnold Toynbee (1852-1883) died at a young age and his great promise as an economic historian was never fully realized, his *Lectures on the Industrial Revolution of the Eighteenth Century in England* (1884) are a magnificent example of the use of the historical approach to understand the fundamental changes that took place in England and the resulting problems of an industrial economy. It was Toynbee who coined the term "Industrial Revolution." The works of William Ashley (1860-1927) and of William Cunningham (1849-1919) on English economic history are still highly respected. Other writers used the historical method to analyze specific topics: Walter Bagehot (1826-1877) wrote *Lombard Street* (1873), a classic study of English banking; and John K. Ingram (1823-1907), in his *History of Political Economy* (1876), produced the first systematic book on the history of economic theory written in English.

SUMMARY

The 1890s witnessed important new developments in microeconomic theory. Although the early marginalists had emphasized the differences in content between their views and those of classical orthodoxy, economists gradually realized that the important difference was in their method, that is, in their use of marginalism and abstract model building. The first generation of marginal writers had applied their technique almost exclusively to the demand side and the household and had developed hardly any theoretical constructs to explain supply, the prices of factors of production, the distribution of income, and the special problems associated with interest and profits. But the new technique of examining the economic forces at work at the margin was employed to derive demand curves for factors of production and to indicate the optimum way for firms to hire several factors. The marginal productivity theory of distribution was developed, raising new and interesting theoretical issues. Since the classical economists had used a residual theory of distribution, the sum of the payments to the factors had necessarily been equal to the total product. The new theory held that each factor received its marginal product, thus raising the issue of product exhaustion. The mathematical properties that production functions must have to cause product exhaustion were discovered, and it was recognized that perfectly competitive markets in long-run equilibrium satisfied these prerequisites. But this solution led to other problems, such as the economic forces determining the long-run average cost curves of firms and the compatibility of constant returns to scale and competition.

J. B. Clark tried to draw ethical conclusions from the marginal productivity theory. Others used it to explain depressions. It was criticized on a number of grounds, most importantly that it was impossible to determine the marginal product of cooperating factors. Economists soon recognized that profits and interest were returns that required special study. A number of theories of profits were offered, all basically concluding that profits arise either because of monopoly power or because of temporary disequilibria in perfectly competitive markets. The classical tradition of explaining interest as a nonmonetary phenomenon continued, but individual time preferences were acknowledged as a subjective cause of interest in addition to the classical objective cause, the productivity of capital. As a result, interest theory could be fitted into the basic supply-and-demand framework emerging during the period. A heated controversy over the proper methodology for economics and the social sciences broke out, which carried on into the twentieth century and influenced both American economic theory and the economics of Alfred Marshall. After we have examined Marshallian economics in the next chapter, we shall be able to summarize and evaluate the relative merits of the marginal utility school's emphasis on demand, the classical emphasis on supply, and Marshall's attempt to deal with these issues and the methodological questions of the time.

SUGGESTED READINGS

Allen, William R. "Irving Fisher, F.D.R., and the Great Depression." *History of Political Economy*, 9 (Winter 1977).

Böhm-Bawerk, Eugen. *The Positive Theory of Capital.* London: Macmillan, 1891.

Clark, John Bates. *The Distribution of Wealth.* New York: Kelley and Millman, 1956.

Coats, A. W. "The Historicist Reaction in English Political Economy, 1870–1890." *Economica*, 21 (May 1954).

Conrad, J. W. *An Introduction to the Theory of Interest.* Berkeley: University of California Press, 1959.

Dorfman, Joseph. "The Role of the German Historical School in American Economic Thought," *American Economic Review*, 45 (May 1955).

Hutchison, T. W. *A Review of Economic Doctrine 1870–1929.* Oxford: Clarendon Press, 1953.

Knight, Frank H. *Risk, Uncertainty and Profit.* Boston: Houghton Mifflin, 1921.

Mitchell, Wesley C. "The German Historical School: Gustav von Schmoller," in *Types of Economic Theory*, II. New York: Kelley, 1969.

Robertson, Dennis H. "Wage-Grumbles," in *Readings in the Theory of Income Distribution.* Philadelphia: Blakiston, 1949.

Schumpeter, Joseph A. *The Theory of Economic Development.* Cambridge: Harvard University Press, 1955.

Seligman, Ben B. "Protest from the Historicists," in *Main Currents in Modern Economics.* New York: Free Press of Glencoe, 1962.

Stigler, George J. *Production and Distribution Theories.* New York: Macmillan, 1941.

Weston, J. Fred. "The Profit Concept and Theory: A Restatement," *Journal of Political Economy*, 62 (April 1954).

Chapter 9
Alfred Marshall and Neoclassical Economics

It would be difficult to overstate the immense contributions of Alfred Marshall (1842-1924) to modern orthodox microeconomic theory. Building on the work of Smith, Ricardo, and J. S. Mill, he developed an analytical framework that still serves today as the structural basis of current economic theory. A truly thorough examination of his ideas would include nearly all of present-day partial equilibrium microeconomic theory; what follows in this chapter should be viewed as the barest introduction to the works of this great thinker.

THE FATHER OF NEOCLASSICISM

Marshall came to economics with an undergraduate training in mathematics and strong humanitarian feelings about improving the quality of life of the poor. His early education and home environment had oriented him toward ordination in the Anglican church, but his undergraduate study at Cambridge revealed a strong preference and aptitude for mathematics. He therefore stayed on at Cambridge after graduation to teach mathematics. Soon, however, he was caught up in reading metaphysics, ethics, and economics. By the late 1860s he had developed such a consuming interest in economics that he decided to become a scholar-teacher rather than a clergyman. He began teaching economics at Cambridge, and under the influence of the writings of two of the early mathematical economists, Cournot and von Thünen, he began to translate Ricardo's and J. S. Mill's economics into mathematics.

Marshall came to the study of economics at a historically propitious time. We have already noted the crumbling of the foundations of classical theory. Malthusian population doctrine maintained that real wages would fall as population increased, but English economic history continued to demonstrate the contrary. J. S. Mill had become so dissatisfied with the wages fund theory that by 1869 he had expressly rejected it. Karl Marx had constructed a novel analysis on a foundation of classical theory and invoked revolution. The German historical school and certain English writers, such as Leslie and Bagehot, had taken exception to several fundamental tenets of classical economic theory. In 1871, Jevons and Menger had attacked its almost exclusive emphasis on supply. The *policies* arising from classical theory were also under siege. Laissez faire, for example, seemed hardly appropriate

Alfred Marshall

in light of the poor living and working conditions of the growing population of English factory workers. Thus, the time was ripe for the appearance of this man of immense scholarship and wisdom who, from 1867 to 1890, carefully forged the principles of supply-and-demand analysis.

Jevons rushed into print claiming to have destroyed the classical theory of value and revolutionized economic theory, but Marshall tried his ideas on his students and colleagues for more than twenty years before cautiously presenting them in 1890 in his *Principles of Economics.* As Keynes has aptly said: "Jevons saw the kettle boil and cried out with the delighted voice of a child; Marshall too had seen the kettle boil and sat down silently to build an engine."[1] The engine of analysis that Marshall built reflects both his personality and the environment in which he was reared. His early religious beliefs, later expressed as a mellow humanitarianism, evoked in him a deep concern for the poor, as well as an optimistic conviction that the study of the economy might provide the means of improving the well-being of the entire society. His scholarship had familiarized him with the attacks of the historically oriented economists, who objected to the notion that economic theory was a body of absolute truths applicable to all times and places. In an inaugural lecture given on his election to professorship at Cambridge in 1885, he addressed himself to this criticism: "For that part of economic doctrine, which can alone claim universality, has no dogmas. It is not a body of concrete truth, but an engine for the discovery of concrete truth."[2]

Marshall was trying to combine his early mathematical training with his background in history to construct an engine of inquiry adaptable to the changing times. Yet, aware of J. S. Mill's hasty conclusion in 1848 that the theory of value was complete, Marshall expected his own contributions to economics also to become obsolete as new theories arose to meet the needs of a continually changing society. He was aware, too, of Jevons's claim to originality and belief that he had replaced the classical cost of production theory of value with a theory that value depends entirely on demand. Marshall hoped, of course, that his own ideas might be both original and enduring, but most of all he wanted to be understood — not only by his fellow economists but by the community at large, particularly the businessman. Thus, even though he had begun to work out the fundamental mathematical structure of his theory by the 1870s, and had developed the basic technique by which to illustrate supply-and-demand analysis with

1. J. M. Keynes, *Essays and Sketches in Biography* (New York: Meridian, 1956), p. 58.
2. *Memorials of Alfred Marshall*, ed. A. C. Pigou (New York: Kelley and Millman, 1956), p. 159.

graphs, he did not actually publish his findings until 1890, and then only with the mathematics and graphs in footnotes and various appendixes. Marshall is a strange admixture of theoretician, humanitarian, mathematician, and historian who tried to point the way out of the methodological controversy of his time, while simultaneously taking the best of the classical analysis and tempering it with the new tools of the marginalists to explain the forces determining prices and the allocation of resources.

Although Marshall is a towering figure in the development of economic theory, his refusal to take rigid positions on theoretical and methodological issues has caused succeeding generations of economists a good deal of pain. In attempting to achieve balanced judgments, he sometimes seems vague and indecisive. He often seems to be saying that it all depends: Ricardo was right but also wrong; abstract theory is good and bad; the historical method can be helpful, but theory is needed, too; payments to the factors of production are price-determining from one point of view, but price-determined from another. Some readers see this flexibility with regard to issues of theory and method as a sign of true wisdom, but others, particularly the more abstract mathematical economists, chafe at what they regard as indecisiveness in Marshall's economics. At all events, his style has given rise to a vast body of literature that tries to uncover what Marshall "really meant."

Scope of Economics

Book I, Chapter I, of Marshall's *Principles of Economics* begins with a broad, flexible definition of economics.

> Political Economy or Economics is a study of mankind in the ordinary business of life; it examines that part of individual and social action which is most closely connected with the attainment and with the use of the material requisites of wellbeing.[3]

The first interesting aspect of this definition is that the concept defined is referred to by two different terms, "political economy" and "economics." Marshall's inclusion of both terms reflects some of the methodological issues of his time. The term "political economy," which was more common than "economics" at the time, implies that economics and politics are related and that economics, as a discipline in the

---

3. Reprinted with permission of Macmillan Publishing Co., Inc., from *Principles of Economics*, 8th ed., by Alfred Marshall, p. 1. Copyright © 1948 by Macmillan Publishing Co., Inc., New York. By permission of Macmillan, London and Basingstoke.

social sciences, is intimately connected with normative judgments. But John Neville Keynes, a colleague and friend of Marshall who was particularly interested in methodological issues, published in 1891 a work entitled *The Scope and Method of Political Economy* in which he clearly distinguished between positive and normative economics: between a science that describes what is and an art that prescribes what ought to be. The term "economics" or "economic science" was preferable to "political economy," asserted Keynes, because these names stressed the positive nature of economics as a science. Unlike Ricardo and J. S. Mill, Marshall chose to call his book *Principles of Economics* rather than *Principles of Political Economy*, and eventually he dropped the term "political economy" in favor of the term "economics."

The second interesting aspect of the definition is its breadth and flexibility — some might say its "flabbiness." How, according to this definition, can economics be distinguished from political science, sociology, psychology, anthropology, and history? Marshall's loose definition springs not from careless, unfocused thinking but from a conscious reluctance to sharply divide economics from the other social sciences. Nature draws no such sharp lines, he points out, and the economist accomplishes nothing by defining the scope of the discipline too narrowly. In Appendix C, entitled "The Scope and Method of Economics," Marshall considers, in his characteristically compromising fashion, the relative merits and feasibility of developing a unified social science as opposed to allowing each discipline to develop separately. The idea of unifying the social sciences appeals to him, but he recalls that both the great Comte and Herbert Spencer failed in their attempts to accomplish it. On the other hand, he observes, the physical sciences have made great strides by means of specialization. He decides ultimately that the issue cannot be resolved in the absence of some concrete question.

> Economics has made greater advances than any other branch of the social sciences, because it is more definite and exact than any other. But every widening of its scope involves some loss of this scientific precision; and the question of whether the loss is greater than the gain resulting from its greater breadth of outlook, is not to be decided by any hard and fast rule.[4]

Marshall suggests that each economist define the scope of economics to suit his own inclination, that some economists are more likely to do their best work within a rather narrow definition of the scope of economics while others work within a broader framework. Those who

4. *Ibid.*, p. 780.

choose a broad definition of economics and extend their analysis toward other areas of the social sciences must exercise extreme caution, he warns, but if they work carefully they perform a great service to economics and the other social sciences.

Marshall introduces one other interesting issue in his discussion of the scope of economics, namely, the complexity of the relationship between the wants of society and its economic activity. Could economics be described as a study of the ways in which economic activity satisfies the wants of society? Marshall would reject this definition because it suggests that wants are somehow an independent given, to which economic activities are secondary. In his discussion of the relationship between wants and activities in Book III, Chapter II, Marshall tries to correct what he regards as the incorrect conclusion reached by Jevons and Menger and their predecessors, who seem to regard "the theory of consumption as the scientific basis of economics." He assesses the relative importance of demand (wants) and supply (activities) in the broadest possible context. His position is that our wants are not something that arise within us independent of our activities; on the contrary, many of our wants are direct outgrowths of our activities. It would be wrong to view a suburban family's desire for a station wagon paneled in simulated wood as the starting point of economic analysis, since this want arises from the family's perception of its role in the society. Marshall suggests that economists begin with a preliminary study of demand, proceed to activities and supply, and then return to demand. This, he contends, will enable them to appreciate the complex interconnections between wants and activities. If forced to choose between the supremacy of either wants or activities in economic analysis, Marshall would opt for activities; this reflects his affinity to classical economics, with its emphasis on supply, and contrasts him with Jevons and Menger, who emphasized demand.

> For much that is of chief interest in the science of wants is borrowed from the science of efforts and activities. These two supplement one another; either is incomplete without the other. But if either, more than the other, may claim to be the interpreter of the history of man, whether on the economic side or any other, it is the science of activities and not that of wants.[5]

Marshall's religiously based humanitarian concerns led him to regard the elimination of poverty as the chief task of economics. He felt that the key to solving these problems lay in the facts and theories of the economists, and his fondest hope was that the engine of inquiry he was constructing might uncover the causes of poverty and eventually dis-

5. *Ibid.*, p. 90.

cern how it might be remedied. In Appendix B of his review of the history of economic theory, he castigates the classical theorists, particularly Ricardo, for not recognizing that poverty breeds poverty, because the poor do not have sufficient income to attain the health and training that would enable them to earn more. Marshall, in contrast to the classicals, wholeheartedly believes in the possibility of significantly increasing the well-being of the working classes.

His discussion of the scope of economics reveals his desires to respond to the criticisms of the historically oriented economist who wanted a broader definition of economics; to discuss the question of whether economics should develop as a narrow, abstract discipline or develop into a unified social science; to answer the marginal utility writers, who held that the theory of consumption should take precedence over the theory of cost and supply; and to take issue with that part of classical economics that had troubled J. S. Mill because it held out so little hope for the elimination of poverty. As usual, Marshall tries to present a balanced judgment on these issues and seldom takes a clear-cut position.

Marshall on Method

Marshall's training and background are also reflected in his views on methodology. His mathematical ability made him fully aware of the power of mathematics as a tool in the hands of the economist, and his close study of Ricardo revealed the insights to be gained by building abstract models. His wide reading of history and the historical economists convinced him of the value of their approach and of the validity of their attacks on classical theory. He realized that the chief fault of classical economics, especially Ricardian economics, was its failure to recognize that society changes. But he saw that a combination of abstract theory and historical analysis could correct this defect, and in Appendix B he praises Adam Smith as a model of method. In his Appendix C on "The Scope and Method of Economics" and Appendix D on "The Uses of Abstract Reasoning in Economics," he bestows lavish praise on the historical method and the German historical school. Marshall's own methodology attempts to blend the theoretical, mathematical, and historical approaches. He acknowledges that some economists will prefer to rely heavily on a single methodology and does not object to this. For Marshall, the use of a different methodology does not imply conflict or opposition, since all economists are engaged in a common task. Each methodology will throw its particular light on the working of the economy and thus increase our understanding of it.

Marshall's attempt to reconcile the methodological controversies of his time made him vulnerable from all sides. The historically oriented economists of Germany and England found his economic methodology too abstract and rigid. In the twentieth century a strong attack against his method was led by an American, Thorstein Veblen, and the so-called institutionalists who followed him. The advocates of an abstract mathematical methodology were irritated by his praise of the historical method and his pointed remarks concerning the limitations of theory and mathematics. In a letter written in 1906 to A. L. Bowley, a friend who was very much involved with the use of mathematics and statistics in economic research, Marshall made a comment capable of both irritating and pleasing opposing methodological camps.

> I have not been able to lay my hands on any notes as to Mathematico-economics that would be of any use to you: and I have very indistinct memories of what I used to think on the subject. I never read mathematics now: in fact I have forgotten how to integrate a good many things.
>
> But I know I had a growing feeling in the later years of my work at the subject that a good mathematical theorem dealing with economic hypotheses was very unlikely to be good economics: and I went more and more on the rules — (1) Use mathematics as a shorthand language, rather than as an engine of inquiry. (2) Keep to them until you have done. (3) Translate into English. (4) Then illustrate by examples that are important in real life. (5) Burn the mathematics. (6) If you can't succeed in (4), burn (3). This last I did often.[6]

Marshall's *Principles* includes steps (3) and (4) and is written in a style intended not for his fellow economists but for any educated reader. His mathematics are placed either in footnotes or in a mathematical appendix. But even though Marshall goes to great lengths to avoid the jargon of economics and illustrates each principle with examples from either current or historical economic experience, underneath it all is a strong, tight, highly abstract theoretical structure.

Just as Marshall refuses to provide a neat and tidy definition of economics, so he generally avoids precise definitions of a number of economic concepts. Classical economics had given the concepts of land, labor, and capital, the so-called factors of production, a much more precise meaning than was appropriate. In the economy land, labor, and capital are often so intermingled that only a gross abstraction can disentangle them from one another. Marshall therefore suggests that "we...arrange the things that are required for making a commodity into whatever groups are convenient, and call them its *factors of production*."[7] Thus no hard and fast definition is laid down: the problem

---

6. Pigou, *Memorials of Alfred Marshall*, p. 427.
7. Marshall, *Principles*, p. 339.

at hand dictates how the factors will be defined. Similarly, in analyzing supply Marshall has to deal with the issue of costs. If supply depends upon the normal costs of a firm, which firm is to be selected as normal? Here again Marshall demonstrates his flexibility, stating that "for this purpose we shall have to study the *expenses of a representative producer* for that aggregate volume."[8] His concept of the average, or representative, firm is not a statistical one, such as an arithmetic mean, mode, or median. Rather he suggests that an industry be surveyed to locate firms managed by people of normal or average ability, firms that are neither newcomers to the industry nor old and established, and firms whose costs disclose that they have normal access to the technology available.

It is important to recognize that Marshall's seeming vagueness, changeability, and occasional lack of theoretical rigor do not result from a disorderly mind; his is a carefully considered methodological position. Marshall's understanding of micro theory and mathematical ability would have enabled him to present his *Principles*, which is some seven hundred pages long, in a much more concise form. He did this, in fact, in his mathematical appendix. But the economy is actually far more complex than can be shown by mathematical economics. Marshall worked out the pure theory of a market economy early in his career; it was reasonably complete by about 1870. Mathematical Note XXI is a one-page version of a general equilibrium model showing the relationships among the demand for final products, the supply of final products, the demand for factors of production, and the supply of factors of production. In 1908 Marshall wrote to J. B. Clark: "My whole life has been and will be given to presenting in realistic form as much as I can of my Note XXI."[9] In his *Principles* Marshall explicitly defends his lack of exactness. After spelling out briefly the conditions that would exist in an economy in long-run equilibrium, Marshall goes on to point out that

> nothing of this is true in the world in which we live. Here every economic force is constantly changing its action, under the influence of other forces which are acting around it. Here changes in the volume of production, in its method, and its cost are ever mutually modifying one another; they are always affecting and being affected by the character and the extent of demand. Further all these mutual influences take time to work themselves out, and, as a rule, no two influences move at an equal pace. In this world therefore every plain and simple doctrine as to the relations between costs of production, demand and value is necessarily false: and the greater the appearance

8. *Ibid.*, p. 317.
9. Pigou, *Memorials*, p. 417.

of lucidity which is given to it by skillful exposition, the more mischievous it is. A man is likely to be a better economist if he trusts to his common sense, and practical instincts, than if he professes to study the theory of value and is resolved to find it easy.[10]

Understanding the Complex — The Method in Action

Marshall has two reasons for regarding the study of an economy as complex and difficult. On the one hand everything seems to depend upon everything else: there is a complex and often subtle relationship between all the various parts of the system. On the other hand "time is a chief cause of those difficulties in economic investigations which make it necessary for man with his limited powers to go step by step."[11] Causes do not instantaneously bring final effects, but work themselves out over time. But as one cause is making its influence felt, such as an increase in demand, other variables in the economy may independently change (for example, supply may increase), so that it is often difficult to isolate a single cause and be certain of its effects. If only the laboratory technique of the physical sciences, where it is possible to hold constant all influences except one and then to observe the results of repeated experiments, were available to the economist, this problem would not exist. But since the methodology of the laboratory is not available to economics, an alternative must be used. Marshall provided this alternative when he carefully developed his basic thought system.

According to this system, since the economist cannot in fact hold constant all the variables that might influence the outcome of a given cause, he must do so on the theoretical level by assumption. We hypothesize that changes in certain elements occur *ceteris paribus*, with other things being equal, in order to make some headway in analyzing the complex interrelationships in an economy. At the start of any analysis, many elements are held constant, but as the analysis proceeds, more elements can be allowed to vary, so that greater realism is achieved. The *ceteris paribus* technique permits the handling of complex problems at the cost of a certain loss of realism.

Marshall's first and most important use of the *ceteris paribus* technique was to develop a form of partial equilibrium analysis. To break down a complex problem, we isolate a part of the economy for analysis, ignoring but not denying the interdependence of all parts of an economy. For example, we analyze the actions of a single household or firm isolated from all other influences. We analyze the supply-and-demand conditions that produce particular prices in a given industry,

10. Marshall, *Principles*, p. 368.
11. *Ibid.*, p. 366.

ignoring for the moment the complex substitute and complementary relationships existing between the products of the industry under analysis and other industries. One important use of the partial equilibrium approach is to make a first approximation of the likely effects of a given cause. It is therefore particularly useful for dealing with policy issues — for example, predicting the effect of a tariff on imported watches. Simple supply-and-demand analysis can be used within a partial equilibrium approach to get some idea of the immediate implications of such a policy. Marshall's procedure is first to limit a problem very narrowly in a partial equilibrium framework, keeping most variables constant, and then to broaden the scope of the analysis slowly and carefully by permitting other things to vary. His method has been called, appropriately, the "one-thing-at-a-time method."

The Problem with Time

One of the chief difficulties in economic analysis is that causes take time to work out their effects. Any analysis or conclusion that correctly explains the short-run effects of a given cause may be incorrect in its conclusions with regard to long-run effects. Marshall's use of the *ceteris paribus* technique corresponds to his method of dealing with time. In the market period, sometimes called the immediate period or very short run, many factors are held constant. More and more constants are permitted to vary as the time period is extended to the short run, long run, and the secular period, also referred to as the very long run. The passage of time influences demand somewhat, but it can be far more disruptive to the analysis of supply.

To deal with the problems caused by time, Marshall defines four time periods. He acknowledges that his distinctions are purely artificial, for "nature has drawn no such lines in the economic conditions of actual life."[12] Marshall's concept of time is not chronological time, measured in clock hours, but is an analytical construct. The various time periods are defined in terms of the economics of the firm and of supply. The *market period* is so short that supply is fixed, or perfectly inelastic. Under these circumstances there is no reflex action of price on quantity supplied, as the period is too short for firms to be able to respond to price changes. The *short run* is defined as a period in which the firm can change production and supply but cannot change plant size. Here there is a reflex action, as higher prices cause larger quantities to be supplied, and the supply curve slopes upward. In the short run, the total costs of the firm can be divided into two components: costs that vary with output, which Marshall terms "special," "direct," or

12. *Ibid.*, p. 378.

"prime" costs, and costs that do not vary with output, which Marshall terms "supplementary" costs and modern texts call "fixed" costs. This distinction between variable and fixed costs in the short run was evidently drawn from Marshall's observation of the business world. It became an important analytical tool in analyzing the actions of the firm. In the *long run*, plant size can vary, and so all costs become variable. The supply curve becomes more elastic in the long run than in the short run, as firms are able to make full adjustment to changing prices by altering plant size. The long-run supply curve for an industry can take three general forms: it can slope up and to the right (costs may increase); it can be perfectly elastic (costs may be constant); or, in unusual situations, it might slope down and to the right (costs may decrease). The *secular period*, or very long run, permits technology and population to vary, so Marshall uses this construct when he analyzes the movement of prices from one generation to another.

Clearly, Marshall's time periods are not measured in days but refer instead to conditions of supply for the firm and industry. For example, the short run in a very capital-intensive industry in which plant size can be changed only very slowly, such as the steel industry, may be as long in chronological time as the long run in an industry in which plant size may be altered rather quickly. Although Marshall contributed to nearly every part of microeconomic theory, the focus of his major attention and the source of his greatest contributions was his analysis of the influence of time on supply. He found the chief difficulties in the analysis of price to be determining the influence of time, and he felt later in life that much more work needed to be done in this area. In a 1908 letter to J. B. Clark, he listed five topics that still needed an immense quantity of work, and at the top of his list was "elaborating the influence of time."[13]

The Marshallian Cross

During the last quarter of the nineteenth century, a controversy arose among economists concerning the relative importance of demand and supply in price, or value, theory. Classical economics as set forth in the *Principles* of J. S. Mill had emphasized supply; Jevons, Menger, and Walras, however, had stressed demand, and Jevons and others went so far as to assert that value depends *entirely* on demand. It is difficult to assess the impact of this controversy on the content and form of Marshall's theory of relative prices. He asserts that the essential elements of his own views on value and distribution were worked out before 1870 but that it would be "foolish if he troubled himself to weigh and

13. Pigou, *Memorials*, p. 417.

measure any claims to originality that he has."[14] Marshall was vexed by criticisms of his supply-and-demand analysis that suggested he had tried to reconcile the positions of the classical and marginal utility schools. He was looking for truth, not just peace, he asserted; his supply-and-demand analysis had, moreover, been formulated before Jevons, Menger, and Walras began to write on the subject.

Marshall believed that a correct understanding of the influence of time and an awareness of the interdependence of economic variables would resolve the controversy as to whether cost of production or utility determines price. The demand curve for final goods slopes downward to the right, as individuals will buy larger quantities at lower prices. The shape of the supply curve depends upon the time period under analysis. The shorter the period, the more important the role of demand in determining price, and the longer the period, the more important the role of supply. In the long run, if constant costs exist and supply is therefore perfectly elastic, price will depend solely on cost of production. In general, however, it is fruitless to argue whether demand or supply determines price. Marshall uses the following analogy to show that causation is not a simple matter and any attempt to find one single cause is doomed to failure:

> We might as reasonably dispute whether it is the upper or under blade of a pair of scissors that cuts a piece of paper, as whether value is governed by utility or costs of production. It is true that when one blade is held still, and the cutting is effected by moving the other, we may say with careless brevity that the cutting is done by the second; but the statement is not strictly accurate, and is to be excused only so long as it claims to be merely a popular and not a strictly scientific account of what happens.[15]

Possibly even more important is Marshall's insistence that marginal analysis has been misused by many economists. They write, he says, as though it is the marginal value (whether cost, utility, or productivity) that somehow determines the value of the whole. For example, in analyzing the prices of final goods, it is not correct, according to Marshall, to say that marginal utility or marginal cost determines price. Marginal analysis simply suggests that "we must go to *the margin to study the action of those forces which govern* the value of the whole."[16] Marginal utility or marginal cost do not determine price, for their values along with price are mutually determined by those factors acting on the margin. Here again Marshall provides a very apt analogy to illustrate his

14. *Ibid.*, p. 418.
15. Marshall, *Principles*, p. 348.
16. *Ibid.*, p. 410.

point. Jevons had isolated the essential elements in price determination: utility, cost, and price. But he was mistaken in trying to find a single cause and in viewing the process as a chain of causation, with cost of production determining supply, supply determining marginal utility, and marginal utility determining price. Marshall holds that this is mistaken because it ignores the interrelationships and mutual causation existing among these elements. If we place three balls in a bowl, one being marginal utility, one being cost of production, and the third being price, it is clearly incorrect to say that the position of any one ball determines the position of the others. But it is true that the balls *mutually* determine each other's positions. Thus demand, supply, and price interact with each other at the margin and mutually determine their respective values.

In Appendix I and the last paragraph of Book V, Marshall attempts to place his theory of price in the context both of Ricardo's theory of value and of the controversy over whether utility or cost of production determines price. Marshall believes that his own theory of price is fundamentally in the Ricardian line. Although the marginal utility writers would hardly have agreed, he suggests that Ricardo recognized the role of demand but gives it limited attention because its influence is so easy to understand, devoting his energies instead to the much more difficult analysis of cost. Marshall finds that Ricardo's cost of production theory of value includes both labor and capital costs. Most historians of economic theory consider this an overly generous interpretation of Ricardo. The main defects in Ricardo's value theory, according to Marshall, were his inability to handle the influence of time and to express his ideas clearly. Marshall rejects the claim of Jevons and other marginal utility writers that they have effectively demolished Ricardo's theory of value and replaced it with a correct version by emphasizing demand almost exclusively. Marshall, viewing his own contribution as merely an extension and development of Ricardo's ideas, felt that his treatment of Ricardo left the basic foundation of the Ricardian theory of value intact. We will postpone our evaluation of Marshall's value theory until we have surveyed his other ideas.

Marshall on Demand

Marshall's suggestion that the influence of demand on price determination is relatively easy to analyze may well be correct. Yet there were some problems in the theory of demand that Marshall was not able to solve satisfactorily. He seemed to recognize these difficulties and avoided them by assumption. His most important contribution to demand theory was his clear formulation of the concept of price elasticity of demand. Price and quantity demanded are inversely related to each other; demand curves slope down and to the right. The degree of relationship between change in price and change in quantity demanded is disclosed by the *coefficient of price elasticity*. The coefficient of price elasticity is

$$e_D = -\frac{\text{Percent change in quantity demanded}}{\text{Percent change in price}} = -\frac{\frac{\Delta q}{q}}{\frac{\Delta p}{p}}$$

The negative sign appears on the right side of the equation, since price and quantity demanded are inversely related. Thus the coefficient is always a positive number. The price of a product times the quantity demanded will equal the total expenditure of the buyers or, alternatively, the total revenues of seller ($p \cdot q = TE = TR$). If price decreases 1 percent and quantity demanded increases 1 percent, total expenditure, or revenue, will remain unchanged and the coefficient will have a value of 1. If price decreases and total expenditure or revenue increases, the coefficient has a value greater than 1, and the commodity is said to be *price elastic*. If the price decreases a given percentage and quantity demanded increases by a smaller percentage, total expenditure or revenue will decrease, the coefficient will have a value less than 1, and the commodity is said to be *price inelastic*. Marshall also applied the elasticity concept to the supply side, and in so doing gave economics another extremely useful tool. Although the notion of price elasticity had been suggested in earlier literature, it was Marshall, with his mathematical ability, who was able to express it precisely; he is therefore considered its discoverer.

According to Marshall, individuals desire commodities because of the utility received through their consumption. The form of the utility function used by Marshall was additive, which is to say that he derived total utility by adding the utilities received from consuming each good. The utility received from consuming good A depends solely on the quantity of A consumed, not on the quantities of other goods consumed. Thus substitution and complementary relationships are ignored. An additive utility function is

$$U = f_1 q_A + f_2 q_B + f_3 q_C + \ldots + f_n q_n$$

The utility function used in contemporary practice explicitly recognizes complementary and substitute relationships and is expressed as

$$U = f(q_A, q_B, q_C, \ldots, q_N)$$

Edgeworth and Irving Fisher were two of Marshall's contemporaries who suggested the more generalized utility function now used. The most important implication of Marshall's use of the additive utility function, which we will discuss shortly, concerns income effects.

Marshall assumed that utility was measurable through the price system. If an individual pays $2 for another unit of good A and $1 for another unit of good B, then A must give twice the utility of B. He also believes that *intergroup* comparisons of utility are possible because in group comparisons personal peculiarities are washed out.

The most important task of the theory of demand is to explain the shape of the demand curve. If, as more of a commodity is consumed, its marginal utility decreases, does it therefore follow that individuals will pay lower prices for larger quantities? Are demand curves, then, negatively sloped? Marshall accepted diminishing marginal utility (Gossen's First Law) and formulated the equilibrium condition that would give maximum utility for an individual consuming many commodities (Gossen's Second Law).

$$\frac{MU_A}{P_A} = \frac{MU_B}{P_B} = \ldots = \frac{MU_N}{P_N} = MU_M \tag{9.1}$$

In equilibrium the consumer will spend so that the last dollar spent for any final good will have the same marginal utility as that spent for any other good. The ratios of these marginal utilities to prices will be equal to, and thus disclose, the marginal utility of money. The marginal utility of money is the marginal utility received by the last dollar of expenditure. If saving is considered as a good, then the marginal utility of money is the utility received from the last dollar of income. The marginal utility of a single good is equal to its price times the marginal utility of money.

$$MU_A = P_A \cdot MU_M \tag{9.2}$$

Let us work through the derivation of a demand curve in order to see some of the problems encountered and Marshall's solution to these problems. If we begin with an individual who is maximizing utility and then lower the price of one good, we can derive the relationship between price and quantity demanded. Using equations (9.1) and (9.2), we shall see that lowering the price, P_A, of good A will lead to an increase in quantity demanded only under certain conditions. Lowering the price of good A will have two effects. The *substitution effect* reflects the fact good A is now relatively cheaper than its substitutes, so that the individual will therefore increase his consumption of good A. The substitution effect will always lead to greater consumption at lower prices and less consumption at higher prices. The *income effect* produced by price changes is more complex. Lowering the price of good A increases an individual's real income. At the lower price he can buy the same quantity of good *A* as before and have income left over that can be spent on good *A* or on other goods. For example, if the price of *A* was $1 and 10 units were previously purchased, lowering the price of *A* to $0.90 increases real income by $1.00. A *normal good* is defined as one whose consumption increases with increases in income. If good *A* is a normal good, its demand curve will slope down and to the right, since, because of the substitution and income effect, lowering its price will increase the quantity demanded.

If good *A* is an *inferior good*, other complications occur. An inferior good is a good whose consumption decreases with increases in income. Hamburger might well be an inferior good in a consumer's budget. As income increases, the quantity of hamburger consumed will decrease as better cuts of beef replace hamburger. If good *A* is an inferior good, then a fall in its price will lead to an increase in its consumption, because of the substitution effect, but a decrease in its consumption because of the income effect. If the substitution effect is stronger than the income effect, the demand curve will be negatively sloped, but if the income effect is stronger than the substitution effect, the demand curve will be positively sloped. The possibility of upward-sloping demand curves is extremely disturbing to the theory of demand. The theoretical possibility clearly exists, but no empirical information has yet been produced to indicate the actual occurrence of upward-sloping demand curves.

Marshall first states the general law of demand: "The amount demanded increases with a fall in price, and diminishes with a rise in price."[17] He then notes that information gathered by Robert Giffen suggests that the demand curve of poorer individuals for bread may slope up and to the right. In other words, for these individuals a rise in the price of bread results in a reduction in the consumption of meat and more expensive foods, and a rise in the consumption of bread. For this reason, inferior goods with a more powerful income than substitution effect are referred to as *Giffen goods* in the theoretical literature. Again, although a considerable body of theoretical literature exists about the so-called Giffen paradox, no acceptable statistical information showing actual upward-sloping demand curves has been produced.

Let us return to the theoretical problems of deriving demand curves and how Marshall handled them. Because he worked with an additive utility function, he ignored substitution and complementary relationships in his formal mathematical treatment of deriving demand curves, although, characteristically, he did discuss these issues. Marshall simply assumes that the income effect of small price changes is negligible, or in other words, that the marginal utility of money remains constant for small changes in the price of any single commodity. Thus if we

17. *Ibid.*, p. 99.

lower the price of good A in equation (9.1) quantity demanded increases and the marginal utility of A decreases until the ratio $\dfrac{MU_A}{P_A}$ is brought into equality with the ratios for other commodities, and all are again equal to the constant marginal utility of money. Marshall's procedure can be studied from another perspective. Using equation (9.2), a fall in the price of good A, assuming that the marginal utility of money is constant, must lead to an increase in its consumption, because of the principle of diminishing marginal utility.

Marshall had two reasons for dismissing these theoretical difficulties by assuming that the marginal utility of money was constant: first, he did not have the theoretical tools to distinguish clearly between the substitution and income effects, and, second, he felt that the income effect of minor changes in the price of a good was so small that no harm was done by ignoring it.

Consumers' Surplus

Marshall's belief that the marginal utility of money was constant for small changes in prices permitted him, or so he thought, to draw certain conclusions in the area now called welfare economics. In this case, too, Marshall's first ventures into the new areas of economic theory have been followed by a large volume of literature interpreting and extending his analysis. The concept of consumers' surplus, first suggested by Marshall, is still being discussed in the literature of welfare economics.

Using equation (9.2), $MU_A = P_A \cdot MU_M$, and assuming that the marginal utility of money is constant, the price of good A and the marginal utility of good A are directly related. Marshall concluded that the price of A is a measure of the marginal utility of good A to a consumer. Demand curves slope down and to the right because of diminishing marginal utility. Their downward slope indicates that consumers will be willing to pay more for earlier consumed units of a commodity than for later consumed units. In the market, however, consumers are able to buy all the units consumed at one price, and since this price measures the marginal utility of the last unit consumed, consumers obtain the earlier units, the intramarginal units, at a price less than they would be willing to pay. The difference between the total expenditures consumers would be willing to pay and what they actually pay constitutes consumers' surplus

Marshall wished to use the concept of consumers' surplus to draw welfare conclusions; therefore he is concerned with the surplus of consumers as a group rather than with the individual consumer's surplus. He works with market-demand curves, not individual-demand curves. Given a market-demand curve as in Figure 9.1 we can analyze consumers' surplus. If the market price is OC, the quantity demanded will be OH. Since DD' is a market-demand curve, there are buyers who would have been willing to pay a higher price than OC. The OMth buyer would have been willing to pay a price of MP but paid only a price of MR. RP then represents that consumer's surplus. All the other intra-marginal buyers also account for a consumers' surplus and the total consumers' surplus is equal to CAD, which is the difference between what consumers spent to buy the commodity, or $OHAC$, and what they would have been willing to spend, or $OHAD$.

CAD is, then, a measure of the monetary gain obtained by consumers in purchasing a commodity. To express this result a little differently, a monopolist practicing perfect price discrimination will work the consumers down their demand curve and in the process collect total revenues of $OHAD$, but in a competitive market, in which all consumers buy at the single price of OC, the total expenditures of consumers are $OHAC$. CAD is therefore the amount the consumers save, or their monetary gain. Marshall, however, wanted to measure the gain in utility, and the monetary gain can be expressed as a gain in utility only if there is an invariable measure to transform price into utility. If the marginal utility of money remains constant as we move down the demand curve from price OD to MP to HA, then Marshall's consumers' surplus is an acceptable means of representing the gain in utility from consuming the good.

Marshall's use of prices to measure utility, then, depends on two assumptions: one, that there is an additive utility function that ignores

Figure 9.1 Consumers' Surplus

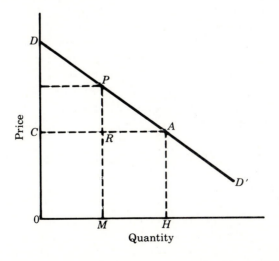

substitution and complementary relationships and, two, that the income effect from small price changes is negligible, in other words, that the marginal utility of money is constant. Edgeworth had suggested using a more generalized nonadditive utility function, and Irving Fisher had shown that although utility could be measured using additive utility functions, this would not be possible if substitution and complementary effects were permitted. Furthermore, there was general criticism of the hedonistic element in the theory of demand as presented by Marshall and others. Marshall responded to these criticisms by making some minor terminological changes, such as *satisfaction* for *utility*, but he basically held to the position that price could be used as a measure of utility. Marshall's awareness of the problems associated with measuring consumers' surplus led him to use the measure only for small changes in price in his applications to welfare economics. For small changes in price, for example around the price *HA* of Figure 9.1, the assumption of constant marginal utility of money does not appear to be unrealistic, particularly if expenditures on the commodity in question represent only a small part of total consumer expenditures. The income effect of small price changes for most commodities is likely to be so small that it can be ignored.

Taxes and Welfare

Marshall used his concept of consumers' surplus to analyze the welfare consequences of taxes. The essence of the analysis can be appreciated by examining the simplest case, a constant-cost industry represented by the perfectly elastic supply curve of Figure 9.2. Assume the industry in equilibrium, with demand being *DD'*, supply *SS'*, and price *HA*. Consumers' surplus is *SAD*. Now a tax of *Ss* is levied, shifting the supply curve to *ss'*. The loss of consumers' surplus is *SAas*, and the gain in tax revenues is *SKas*. The loss in consumers' surplus is greater than the gain in revenues by *KAa*. Taxes on constant-cost industries, therefore, appear undesirable. The analysis can be similarly used to show that a subsidy to a constant-cost industry is undesirable, because its net costs would be greater than its net benefits. Assume that demand is *DD'*, supply is *ss'*, and price is *ha*. A subsidy in the amount of *Ss* will shift downward the supply curve to *SS'*. The gain in consumers' surplus is *SAas*, which is *ALa* less than the total expenditure for the subsidy *SALs*.

Marshall then extends the analysis to cover industries with diminishing returns (upward-sloping supply curves) and those with increasing returns (downward-sloping supply curves).[18] Assuming decreasing

18. *Ibid.*, pp. 468–476.

returns exist, a tax will result in increased welfare if the supply curve is sloped steeply enough so that the gain in the tax is greater than the loss in consumers' surplus. In the same way, a subsidy to a decreasing-cost industry will increase welfare, since the gain in consumers' surplus will be greater than the cost of the subsidy. Marshall thus concludes that there might be advantages to the society from taxing certain decreasing-returns industries and using the collected revenues to subsidize increasing-returns industries. The whole analysis rests on the dubious notion that utility can be measured by the consumers' surplus; its practical value for use in making policy is questionable. Marshall's purpose in presenting the analysis is not so much to give a set of precise rules for taxes and subsidies, but rather to show that unregulated markets do not always result in an optimum allocation of resources. Professor Pigou took these seminal suggestions of Marshall to form an extended theory of welfare economics.

Marshall on Supply

Marshall laid the foundation for the currently accepted analysis of cost and supply that is taught in undergraduate courses. His most important contribution to the theory of supply was his concept of the time period, particularly the short run and the long run. He correctly perceived the shapes of industry supply curves in the market period, short

Figure 9.2 Taxes, Subsidies, and Consumers' Surplus

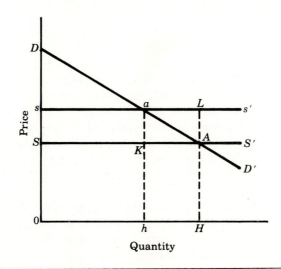

run, and long run, even though his explanation of the economic reasons
for these shapes was often deficient and confused, and sometimes
incorrect.

The market period causes no difficulties; here supply is perfectly
inelastic. In the short run, modern micro theory explains the shape of
supply curves for the firm and for the industry as depending upon the
principle of diminishing returns. Marshall pointed out that for analytical
purposes it is useful to divide the firm's costs in the short run into fixed
costs and variable costs. Marshall did not, however, establish a precise
relationship between his distinction between fixed costs and variable
costs and the derivation of the short-run cost curves of the firm based
on the principle of diminishing returns. His main application of the
principle of diminishing returns was to land, usually in the context of
long-run analysis.

He did use his distinction between fixed and variable costs in the
short run to show that a firm would continue to operate in the short
run, even if it was incurring a loss, as long as it was covering its total
variable costs. Under these circumstances the firm actually minimizes
losses by operating: shutting down would result in a loss equal to total
fixed costs, but the losses incurred by operating are less than total fixed
costs as long as total revenue exceeds total variable costs. This has
become a standard textbook example of the economics of the firm in
the short run. The supply curve of the firm in the short run in a perfectly competitive industry is, therefore, equivalent to that portion of
its marginal cost curve above its average variable cost curve. With his
characteristic realism, Marshall goes on to conclude that the real supply
curve for the firm in the short run is not likely to be its marginal cost
curve in the situation where prices have fallen below average costs and
losses are incurred. He says that firms would be hesitant to sell at a
price that does not cover all their costs, both fixed and variable, since
they are concerned about "spoiling the market." Spoiling the market
means selling at low prices today and preventing the rise of market
prices tomorrow, or selling at prices that incur the resentment of other
firms in the industry. Thus the true short-run supply curve, when losses
are incurred, is not the portion of the marginal cost curve between the
average variable and average cost curves, but a supply curve to the left
of the marginal cost curve. In this discussion Marshall drops the assumption of perfectly competitive markets, since under a strict definition of
perfect competition, no firm would be concerned about glutting the
market or about the consequences of its actions on other firms in the
industry. The inspiration for Robinson's *Imperfect Competition* and
Chamberlin's *Monopolistic Competition* can be found in part in Marshall's discussion of the operation of markets when the assumption of
perfect competition is dispensed with.

Although Marshall's discussion of long-run firm cost curves and
supply curves and industry supply curves is clearly deficient by modern

standards, his early attempts in these areas provoked an interesting series of articles in the 1920s and 1930s, the most important being by Knight, Sraffa, and Viner. Marshall indicates the long-run forces that determine the shape and position of the firm's cost and supply curves. First there are those forces internal to the firm. As the size of the firm is increased, internal economies of scale lead to decreasing costs, and internal diseconomies result in increasing costs. Marshall's discussion of the economic reasons for internal economies of scale is reasonably satisfactory; his discussion of internal diseconomies is minimal, and he does not really confront the issue of the relationship between economies and diseconomies and its influence on the optimum size of the firm.

Marshall's discussion of external economies and diseconomies nevertheless precipitated a plethora of literature on the theoretical issues implicit in his analysis. Marshall wanted to reconcile the upward-sloping short-run supply curves of firms and industries with historical evidence suggesting that, in some industries, costs and prices have decreased over time. He based this reconciliation on his notion of external economies. External economies — Marshall never makes it clear whether these are external to the firm or to the industry — result in the downward shift of firm and industry cost curves and supply curves as an industry develops. Under these circumstances the industry's long-run supply curve will slope downward: larger quantities will be supplied at lower prices. The major causes of external economies are the reductions in costs that take place for all firms in an industry when all the firms locate together and share their ideas. Localization also brings cost-saving subsidiary industries and skilled labor to the area.

Marshall's examination of costs and supply raised a number of important theoretical issues examined between 1900 and 1940: What are the economic reasons for the shape of cost and supply curves? Why do supply curves rise in the short run while costs and prices fall in the long run for some industries? Are internal and external economies compatible with competitive markets?

Marshall on Distribution

Marshall's explanation of the forces determining the prices of the factors of production and the distribution of income was consistent with the rest of his analysis. Here, as elsewhere, he often generously acknowledged the merits of criticism of his theories, for example, those attacking his marginal productivity theory of distribution. The same basic supply-and-demand analysis and the distinction between short run and long run used to explain the prices of final goods are also used to explain rents, wages, profits, and interest. The demand for a factor of production is a derived demand that depends on the value of the marginal product of the factor. Marginal products are, however, difficult to disentangle, since technology usually requires that an increase in one factor will require more of other factors. Marshall solves this problem of measuring marginal products by computing what he terms the *net product at the margin*. If an additional laborer requires a hammer, then the net product of the labor is the laborer's addition to total revenue minus the added cost of the hammer. Marshall then points out that it is incorrect to call the theory of factor pricing a marginal productivity theory of distribution, since marginal productivity measures only the demand for a factor, and factor prices are determined by interaction of demand, supply, and price at the margin. After explaining his concept of marginal productivity and its measurement with respect to labor and wages, Marshall advocates a cautious interpretation of the marginal productivity theory.

> This doctrine has sometimes been put forward as a theory of wages. But there is no valid ground for any such pretension. The doctrine that the earnings of a worker tend to be equal to the net product of his work, has by itself no real meaning; since in order to estimate net product, we have to take for granted all the expenses of production of the commodity on which he works, other than his own wages.
>
> But though this objection is valid against a claim that it contains a theory of wages, it is not valid against a claim that the doctrine throws into clear light the action of one of the causes that govern wages.[19]

The proportions in which factors are combined, he says, will depend upon their marginal products and their prices. An entrepreneur interested in maximizing profits will want to produce a given level of output at the lowest possible cost, which will lead the firm to use factors of production in such a way that the ratios of their marginal physical products to their prices will be equal. Otherwise it will be possible to substitute at the margin and achieve lower costs. Marshall does not dwell on the issue of product exhaustion and Euler's theorem and accepts the Wicksteed-Flux conclusion that, in long-run competitive equilibrium, the total product is exhausted when each factor receives the value of its marginal product. Marshall's analysis of the returns to the separate factors of production — wages, rents, profits, and interest — is not particularly interesting. However, his development of the concept of quasi-rent in connection with his theory of factor prices and distribution deserves attention.

Quasi-rent

With his concept of quasi-rent, Marshall not only provided insight into the workings of a market system but also threw new light on an aspect

19. *Ibid.*, p. 518.

of the controversy between classical and marginal utility economists. Classical economics had held that payments to the factors of production, with the exception of land, were price-determining. Prices of final goods depended upon costs of production at the margin. And since there is no rent at the margin, the classical doctrine, in the hands of J. S. Mill, held that wages, profits, and interest were price-determining. Prices were thus basically determined on the side of supply. The marginal utility writers joined the early critics of the classical cost doctrine in holding that payments to the factors of production are price-determined. Marshall's analysis indicates that whether a factor payment is price-determining or price-determined depends upon the time period under consideration (which significantly influences the elasticity of the supply curve of the factors) and the particular perspective from which the analysis is made. Let us examine the payments called rent, wages, profits, and interest.

The return to land has historically been termed "rent." Ricardo in his analysis of land rent had assumed that the supply of land was perfectly inelastic and that there were no alternative uses of land. The payment to the landlord for the use of land was price-determined rather than price-determining. The high price of corn was the cause of high rents. Although there were some criticisms of this theory from minor economists, the basic Ricardian analysis of rent remained unchanged through J. S. Mill to the time of Marshall. Marshall recognized that the issues were much more complex. Whereas the rent of land, when viewed from the perspective of the whole economy, was price-determined and therefore not a cost of production, from the perspective of the individual farmer or firm, rent was a cost of production and therefore price-determining. The farmer who wants to rent land to grow oats must pay a price sufficient to keep the land from alternative uses. Unless the rent the oat farmer is willing to pay is higher than that of the barley farmer or the real-estate developer, the oat farmer will not be able to rent the land in a competitive market. From the perspective of the individual farmer or firm, therefore, land rent is a cost of production that must be paid just as labor and capital costs must be paid.

Marshall also held that, under certain circumstances, land rent was price-determining even from the point of view of the whole economy. For an economy with unsettled land that costs nothing, like the United States in the nineteenth century, rent may be considered as price-determining. Marshall reasoned that the original pioneers considered as part of their return for land settlement not only the immediate return from farming, but also the appreciation in land prices that would take place as population moved toward the frontier areas. This expected land price appreciation is, therefore, part of the necessary supply price that must be paid in order to induce individuals to endure the hardships and dangers of frontier life. The rising land prices, equal to the capitalized value of the rising rents, can therefore be considered as a social cost. Rent under these circumstances is price-determining from the perspective of the economy. Consider the elasticity of the supply curve. From the perspective of the economy, the supply curve of land is perfectly inelastic in a country where all the land is settled, and rent is therefore price-determined. For a country with unsettled land, the supply curve of land slopes up and to the right; with higher rents larger quantities of land will be settled and rent is price-determining. In a letter to Edgeworth, Marshall comments that

> it is *wisest not* to say that "Rent does not enter into cost of production": for that will confuse many people. But it is *wicked* to say that "Rent *does* enter into cost of production," because that is *sure* to be applied in such a way as to lead to the denial of subtle truths.[20]

Marshall went on to show how the returns called wages, profits, and interest in the short run have some of the characteristics of rent. The wage paid to a particular type of labor, for example, an accountant, in long-run equilibrium will be just sufficient to bid those persons in that occupation away from other occupations and hold them in their present use. This long-run wage is the supply price that must be paid by society in order to elicit the quantity supplied. Wages are therefore price-determining. Suppose there is an increase in the demand for the services of accountants and thus an increase in the wage of accountants. In the short run the supply of accountants is less elastic than in the long run. Increases in wages will not greatly influence quantity supplied, and so the short-run wage will rise above the long-run wage. This higher short-run wage, then, has no connection with the price necessary to keep individuals in the occupation and is therefore price-determined, not price-determining. The key to understanding these issues is in the elasticity of the supply curve. In the very short run, the supply curve of a particular kind of labor can be thought of as perfectly inelastic. An increase in demand will result in higher wages with the quantity of labor supplied remaining constant. During the short run the wage will fall slightly as individuals with acceptable training who were working in other occupations enter the occupation. In the long run the supply curve will become even more elastic, as wages fall to the long-run equilibrium value, the necessary supply price. In the short run and market period, therefore, wages are price-determined and are like rent. Marshall called these payments quasi-rents. "And thus even the rent of land is seen, not as a thing by itself, but as the leading species of a large genus."[21] With this concept of quasi-rent, Marshall illuminated the con-

---

20. Pigou, *Memorials*, p. 436.
21. Marshall, *Principles*, p. 412.

troversy as to whether the payments to the factors of production were price-determining or price-determined. It all depends on the time period: in the long run wages are price-determining, but in the short run wages are price-determined and therefore like rent.

Marshall also applied his concept of quasi-rent to the analysis of profits in the short run. In perfectly competitive markets in long-run equilibrium, each firm will earn only a normal rate of profits. Normal profits are a cost of production and must be paid by the firm to hold capital in the firm, just as normal wages must be paid to attract and hold labor. If a firm does not earn normal profits in the long run, capital will leave the firm for other firms and industries where a normal rate is earned. Thus, in the long run, normal profits are a necessary cost of production and therefore price-determining. But in the short run the return called profits can be considered a quasi-rent, and they are price-determined. In the short run the costs of the firm can be divided into variable and fixed costs. The revenues of the firm must be sufficient in the short run to pay the opportunity costs of all the variable factors, or they will leave the firm. What is left over is the return to the fixed factors, which in the short run are perfectly inelastic in supply. Profits in the short run are a quasi-rent to the fixed factors and are price-determined. If total revenues exceed total costs, above-normal profits are made, but where competition prevails these will be eliminated in the long run. If total revenues exceed total variable costs but are less than total costs, losses are incurred, but these losses will disappear in long-run equilibrium. Profits, like wages, then, can be either price-determining or price-determined, depending on the time period under examination.

Marshall also applied his concept of quasi-rent to the analysis of interest in the short run. In the long run there will be a normal rate of interest, which is a necessary cost of production and therefore price-determining, although an old capital investment may earn above or below a normal rate of interest, depending upon supply and demand in the market. But since the capital is fixed, or sunk, in the short run, its return is a quasi-rent.

The analysis of quasi-rent in the broadest perspective can be used to point out some of the essential differences between classical economics, with its emphasis on the supply side, and the marginal utility writers who emphasized demand. If the supply of factors of production is fixed, any factor's return is a quasi-rent, and factor prices are price-determined. The return to the factors is considerably influenced by the level of demand. In the long run the supply of factors is not fixed, and long-run equilibrium prices of final goods must therefore be sufficient to pay for all of the socially necessary costs incurred in production. Under these circumstances the payments to the factors of production are price-determining, and the analysis of final prices must give greater attention to the role of supply. Analytically the returns called wages, profits, rents, and interest have much in common over the various time periods. While, admittedly, nature provides no sharp divisions between time periods, Marshall's theory of generalized time periods with its accompanying doctrine of quasi-rent penetrated deep into the complex issues raised by the forces determining relative prices.

Stable and Unstable Equilibrium

Marshall saw demand schedules as indicating the maximum price individuals would be willing to pay for a given quantity of a commodity. Quantity is thus the independent variable, and demand price is the dependent variable. Supply schedules, on the other hand, indicate the minimum price at which sellers would be willing to supply a given quantity of a commodity. Again, quantity is the independent variable and price the dependent variable. In Book V, Section III, Paragraph 6, of his *Principles of Economics*, Marshall explains the process of reaching equilibrium in markets. Since he regards quantity as the independent variable, the adjustments that bring about equilibrium are discussed largely in terms of quantity adjustments. If at a given quantity demand price exceeds supply price, "then sellers receive more than is sufficient to make it worth their while to bring goods to market to that amount; and there is at work an active force tending to increase the amount brought forward for sale."[22]

Figure 9.3 reproduces Marshall's graphic representation of the process by which equilibrium is reached. At quantity R_1 demand price R_1d_1 exceeds supply price R_1s_1, and thus a larger quantity will be brought to the market by sellers. At quantity R_2 supply price R_2s_2 exceeds demand price R_2d_2 and sellers reduce the quantity brought to the market. Equilibrium is brought about by changes in quantity as sellers respond to the relative level of demand and supply prices. The equilibrium achieved is a stable equilibrium, since any displacement from equilibrium will produce forces returning the market to equilibrium.

Walras and current economic theory follow a quite different set of behavioral postulates in analyzing market forces, seeing price as the independent variable. For them demand schedules show the quantities individuals are willing to buy at various prices, and supply schedules indicate the quantities sellers are willing to offer at various prices.

Which is correct: to regard price as the independent variable, as Walras did, or quantity as the independent variable, as Marshall did? Since this question involves assumptions about the way buyers and

22. *Ibid.*, p. 345.

sellers behave in a market, it can be decided only by empirical research. The analytical consequences of these two ways of describing market behavior can, however, be theoretically deduced. Marshall concluded that it made no theoretical difference, but he was wrong.

The issue is further confused by a historical anomaly: although modern theory followed Walras in regarding price as the independent variable, it followed Marshall in placing price on the vertical axis in supply-and-demand graphs. Mathematical convention places the dependent variable on the vertical axis. An equation of a linear demand curve written $p = a - bq$ implies that price is the dependent variable, yet the behavioral postulates of modern theory regard price as the independent variable.

It is true that Walras and Marshall reach the same conclusions if the demand curve is downward-sloping and the supply curve is upward-sloping. Referring again to Figure 9.3, we see that, under Marshall's analysis, changes in quantity would bring about an equilibrium quantity of $0H$. Walras and modern theory, however, using price as the independent variable, would analyze the forces bringing about equilibrium as follows. At a price of P_2 quantity demanded is $P_2 d_1$, which is less than quantity supplied, $P_2 s_2$, so there is an excess supply. Competition among sellers will force price down until a price is reached where the market clears, that is, where quantity supplied equals quantity demanded. At price $0P_1$, which is less than the equilibrium price, there

Figure 9.3 Reaching Equilibrium

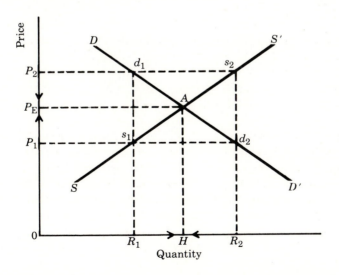

is an excess demand; quantity supplied, $P_1 s_1$, is less than quantity demanded, $P_1 d_2$. Competition among buyers will, therefore, force price up until the market clears.

A market represented by the supply-and-demand curves of Figure 9.3 will reach a stable equilibrium. Using the analysis of Walras and modern theory, any price other than $0P_E$ will set in motion forces that will return price to $0P_E$. $0P_E$ is an equilibrium price, since if price is at $0P_E$ it will remain there. The equilibrium is stable; if something should cause the price to move from $0P_E$, it will return to $0P_E$. But the equilibrium is also stable equilibrium under Marshall's analysis. Quantity $0H$ is a stable equilibrium quantity, since for any quantity other than $0H$, demand price would be either greater or less than supply price, and market forces would return the quantity to $0H$.

Unstable equilibrium is possible when the supply curve is downward-sloping. In unstable equilibrium, if price or quantity attain their equilibrium values, they will remain there; but if the system is disturbed, it will not return to these equilibrium values. An egg laid on its side is in stable equilibrium; if disturbed it will return to its original position of rest. But an egg laid on its end is in unstable equilibrium; if left alone it will remain on its end, but if disturbed it will not return to its original state of equilibrium. Panel (a) of Figure 9.4 represents stable equilibrium using Marshall's analysis with quantity as the independent variable.

At a quantity greater than $0H$, supply price exceeds demand price, that is, the minimum supply price sellers will accept exceeds the maximum price buyers are willing to pay, and sellers will consequently reduce quantity offered to $0H$. If quantity were less than $0H$, sellers

Figure 9.4 Stable and Unstable Equilibrium

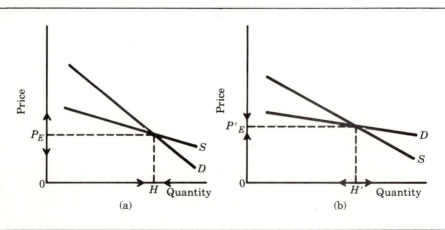

(a)   (b)

would expand quantity, since demand price would exceed supply price. However, if price is the independent variable, panel (a) of Figure 9.4 represents an unstable equilibrium. At a price less than $0P_E$, quantity supplied exceeds quantity demanded and competition among sellers will force the price further down. If price were higher than $0P_E$, the excess demand would force price further up.

Panel (b) of Figure 9.4 shows that a stable equilibrium when quantity is the independent variable can be an unstable equilibrium when price is the independent variable. A comparison of panels (a) and (b) indicates that when a supply curve slopes down and to the right, the stability of equilibrium will depend upon the relative slopes of the supply-and-demand curves and the behavioral assumptions used. Marshall and Walras did have an element in common, which led them both to conclude that with upward-sloping supply curves stable equilibrium is achieved. Both their analyses were in a static framework. For Walras quantity supplied and quantity demanded in the present period depend upon price in the present period; for Marshall supply price and demand price in the present period depend upon quantity in the present period. Thus both Marshall and Walras assumed static behavior.

Economic Fluctuations, Money, and Prices

Although Marshall's overriding concern was with microeconomic theory, he contributed significantly to macroeconomics by studying the influence of monetary forces on the general level of prices. Although some of Marshall's earliest writings (1871) concerned the quantity theory of money, he did not publish any systematic work on money until 1923, when he published a book called *Money, Credit, and Commerce*. But his ideas on macroeconomic topics, though not yet published, were well developed in his lectures and in evidence presented before governmental commissions. The first five editions of his *Principles* carried the subtitle "Volume I," but in the sixth edition, in 1910, he changed this to "An Introductory Volume." In 1895, with the publication of the third edition of the *Principles*, Marshall announced three prospective volumes: Modern Conditions of Industry and Trade; Credit and Employment; and The Economic Functions of Government. He published *Industry and Trade* in 1919 but never was able to write the other two volumes. What Marshall did write on macroeconomics primarily concerns economic stability or instability and the forces determining the general level of prices.

Marshall basically accepts J. S. Mill's views on the stability of the economy: there can never be an insufficiency of aggregate demand, since a decision to save necessarily involves a decision to invest. It is impossible to have general overproduction. This line of reasoning was started by Adam Smith, elaborated by James Mill, Ricardo, and J. B. Say, and is now known in the literature as Say's Law. Still, there were fluctuations in economic activity during Marshall's time, and some writers, particularly J. A. Hobson in England, were advocating underconsumptionist theories. Marshall believed that an understanding of the causes of economic fluctuations was "not to be got by a study of consumption, as has been alleged by some hasty writers."[23] Marshall's explanation of the causes of economic fluctuations follows J. S. Mill, who stressed the influence of business confidence. During an upswing, business confidence is high and credit expands rapidly; during a downswing, businessmen become pessimistic and credit rapidly contracts. Mill's acceptance of Say's Law led him to hold that depressions could not be attributed to any fundamental problem within the system. Marshall suggests two public policies to deal with depression and unemployment. The first is to control markets so that credit is not overexpanded in periods of rising business confidence, since overexpansion may lead to recession. If depression does occur, governments can help restore business confidence by guaranteeing firms against risks. Marshall is not totally satisfied with this solution, since it would be difficult to implement without some adverse results. Guaranteeing businesses against risk, for example, would insure both competent and incompetent businessman and thus interfere with market processes that reward the capable and punish the incapable.

Although Marshall's contribution to the understanding of the causes of business fluctuations was meager, his explanations of those forces that determined the general level of prices are significant. He recognized that his microeconomics analysis was based on the assumption that full employment existed and that there were no important changes in the general level of prices. His analysis of the determinants of the general level of prices is a quantity theory of money constructed within the framework of his basic supply-and-demand analysis.

SUMMARY AND CRITICAL EVALUATION OF MARSHALL

Although over a century has passed since Marshall began his study of economics, his contributions to microeconomics still provide the basis of orthodox undergraduate theory. Like most writers of economics he built upon the work of great theorists of the past; unlike many great thinkers and innovators, however, Marshall did not stress his differences with past writers but acknowledged his borrowing from their ideas. He regarded his work as a continuation of the work of Smith, Ricardo, and

23. *Ibid.*, p. 712, fn.

J. S. Mill and was always generous in his interpretation of their works. His writing is characterized by modesty, a quality rare in the writings of seminal thinkers.

Marshall came to economics with a strong background in mathematics and a deep humanitarian desire to help those in lower-income groups. Yet he believed that it was possible to separate the normative and positive elements of economics and busied himself in developing what he regarded as a positive, value-free science, on the theory that if we understand what is, society can make better choices about what ought to be. He dealt with many methodological and theoretical issues, some of which had been discussed in the literature of economics since the 1830s. Classical orthodox theory had not agreed upon a uniform methodology. Adam Smith had amalgamated theory, history, and description in the *Wealth of Nations*, his weakest link being theory. Although he was not specifically concerned with methodology, Ricardo had presented, without using mathematics, a methodology almost completely in the abstract, deductive theoretical mold. Ricardo's weak point had been history and description. J. S. Mill followed Smith in attempting to forge a structure in which theory, history, and description reinforced and complemented one another. Yet these men had many elements in common. They presumed that economic theory was universally true, equally applicable to different periods in history and to societies with markedly different structures. They also commonly assumed that an understanding of the whole economy was best achieved by starting at the level of the household and the firm. Human nature and behavior were antecedent to the culture. Another common element was an overriding belief that economic conflicts were harmoniously worked out in free markets. Whatever the inadequacies of free markets, they were to be preferred to government intervention in the economy. The only obvious flaw in this harmonious natural order was the conflict between the landlords and the industrialists. Aside from that, scarce resources would be efficiently allocated by the market without government direction, and the free play of markets would assure a full utilization of resources. In the classical analysis of the forces determining relative prices, prices were commonly assumed to depend upon the cost or supply side in the long run.

These classical ideas were not accepted by everyone. A literature developed in the post-Ricardian period criticized the classical theory of value and further suggested that utility and demand were the crucial factors determining relative prices, rather than cost and supply. Other writers had taken the Ricardian labor theory of value and used it to show that labor was being exploited, thereby calling into question the harmonious operation of the economic process in the classical system. This line of thinking reached its fruition in Marx, who used the classical tools to reach quite different conclusions. The systems presented by

Auguste Comte, Karl Marx, and Herbert Spencer called into question the methodological foundations of classical theory, which defined the scope of economics narrowly and viewed human behavior as antecedent to culture and society. Some writers in Germany and England attacked the abstract nature of classical theory and tried to formulate a broader, historically oriented approach to understanding the economy. Finally, the basic theoretical structure was assailed by Jevons, Walras, and Menger, who wanted to replace the cost of production theory of value with an almost exclusive emphasis on the role of demand and marginal utility.

Marshallian economics is the product of these methodological and theoretical controversies. Marshall consistently refused to take a partisan approach to these issues, and his conclusions therefore failed to satisfy the dogmatic thinkers on both sides. He believed there was merit in a narrow definition of the scope of economics, but he also held out the hope that a unified approach in the social sciences would prove fruitful. Since each methodological approach has its benefits as well as its costs, he considered it pointless to waste time arguing over a unique methodology for economics. Economists should use the approach that fits their training and temperament, and different methodologies should be regarded as complementary rather than mutually exclusive. Equally pointless are controversies over whether prices are determined by supply alone or by demand alone. Prices, Marshall pointed out, are the result of a vast set of complex, interacting forces. It is incorrect to view the process of price determination as a simple chain of causal relationships in which utility determines demand, which then determines price, or cost determines supply, which then determines price. Nor do marginal values, whether on the side of utility or of cost, determine prices. We go to the margin to examine the forces at work and to improve our understanding of them, but when we go to the margin we find that utility, cost, and price mutually determine each other's values and that simple causal chains do not exist. The margin, partial equilibrium, *ceteris paribus*, time periods, the representative firm, and factors of production are all abstract theoretical constructs that help us to break up complex problems for analysis. This analytical progress is achieved, however, at a cost of realism, and the economist must therefore supplement pure theory with descriptive and historical material.

Although Marshall attempted to take noncommittal positions on many of the methodological and theoretical issues of his time, he usually leans in the direction of certain elements in the classical theory. He defines the scope of economics more broadly than Jevons, Menger, and Walras and prefers the methodology of Smith and J. S. Mill. He feels that although prices depend upon a complex set of forces in the long run, the classical economists were basically correct in emphasizing the importance of cost and supply. The concept of opportunity cost gives some insights into the allocation of resources in the short run when supply is relatively fixed, but in the long run a more fundamental insight into the pricing process can be achieved by considering the real costs of production, the efforts of labor, and the waiting or abstinence of the capitalists. Marshall was never able to dispense completely with Bentham's hedonistic psychology, although he was well aware of the criticism it incurred.

The fundamental framework of present-day undergraduate microeconomic theory derives from Marshall's *Principles*. Although there have been many important contributions to micro theory since then, most have been additions to technique, not to substantive analysis. The only exception is the contribution to the theory of market structures initiated by Joan Robinson and Edward Chamberlin in the 1930s. The great weakness in Marshall's system was his failure to examine the forces determining the levels of income and employment. But when that treatment was undertaken in the 1930s by J. M. Keynes, it was formulated within the basic Marshallian framework of supply-and-demand analysis applied to aggregate variables.

SUGGESTED READINGS

Coats, A. W. "Sociological Aspects of British Thought." *Journal of Political Economy*, 75 (October 1967).

The Eastern Economic Journal. Vol. 8, No. 1 (January/March 1982). Complete issue on Alfred Marshall.

Frisch, Ragnar. "Alfred Marshall's Theory of Value." *Quarterly Journal of Economics*, 64 (November 1950).

Guillebaud, Claude W. "Some Personal Reminiscences of Alfred Marshall." *History of Political Economy*, 3 (Spring 1971).

Homan, Paul T. "Alfred Marshall" in *Contemporary Economic Thought*. New York: Harper, 1928.

Keynes, J. M. "Alfred Marshall" in *Essays and Sketches in Biography*. New York: Meridian, 1956.

Marshall, Alfred. *Principles of Economics*. 9th ed. London: Macmillan, 1961.

Petridis, Anastasios. "Alfred Marshall's Attitudes to the Economic Analysis of Trade Unions: A Case of Anomalies in a Competitive System." *History of Political Economy*, 5 (Spring 1973).

Pigou, A. C., ed. *Memorials of Alfred Marshall*. New York: Kelley and Millman, 1956.

Robertson, H. M. "Alfred Marshall's Aims and Methods Illustrated from His Treatment of Distribution." *History of Political Economy*, 2 (Spring 1970).

Shove, G. F. "The Place of Marshall's 'Principles' in the Development of Economic Thought." *Economic Journal*, 52 (December 1942).

Viner, Jacob. "Marshall's Economics, in Relation to the Man and to His Times." *American Economic Review*, 31 (June 1941).

Whitaker, John K. "Alfred Marshall: The Years 1877 to 1885." *History of Political Economy*, 4 (Spring 1972).

———. *The Early Economic Writings of Alfred Marshall, 1867-1900*. New York: Free Press, 1975.

———. "Some Neglected Aspects of Marshall's Economic and Social Thought." *History of Political Economy*, 9 (Summer 1977).

Chapter 10

The Development of Modern
Microeconomic Theory

When British and American students, graduate and undergraduate, studied economics in the early 1900s, they studied a form of Marshallian economics that blended equilibrium analysis, historical and institutional facts, and common sense. Although much of the historical and institutional material, as well as some of the common sense, have disappeared, the undergraduate microeconomics taught today is still strongly rooted in Marshallian economics. Graduate microeconomics, however, is now almost totally devoid of Marshallian analysis. Depending heavily on mathematical modeling and Walrasian general equilibrium economics, it focuses on such topics as dynamic choice theory under uncertainty, set theoretic choice theory, and principal-agent problems. The story of how and why we moved from an emphasis on Marshallian economics at both the graduate and undergraduate levels to this bifurcated state is an important part of the story of the development of modern microeconomics. The first episode of this story recounts the development of micro theory from the Marshallian economics at the turn of the century to the 1950s, when the core of modern graduate school theory began to emerge.

THE MOVEMENT AWAY FROM
MARSHALLIAN ECONOMICS

Marshall's engine of analysis, combining supply and demand curves with common sense, could answer certain questions, but others exceeded its scope. Supply-and-demand analysis was partial equilibrium analysis applied to problems of relative prices. But many of the questions economists were trying to answer, such as what determines the distribution of income or what effect certain laws and taxes would have, either introduced problems beyond the applicability of partial equilibrium analysis or violated its assumptions. Nonetheless, economists continued to apply partial equilibrium arguments to such issues, assuming that the aggregate market must constitute some as yet unknown combination of all the partial equilibrium markets.

Most economists were content with this state of affairs for quite a while. After all, Marshallian economics did provide a workable, if not formally tight, theory that was able to answer many real-world questions. It was the middle ground. Marshallian economists were engineers rather than scientists, and engineers are interested not in pondering underlying forces but in building something that works. As Joan Robinson put it, Marshall had the ability to recognize hard problems and hide them in plain sight.

Marshallian economics attempted to walk a fine line between a formalist approach and a historically institutional approach. It is not surprising that in doing so it created critics on both sides. In the United States, a group called the institutionalists wanted simply to eliminate the theory, arguing that history and institutions should be emphasized and the inadequate theory dropped. Other critics, whom we will call formalists, went in the opposite direction: they believed economics should be a science, not an engineering field. These formalists agreed with the institutionalists that Marshallian economic theory was inadequate, but their answer was not to eliminate the theory; they wanted to provide a better, more rigorous general equilibrium foundation that could adequately answer the more complicated questions.

THE FORMALIST REVOLUTION IN MICROECONOMICS

The Marshallians remained the predominant group in the United States until the 1930s, but in the mid-1930s the formalists began a program of theoretical research that would eventually reformulate microeconomics into its present highly mathematical structure. This program, which we will term the "formalist revolution," remained within the general sphere of neoclassical economics but significantly altered its methods. Consequently, modern economics is essentially neoclassical economics altered by mathematical economists in four ways.

1. The formalists provided greater range and precision to the existing theory. As economists moved away from Marshall and toward a more formal analysis, they also adopted a more formal language of exposition — mathematics. Marshall's immediate followers used geometry to extend and formalize his analysis. During the late 1930s and the 1940s Marshallian geometry was gradually replaced by multivariate calculus, which could be used to model multidimensional problems instead of the two or three dimensions graphical techniques allowed. Later, new techniques were added, such as optimal control theory (the calculus of functions rather than of variables), game theory, and set theory.

2. The new methods expanded the existing theory to include a wider range of phenomena. For example, modern graduate microeconomics analyzes choice under certainty, whereas in Marshall's day economics had no such formal analysis.

3. Economics moved from contextual to noncontextual argumentation, rendering it less representative of the real world and more abstract.

4. Although the new methodology was generally more abstract, some very practial techniques developed, such as linear programming, now commonly used by businesses to study the efficient use of resources.

Some Historical Roots of Modern Microeconomics

The formalist revolution that engendered modern graduate microeconomics is rooted in the thought of several nineteenth- and early-twentieth-century figures. The first of these great pioneers in stating hypotheses in mathematical form was A. Cournot, who published his *Researches into Mathematical Principles* in 1838. Cournot expected that his attempts to bring mathematics into economics would be rejected by most economists, but he adhered to his method nevertheless, because he found the literary expression of theory that could be expressed with greater precision by mathematics to be wasteful and irritating.

Léon Walras and Vilfredo Pareto, who succeeded Walras as professor of economics at Lausanne, are other early devotees of mathematical economics. Whereas Marshall had focused on partial equilibrium, Walras, using algebraic techniques, focused on general equilibrium. His general equilibrium theory has substantially displaced Marshallian partial equilibrium theory as the basic framework for economic research. Pareto, whose name is familiar to many students of economics from its use in the phrase "Pareto optimal criteria," began in the early 1900s to apply marginal analysis to questions of economic policy. Jevons, whose contribution to demand theory we examined in Chapter 7, in 1870 advocated a more extensive use of mathematics in economics.

Jevons was followed by another pioneer in formalist economics, F. Y. Edgeworth, who pointed out in 1881 that the basic structure of micro theory was simply the repeated application of the principle of maximization. This finding raised the question, why reexamine the same principles over and over again? By abstracting from the specific institutional context and reducing a problem to its mathematical core, one could quickly capture the essence of the problem and apply that essence to all such microeconomic questions. Following this reasoning,

Edgeworth declared that both an understanding of the economy and a basis for the formulation of proper policies were to be found in the consistent use of mathematics. He accused the Marshallian economists of being seduced by the "zigzag windings of the flowery path of literature."[1]

Irving Fisher, writing in the last decade of the nineteenth century, was an early American pioneer of formalism who supported and extended Simon Newcomb's advocacy of increased use of mathematics in economics. The formalist position was not well received in the United States, however, until nearly the middle of the twentieth century. All these pioneers were, therefore, unheeded prophets of the future. Inattention to their efforts can be attributed partly to the strength of Marshall's analysis, a judicious blend of theory, history, and institutional knowledge. Unable to compete with the Marshallian approach, early mathematical work in economics was practically ignored by mainstream economists until the 1930s.

In the early 1930s this situation began to change. Expositions of the many geometric tools that now provide the basis for undergraduate microeconomics began to fill the journals. The marginal revenues curve, the short-run marginal cost curve, and models of imperfect competition and income-substitution effects were "discovered" and explored during this period. Though rooted in Marshall, these new tools *formalized* his analysis, and as they did so they moved farther and farther from the actual institutions they represented. The Marshallian approach to interrelating theory and institutions had been like a teeter-totter: it had worked as long as the two sides balanced. But once the theory side gained a bit, the balance was broken and economics fell hard to the theoretical side, leaving history and institutions suspended in air.

History and institutions were abandoned because the new formalized tools required stating precisely what was being assumed and what was changing, and stating it in such a way that the techniques could handle the entire analysis. History and particular institutions no longer fit in. One could no longer argue, as in the earlier Marshallian economics, that "a reasonable businessman" would act in a certain way, appealing to the reader's sensibility to know what "reasonable" meant. Instead "reasonableness" was transformed into a precise concept — "rational" — which was defined as making choices in conformance with certain established axioms. Similarly, the competitive economy was defined as one in which all individuals are "price takers." Formalism required noncontextual argumentation, abstracted from any actual setting, in which assumptions are spelled out.

1. F. Y. Edgeworth, *Papers Relating to Political Economy* (Burt Franklin, 1925), II, 282. See Bruce Larson, "Edgeworth, Samuelson and Operationally Meaningful Theorems," *History of Political Economy*, 19, No. 3 (1987), pp. 351-357, who argues that Edgeworth is a precursor of Samuelson.

Though the use of geometry as a tool in Marshallian analysis was a relatively small step, it was the beginning of the end for Marshallian economics. When geometry disclosed numerous logical problems with Marshallian economics, the new Marshallians responded with further formalization. Thus, by 1935 economics was ripe for change. Paul Samuelson summed up the situation.

> To a person of analytic ability, perceptive enough to realize that mathematical equipment was a powerful sword in economics, the world of economics was his or her oyster in 1935. The terrain was strewn with beautiful theorems waiting to be picked up and arranged in unified order.[2]

Since many economists had by this time acquired the requisite analytic equipment, the late 1930s and early 1940s witnessed a revolution in microeconomic theory, which formalism won. Cournot, Walras, Pareto, and Edgeworth unseated Marshall to become the forefathers of modern graduate microeconomics, relegating Marshallian economics to a role in undergraduate education.

The first step in the formalization of micro theory was to extend the marginal analysis of the household, firm, and markets and to make it more internally consistent. As economists shifted to higher-level mathematical techniques, they were able to go beyond partial equilibrium to general equilibrium, because the mathematics provided a method by which to keep track more precisely of items they had formerly kept somewhat loosely in the back of their heads. The second step was to reformulate the questions in a manner consistent with the tools and techniques available for dealing with them. The third step was to add new techniques to clarify unanswered questions. This process is continuing today.

Paul Samuelson

Of the many economists involved in this formalization, Paul Samuelson has played the largest role. Born in 1915, Samuelson began graduate economics studies at Harvard in 1935, after acquiring a strong undergraduate background in mathematics. There he proceeded to publish significant articles applying mathematics to both micro- and macroeconomic theory. He received his Ph.D. in 1941 at the age of twenty-

2. Paul Samuelson, "The General Theory: 1946," in *Keynes' General Theory: Reports of Three Decades*, ed. Robert Lekachman (New York: St. Martin's Press, 1964), p. 315.

six, and by the time he was thirty-two had become a full professor at the Massachusetts Institute of Technology and the first recipient of the American Economics Association's John Bates Clark Award, given to economists under forty who have made significant professional contributions. Samuelson later became the first American to receive the Nobel Prize in economics.

The sources of Samuelson's intellectual inspiration were Cournot, Jevons, Walras, Pareto, Edgeworth, and Fisher, all of whom contributed piecemeal applications of mathematics to economic theory. Using his mathematical background, Samuelson extended their work and laid down the mathematical foundations of orthodox economic theory. Like Edgeworth, he had harsh words for Alfred Marshall, whose ambiguities, he said, "paralyzed the best brains in the Anglo-Saxon branch of our profession for three decades."[3] He went on to say

> I have come to feel that Marshall's dictum that "it seems doubtful whether any one spends his time well in reading lengthy translations of economic doctrines into mathematics, that have not been done by himself" should be exactly reversed. The laborious literary working over of essentially simple mathematical concepts such as is characteristic of much of modern economic theory is not only unrewarding from the standpoint of advancing science, but involves as well mental gymnastics of a peculiarly depraved type.[4]

Samuelson's works provide an interesting perspective on the methodological changes in economics since Marshall.

The direction Samuelson's contribution to economic theory would take is evident in his Ph.D. dissertation, completed in 1941 and published in 1947 as *Foundations of Economic Analysis*. A subtitle, *The Operational Significance of Economic Theory*, was eliminated in the published edition, and the statement "Mathematics Is a Language" added to its title page. The book undertakes to analyze mathematically the foundations of modern micro and macro theory. In the introductory chapter, Samuelson explains that his purpose is to work out the implications for economic theory of the following statement: "The existence of analogies between central features of various theories implies the existence of a general theory which underlies the particular theories and unifies them with respect to those essential features."[5]

3. Paul A. Samuelson, "The Monopolistic Competition Revolution," in *Competition Theory*, ed. R. E. Kuenne (New York: John Wiley, 1967), p. 109.
4. Samuelson, *Foundations of Economic Analysis* (Cambridge: Harvard University Press, 1955), p. 6.
5. *Ibid.*, p. 3. (Complete sentence is italicized in the original.)

Equilibrium and Stability

According to Samuelson, the theoretical structure that underlies and unifies the individual elements of micro and macro theory rests on two very general hypotheses concerning the conditions, first, of equilibrium and, second, of its stability. For problems of comparative statics, the conditions of equilibrium can be placed in the familiar maximization framework in which much of the previous work in micro theory had been done. Samuelson illustrates the unity of this approach by working through the firm's minimization of costs and maximization of profits, the consumer's maximization of satisfaction, and welfare theory. And whereas previous economists had paid less attention to dynamic analysis, Samuelson demonstrates that once the dynamic properties of a system are specified, its stability can be assessed. Equilibrium and

Paul Samuelson

stability conditions thus emerge as the two-part structure underlying economic theory.

Although Samuelson's *Foundations* and his subsequent work have dealt almost exclusively with mathematical economic theory, he is sensitive to the relationship between mathematical economics and the process of economic research. He consistently attempts to formulate operationally meaningful, not merely elegant, theorems — in other words, to provide testable hypotheses useful in economic research. "By a *meaningful theorem*," he says, "I mean simply any empirical data which could conceivably be refuted, if only under ideal conditions."[6]

Formalists, Mathematics, and Pedagogy

Mathematical economics has made it possible to state economic theory concisely and precisely and, by mathematical manipulations, to deduce the theoretical implications of a given set of assumptions. The formalists mathematically exposed inconsistencies and corrected logical errors in the literary reasoning that had been used to extend partial equilibrium analysis. As they did, their mathematical techniques undermined the reason for using partial equilibrium analysis. Recognizing this, Samuelson went back to Walras to observe how he approached interconnected markets. Starting from Walras's analysis, and applying algebra and calculus, Samuelson was able to determine the stability conditions necessary for equilibrium. This provided economic reasoning with a much more solid theoretical ground and an analytical core of multimarket equilibrium that would serve as the foundation of modern microeconomics.

But the introduction of formalism presented a pedagogical problem: the Walrasian general equilibrium approach is very difficult. In order to master it, one must learn a new language, mathematics, and be able to grasp highly abstract, noncontextual argumentation. But most economics undergraduates have no intention of becoming economists and hence have little incentive to acquire the considerable mathematical skills necessary to comprehend the complexities of general equilibrium interactions. This pedagogical problem has occasioned the current bifurcation of microeconomics, since the preferred graduate economics theory is too difficult for the typical undergraduate. Paul Samuelson responded to the special needs of undergraduate education by writing an elementary economics textbook, which has sold three million copies and gone through many editions. Samuelson's text dominated the field for some thirty years from its first edition in 1947, and most other introductory texts have copied his format. This elementary text shaped

6. *Ibid.*, p. 4.

modern undergraduate economics, just as his *Foundations* did graduate economics.

In his undergraduate text Samuelson graphically presented microeconomics as a logical extension of the interactions of rational individuals within a competitive market structure. Retaining the Marshallian tools but eliminating most of the platitudes and homey analogies of earlier economics texts, Samuelson constructed a largely noncontextual theory more consistent with general equilibrium analysis. Thus arose the current divided worlds of graduate and undergraduate economics. Undergraduate introductory texts kept the Marshallian approach, emphasizing two-dimensional graphical techniques rather than multivariate calculus, and graduate microeconomics moved on to the formalist approach far more consistent with Walras and Cournot than with Marshall. With the ever-increasing sophistication of the techniques used in graduate micro theory, the split has widened.

Some carryover from graduate education has of course occurred, since graduate students, once they become teachers, naturally tend to teach what they have been taught. Upper-level textbooks in subjects such as public finance and intermediate microeconomics are beginning to reflect the change and are becoming less Marshallian. But since introductory texts have not changed, the dichotomy between undergraduate and graduate microeconomics continues to be significant.

The Progression of General Equilibrium Theory

General equilibrium theory developed in part as a means of formally exploring Adam Smith's questions. Will the unfettered use of markets lead to the common good, and if so, in what sense? Will the invisible hand of the market promote the social good? What types of markets are necessary for that to be the case? Since they involve the entire system, these are essentially general equilibrium questions, not questions of partial equilibrium. They could not, therefore, be answered within the Marshallian framework, although they could be discussed in relatively loose terms, as indeed they were before formal general equilibrium analysis developed.

In the 1930s two mathematicians, Abram Wald (1902–1950) and John von Neumann (1903–1957), turned their attention to the study of equilibrium conditions in both static and dynamic models. They quickly raised the technical sophistication of economic analysis, exposing the inadequacy of much of previous economists' policy and theoretical analysis. Their work was noted by economists such as Kenneth Arrow and Gerard Debreu, who extended it and applied it to Walras to produce a more precise formulation of his general equilibrium theory. Following Wald's lead, Arrow and Debreu then rediscovered the earlier writings of Walras and Edgeworth. So impressed were they by these writers that they declared Walras and Edgeworth, not Marshall, to be the rightful forefathers of modern microeconomics.

General equilibrium theorists have found the answer to the question "Does the invisible hand work?" to be yes, as long as certain conditions hold true. Their proof, for which Arrow and Debreu received Nobel prizes, was a milestone in economics because it answered the conjecture Adam Smith had made to begin the classical tradition in economics. Much subsequent work has been done in general equilibrium theory to articulate the invisible hand theorem more elegantly and to modify its assumptions, but by first proving it Arrow and Debreu earned a place in the history of economic thought.

The Expanding Domain of Microeconomics

Economists have applied the micro model that explains household consumer behavior and firm behavior using the tools of rationality and maximization to areas that were formerly the exclusive province of sociology and political science. In this sense, economists have become imperialistic in the post–World War II period. The formalization of theory as a methodological program, which now dominates economics, has also infiltrated into other disciplines, notably, political science, history, sociology, and geography. Techniques developed largely by econometricians are widely used in the social sciences and history. One example of this expanded use of economic models to explain what was previously regarded as noneconomic behavior is the work of Gary Becker.[7] He has used microeconomic models to study decisions about courtship, marriage, and childbearing.

The simple-maximization micro model based on the assumption of rational individuals has a potentially infinite application, and recent years have seen it used in widely diverse areas. These incursions of economic ideas into other disciplines have sometimes been treated facetiously by those who claim that the economic approach is too simple. In one sense they are right. The ideas and policy conclusions of the "economics of everything" are often simple. But mere simplicity does not make them wrong. Market incentives make a difference in people's behavior, and noneconomic specialists have often not included a sufficient consideration of these incentives in their analyses. But analyses can go astray when *only* economic incentives are considered and insufficient attention is paid to institutional and social incentives. Unfortunately, given modern economists' training in noncontextual modeling, this is often what occurs.

---

7. See Richard B. McKezie and Gordon Tullock, *The New World of Economics* (Homewood, Ill.: R. D. Irwin, 1975), for other examples.

Gains of Formalism

The results of the mathematical reformulation of microeconomics are impressive. As economists worked through the problems, they began to perceive the relationship between prices and LaGrangian multipliers (the values of the constraints). The question of whether prices were inherent in economic systems had been debated previously, but now mathematical economists could show that prices occurred naturally in a maximization process and that even in the absence of markets, constrained maximization will still have a "price" (called a shadow price). If prices do not exist, another rationing device must replace price.

They also showed how one can easily reformulate a maximization problem subject to a constraint into a constrained minimization problem: by switching constraints and objective functions, the problem "Maximize output subject to technical production constraints" is equal to the problem "Minimize cost subject to producing a certain output." Such a reformulation, which is called "analyzing the dual," affords insight into the nature of the maximization problem by showing how slight changes in the output or constraints change the situation.

These developments had both practical and theoretical significance. On the practical side, the understanding of shadow prices and duals led to significant developments in modern management techniques. On the theoretical side, the analysis of the dual added to economists' analysis of scarcity a symmetry that deepened their understanding of the problem. What previously took volumes to present (often incorrectly) could be covered in one or two pages (for those who knew the language). Given the earlier misuse of informal models and confusion about their implications, most economists saw these developments as a significant gain. The 1987 winner of the Nobel Prize in economics, Robert Solow, commented:

> I detect a tendency...to idealize the old, nonformalist days in economics. I lived through those days and I was educated when that was the way economics was done, and let me tell you — they were not so great at all. They were pretty awful, in fact. My nonformalist education was full of vagueness and logical inconsistency and wishful thinking and mere prejudice and *post hoc propter hoc*, and pontification was everywhere in the classes I took and the lectures I went to.[8]

8. Unpublished transcript of a comment by Robert Solow on a paper by David Colander at the 1986 American Economic Association meetings.

The Development of Econometrics

Allied with the use of mathematics to formalize microeconomic theory was the development of better tools by which to test empirically the new mathematically formulated hypotheses. Prior to the formalization of economic theory, economists employed discourse not only to state economic theories and hypotheses but also to test them. Testing of hypotheses was based either on present circumstances or history, but in either case the use of statistics was minimal. This essentially heuristic approach did not permit hypotheses to be tested in a manner acceptable to modern neoclassical economists.

Although mathematics, in its broadest sense, can be used at every stage of economic research, the term *mathematical economics* refers only to the application of the mathematical technique to the formulation of hypotheses. It is formal, abstract analysis used to develop hypotheses and clarify their implications. The term *statistics* refers to a collection of numerical observations, and *statistical analysis* to the use of such data to test hypotheses. *Econometrics* combines mathematical economics as it is applied to the formulation of hypotheses, and statistical analysis as it is used to test hypotheses. Thus econometrics fuses two stages of economic research.

The 1960s and 1970s saw enormous advances in formal statistical testing and in an understanding of econometric methods. Advances in computer technology made it possible to conduct intensely complicated empirical work. Statistical tests that earlier would have taken days could be done in seconds on the computer. The initial hopes for econometrics were large. Some believed that econometrics would make economics a science in which all theories could be tested. During this time, logical positivism and Popperian falsificationism were the reigning methodologies, and the errors of the past — formulating theories in such a way as to be untestable — were to be avoided.

Malthus's statement of the population doctrine is a good example of such an untestable formulation. In the first edition of his *Essay on Population*, Malthus presented the hypothesis that population tends to grow at a faster rate than the food supply. The rate of population growth will equal the rate of growth of the food supply only as a result of forces that reduce the birth rate and increase the death rate. Over the long run, which is the period to which the theory applies, he concludes that the growth of population is incompatible with a rise in per capita income. The hypothesis is thus in part capable of being statistically refuted. In the second and subsequent editions of his *Essay on Population*, however, Malthus states the population thesis in such a way that it cannot be tested empirically; he adds an unmeasurable check on population, the "growth of moral restraint," by which he means the postponement of marriage and abstinence from premarital sexual activity. When moral restraint as a check on birth rates is added to the theory, an observed population increase may be combined with a rising, falling, or constant per capita income and still be compatible with the theory. Thus the population theory becomes impossible to test empirically.

In the 1950s and 1960s economists believed that they could avoid such problems. Unfortunately, econometric testing of theories proved much more difficult in practice than researchers first hoped, for four major reasons. First, the validity of classical statistical tests depends upon the theory being developed independently of the data. In reality, however, most empirical economic researchers "mine the data," looking for the "best fit" — that is, the formulation of the theory that achieves the highest r^2, t, and F statistics (statistics that measure the likelihood that the theory is correct). Data mining erodes the validity of the statistical tests. Second, even where statistical tests are conducted appropriately, the limited availability of data makes it necessary to designate proxies, which may or may not be appropriate; the validity of the tests depends upon the appropriateness of the proxy, but there is no statistical measure of the appropriateness of a proxy. Third, almost all economic theories include some immeasurable variables that can be, and often are, relied upon to explain statistical results that do not conform to the theory. Fourth, replication of econometric tests generally is impossible since economists can seldom, if ever, conduct a controlled experiment.

As a result of these limitations, some economists have developed a cynical view of testing. Edward Leamer nicely captured this view when he wrote that

> the econometric modeling was done in the basement of the building and the econometric theory courses were taught on the top floor (the third). I was perplexed by the fact that the same language was used in both places. Even more amazing was the transmogrification of particular individuals who wantonly sinned in the basement and metamorphosed into the highest of high priests as they ascended to the third floor.[9]

Similarly, Solow has stated:

> I do not think that it is possible to settle these arguments econometrically. I do not think that econometrics is a powerful or usable enough tool with macroeconomic time series. And so one is reduced to a species of judgment about the structure of the economy. You can always provide models to support your position econometrically,

9. E. E. Leamer, *Specification Searches* (New York: Wiley, 1978).

but that is too easy for both sides. One was never able to find common empirical ground.[10]

Cynicism toward testing has led many researchers to take a cavalier attitude toward their statistical work. The result is that many studies cannot be duplicated, much less replicated, and that "inadvertent errors in published empirical articles are a commonplace rather than a rare occurrence."[11] Leamer suggests that one way out of the dilemma is to use Bayesian econometrics, in which a researcher's degree of belief is taken into account in any statistical test, but the process is so complicated that most researchers simply continue to do what they do. It is this difficulty of empirical testing that has spawned the rhetorical and sociological methodologies we described in Chapter 1.

Evolving Techniques

The evolution of microeconomics has entailed a progression from one mathematical language to another, each of which has been able to resolve some of the ambiguities that marred its predecessor. Initially, economists such as Paul Samuelson and John Hicks translated the geometry of the 1930s to the multivariate calculus of the 1960s. The partial differentials of calculus represented the interrelationships among sectors; the sign of the second partial derivative illustrated stability conditions; and the sign of the first derivatives captured the interactive effects. Cross partial elasticities of demand, linear homogeneous production functions, homothetic demands, and constant elasticity of substitution (CES) production functions all appeared in microeconomic terminology. But multivariate calculus requires one to assume continuity and poses the maximization problem in a highly rarefied way. In response to these shortcomings of calculus, economists modified the maximization problem in a number of ways, some of which made microeconomics more practical and useful in business while others provided deeper understanding of the economy.

By the 1970s the possibilities of comparative static calculus had begun to be exhausted, and the cutting edge of theoretical work was being done in *dynamic calculus*, in which time is explicitly taken into account. To see why dynamic calculus is relevant, consider the production problem. The intermediate micro approach is to say that the firm faces a production problem: given a set of inputs and relative prices, it

10. Robert Solow in *Conversations with Economists*, ed. Arjo Klamer (New Jersey: Rowman and Allanheld, 1984), p. 137.
11. William Dewald et al., "Replication in Empirical Economics," in *American Economic Review*, 76 (September 1986), pp. 587–588.

chooses an optimal quantity of output. But where is time in the model? It is suppressed, so how the model actually works is unclear. Adopting a *comparative static interpretation* provides a somewhat temporal dimension. The problem is considered twice: before and after a single change. Thus it becomes an analysis of two points in time. No consideration is given, however, to how one gets from one point to the other or to how long that time period is.

For a better analysis of the process of getting from one point to the other, the mathematical formulation of the problem must explicitly include the time path along which one goes from the initial state to the end state. The calculus that accomplishes this is *optimal control theory*. Students typically learn optimal control theory in the calculus course following differential equations, which follows multivariate calculus. The solution sets are similar, but instead of being expressed in LaGrangian multipliers, they are expressed in Hamiltonians and bordered Hessians.

After increasing the complexity of the calculus it used, micro analysis expanded away from it, for both practical and theoretical reasons. Practically, it moved toward linear models because linear algorithms existed by which one could more easily compute numerical solutions. Thus, a simple linear formulation was more relevant to real-world problems, and *linear*, *network*, and *dynamic programming* were added to the economist's tool kit. In theoretical work, the formulation of the general equilibrium problem soon went beyond calculus to *set theory* and *game theory*. Economists preferred these approaches because they were more precise and did not require assumptions of continuity as calculus did. As the techniques changed, so did the terminology; such terms as "upper-semi continuous" and "a Cournot-Nash equilibrium" became commonplace in graduate micro courses.

Another significant change in microeconomics is evident in its handling of uncertainty. Economic decisions must be made in the face of an uncertain future. Marshall did not attempt to tackle the uncertainty problem directly. Modern microeconomics, however, formally confronts uncertainty, though often with stochastic rather than static processes. To analyze such models, microeconomics uses *applied statistical decision theory*, a blend of statistics, probability theory, and logic.

DEVELOPMENTS IN MICROECONOMICS:
DEMAND THEORY AND
WELFARE ECONOMICS

Although we cannot provide more than an overview of the changes currently underway in microeconomics, we can illustrate some of their implications by examininig developments in two areas, demand theory and welfare theory.

The Progression of Demand Theory

In the neoclassical model, the theory of demand — that as price falls the quantity demanded will increase — was based upon assumptions about utility maximization. Marshall assumed that the utility received from consuming a good depends exclusively on the quantity of that good consumed. In mathematical terms he assumed that individuals' utility functions were additive. Marshall's theory of demand also assumed that utility was cardinally measurable and that the principle of diminishing marginal utility held true.

A key debate in the early 1900s concerned the validity of the law of demand. Some economists questioned the assumptions, arguing either that utility was not cardinally measurable or that the theory of diminishing marginal utility did not hold true. Others, such as Giffen, argued that empirical evidence contradicted the law of demand. Still others contended that demand theory was based on an inadequate, hedonistic psychology. Modern demand theory evolved, in part, in response to economists' attempts to answer these questions.

Although a number of economists contributed to the revision of demand theory, the work of J. R. Hicks has had the greatest impact. In 1934 Hicks and R. G. D. Allen restructured demand theory by demonstrating that basing demand on indifference curves eliminates the assumptions of cardinal measurement of utility and diminishing marginal utility. They also showed that a generalized utility function allows for substitute and complementary relationships. Although indifference-curve techniques had been developed by Edgeworth, Pareto, and Fisher, they had not been used in the literature to any extent since their initial development. With their reintroduction in the 1930s, however, indifference curves became an accepted and frequently used tool of microeconomic theory.

Giffen's empirical results, alleging an upward-sloping demand curve, provoked further interest in a study of demand. With his new technique of indifference curves, Hicks was able to separate theoretically the income and substitution effect. If the price of good A is decreased, the substitution effect will produce an unambiguous result: the quantity demanded will increase. In cases involving what are now called "Giffen goods," in which the good is strongly inferior, the income effect can offset the substitution effect and cause the demand curve to slope upward. Although these developments demonstrated the theoretical possibility of upward-sloping demand curves, no one could demonstrate empirically a positively sloped demand curve.[12]

12. In their article Hicks and Allen referred to a 1915 work by E. Slutsky that distinguished between normal and inferior goods. But not until Hicks and Allen discovered this earlier work was it generally introduced into the literature, which demonstrates that a first statement of a theoretical proposition is not as significant as a meaningful application of a proposition.

The Problem of Inadequate Psychological Foundations

Developments of demand and utility theory expanded the applicability and clarified the meaning of the theory of consumer behavior, but they did not answer criticism of its underlying hedonistic psychological assumptions. The intellectual origins of utility theory can be found in the work of Jeremy Bentham. By the 1930s psychologists had rejected Bentham's explanation of behavior, asserting that economics was built upon false psychological premises. Psychologist William McDougall stated this criticism succinctly early in the 1920s.

> Political economy suffered hardly less from the crude nature of the psychological assumptions from which it professed to deduce the explanations of its facts and its prescriptions for economic legislation. It would be a libel, not altogether devoid of truth, to say that classical political economy was a tissue of false conclusions drawn from false psychological assumptions.[13]

Attacked on this issue by those outside the profession as well as by heterodox economists, especially Thorstein Veblen, mainstream economists became uneasy. Marshall attempted to ameliorate the situation by changing some of his terminology in subsequent editions of his *Principles*. But because he had no alternative explanation, he never succeeded in purging hedonistic psychology from his theory of consumer behavior. Some economists argued that indifference-curve techniques solved these problems by explaining consumer behavior without assuming cardinal measurement of utility or diminishing marginal utility. But most economists disagreed, since indifference curves contain most of the inherent assumptions of cardinal measurement and diminishing utility.[14]

Though most modern economists use indifference-curve techniques, many recognize their limitations, one of which is that the concept of a consumer being "indifferent" to various bundles of goods is nonoperational. The concept of the indifference curve is completely theoretical: there is no way of empirically measuring "indifference" or constructing indifference curves. Furthermore, the theory still rests on two major psychological assumptions, that consumers are introspective and that they are trying to maximize. Since the indifference curve is merely a

---

13. William McDougall, *An Introduction to Social Psychology* (Boston: John W. Luce, 1923), pp. 10–11.
14. F. H. Knight, "Realism and Relevance in the Theory of Demand," *Journal of Political Economy* 36 (December 1944); Dennis Robertson, "Utility and All What?" Economics Journal 64 (December 1954).

construct without empirical content, the theory of consumer behavior becomes tautological. First we assume that consumers are free to purchase any goods consistent with their incomes and preferences. Since we have no way of determining preferences except as revealed by actual purchases, it follows that what is actually purchased must be preferred. And since the consumer is assumed to be maximizing, purchase equals maximizing. Such a tautological theory tells us nothing about consumer behavior.

Versions of this critique have been expressed by eminent orthodox theorists. George Katona has suggested that "statements about 'maximizing' are too general to contribute to a real understanding of consumer motivation."[15] The tautological nature of the theory is suggested by the fact that it tells us only that "a person does what he deems best."[16] James Duesenberry comments on existing theory as follows:

> The preference system analysis of consumer behavior is a somewhat remarkable tour de force. It seems to say something about consumer behavior without saying anything about the motivation of the consumers in question. In its present form it is a more or less deliberate attempt to sidestep the task of making any psychological assumptions.[17]

Paul Samuelson's view in 1947 of the theory of demand based upon indifference techniques is also critical.

> Thus, the consumer's market behavior is explained in terms of preferences, which are in turn defined only by behavior. The result can very easily be circular, and in many formulations undoubtedly is. Often nothing more is stated than the conclusion that people behave as they behave, a theorem which has no empirical implications, since it contains no hypothesis and is consistent with all conceivable behavior, while refutable by none.[18]

Out of this dissatisfaction with the indifference-curve approach emerged a new theory of demand, but it retreated even further from any assumptions about psychological motivation and the concept of utility. Called the "revealed preference approach," its major developer was Paul Samuelson. The primary assumption required for this theory

15. George Katona, *Psychological Analysis of Economic Behavior* (New York: McGraw-Hill, 1951), p. 70.
16. *Ibid.*
17. James Duesenberry, *Income, Saving, and the Theory of Consumer Behavior* (Cambridge: Harvard University Press, 1952), p.17.
18. Samuelson, *Foundations*, pp. 91–92.

to deduce a downward-sloping demand curve is that the consumer's preferences are consistent, or "transitive." Whether the consumer is maximizing or merely following Freudian urges is of no consequence to the theory: it is completely behavioristic, requiring the economist merely to *record* the consumer's choices as manifested in the market. Unfortunately, the revealed preference approach was not proven operationally significant. Although it freed micro analysis from its tautological theory of utility maximization, revealed preference is a theory of demand without a theory of consumer behavior; it is thus without much operational content.

Recent Developments in Utility Theory

Along with the increasing formalization of demand theory and the utility theory underlying it, there have been other changes, two of which deserve attention. One is an extension of utility analysis to include risk, and the second is a modified conceptualization of the utility approach. The inclusion of risk allows utility analysis to focus on choices made under uncertainty. It is based on the *theory of expected utility* developed by John von Neumann and Oskar Morgenstern in 1944 and extended by J. L. Savage in 1953. They listed a series of reasonable axioms about human behavior and deduced a method of changing uncertainty states into certainty equivalents consistent with those axioms. For example, suppose one must decide whether to go fishing or to study. Going fishing would yield ten "utiles." Studying would result in a 50-percent chance of getting an A, which would yield fifteen utiles, and a 50-percent chance of not getting an A, or a yield of zero utiles. Given this information, along with one's risk preference, we can calculate expected utiles for each alternative by multiplying the probability of occurrence by the utility one derives from the occurrence of that event. Assuming one is risk-neutral, in this case one would choose fishing, since it yields 10 expected utiles compared to 7.5 expected utiles for studying.

Another method of extending utility theory to handle uncertainty is Kenneth Arrow's *state preference theory*, which is used to extend general equilibrium theory to include risky situations. Commodities in state preference must always be considered contingent on things outside themselves; thus "a suit" would not be a sufficient description of a commodity whose preference order can be determined. Instead, one must rank all contingent commodities (a blue suit if Ellen calls; a brown suit if Bill calls; jeans if Joe calls). Individuals are assumed to have clear preferences among *contingent* commodities, not simply among commodities.

The second change in utility theory that deserves mention is modified conceptualizations of the theory. Probably the best known and most widely used of these new conceptualizations of utility theory is the *human capital approach*, which explicitly treats time as a commodity and develops a household production function. The importance of time was generally recognized before, but except for analysis of labor supply, it was not formally built into the analysis, and the myriad logical results of its inclusion had not been drawn.

Lancaster's *characteristic analysis* provides an alternative method of expanding utility theory to capture a broader range of issues. Rather than specifying commodities, such as a car, as arguments in the utility function, it specifies characterisics. A commodity is a bundle of characteristics, in this case a red, fourteen-foot-long, five-foot-high, gas-powered mode of transportation. Lancaster argues that individuals' preferences are for characteristics, not for commodities. Using Lancaster's approach, marginal decisions are impossible, and the decision process is modeled as a linear-programming (nonmarginal) maximizing problem.

Modern Demand Theory in Perspective

The primary function of a theory of demand or household consumer behavior is to explain the shape of demand curves. Demand theory has come almost full circle, starting with J. S. Mill and ending with revealed preference theory. Mill was one of the first to recognize a functional relationship between price and quantity demanded, although he did not graph demand curves or explicitly state them in mathematical form. After the time of J. S. Mill, economics tried to tie demand theory to notions of measurable utility based upon hedonistic psychological assumptions. As psychologists backed away from pleasure-pain theories, so did economists, but with considerable reluctance. Marshall tried to purge hedonism from his demand theory by changing the terminology but retaining the essence of his analysis.

Modern demand theory is a theory of demand without a theory of consumer behavior, which would seem to indicate that economists would be better off without the assistance of psychologists. The attention given the theory of demand today seems disproportionate to the benefits to be gained from it; its contribution amounts to little more than a statement that demand curves are negatively sloped because that is what we find in the marketplace. In considering recent developments in utility theory, moreover, one is left with the feeling that although its theoretical underpinnings have been intensively explored, these explorations have had little effect on the way in which economics is practiced.

Welfare Economics

A second area of economics that demonstrates the development of modern microeconomic theory is welfare economics, the branch of economics that draws policy prescriptions from theory. Welfare economics comprised an integral part of classical economics, most of whose theoretical arguments were specifically designed to support policy positions. But as classical evolved into neoclassical economics in the last quarter of the nineteenth century, economists began to distinguish between economic theory and policy. Increased attention to demand helped to change economists' thinking about welfare. To Smith, Ricardo, and J. S. Mill, increasing welfare had meant, for the most part, increasing output, but with developing notions of marginal utility in the 1870s, the concept of welfare came to be framed in terms of psychology rather than physical output.

As this change occurred the classical conclusion of the "invisible hand" theory, that laissez faire would produce maximum welfare, came under attack, and some economists began to investigate aspects of the economy in which unregulated markets did not necessarily achieve this goal. As the debate proceeded, the loose, contextual classical argument in favor of laissez faire as a policy prescription became a formal, noncontextual argument centered on whether the market will optimally allocate a fixed quantity of resources among alternative uses within the framework of a subjective theory of prices. Discussions of growth, political and economic interaction, and evolving institutions disappeared and were replaced by an abstract, noncontextual theoretical model.

Henry Sidgwick (1838–1900), a moral philosopher who turned to economics with his 1883 *Principles of Political Economy*, devoted a good deal of attention to exceptions to the general rule that laissez faire will produce maximum welfare. A sensitive liberal humanitarian, he noted with approval the movement toward greater government intervention in the economy; yet he also firmly believed in the beneficial effects of an economic structure that rewarded individual incentives and would change it only where it proved to be deleterious.

As economic theory became more formal, so too did the determination of when welfare actually increased. Building on Sidgwick's work, A. C. Pigou, who succeeded Marshall at Cambridge, tried to develop a formal welfare theory that could be applied to economic policy. While distinguishing between normative and positive analysis, however, he himself made some obvious value judgments: that working at home is better than working in a factory, that browsing in a museum is preferable to drinking in a pub. Such judgments, because they were agreed upon by most learned individuals, seemed acceptable in Marshallian contextual analysis, but in subsequent formalist noncontextual arguments they were not.

In the attempt to develop a value-free welfare economics, economists went back to the Italian economist Vilfredo Pareto, who initially proposed ordinal measurement of utility. Pareto argued that individuals in a market will voluntarily exchange as long as there is some benefit to them, and that production and exchange will cease at maximum welfare. At a "Pareto optimum" it is not possible to make someone better off without making someone else worse off. Economists in the 1930s thought they could use Pareto optimality to evaluate the performance of an economy without making value judgments. Accordingly, they began to try to formulate precisely the conditions for the general economy to reach a Pareto optimum. This writing was extremely fertile, leading to a much better understanding of the welfare implications of the economy and the allocation of resources in social economic systems. Three Nobel Prize winners in economics, Arrow, Samuelson, and Hicks, contributed significantly to this literature. As economists adopted Pareto optimality as their central welfare criterion, income distribution lost its role as a key economic issue, since Pareto optimality considers welfare implications *given* the distribution of income.

Despite its widespread use by economists, however, as elegantly pointed out in the work of A. K. Sen, Pareto optimality does not provide a value-free welfare economics.[19] It assumes that if a move makes everyone better off, society is better off. This may be an unobjectionable value judgment for many, but it is a value judgment nonetheless. Using Pareto optimality as a criterion to determine welfare violates Hume's dictum that you cannot derive a "should" from a fact. Even if one accepts Pareto optimality as being acceptably free of normative elements, it does not provide much help in policy making. Most political actions will hurt some people in helping others, even if only in a small way. For example, any action will affect the entire price vector of all goods, inevitably helping some and harming others. Pareto optimality provides no guide to dealing with such effects.

The limitations of Pareto optimality occasioned much literature on the subject. Some economists suggested, for example, the *compensating variation approach*, in which the gainers could compensate the losers. This led to a number of paradoxes. Tibor Scitovsky demonstrated that there are a number of cases where gainers can compensate losers, but where losers can also compensate gainers. A second, more widely used approach was introduced by Abram Bergson in 1938. He included welfare criteria in initial assumptions by using a social welfare function in an ordinal form to specify the preferences of society. Since this is the approach used by most economists today, there has been widespread discussion of what form this social welfare function should take. Proponents from several camps have advanced a variety of functions,

19. A. K. Sen, *Social Choice and Welfare* (Oxford: Basil Blackwell, 1982).

including the additive, multiplicative, and the Maximin (maximizing the welfare of the least-well-off individual), which was proposed by the philosopher John Rawls.[20] These unspecified, abstract social welfare functions are so formalized that most models are never applied to policy. Although they theoretically resolve the problem of introducing normative arguments into economics, they serve little practical role.

The concept of the social welfare function did, however, raise a number of theoretical issues. Some economists asked, for example, whether it was possible to move from individuals' welfare functions to a social welfare function, and by what means. Voting was suggested as a means, which led to Kenneth Arrow's famous work on the voting paradox, *Social Choice and Individual Values* (1951), in which he demonstrated that, given some reasonable assumptions, it is impossible to arrive at a unique social welfare function. Arrow's work opened up a new branch of highly abstract welfare economics called social choice theory.

Externalities

Even though Pareto optimality has proven an insufficient base for developing a solid welfare theory, it has left its mark on the profession. Specifically, it is central to the question of whether perfectly competitive markets lead to an optimum allocation of resources, and hence it is basic to the structure of modern micro theory. A. C. Pigou was one of the first economists to specifically introduce such considerations into economic analysis. Pigou showed that firms' marginal cost functions may not accurately reflect the social costs of production and that the demand curves of individuals may not accurately reflect the social benefits from consumption. He examined the divergencies between private benefit and social benefit, and between private costs and social costs. These divergencies, known variously as externalities, third-party effects, and spillover effects, are considered to justify government action. The costs a firm considers in its profit-maximizing decisions are private costs borne by the firm. But social costs, such as pollution, are not borne by the firm; thus there is a divergence between private and social cost at the margin. A free market will therefore result in the production of an excessive quantity of goods whose marginal social cost exceeds their marginal private cost.

Let us express this in the broadest possible terms. One problem of economics is to analyze the relative scarcity arising because the desires of individuals for goods and services exceed the ability of the economy to provide them. A conflict then exists between the benefits derived

20. John Rawls, *A Theory of Justice* (Cambridge: Harvard University Press, 1971).

from consumption and the costs incurred in production. According to marginal analysis, the optimum solution to this conflict is to produce and consume goods up to the point where marginal benefits equal marginal costs. Ignoring issues of the distribution and level of income, a free competitive market would provide a maximum of economic welfare and optimally resolve this conflict, as long as market demand and supply curves correctly reflect all costs and benefits in the society. Pigou's contribution to welfare economics was an analytic framework to deal with externalities where market demand and supply curves do not adequately reflect social benefits and costs.

Whereas the externality structure is generally accepted, the policy implications are not. Externalities are difficult, if not impossible, to measure, and some economists argue that they have yet to see one. Moreover, even if externalities exist, it is not clear that anything should be done about them. Given the influence of politics on economic policy, the actual policy undertaken by government may not in any way reflect the "theoretically correct" policy. Consideration of these issues has led to a burgeoning "public choice" literature focusing on the interrelationship of economics and politics.

Welfare Economics in Perspective

Even if all the issues raised by recent work in theoretical welfare economics could be successfully handled, some fundamental questions are still to be answered. Suppose we had a theory that gave unambiguous answers about the economic welfare consequences of various actions or policies. Presumably welfare theorists would regard this as a significant contribution to the larger task of answering questions about social welfare. The economic part of the jigsaw puzzle would be solved, but a complete solution would await developments in the other social sciences and possibly in the humanities. A number of writers from the nineteenth century up to the present have questioned this fragmented approach of economists to questions of social welfare. Although this criticism has taken various forms, its basic thrust is that one part of social welfare, economic welfare, cannot be isolated for analysis. Social welfare, according to them, is not many separate problems but one big problem. Economists have been reluctant to tackle the question of social welfare for a number of reasons, the most important being the desire to keep economics a positive science. It is, of course, always dangerous to evaluate a contemporary development in economic theory such as welfare economics, but it appears that economists will either have to abandon the study of welfare economics or join other disciplines in a search for a theory of social welfare that explicitly recognizes the necessity of normative judgments.

PROBLEMS IN MODERN MICROECONOMICS

This discussion of the successes of modern microeconomics should be seen as both a tribute to the field's accomplishments and a prelude to our consideration of the problems it still faces. Most economists would agree that the formalization of economics has made some significant gains, but it has also had its costs. Each advance we have discussed has deepened our understanding of a particular area, but one cannot avoid concluding that the overall improvement to microeconomic theory is not equal to the sum of its parts; in some ways, an improved part may even be a step backward for the whole. A primary example is the significant shift in the method of argumentation from contextual analysis to noncontextual analysis that has accompanied the expression of formalist economics. Contextual analysis assumes that the reader will understand the nature of the decision maker and the institutional structure. Since these are taken as given, only the particular context that the writer is introducing need be considered. Most classical analysis was contextual.

Contextual analysis is efficient, but it is also subject to misinterpretation if the assumptions of the writer do not correspond with those of the reader. Incompletely explored assumptions can lead to quite preposterous conclusions. This is why economics evolved to noncontextual analysis, which avoids the problems of contextual analysis by spelling out each assumption. But because of the need to fully specify the assumptions and to take nothing for granted, noncontextual analysis creates a danger of its own: the analysis becomes lost in itself. This is what some critics argue has happened to economics.

To see more clearly the problem that can develop from noncontextual argumentation, let us consider the underlying theory of modeling. A model is a simplified representation of reality. It makes an enormous number of simplifying assumptions, but if it is a good model the incorrect assumptions on both sides will cancel each other out. Ideally, as a model is expanded — if it is to remain a good representation of reality — there must be an equal marginal relaxation of assumptions so that the balance remains. But the decision as to what an equal marginal relaxation of assumptions is can only be made contextually, with knowledge of institutions and reality, because reality is ultimately what the model is designed to describe. And this skill is exactly what is no longer taught. The models that have been developed do not allow equal marginal relaxations of the assumptions, and thus produce results that do not accord with reality. And more complicated models do not necessarily add more insight; since the assumptions of the model are often interrelated, relaxing one assumption without relaxing the opposing interrelated assumption often yields a poorer, not a better, model.

With formalization has also come a loss of general focus. In Marshallian economics, the focus was on the general questions, and the specifics were hazy. Modern formalist economics focuses on the specific questions, paying little attention to general questions about how the specifics interact. Many critics believe that as this change has occurred, modern economics has lost sight of which questions are important and which are not, and that economists spend inordinate amounts of time discussing (in a highly abstract, formal manner) the modern-day equivalent of how many angels can dance on the head of a pin. Kenneth Boulding expressed the problem somewhat differently when he called modern economics "the celestial mechanics of a nonexistent world."

This loss of general focus was inevitable; as the tools of microeconomics have become more and more complicated, so have the areas of inquiry. The training of economists focuses so much on mathematics and techniques that sensitivity and workable rules of thumb for applying the analysis to reality must be discarded. Economists today are forced to concentrate on one subarea and one set of tools. Thus the formalist approach had led to a breakdown of communication among economists. A search theorist will often have little to say to a social choice theorist, who in turn will have little to say to a general equilibrium theorist. The tools they use and the questions they ask are different.

Critics argue that, in the absence of a set of general directions of inquiry, sociological factors direct the profession: economists ask the questions that meet their own immediate needs, questions that can be most easily developed into articles and thereby lead to tenure and promotion, not the questions whose solutions are necessarily most relevant to society as a whole. Modern microeconomics has resolved problems, but not in the way that best fits reality. Rather, it has done so in a way that best fits the mathematics.

All this is not to say that the formalist revolution should never have taken place. There were serious problems with Marshallian economics. But there were also advantages to the Marshallian approach, and these were lost. The current goal is not to abandon the advances but to find a way to integrate the best of both approaches.

Backtracking

If the critics of modern microeconomics are correct, economics went astray somewhere in the past. In "The Uses of the Past,"[21] (unpublished manuscript), Axel Leijonhufvud has argued that knowledge of the

21. Axel Leijonhufvud, "The Uses of the Past" (unpublished paper presented to the History of Economics Society, 1987).

history of thought allows one to backtrack and to try to figure out where one has been. In doing so, he argues, one can perhaps direct economics onto a more useful and relevant track. Many economists believe that economics went wrong in the 1930s when the monopolistic competition revolution emerged and then shortly thereafter died, swamped by the Keynesian and mathematical Walrasian revolutions. James Tobin states that

> the neglected revolution of the early 1930s (the monopolistic competition revolution) reminds us that microeconomics has yet to resolve a crisis of its own. For both "micro" and "macro" monopolistic and imperfect competition would be a firmer foundation, one which would in both spheres cast doubt on the all too prevalent view that "the market" always works out for the best.[22]

In the final section of this chapter we briefly consider the monopolistic competition revolution, why it didn't spread, and how it ties into some recent work that seems to offer a relevant line of inquiry into the future. We begin by considering the reasons the monopolistic competition revolution developed, then look at why it failed, and finally appraise some recent developments that are reintroducing this concept into economics.

The Monopolistic Competition "Revolution"

For classical economists up to and including Marshall, "competition" was a vague term. Marshall assumed perfect competition in his formal models, but in accompanying discussions he often relaxed his model to deal informally with markets in between monopoly and competition. Classical economists no doubt felt they knew what they meant by "competition" and did not need to define it. Their vague use of the term allowed competition to serve as the answer to all economic problems. In laissez faire economic philosophy, the consensus was that competition would solve any problem that arose. Once the formalists began to scrutinize laissez faire thought, however, they demanded a precise definition of this pivotal concept and reproached Marshall for continuing to use the term without providing one.

Some economists argued, too, that Marshall's analysis did not correspond with empirical observation. In *Risk, Uncertainty, and Profit* (1921), for example, Frank Knight argued convincingly that the theoretical model of competitive markets failed to correspond to the

---

22. James Tobin, "The Half-Century Crisis of Microeconomics," mimeographed (Yale University, 1984). p. 1.

markets actually found in the economy. The major empirical problem was that for Marshallian competition to work, there had to be many small firms; but during this period large firms were becoming increasingly powerful, which lessened the impact of competition on the market. John Clapham similarly pointed out in 1922 that many of the concepts concerned with cost conditions in industries, such as increasing, constant, and decreasing costs, were empty economic boxes.

In 1926 Piero Sraffa challenged Marshall contending that there was an internal inconsistency in the Marshallian analysis of decreasing-cost situations, since decreasing costs "are clearly incompatible with the conditions of particular equilibrium of a commodity."[23] If decreasing costs are incompatible with perfectly competitive markets, Sraffa declared, then downward-sloping cost curves implied that the deterrent to selling larger quantities of output was not on the side of supply and cost but of demand.[24] If costs were continually declining, competition could not continue to exist, at least as Marshall had described it; monopoly, not competition, would be the dominant market structure. Marshall and some subsequent theorists had devoted some attention to monopoly, but their analysis generally continued to assume perfectly competitive markets. Because of the persistent divergence between empirical observation and theory, greater interest was aroused in the structure of markets at intermediate stages between monopoly and perfect competition.

These criticisms occasioned a number of works that had significant implications for modern theory, including Jacob Viner's integration of firms' long-run and short-run cost curves, Joan Robinson's theory of imperfect competition, and Chamberlin's theory of monopolistic competition. Viner reconciled observation with theory by formally separating the long run from the short run. In his model, which has since become the mainstream model, capital is assumed to be fixed in the short run and diminishing marginal returns cause the short-run marginal cost curve to be upward-sloping regardless of whether there are increasing, decreasing, or constant returns to scale. Mathematically this solved the problem of reconciling theory with empirical observation — as long as one analyzed only the short run and did not try to integrate it with the long run. That is what economists did with general equilibrium

23. Piero Sraffa, "The Laws of Returns under Competitive Conditions," *The Economic Journal*, 1926. The quotation is taken from an article in American Economic Association, *Readings in Price Theory* (Chicago: R. D. Irwin, 1952), p. 185.
24. Joan Robinson writes at the beginning of her book, "Mr. Sraffa's article must be regarded as the fount from which my work flows, for the chief aim of this book is to attempt to carry out his pregnant suggestion that the whole theory of value should be created in terms of monopoly analysis." Joan Robinson, *The Economics of Imperfect Competition* (London: Macmillan, 1933), p. v.

theory, and the basic long run–short run distinction that underlies the definition of capital stems from Viner's work.

Joan Robinson's major contribution (which she later disavowed) was the rediscovery of the marginal revenue curve. Cournot had used this tool in 1838, but since Marshall had passed it by, it had to be rediscovered by Robinson and others. Her model of "imperfect competition," in which a firm equated marginal revenues and marginal cost, is now standard economics. Chamberlin's work, though similar to Robinson's, was more far-reaching. It attempted a thorough reconstruction of the theory of value. Chamberlin writes, "Monopolistic competition... is a challenge to the traditional viewpoint of economics that competition and monopoly are alternatives and that individual prices are to be explained in terms of either the one or the other."[25] The subtitle of his book, "A Re-orientation of the Theory of Value," reflects Chamberlin's belief that this new theory "contains, not a technique, but a way of looking at the economic system; and changing one's economic *Weltanschauung* is sometimes very different from looking into the economics of the individual firm or adding new tools to one's kit."[26]

Chamberlin held that the various models of duopoly, such as Cournot's, and Marshall's entire analysis of markets were all based upon a fundamental error: they ignored the interdependence of firms. Although the Marshallian theories of pure competition and monopoly describe polar markets, they share a common assumption, namely, that each firm is independent of other firms and that firms do not recognize their mutual interdependence. In Marshallian theory, when Farmer Brown sells more output, there is no direct effect on price and no indirect effect in the form of a reaction by other farmers. However, when a monopolist sells more output there is a direct effect, a fall in price, but no indirect effect, since Marshall assumes that no other firms are affected. Chamberlin's theory demonstrated that a firm's actions usually do have indirect effects and that firms will recognize this fact and be aware of their consequent interdependence with other firms. Chamberlin called such markets "monopolistic competition markets," since they contain elements of both monopoly and competition.

The Revolution That Wasn't

Chamberlin drew broad implications from his ideas. He noted that for a long time economic theory had loosely identified free enterprise with competition, but when he examined the actual outcome typical of a

25. E. H. Chamberlin, *The Theory of Monopolistic Competition*, 6th ed. (Cambridge: Harvard University Press, 1950), p. 204.
26. *Ibid.*, pp. 204-205.

free enterprise system, he found not pure competition but monopolistic competition. An essential characteristic of free enterprise seemed to be "the attempt by every businessman to build up his own monopoly, extending it wherever possible and defending it against the attempts of others to extend theirs."[27] If Chamberlin is correct, we can no longer follow the Smithian-Marshallian tradition of equating perfectly competitive markets with the ideal for purposes of welfare economics. Chamberlin held that in many cases it would be impossible to establish perfectly competitive markets; he even questioned the desirability of such markets. The overstandardization of products that might result from them, for example, would not necessarily be desirable: "Differences in taste, desires, incomes, and locations of buyers, and in the uses buyers wish to make of commodities all indicate the need for variety."

E. H. Chamberlin

27. *Ibid.*, pp. 213-214.

Such problems, he felt, dictate "substituting for the concept of a 'competitive ideal' an ideal including both monopoly and competition. How much and what kinds of monopoly, and with what measure of social control, became the questions."[28]

There was so much common sense and insight in the monopolistic competition model that many economists in the late 1930s and early 1940s expected it to revolutionize mainstream economics. That didn't occur. By the mid-1950s the monopolistic competition revolution was being relegated to undergraduate and history of thought textbooks.

Why Did the Monopolistic Competition Revolution Fail?

A central reason the monopolistic competition revolution failed was that it was difficult to formalize it and to draw implications from it. It was difficult, if not impossible, to separate out selling costs from product differentiation costs and hence to determine what to include as a cost and what to include as a variable that changed the demand curve. (If you buy a case of Pepsi or Classic Coke because these products are consumed regularly by sexy-looking people on television, it is not easy to separate out the product from the advertising.) Also, since most U.S. industries are, in effect, oligopolies, there is interdependence among the decisions of various firms; in making any decision, each firm takes into account the expected reaction of other firms in the industry. Chamberlin tried to solve these problems analytically, but he lacked the technical ability to do so adequately.

A second reason for the failure of the monopolistic competition revolution was that Chamberlin's analysis was essentially partial equilibrium with acknowledged Marshallian roots. In 1940 Robert Triffin raised questions concerning the integration of monopolistic competition with general equilibrium analysis, and at present general equilibrium theory is still largely formulated in terms of the competitive model.[29] The departure of graduate economics into Walrasian general equilibrium left behind the monopolistic competition revolution, which in the 1930s had seemed a contribution equal to Keynes's. But the fact that the monopolistic revolution died in no way negated the problems it had attempted to address. Even though most industries continue to be positioned somewhere between monopoly and competition, much of modern economic theory does not deal with this reality. George Stigler states that no economist has "any professional knowledge on which to

28. *Ibid.*, pp. 214–215.
29. Robert Triffin, *Monopolistic Competition and General Equilibrium Theory* (Cambridge: Harvard University Press, 1940).

base recommendations (concerning antitrust and monopolies) that should carry weight with a skeptical legislator."[30]

New Directions in Monopolistic Competition Theory

Recent research has been directed toward an examination of monopolistic competition. Work by Darius Gaskins, Steven Salop, and Joseph Stiglitz has examined strategic pricing and has shown that when interfirm responses are considered, competition will not lead to efficient pricing. Joseph Stiglitz, George Akerof, and Janet Yellen, among others, have explored the monopolistically competitive underpinnings of a macro-model and found that these underpinnings lead to Keynesian conclusions. This work unlike Chamberlin's and Robinson's, is more formal and uses complex mathematical techniques. Thus, whereas the work of these earlier writers was not compatible with modern micro theory, the new work is, and the lost revolution may yet occur.

The reemergence of the monopolistic competition revolution is also occurring from another direction, namely, from economists who contend that the domain of modern microeconomics is too narrow and needs to be expanded to include political and anticompetitive actions. An early statement of this view was Gordon Tullock's analysis of the welfare loss due to monopoly. Tullock argued that the loss in efficiency from monopoly that traditional welfare economics focuses on is only a small part of the actual welfare loss; the time and money spent on achieving monopoly was far more significant.

Similar arguments were proposed by Jagdish Bhagwati and Mancur Olson, whose combined work has been called "neoclassical political economy."[31] This theory assumes that people maximize not only *within* an assumed institutional structure but also to *achieve* an institutional structure most beneficial to them, and that these two maximizing procedures must be analyzed simultaneously. This approach has led to the reintroduction of a type of monopolistic competition, since it accords with Chamberlin's thesis that individuals are continually trying to create monopolies for themselves. But the emphasis is reversed: the new analysis yields not monopolistic competition but competitive monopolies, in which the desire to achieve monopoly is the central driving force held in check only by the attempts of others to get a part of that monopoly for themselves. Thus the creation of monopoly provides competition for existing monopolies and that competition occurs only in the presence of monopoly.

---

30. George Stigler, "The Economists and The Problem of Monopoly," *The American Economic Review* (May 1982), Vol. 72, p. 6.
31. David Colander, ed., *Neoclassical Political Economy* (Boston: Ballinger, 1984).

MODERN MICROECONOMICS — A SUMMARY

Our coverage of developments in modern micro theory has not included all the additions to present day theory. For example, we haven't discussed the many improvements made in the theory of supply and costs which remove some of the internal inconsistencies in the Marshallian formulation. Nor have we presented the theoretical developments in various applied fields such as international trade, labor, and public finance, which fall into the domain of micro theory. Our coverage has been selective, dealing principally with the increased formalization of economic theory and with topics in the theory of monopolistic competition, welfare theory, and demand theory. Nonetheless, the chapter conveys a sense of the direction micro theory has taken.

During the period from 1890 to the 1930s, microeconomists worked to improve the logical structure of micro theory laid down by Marshall and apply the Marshallian apparatus to questions of economic welfare. Some economists during this period, unconvinced by Marshall's arguments against the use of mathematics in economics, advanced an even more rigorous theoretical structure for micro theory. The most important advocates of this new mathematical economics were Vilfredo Pareto in Europe, F. Y. Edgeworth in England, and Irving Fisher in the United States.

The most fundamental contribution in the period from 1930 to the present was more methodological than theoretical; we have termed this the formalization revolution in microeconomics. Economists soon found that the increased mathematical precision they sought could not be achieved within the Marshallian framework; so modern microeconomic theory rejected Marshall's attempt to blend theory and institutions in a partial equilibrium framework. Instead, they adopted a general equilibrium framework almost devoid of contextual argument and analysis. While a number of theorists from Europe and the United States have spearheaded these modern developments, the most important has been Paul Samuelson. E. H. Chamberlin's theory of monopolistic competition, on the other hand, runs counter to the increased formalization of economic theory. Though rich in contextual argument, it could not be used in a mathematical or general equilibrium framework.

While some within the profession are alarmed by the increased formalization of economic reasoning over the past fifty years, the mainstream microeconomics taught and researched at graduate schools in the United States is now highly mathematical. The study of economic history, the history of economic theory, and institutions in the applied fields has almost ceased. Some economists who object to this formalization will be examined in Chapter 12 after the discussion of recent developments in macroeconomics.

SUGGESTED READINGS

Backhouse, Roger. *A History of Modern Economic Analysis*. New York: Basil Blackwell Ltd., 1985.

Becker, Gary. *A Treatise on the Family*. Cambridge: Harvard University Press, 1981.

Chamberlin, Edward H. *The Theory of Monopolistic Competition*. Cambridge: Harvard University Press, 1962.

Clapham, J. H. "Of Empty Economic Boxes." *Economic Journal*, 32 (1922), pp. 305-314.

Cournot, Antoine Augustin. *Researches into the Mathematical Principles of the Theory of Wealth*, 1838. Translated by Irving Fisher. New York and London: Macmillan, 1927.

Hicks, John R. *Value and Capital*. Oxford: Clarendon Press, 1946.

Lancaster, Kevin J. "A New Approach to Consumer Theory." *Journal of Political Economy*, 74 (April 1966), pp. 132-157.

Little, I. M. D. *A Critique of Welfare Economics*. London: Oxford University Press, 1957.

Musgrave, Richard A. *The Theory of Public Finance*. London: McGraw-Hill, 1959.

Reder, Melvin W. "Chicago Economics: Permanence and Change." *Journal of Economic Literature*, 1 (March 1982), pp. 1-38.

Robinson, Joan. *The Economics of Imperfect Competition*. London: Macmillan, 1933.

Samuelson, Paul A. *Foundations of Economic Analysis*. Cambridge: Harvard University Press, 1955.

Sraffa, Piero. "The Laws of Returns Under Competitive Conditions." *Economic Journal*, 36 (December 1926), pp. 535-550.

Whitaker, J. K., ed. Introduction to *The Early Writings of Alfred Marshall, 1867-1890*. London: Macmillan, 1975.

Chapter 11

The Development of Modern Macroeconomics

Interest in macroeconomic issues has fluctuated throughout the years, reaching its nadir around the turn of the century. The attitude of the economics profession toward it at that time could be characterized mainly as benign neglect. The macroeconomic thinking that did exist, moreover, was somewhat confused. Alfred Marshall, who had codified and organized microeconomics in his *Principles of Economics*, always intended to do the same for macroeconomics, but he never truly did. He essentially limited his discussion of macroeconomics to a determination of the general level of prices, as did F. W. Taussig in his introductory textbook popular during the first part of the twentieth century and F. B. Garver and Alvin H. Hansen in their leading book of the 1930s. This is in striking contrast to the typical modern text, half of which may concern macroeconomic issues.

HISTORICAL FORERUNNERS OF MODERN MACROECONOMICS

Mercantilists specifically wanted to understand the forces that determine the capacity of an economy to produce goods and services and to ascertain whether the actual level of output reached the potential level. Many mercantilists perceived a fundamental conflict between private and public interest and therefore believed that the economy would fail to achieve its output potential unless the government intervened. Their argument was twofold: first, following Jean Bodin, they believed that private interest led to monopoly and that monopoly restricted output; second, they believed that when individuals either saved or bought foreign goods, a shortage of demand for domestic goods ensued, which weakened the economy. The mercantilist policy position was that the government should regulate domestic and foreign trade so that the economy would show a balance-of-payments surplus and should control the money supply.

As mercantilism evolved into classical economics, attitudes toward government intervention changed dramatically. Unlike the early mercantilists, Adam Smith believed that competitive market forces were sufficiently strong so that private interests, as though led by an "invisible hand," would be directed to work for the public interest. The economy would reach its output potential only if the government followed a laissez faire policy. Smith's analysis in favor of laissez faire was a contextual argument, made in view of feasible alternatives. He agreed with the mercantilists that monopolies reduced output, but he felt that the methods intended to control them — government control of trade and allocation of monopolies — made matters worse, not better. Thus, he felt the preferable policy was to rely on laissez faire and competition to bring about utilization of resources as fully as possible.

The mercantilist underconsumption arguments came under much heavier attack by Smith and other classical economists. They argued that savings would automatically be translated into investment spending, since a decision to save is a decision to invest. This proposition that a laissez faire economy would automatically produce full utilization of resources was called Say's Law, and became a central element of pre-Keynesian economic thinking. Classical economists also attacked the mercantilist argument for increasing the stock of gold by running a trade surplus, contending that the wealth of a nation is measured not in precious metals but by real output, and that a country would be better off allowing free trade, thereby gaining the advantage of foreign competition.

Classical economists, particularly Smith and J. S. Mill, agreed that market forces didn't work perfectly but felt that the market worked better than the alternatives. With the exception of Thomas Malthus, it was left from 1800 through 1930 to such heterodox, nonmainstream economists as Karl Marx, Mikhail Tugan-Baranowsky, and J. R. Hobson to assert that the economy might have an aggregate, or macroeconomic, problem. The classical conviction that markets be relied upon to control the economy shifted the focus of economic inquiry from monetary and financial forces to real forces, and the classical analysis of macroeconomic issues generally accepted a dichotomy between real and nominal forces.

Quantity Theory of Money

Orthodox theory maintained an interest in at least one macro question: what determines the general level of prices? A few orthodox theorists also paid some attention to the question of stability in their study of business cycles. First let us examine the attempts to explain the forces determining the general level of prices, or put another way, the forces determining the value of money. Then we will examine pre-Keynesian business cycle theory.

One way orthodox theory addressed the question of the value of money, or the general level of prices, was by utilizing the basic supply-and-demand approach developed in micro theory. The supply of money was assumed to be determined by the monetary authorities, so some orthodox economists contended that the basic issues to be analyzed were on the side of demand. The household and firm are assumed to be rational and to have a demand for money to be used for various purposes. Walras, Menger, and others developed a supply-and-demand analysis explaining the value of money, but the most famous of these theories is probably the one developed by Marshall, which has become known as the Cambridge cash-balance version of the quantity theory of money. The first clear statement of the quantity theory of money was made by David Hume in 1752. This theory, as it came down through the literature, held that the general level of prices depended upon the quantity of money in circulation. Marshall's version of the quantity theory was an attempt to give microeconomic underpinnings to the macro theory that prices and the quantity of money varied directly. He did this by elaborating a theory of household and firm behavior to explain the demand for money. Marshall reasoned that households and firms would desire to hold in cash balances a fraction of their money income. If M is money (currency plus demand deposits), Y is money income, and k is the proportion of income households and firms desire to hold in the form of money, then the fundamental cash-balance equation is

$$M = kY$$

Since Marshall accepted Say's Law, full employment is assumed. An increase in the quantity of money, assuming k remains constant, will lead to an increase in money income, Y. Since full employment is assumed, an increase in the quantity of money will result in higher prices and a consequent increase in money income; real income, however, does not change. Decreases in the quantity of money result in a fall in money income as prices fall; real income again remains constant. We shall not examine the many different aspects of Marshall's formulation; the important point is that Marshall's version of the quantity theory made an attempt to integrate the microeconomic behavior of maximizing firms and households with the macro question of the general level of prices.

A group of economists, the most prominent being the American Irving Fisher, developed another form of the quantity theory, known as the transactions version. However, they showed little interest in finding a micro foundation for the macro analysis of the general level of prices. In this version,

$$MV = PT$$

where M is the quantity of money, V is the velocity of money, P is a measure of the price level, and T is the volume of transactions.

Although these two approaches have important differences, they have one element in common: they were both designed to explain the forces that determined the general price level. They were not used to explain the level of real income, since this was assumed to be at full employment and fixed by nonmonetary forces in the economy. Knut Wicksell did not like the quantity theory of money because it failed to explain "why the monetary or pecuniary demand for goods exceeds or falls short of the supply of goods in given conditions."[1] Wicksell tried to develop a so-called income approach to explain the general level of prices, that is, to develop a theory of money that explains fluctuations in income as well as fluctuations in price levels. Although he was not successful in developing a complete theory of income determination, he did manage to state a reasonably complete theory of the forces determining the level of investment expenditures. J. M. Keynes, a student of Alfred Marshall, used the basic Cambridge cash-balance version of the quantity theory of money in his *Tract on Monetary Reform*, published in 1924. By 1930, however, he had moved to an income approach to the theory of money.

> Formerly I was attracted by this line of approach. But it now seems to me that the merging together of all different sorts of transactions — income, business and financial — which may be taking place only causes confusion, and that we cannot get any real insight into the price-making process without bringing in the rate of interest and the distinctions between incomes and profits and between savings and investment.
>
> The "Real-balances" Equation discussed above is descended from a method of approach long familiar to those who have heard Professors Marshall and Pigou in the lecture-rooms of Cambridge. Since this method has not been employed elsewhere in recent times I call it the "Cambridge" Quantity Equation; but it has a much longer descent, being derived from Petty, Locke, Cantillon and Adam Smith.[2]

1. Knut Wicksell, *Lectures on Political Economy* (London: Routledge and Kegan Paul, 1935), II, 160 (originally published in Swedish in 1901 and 1906).
2. J. M. Keynes, *A Treatise on Money* (New York: Harcourt Brace, 1930), I, 229.

Thus Keynes in 1930 broke with the classical-neoclassical "traditional method of setting out from the total quantity of money irrespective of the purposes on which it is employed"[3] and developed an analysis based on income flows. Several other writers employed the income approach, but none of them, including Keynes in his *Treatise* and Wicksell, attempted to formulate a theory explaining the determination of the level of income, nor did they reject the proposition of Say's Law that the automatic forces of the market would produce full employment.

Business Cycle Theory

Although fluctuations in business activity and in the level of income and employment had been occurring since the beginning of merchant capitalism and were acknowledged by orthodox theorists, economists made no systematic attempts to analyze either depression or the business cycle until the 1890s. Heterodox theorists had pursued these issues with greater vigor, most importantly Marx. But Marx's works were largely ignored by orthodox theory. Thus, up to the last decade of the nineteenth century, orthodox economic theory consisted of a fairly well developed theoretical micro structure explaining the allocation and distribution of scarce resources, a macro theory explaining the forces determining the general level of prices, and a loose set of notions concerning economic growth. Prior to 1890, orthodox "work on depressions and cycles had been peripheral and tangential."[4]

One major exception to this generalization is the work of Clement Juglar (1819-1905), who in 1862 published *Des crises commercials et de leur retour périodique en France, en Angleterre et aux États-Unis.* The second edition of this work, published in 1889, was considerably enlarged with historical and statistical material. Juglar is a spiritual predecessor of W. C. Mitchell in that he did not build a deductive theory of the business cycle, but rather collected historical and statistical material that he approached inductively. His main contribution was his statement that the cycle was a result not of forces outside the economic system but of forces within it. He saw the cycle as containing three phases that repeated themselves in continuous order.

The periods of prosperity, crisis, liquidation, although affected by the fortunate or unfortunate accidents in the life of peoples, are not the result of chance events, but arise out of the behavior, the activi-

3. *Ibid.*, I, 134.
4. Alvin Hansen, *Business Cycles and National Income* (New York: W. W. Norton, 1951), p. 225.

ties, and above all out of the saving habits of the population, and the way they employ the capital and credit available.[5]

Although Juglar's work initiated the study of the business cycle, the modern orthodox macro analysis of economic fluctuations is grounded in the writings of a Russian, Mikhail Tugan-Baranowsky (1865-1919). His book *Industrial Crises in England* was first published in Russian in 1894; German and French editions followed. After reviewing past attempts to explain the business cycle, he pronounced them all unsatisfactory. The chief intellectual influences on Tugan-Baranowsky were Juglar and Marx, particularly Marx. Tugan-Baranowsky's main contribution to our understanding of the business cycle was his statement of two principles: (1) that the economic fluctuations are inherent in the capitalist system because they are a result of forces within the system and (2) that the major causes of the business cycle are to be found in the forces determining investment spending. The modern Keynesian analysis of income determination, with its emphasis on the inherent instability of capitalism and the role of investment, runs from Marx through Tugan-Baranowsky, Juglar, Spiethoff, Schumpeter, Cassel, Robertson, Wicksell, and Fisher on the orthodox side; and from Marx, Veblen, Hobson, Mitchell, and others on the heterodox side.

The history of that part of macroeconomics dealing with the forces determining the level of income is in some respects a "nonhistory." Some of the mercantilists, the physiocrats, and a host of heterodox economists who followed had suggested earlier that there were forces inherent in capitalism that would bring about depressions, but their theories had been almost universally repudiated by Say's Law. After 1900 more serious work was done on business cycles by orthodox theorists, but curiously enough this work existed side-by-side with a continuing fundamental belief that the long-run equilibrium position of the economy would provide full employment. No one, neither heterodox nor orthodox, had been able to challenge this belief, because no one had built a theory of income determination to show that equilibrium at less than full employment was possible. When J. M. Keynes in 1936 developed a theory arguing that equilibrium at less than full employment could exist, a new phase of orthodox macro theory commenced. The developments that followed and Keynes's contributions to them are discussed in the remainder of this chapter.

---

5. Clement Juglar, *Des crises commercials*, 2nd ed. (Paris: Guillaumin, 1889), p. xix, quoted in T. W. Hutchison, *A Review of Economic Doctrines 1870-1929* (Oxford: Clarendon Press, 1953), p. 372.

Neoclassical Macroeconomics

Why did Marshall, and others using his framework, have a problem with macroeconomics? The reason is inherent in the partial equilibrium nature of supply-and-demand analysis. It analyzes a specific market, holding everything else constant. To use supply and demand curves correctly, one must assume that everything in the market being analyzed remains constant except price and quantity. But since all other things cannot be assumed to remain constant in an entire economy, Marshall's framework is inappropriate. The only way to extend the arguments from partial to general equilibrium is to use complicated mathematics or simply to have faith; early-twentieth-century neoclassical economists used little of the former and much of the latter, especially when the aggregate economy seemed to be working.

A few economists anticipated the problems to come. In the early 1900s two Swedish economists, Gunnar Myrdal and Erik Lindahl, working from the writings of Knut Wicksell, examined the possibility of an inequality between savings and investment. They argued that a difference between ex-ante and ex-post savings and investment could significantly affect the aggregate economy. Although their work had been done in the 1920s and early 1930s, it was not translated into English until the late 1930s, after the Depression had necessitated a reconsideration of the problem of unemployment and other macroeconomic issues by the British neoclassicals.

The work done by British economists influenced by these events is now called the disequilibrium monetarist approach, or neoclassical monetary theory. Its most notable representative, Dennis Robertson, held that there could be temporary monetary disturbances in which the flow of savings would not equal the flow of investment. Although accepting Say's Law for the long run, Robertson contended that disequilibrium could occur because individuals had to make plans before knowing the plans of others, so their actions in the market would not be coordinated. These temporary disturbances would cause fluctuations in real income. Ultimately the economy would right itself, but there could be a sequence of time periods within which the interconnected flows would be in disequilibrium.

In their research, these disequilibrium monetary theorists sought to determine exactly how individuals' adjustments affected the aggregate economy. Robertson considered a "sequence equilibrium" in which individuals *progressively* adjusted their plans; then he analyzed a series of these sequence disequilibria in order to discover how the long-run forces pushing toward equilibrium interacted with the short-run disequilibrium forces. His model allowed for temporary unemployment but held that unemployment caused by too little investment spending would be eliminated in time. It followed that something other than lack of investment would be the cause of extended unemployment. Robertson's painstaking theoretical work became so enormously complicated that few economists of his time read it. Modern researchers have rediscovered him, however, and his analysis has provided the basis of some recent work in macroeconomic theory.

Another economist working with Robertson to extend neoclassical monetary theory was J. M. Keynes. His work focused on potential short-run problems with the quantity theory. In his two-volume *Treatise On Money*, Keynes argued that the velocity of money could fluctuate in the short run and that there would be temporary unemployment as it did. Such temporary unemployment was not inconsistent with Say's Law, which stated only that these problems would adjust in the long run.

Most neoclassical economists of this period were not disequilibrium monetary theorists, however, but subscribed to a much simpler view of the cause of unemployment. Using Marshall's partial equilibrium approach, they focused on monopoly as the cause of any extended unemployment, believing that the real wage must be above a market-clearing wage in order for unemployment to occur. Something had to be preventing the real wage from falling, and most neoclassical economists considered unions the culprit. Their approach to eliminating unemployment was to lower the real wage by abolishing unions.

The Depression of the 1930s changed the context within which society and economists viewed the market. Prior to that time, the neoclassical arguments in favor of laissez faire had been based not only on economic theory but also on a set of philosophical and political judgments about government. The general political orientation of almost all individuals except radicals in the early 1900s was against government involvement in the economy. Within that context the concepts of many government programs we now take for granted, such as social security and unemployment insurance, would have seemed extreme. But with the onset of the Depression, attitudes began to change. Many people felt that if the free market could lead to such economic distress as existed during the Depression, it was time to start considering alternatives. As economists began to analyze the aggregate economy in greater detail, many became less confident of their policy prescriptions and much more aware of the shortcomings of a theory based only on partial equilibrium analysis and faith. Consequently, economists began to advocate a variety of policy proposals to address unemployment that were inconsistent with their "classical" views. In the early 1930s, for example, A. C. Pigou in England and several University of Chicago economists in the United States advocated public works programs and deficits as a means of fighting unemployment.

KEYNESIAN MACROECONOMICS

It was within this context of economic upheaval, concern about unemployment, and questioning of the underlying macroeconomic theory
that what we now know as macroeconomics developed. The history of
modern macroeconomics must begin with a consideration of Keynes,
the economist most responsible for changing the focus of economics.

Keynes the Man

John Maynard Keynes's father, J. N. Keynes, was an important economist in his own right, but his son's accomplishments would quickly
eclipse his own. In this and in several other ways J. M. Keynes's life is
like that of J. S. Mill. Both had fathers who were contemporaries and
friends of brilliant economists: James Mill was a friend of David
Ricardo, and J. N. Keynes a friend of Alfred Marshall. Both the
younger Keynes and the younger Mill received the high-quality education typically provided to children of intellectuals, an education that
equipped their innately brilliant minds to break new ground and to
persuade others with the force of their writing. Both Mill and Keynes
rejected the basic policy implications of their fathers' economics and
proceeded in new directions. But here the similarities end, for J. S. Mill
was unable to break completely with the theoretical structure of his
father and Ricardo; ultimately he constructed a halfway house between
classical and neoclassical theory. Keynes's break with the past — that is,
with the laissez faire tradition running from Smith through Ricardo,
J. S. Mill, and Marshall — was more complete. This was possibly
because, although he was familiar with the basic Marshallian partial
equilibrium analysis, he constructed a new theoretical structure to deal
with the aggregate economy that revolutionized both economic theory
and policy.

Keynes does not fit the stereotype of the intellectually narrow
twentieth-century economist. He was criticized, in fact, for devoting
too little of his time to economic theory and spreading his interests too
broadly. Even as a student at Eton and Cambridge he displayed this
proclivity to pursue a wide range of interests, and hence came to be
known as a dilettante. His education completed, he entered the British
government's Indian Office as a civil servant, where he remained for
two years before returning to Cambridge. He was never exclusively an
academic. His continuing interest in economic policy led him to take
a number of government posts throughout his life. He was active in
business affairs both for himself and as bursar of King's College, and his
ability in business is manifested by the fact that his net worth rose from
near bankruptcy in 1920 to more than $2 million by his death in 1946.

Keynes was interested in theater, literature, and the ballet; he married a ballerina and associated with a group of London intellectuals known as the Bloomsbury group, which included such notables as Clive Bell, E. M. Forster, Lytton Strachey, and Virginia Woolf. His unique mixture of talents enabled him to be an accomplished mathematician as an undergraduate, to write a book on probability theory, and to be a powerful and effective prose stylist, which is evident in the sheer

John Maynard Keynes

literary mastery of both his *Economic Consequences of the Peace* and his essays, collected into two books as *Essays in Persuasion* and *Essays in Biography*.

The single most important aspect of Keynes the economist is his orientation toward policy. He went to the Versailles peace conference as a representative of the British Treasury Department but resigned abruptly in 1919, disgusted with the terms of the Versailles treaty, which imposed large reparations on Germany that Keynes thought could never be paid. He received international acclaim for his criticism of the terms of the treaty, published in 1919 in his *Economic Consequences of the Peace*. In 1940 he wrote *How to Pay for the War*, and in 1943 he advanced a proposal called the Keynes Plan for an international monetary authority to be put into effect after World War II. As head of the British delegation to Bretton Woods, he was instrumental in the formation of the International Monetary Fund and the International Bank, which emerged from the Bretton Woods conference. But his most important contributions to policy and theory are contained in his 1936 book *The General Theory*, which created modern macroeconomics and still forms the basis of most of what is taught in undergraduate macroeconomics. Paul Samuelson captured its importance when, reflecting on the Keynesian era, he wrote, "*The General Theory* caught most economists under the age of thirty-five with the unexpected virulence of a disease first attacking and decimating an isolated tribe of South Sea Islanders."[6]

The Contextual Nature of the General Theory

Possibly no book in economic theory has a more presumptuous first chapter than Keynes's *General Theory*. To be sure, other economists had proclaimed their own originality and brilliance, but Keynes did it with such force that it seemed convincing. This lack of modesty apparently went back to Keynes's youth. When he took the civil service exam upon graduation from college and did not receive the top score in economics, his response was "I evidently knew more about Economics than my examiners."[7] While Keynes was working on *The General Theory*, he wrote to George Bernard Shaw that he was writing a new book that would revolutionize the way the world thinks about economic problems. The first chapter of *The General Theory* is one para-

6. Paul, Samuelson, "The General Theory: 1946," in *Keynes's General Theory: Reports of Three Decades*, ed. Robert Lekachman (New York: St. Martins Press, 1964), p. 315.
7. R. F. Harrod, *The Life of John Maynard Keynes* (New York: Harcourt Brace, 1952), p. 121.

graph long. Here Keynes simply states that his new theory is a general theory, in the sense that previous theory is a special case to be placed within his more general framework. By "previous theory" Keynes meant both classical and neoclassical economics, which he defined as the economics of Ricardo, as it pertains to Say's Law, and of those who followed in this belief: J. S. Mill, Marshall, Edgeworth, and Pigou.

We stated above that the single most important aspect of Keynes the economist was his policy orientation, but his most important work, *The General Theory*, in spite of its policy overtones, is essentially a theoretical book whose major audience was to be found among professional economists. Keynes wrote,

> This book is chiefly addressed to my fellow economists. I hope it will be intelligible to others. But its main purpose is to deal with difficult questions of theory, and only in the second place with the application of this theory to practice.[8]

We can reconcile this seeming contradiction by understanding the way in which Keynes used theory. Many economic theories are what might be called noncontextual, that is, developed in an institutional void. Such theories are best understood by deductive logic; they begin at first principles from which they then deduce conclusions based on carefully stated assumptions. In making these assumptions, one does not take reality into account but tries instead to understand the inherent logic of the interactions among the assumptions. Such theories might be called analytic theories. General equilibrium analysis, done correctly, is an analytic theory. Because the assumptions are inevitably far removed from reality, drawing policy conclusions from broad-ranging analytic theories is extremely complicated.

Keynes used a different kind of theory, one that might be called "realytic," since it is a compromise between a realistic and analytic approach. A realytic theory is contextual; it blends inductive information about the economy with deductive logic. Reality guides the choice of assumptions. Realytic theories are less inherently satisfying, but since they correspond closely to reality, it is easier to draw policy conclusions from them. Keynes did not start from first principles in *The General Theory* but instead used reality to guide his choice of assumptions. Thus, although he concentrated on theory, he never lost sight of its policy implications.

An example might make the distinction between realytic and analytic theories clearer. Keynes assumed prices and wages to be relatively constant without attempting to justify those assumptions. Al-

8. J. M. Keynes, *The General Theory of Employment, Interest, and Money* (London: Macmillan and Co., Ltd., 1936), p. 3.

though he briefly discussed in *The General Theory* the implications of flexible prices, arguing that they do not solve the unemployment problem, a thorough consideration of their implications was of little concern to him; for the problem at hand — what to do about unemployment — it was reasonable to assume fixed wages and prices. He could do this using his realytic approach, whereas a truly analytic model would not have permitted such assumptions. Keynes left it to others to provide an analytic basis for his theory. Much of the subsequent development of macroeconomic thinking has been an attempt to provide an analytic base for macroeconomics.

Keynes began working on *The General Theory* immediately after he had completed his two-volume *Treatise on Money*, which used the quantity theory of money to discuss cyclical fluctuations. In *The General Theory* Keynes abandoned this approach, much to the chagrin of his colleague Dennis Robertson, with whom he had previously worked closely, and adopted instead the simple, new approach that has since become the core of undergraduate macroeconomics. To provide himself with a heftier target, Keynes lumped together the neoclassical disequilibrium monetary approach and the earlier classical approach, exaggerated their beliefs, and called them collectively "classical theory." In so doing he created a caricature of classical thought that emphasized its differences from his new approach but concealed many of its subtleties.

The Demand for Output as a Whole

One of the best ways to appreciate Keynes's contribution is to look at him through the eyes of one of his early converts, Abba Lerner.

> We had heard that some very strange things were happening in Cambridge. We couldn't quite make out what it was, something about the elasticity of demand for output as a whole, and we knew that was nonsense, because we were brought up properly on Marshall, and we knew all about elasticity and demand curves. We knew that if you drew a demand curve you had to assume all the other prices were fixed; otherwise you wouldn't know what the demand curve for this item was. If you were to draw a demand curve for another item (for example, say you wanted to look at the consumer surplus which you could enjoy from being able to buy some item for less than you would have been willing to pay), it was your duty to wipe out the first demand curve because the first one was allowing the price to vary. You had to have the prices fixed for everything else if you were going to draw a demand curve. Knowing this, we knew that demand curves, demand and elasticity, referred only to partial analysis, and,

yet, somehow in Cambridge they must have known that and still, very perversely, they were talking about elasticity of demand for output as a whole.

Well, Joan Robinson started explaining it to us, but we didn't understand her, and so we arranged to have a weekend meeting symbolically at a place called Bishop's Stortford, halfway between London and Cambridge. There was a London contingent and a Cambridge contingent, and we spent a whole weekend trying to find out what they were doing. Joan Robinson was in charge. She was aided by a few other people from Cambridge and Oxford. Her husband [Austin Robinson] dropped in for a while; R. F. Kahn came once, James Meade was also there. I think there were one or two others but I've forgotten now who they were. Mainly, however, it was Joan Robinson in charge, and as we would try to understand, she'd say, "Yes, that's right; now you're getting the idea...No, no; now you've gone backwards." When the weekend was over we still didn't know what they were talking about. However, we were sufficiently impressed to publish an article by Joan Robinson, which we didn't understand, on the demand for output as a whole. This was the first we saw of the Cambridge idea.

The weekend meeting had not been too successful; we still couldn't understand each other — at least we couldn't understand them. They were confident that we were either just very stupid or backward — and we thought they were crazy, obviously doing something that didn't make any sense, but we couldn't quite put our finger on what was wrong.[9]

Why was it so difficult for good Marshallian economists to understand Keynes's argument? To see the problem, consider Figure 11.1 in which we draw a normal demand and supply curve. Because it is partial equilibrium analysis, the price on the vertical axis is a relative price (relative to the general price level). Quantity of good per-unit time is on the horizontal axis. Partial equilibrium supply and demand curves are drawn on the assumption that all other prices and income (as well as everything else) remain constant. If that assumption does not hold, the partial disequilibrium adjustment mechanism and the analysis breaks down. Let us say, for example, that price is P_o, quantity demand is Q_d, and quantity supplied is Q_s. The standard adjustment mechanism is the following: because quantity supplied is greater than quality demanded, the relative price of good X falls. The process continues until equilibrium price, P_e, and quantity, Q_e, are reached.

9. This statement is from an unpublished transcript of a recording of a Boston University Seminar (April 24, 1972) in which Alvin Hansen and Abba Lerner were discussing their roles in the Keynesian revolution.

Now consider what happens if all other things do not remain equal. Specifically, let us say that a decrease in quantity supplied lowers income. Since demand depends upon income as well as price, this means that as quantity supplied falls, the demand curve shifts back to, say, D_1. Now there are two disequilibrium adjustment forces, the price adjustment force, (a) and the income adjustment force (b). As you can see, these forces are pushing in opposite directions. The relative price effect (the movement down along the demand curve) brings us closer to equilibrium, but the income effect shifts the demand curve to the left, moving us further from equilibrium. Without knowing the relative magnitudes of the shift, we cannot say whether an equilibrium will be achieved. Moreover, even if an equilibrium will be achieved, supply-and-demand analysis does not tell us what it will be, since the final equilibrium will not be at P_e and Q_e but at the intersection of the shifted demand curve and the supply curve.

What happens if we try to use supply-and-demand analysis to discuss the aggregate economy? Because the analysis is of the aggregate economy, there is no relative price effect (unless one assumes prices flexible and wages constant, which Keynes did not assume in his simple model). There is only a general price level, so it is unclear what the aggregate

Figure 11.1 Partial Equilibrium Adjustment to Equilibrium

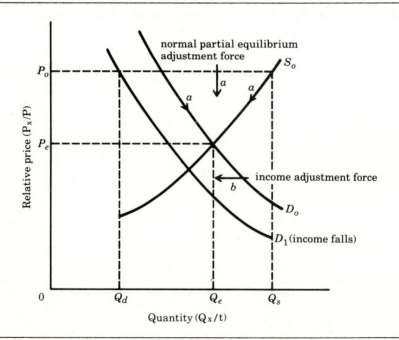

equivalent to the partial equilibrium supply and demand curves will be. One way to determine the aggregate would be to ask the same questions that are asked in the partial equilibrium case: what will happen to quantity supplied if the price level rises? The classicals' answer is that nothing will change, assuming as they did that there is a dichotomy between the real and nominal sectors. Thus the supply curve will be perfectly inelastic. If we now invoke Say's Law (supply creates its own demand), we can also draw an aggregate demand curve coincidental with the aggregate supply curve. The two curves are not only perfectly inelastic; they are also coincidental at the full employment level of income, as in Figure 11.2(a). Because the two curves are coincidental, the price level is indeterminant; but that indeterminancy is consistent with classical thought, in which the price level was determined by the quantity theory of money. Figure 11.2(b) shows how the price level is determined. The price level is on the vertical axis, and the money supply on the horizontal axis. Figure 11.2(b) graphs the relationship between money and prices as it exists in the quantity theory, assuming a constant velocity. When the money supply increases, the price level increases by an equal amount. Figure 11.2 is the classical analysis in a nutshell. The aggregate real economy is always in equilibrium. The quantity of money is determined by the price level, and Say's Law assures that real equilibrium is at full employment.

Good Marshallians understood the above argument. That's why Lerner and his cohorts knew it was foolish to think about a demand

Figure 11.2 Classical Aggregate Equilibrium

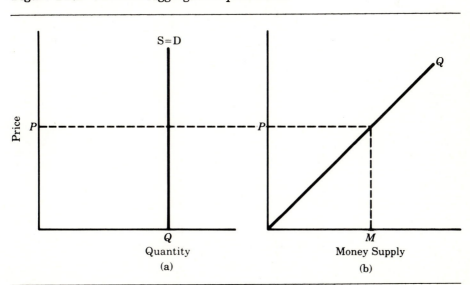

curve for aggregate output. Keynes and Joan Robinson also knew this argument, but the demand curve for output as a whole that they were talking about was no ordinary partial equilibrium demand curve relating relative price and quantity. It is based on the consumption, investment, and government spending functions.

To understand how Keynes's aggregate demand analysis differs from a partial equilibrium demand analysis, it is helpful to consider Keynes's objection to classical analysis. Keynes's argument with the classicals can be understood by asking what would happen if for some reason planned demand did not equal planned supply, so that the economy was in a position such as that represented in Figure 11.3, rather than in Figure 11.2(a). What might bring about an equilibrium between aggregate supply and aggregate demand? In this case, as you can see in Figure 11.3, a fall in the price level, which could only be brought about by a change in the money supply, would have no effect in bringing about an aggregate equilibrium. The dichotomy assumption prevented it. Keynes argued that, assuming an *initial* equilibrium, the economy *stayed* in equilibrium, given the classical assumptions (in particular, the dichotomy assumption); but if the economy was in disequilibrium, it had no way to achieve equilibrium.

Keynes continued his argument by stating that when there was aggregate disequilibrium, an infinitely falling price level luckily was not an economy's fate. Wages and prices were not perfectly flexible, they were institutionally fixed. And because they were fixed, aggregate disequilibrium adjustment did not occur through wage and price adjust-

Figure 11.3 Keynesian Aggregate Disequilibrium

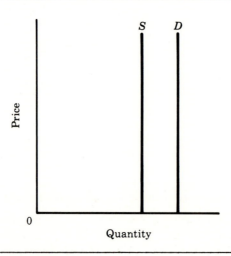

ments; it occurred in a different way. Keynes's model was designed to focus on that alternative path of adjustment.

To understand Keynes's aggregate adjustment analysis, think back to the problem of determining the final equilibrium in the case where supply and demand were interconnected. What prevented us from determining the equilibrium in that example was not knowing how much the demand curve would shift when the quantity supplied shifted. If we had known that, we could have determined whether there would be an ultimate equilibrium and, if so, what that equilibrium would be.

Marshallian analysis of equilibrium prices and quantities for individual micromarkets solves the problem of the interrelatedness of the supply and demand curves by using partial equilibrium analysis. In short, the interrelatedness is ignored. Theoretical perfection is sacrificed in order to make headway in practical analysis. This approach is quite reasonable for understanding individual micromarkets, but unsatisfactory when applied at the level of aggregate supply and demand. Keynes recognized that ignoring the interconnection of aggregate supply and demand made it impossible to understand forces determining the level of income and employment. He therefore assumed an explicit connection between aggregate supply and demand by postulating a relationship between the income and consumption of an economy. Income (supply) and consumption (demand) had a stable relationship, so that as income fell, one could determine the position of the aggregate demand function. The relationship between income and consumption was called the "consumption function," and the coefficient relating changes in demand spending (consumption) to changes in supply (income) was the "marginal propensity to consume."

Keynes argued that the marginal propensity to consume was less than one, so that the difference between income and consumption decreased as income fell. For example, if income (supply) decreases by $1,000, but individuals had been saving 20 percent of their income, consumption (demand) will fall by only $800. As income continues to fall, any gap between aggregate supply and aggregate demand will continue to decrease, and eventually the two will meet at equilibrium. In Keynes's simple model, prices were fixed and changes in income provided all the adjustment. The assumption that the marginal propensity to consume is less than one is the key to explaining why income stops falling. If the marginal propensity to consume is equal to one, stable equilibrium is not possible.

Since this process "multiplies" an initial shock, Keynes used the term *multiplier* to relate how much income must change in response to an exogenous shock. The size of the multiplier depended upon the marginal propensity to consume. For example, if the marginal propensity to consume ($\Delta C/\Delta Y$) is 0.75 and the marginal propensity to save

($\Delta S/\Delta Y$) is 0.25, the multiplier is 4. From national income data for the United States, Keynes estimated the multiplier to have a value of about 2.5. Keynes's theory demonstrated that the total shift in demand and supply would be a multiple of the initial gap, and hence the multiplier became a key element of Keynes's analysis.

The multiplier analysis is shown graphically in Figure 11.4 where $b = \dfrac{\Delta C}{\Delta Y}$. In it we draw a standard consumption function (with slope equal to a marginal propensity to consume of 0.5) and add to it investment and government expenditures, which for simplicity we assume to be independent of income. This gives us the aggregate (income) spending function. Aggregate production or supply corresponds to total production and is represented by the 45-degree line. Initially the economy is in equilibrium at Y_a. Suppose investment falls by ΔI, or 200. If Y_a equals \$1,000, the economy is now in disequilibrium, with production at \$1,000 and spending at \$800. Since production is greater than spending, income falls as producers decide to produce less, decreasing both the quantity supplied and the quantity demanded. As income falls, production and spending become closer (the quantity demanded decreases by less than the quantity supplied) until finally, at income Y_e, aggregate supply and demand are equal. The distance between the initial income, Y_a, and the new equilibrium, Y_e, is two times the initial gap ($2 \, \Delta I$), or 400.

Figure 11.4 Keynesian Consumption Function Analysis

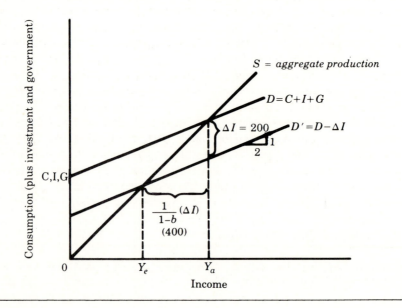

With his theory Keynes provided an explanation for the Depression: a gap between aggregate production and spending would lead to a multiplied effect on income. He also provided a way out of the Depression: increase spending by a portion of the gap and rely on the multiplier to increase income by the remainder.

Precedents for Keynes's Analysis

In explaining why the level of income was volatile, Keynes stressed the role of investment spending. In this he followed Tugan-Baranowsky, who had argued that a change in investment spending would lead to changes in income of a greater magnitude than the original change in investment spending. Most economists did not accept this view, and no formal theoretical explanation of this process was developed.

The Depression of the 1930s changed all that. With 25-percent unemployment, the self-regulating nature of the market system could no longer simply be assumed. Noneconomists were advancing various proposals for public works programs, arguing that these would increase employment, and a number of classical economists favored such proposals even though they conflicted with classical theory.

In 1931 R. F. Kahn, a colleague of Keynes at Cambridge, provided a formal basis for these proposals with his employment-multiplier analysis.* (Michael Kalecki advanced a similar analysis, but since his work was in Polish it was not known to most American and English economists.) Kahn argued as follows: suppose N is total employment and N_1 is employment in public works. A change in employment in the public works sector will increase income. As workers spend this income, other employers will find that they need more employees, and they, too, will increase employment. For example, if the employment multiplier is 3, then a public works project employing 1,000 more laborers will increase total employment by 3,000. Kahn called the coefficient that relates these changes the employment multiplier. Although it was expressed in terms of employment rather than income, it was identical to Keynes's multiplier.

*R. F. Kahn, "The Relation of Home Investment to Unemployment," *Economic Journal*, 51 (June 1931).

What Keynes Really Meant

In the 1930s and 1940s Keynes's arguments were extremely controversial, but since most economists were focusing their attention on the problems of war production, war finance, and postwar reconstruction, they did little work on macroeconomic theory. That changed in the late 1940s; the war ended and economists began working in earnest on Keynes's theory and on relating it to policy.

Because there were many strands of reasoning in Keynes's theory and many interconnected arguments, it was not at all clear what he really meant. He himself provided little assistance in clarifying his meaning. In the ten years after publishing *The General Theory*, he was intricately involved in practical problems of paying for the war and setting up a postwar monetary system. Then in 1946 he died. Not surprisingly, his meaning has been fiercely debated ever since. We will not enter the "What Keynes Really Meant Sweepstakes" here, but we should point out that the presentation of his ideas given above is not the one found in most introductory or intermediate macro textbooks. It is one of many interpretations of Keynes's model and is presented here because it is a helpful way to contrast micro-and macroeconomics and to provide insight into some modern developments in macroeconomics. Before considering those modern developments, however, we will present the prevailing interpretation of Keynes's model from the 1940s to the present.

The Rise of the Consumption Function Model: 1940–1960

Keynes's model was not initially interpreted as an adjustment model of the aggregate economy. Initially the focus was on the consumption function and the multiplier. In the 1940s and 1950s, economists explored this multiplier model, developing it in excruciating detail. It was expanded to include international effects, various types of government expenditure, and different types of individual spending. Terms such as "the balanced budget multiplier" became standard parts of economic terminology, and every economics student had to learn Keynes's model.

This now-standard consumption function model and the monetary and fiscal policies that were and are generally called Keynesian are not to be found in Keynes's book. There is not a single diagram in *The General Theory*, nor any discussion of the use of monetary and fiscal policy. How, then, did the consumption function model (done algebraically and geometrically) become the focal point of the macroeconomic debates of the 1950s? Part of the reason is that it seemed to provide a better description of current reality than did the alternatives. But other factors were also at work. The initial policy debates about the validity of Keynesian economics focused on fiscal policy (government deficits during the war had pulled the Western world out of the Depression). Since the consumption function model nicely captured the effects of fiscal policy, it tended to become the Keynesian model. We suspect that sociological reasons also played a role in both the initial adoption and long-term acceptance of the model. The need for truth, which we discussed in Chapter 1, is often tempered by other needs of the profession — specifically, teaching requirements and the necessity for journal articles. The consumption function model fit those needs beautifully.

It was in the United States that the consumption function analysis caught on, with Paul Samuelson and Alvin Hansen developing it into the primary Keynesian model. Samuelson's textbook introduced it into pedagogy, other books copied Samuelson's, and soon the consumption function model was Keynesian economics. The consumption function analysis had many pedagogical advantages: it was easy to teach and learn. It allowed macroeconomics to develop as a separate field by providing a core analytical structure for the course, just as supply-and-demand analysis had for microeconomics.

Simultaneously, Keynesian policy came to mean fine-tuning through monetary and fiscal policy. Abba Lerner was an influential force in directing Keynesian analysis toward fine-tuning through monetary and fiscal policy. In his *Economics of Control* (1944) Lerner advocated that the government should not follow a policy of "sound finance" (always balance the budget); it should instead follow a policy of "functional finance," which considered only the *results* of policies, not the policies themselves. Functional finance allowed the government to "drive" the economy, and in an oft-repeated metaphor, monetary and fiscal policy were portrayed as government's steering wheel. Lerner contended that fiscal and monetary policy were the tools government should use to achieve its macroeconomic goals: high employment, price stability, and high growth. The size of the deficit was totally irrelevant: if there was unemployment, the government should increase the deficit and the money supply; if there was inflation, the government should do the opposite.

Lerner's blunt statement of the "Keynesian" argument offended the sensibilities of many Keynesians and provoked much discussion, even causing Keynes to disavow Keynesianism.[10] Evsey Domar, a well-known Keynesian at the time, said, "Even Keynesians, upon hearing Lerner's argument that the size of the deficit did not matter, recoiled

10. David Colander, "Was Keynes a Keynesian or a Lernerian?" *Journal of Economic Literature*, 22 (December 1984), p. 1572.

and said, no he had it wrong, in no uncertain terms."[11] But Keynes soon changed his mind and agreed with Lerner, as did much of the economics profession, and it was not long before Keynesian economic policy became synonymous with functional finance.

Monetary and fiscal policies were, moreover, politically palatable. Many economists and others believed the Depression proved that the government had to assume a much larger role in directing the economy. Using monetary and fiscal policy kept that role to a minimum. Markets could be left free to operate as before. The government would not directly determine the level of investment; it could simply affect total income indirectly by running a budget deficit or surplus. The legitimization of deficits had a second desirable characteristic: it allowed government to spend without taxing.

Keynes's Philosophical Approach to Policy

Policy necessarily combines theory with normative judgments. Understanding the Keynesian revolution, therefore, requires a consideration of the general philosophical views of economists at the time, and of Keynes in particular. Keynes was not a radical, although he was so accused after publishing *The General Theory*. We would hardly expect a person of his background, education, and experience to argue for drastic changes in the institutional structure of his society. Keynes was basically conservative in his views about altering the structure of society, generally advocating only such changes as would preserve the essential elements of capitalism. His view was that if the worst defects of the system were not removed, individuals would discard the capitalistic system and lose much more than they gained. His rejection of Marxism reflects both a criticism of Marx's economics and a recognition that a Marxian social system would destroy the social class of which Keynes was very much a part.

> How can I accept a doctrine which sets up as its bible, above and beyond criticism, an obsolete economic textbook which I know to be not only scientifically erroneous but without interest or application for the modern world? How can I adopt a creed which, preferring the mud to the fish, exalts the boorish proletariat above the bourgeois and the intelligentsia who, with whatever faults, are the quality in life and surely carry the seeds of all human achievement?[12]

11. The quotation is from an unpublished interview held with Evsey Domar by the authors.
12. J. M. Keynes, "A Short View of Russia," in *Essays in Persuasion* (New York: Harcourt, Brace, 1932), p. 300.

Keynes was dismayed by the growth of totalitarian government and dictatorship in Germany, Italy, and Russia. He was willing to admit that these changes in social organization might solve some economic problems, but such a solution, he felt, would be purchased only at the cost of individualism and its economic and political advantages. The economic advantages of individualism, stemming from the use of self-interest to achieve greater efficiency and innovation, are well known to economists.

But, above all, individualism, if it can be purged of its defects and its abuses, is the best safeguard of personal liberty in the sense that, compared with any other system, it greatly widens the field for the exercise of personal choice. It is also the best safeguard of the variety of life, which emerges precisely from this extended field of personal choice, and the loss of which is the greatest of all losses of the homogeneous or totalitarian state.[13]

Keynes's broad philosophical views on the structure of the good society led to attacks from two sides: those to the left of him considered him an apologist for capitalism and for his own class, and those to the right regarded him as a wild-eyed reformer-socialist seeking to dismantle the capitalistic system. We have already seen his response to the Marxist approach. His response to criticism from the right was at least more conciliatory. He writes, "While, therefore, the enlargement of the functions of government...would seem...to be a terrific encroachment on individualism, I defend it, on the contrary, both as the only practicable means of avoiding the destruction of existing economic forms in their entirety and as the condition of the successful functioning of individual initiative."[14] Keynes found one of the chief benefits of capitalism to be the free play it gives individualism. What abuses do come from individualism, he believed, could be corrected without destroying capitalism. The chief defects or faults of capitalism, he said, "are its failure to provide for full employment and its arbitrary and inequitable distribution of wealth and incomes."[15]

The question postwar economists faced was this: what policies can we use to preserve the best of capitalism and simultaneously excise its greatest faults? Keynes's views on policy, while conservative, were too liberal for most people in the United States. His more conservative monetary and fiscal policy, which required little direct government intervention in the economy, was the most acceptable aspect of his policy to United States economists. And even those policies were

13. Keynes, *The General Theory*, p. 380.
14. *Ibid.*
15. *Ibid.*, p. 372.

attacked by some conservatives, who considered Keynesians socialists. Lorie Tarshis, who wrote the first Keynesian introductory textbook, discovered this when a conservative group led a drive to stop alumni from giving to any school that used his book and to have him fired from Stanford University, where he taught. During the McCarthy era in the 1950s, Keynesians were often equated with Communists by critics on the right. Within such a political climate, it is not surprising that Keynesians in the United States chose the least radical interpretation of Keynes.

From the Consumption Function to
IS-LM Analysis: 1960–1975

The consumption function model had proved to be inadequate for some theoretical debates because it did not include an analysis of the interconnection between the financial and real sectors. For the policy debates in the early 1950s, which had focused on fiscal policy, this had not mattered; but as soon as the debates began to include monetary policy, it did, and a new model was needed. Sir John Hicks's *IS-LM* analysis filled this need, superseding the consumption function model by the late 1950s and being adopted as the mainstream Keynesian model. It still forms the basis of most intermediate macroeconomic textbooks.

The *IS-LM* model was devised by Hicks in 1937 as a method of elucidating the difference between the Keynesian and classical theories of income determination. It was able to integrate the money market with the goods market, which the simple consumption function model did not do. To grasp the significance of this integrative effect, consider the aggregate adjustment process underlying Keynes's consumption function. The highly simplified analysis presented in Figures 11.3 and 11.4 assumes a complete dichotomy between the real and nominal sectors: by assumption, when the price level falls, the money supply falls by the same amount. Because of that assumption price-level changes fail to bring about equilibrium in the model, since the aggregate demand curve is perfectly price inelastic. The simple Keynesian consumption function model avoided addressing this issue by assuming fixed prices. Keynes's book, however, the full title of which was *The General Theory of Employment, Interest, and Money*, included a long discussion of the role of money and interest rates. Thus, the simple Keynesian model was obviously an incomplete exposition of Keynes's analysis.

When Keynes analyzed what would happen if the price level fell but the nominal money supply remained constant, he determined that since the real money supply is the nominal money supply divided by the price level, a fall in the price level would increase the real money supply, and that increase would lower interest rates, thereby increasing investment and income. Thus the price level was a factor in determining equilibrium income. In terms of an aggregate supply-and-demand model, this price-level effect means that the aggregate demand curve would not be perfectly price inelastic, but downward-sloping. The reason for this is different from the reason that the partial equilibrium demand curve is downward-sloping. The aggregate demand curve slopes down because a fall in the price level increases the real money supply and the real money supply affects aggregate demand. Thus Keynes provided a price adjustment mechanism so that price-level fluctuations can bring about an aggregate equilibrium. Keynes felt, however, that since this effect was relatively weak, and since in reality prices did not fluctuate enough for this to be a useful policy, it was much easier to change the *real* money supply by changing the *nominal* money supply, and not by waiting for prices to change.

This alternative mechanism for bringing about an aggregate equilibrium has become known as the Keynes Effect. The Keynes Effect establishes a link between the real and nominal sectors via the interest rate and investment. A decrease in the money supply raises interest rates, which decreases investment; an increase in the money supply causes a fall in interest rates, which increases investment. The change in investment, in turn, affects income through the multiplier effects of the simple consumption function model. The flow of causation is

$$\Delta P \to \Delta M \to \Delta i \to \Delta I \to \Delta Y$$

With the Keynes Effect the dichotomy assumption is discarded and price-level fluctuations can bring about equilibrium between aggregate supply and demand by increasing the real money supply, which in turn increases the aggregate quantity demanded.

Pigou and others contended in debates with Keynesians that, at least in theory, a fall in the price level did not have to work through a change in interest rates to effect a classical equilibrium. It could work directly on aggregate demand. Pigou reasoned that a fall in the price level makes the holders of money wealthier, and because they are wealthier they will spend more, increasing aggregate demand.[16] The effect of price-level changes on aggregate demand is therefore called the Wealth Effect, or the Pigou Effect. Debate about these issues and the relative roles of monetary and fiscal policy filled the journals in the 1960s.

16. Pigou agreed that whereas, in reality, this effect would be minuscule, it preserved a classical aggregate adjustment mechanism without resorting to the Keynes Effect.

The consumption function model does not allow for the Keynes Effect or the Pigou Effect; if we were to try to include them, the diagrams would quickly become enormously complicated. Thus it was natural that economists would turn to a model more suitable to the issues being debated. *IS-LM* analysis afforded such a model; it provided a neat geometric method of capturing the interrelationships between the real and nominal sectors. *IS-LM* analysis combined Keynes's analysis of the money market with his analysis of the goods market and demonstrated how equilibrium would be achieved through forces in both of these markets. The interconnection between the goods market and the money market occurs because the interest rate also affects investment, which is part of aggregate demand. Lower interest rates make borrowing cheaper, through increasing investment; higher interest rates decrease investment. Since investment is a part of aggregate demand, any change in investment has a multiplied effect on income via the multiplier.

The problem Hicks's *IS-LM* (Investment = Savings — Demand for Liquidity = Money Supply) analysis addressed was how to combine Keynes's analysis of the money market with the savings and investment market. Since there are feedback loops between the two markets, it is not a trivial problem. An increase in investment for example, will increase income, which will increase the demand for money, shifting the demand for money curve up. As it does so it increases the explicit interest rates in the money market. That rise in the interest rate will offset some of the initial rise in investment, which in turn offsets some of the effect on income. The smaller effect on income means the demand for money will not change so much, which means that determining the ultimate equilibrium is no inconsiderable exercise.

The *IS-LM* model reduces the above discussion to a simple two-dimensional diagram. In *IS-LM* analysis, the money market is represented by an *LM* curve, which graphs the combination of interest rates and income levels at which the money market is in equilibrium, that is, when the amount of money desired for liquidity purposes equals the quantity of money. Similarly, the goods market is represented by the *IS* curve, which graphs the combination of interest rates and income levels for which the goods market is in equilibrium, defined as equality between the desire to invest and the desire to save.

IS-LM analysis is shown in Figure 11.5. Aggregate equilibrium is at (i_0, Y_0), where the *IS* curve intersects the *LM* curve. The *IS-LM* curves neatly show the effect of expansionary or contractionary monetary and fiscal policy. In Figure 11.5(a), expansionary fiscal policy shifts the *IS* curve to the right (IS_0 to IS_1), increasing income (Y_0 to Y_1) and interest rates (i_0 to i_1). In Figure 11.5(b), contractionary monetary policy shifts the *LM* curve to the left, decreasing income (Y_0 to Y_2) and increasing interest rates (i_0 to i_2).

Monetarists

In the 1950s and 1960s, the primary foil to the Keynesians was the monetarists. Under the leadership of Milton Friedman, they provided an effective opposition to Keynesian policy and theory. The consumption function model used by 1950s Keynesians had no role for money to play, nor did it consider prices or the price level. This initial lack of concern about money supply and prices manifested itself in policy based on Keynesian analysis. In "The Treasury Accord," which developed during World War II, the Federal Reserve Bank agreed to buy whatever bonds were necessary to maintain the interest rate at a fixed level. This entailed relinquishing all control of the money supply. Monetarists argued that the money supply played an important role in the economy and should not be limited to a role of holding the interest rate constant. Thus the rallying cry for early monetarists was that money mattered.

Keynesians were soon willing to concur with the monetarists that money mattered, but they felt that the monetarists differed from them

J. R. Hicks

in believing that *only* money mattered. The debate was resolved by the *IS-LM* Keynesian-neoclassical synthesis, in which the monetarists assumed a highly inelastic *LM* curve and Keynesians assumed a highly elastic *LM* curve. Thus, at least in terms of the textbook presentation, monetarist and Keynesian analyses came together in the general *IS-LM* model, about which they differed slightly on some parameters.

THE CURRENT STATE OF MACROECONOMICS

Problems with *IS-LM* Analysis

IS-LM analysis is part of any economist's toolbox; it provides the framework most economists initially use in tackling macroeconomic analysis. By the 1960s, however, it had been well explored in the literature and found wanting in several ways. First, it forced the analysis into a comparative static equilibrium framework. In the view of many economists, Keynes's analysis concerned — or should have concerned — speeds of adjustment. They felt Keynes was arguing that the income

Figure 11.5 Monetary and Fiscal Policy

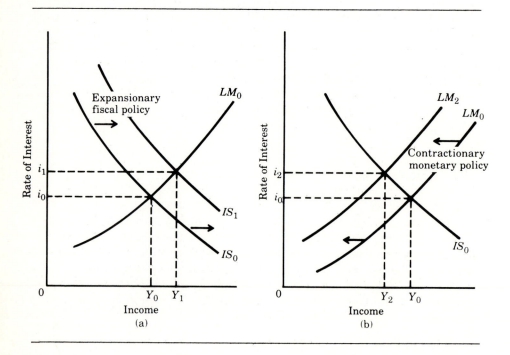

adjustment mechanism (the multiplier) occurred faster than the price or interest rate adjustment mechanisms. Comparative static analysis lost that aspect of Keynes.

Second, in *IS-LM* analysis the interrelationship between the real and nominal sectors had to occur through the interest rate and could not occur through other channels. Monetarists were unhappy with this because they felt money could affect the economy through several channels. Many Keynesians were unhappy with the framework because it shed little light on the problem of inflation, which in the 1960s was beginning to be seen as a serious economic problem. Third, the demand for money analysis used to derive the *LM* curve was not based on a general equilibrium model; instead it was assumed in a rather *ad hoc* fashion. Thus it had not truly integrated the nominal and real sectors. Because it did not capture the true role of money and the financial sector, it trivialized the function of money and the financial sector. It made it seem as if a fall in the price level could bring about an equilibrium — when, in fact, most economists felt that a falling price level would make matters worse, not better. Nonetheless, the *IS-LM* model was adopted. It was neat, it served its pedagogical function well, it was a rough and ready tool, it provided generally correct insight into the economy, and it was the best model available.

Dissatisfaction with existing analysis, however, led many macroeconomists to turn to other models in their research. This led to a dichotomy. While *IS-LM* analysis remained the key undergraduate model in the 1970s and 1980s, graduate research started to focus on quite different issues. Modern theoretical debates in macroeconomics have little to do with the shapes of the *IS-LM* curves. Instead, they approach macro issues from a microeconomic perspective, and they deal with issues such as the speeds of quantity and price adjustment. In a sense, modern researchers have skipped the Keynesian *IS-LM* interval and returned to the macroeconomic debate as it existed in the 1930s, when issues were framed in microeconomic terms.

The Microfoundations of Macroeconomics

Microfoundations literature developed as economists attempted to grapple with the problem of inflation and integrate it into the Keynesian model. One of the first tasks economists undertook was to explain the underlying theory of the Phillips curve, an empirical relationship between inflation and unemployment that had been discovered in 1958 by A. W. Phillips. This discovery opened up a number of theoretical questions, such as "Why does inflation occur?" "Why is the relationship between inflation and unemployment stable?" and "Will this stable relationship continue?"

Its novelty of approach, as much as the profundity of its answers, distinguished the microfoundations literature. It established new ways of looking at unemployment. Whereas Keynesian analysis pictured unemployment as an equilibrium phenomenon in which individuals could not find jobs, the microfoundations literature pictured unemployment as a temporary phenomenon — the result of the interaction of a flow of workers leaving work and new workers entering. It argued that intersectoral flows were an important cause of unemployment and that these flows were the natural result of dynamic economic processes. For the new microeconomics, unemployment was a micro, not a macro, issue.

Microfoundations economists argued that to understand unemployment and inflation economists must look at individuals' and firms' microeconomic decisions and relate those decisions to macroeconomic phenomena. Search theory, the study of an individual's optimal choice under uncertainty, became a central topic of macroeconomics, as did a variety of new dynamic adjustment models. As researchers began focusing more and more on these models, they focused less and less on *IS-LM* models. The initial microfoundations models had been partial equilibrium models, but once the microfoundations box had been opened, economists needed to derive some method of combining the various markets. The obvious choice was to use general equilibrium models. Thus general equilibrium analysis, which we saw in Chapter 10 had become the central model of microeconomics, was ushered into macroeconomics along with microfoundations literature.

Microfoundations literature was cemented into the profession's consciousness by its accurate prediction about inflation. Advocates of the microfoundations approach argued on theoretical grounds that the Phillips curve tradeoff was only a short-term phenomenon and that once the inflation became built into expectations, the unemployment-inflation tradeoff would disappear. The long-run Phillips curve would be close to vertical and the economy would gravitate toward a "natural rate of unemployment."

The policy implications of the new microfoundations approach were relatively strong. Its analyses removed the potential for government to affect the natural rate of long-run unemployment through expansionary monetary and fiscal policy. Attempts to do so would work in the short run by temporarily fooling workers, but expansionary policy would simply cause inflation in the long run. According to the new microeconomics, government's attempt to reduce unemployment below its natural rate was the cause of inflation in the late 1970s.

Keynesian monetary and fiscal policies were not, however, completely ruled out; in theory, at least, they could still be used temporarily to smooth out cycles. Thus, in the early 1970s a compromise arose between Keynesians and the advocates of microfoundations economics:

in the long run the classical model is correct, the economy will gravitate to its natural rate. In the short run, however, because individuals are assumed to adjust their expectations slowly, Keynesian policies can have some effect.

The Rise of New Classical Economics

In the mid-1970s the term "rational expectations" first appeared on the macroeconomic horizon. The rational expectations hypothesis was a by-product of the microeconomic analysis of Charles Holt, Franco Modigliani, John Muth, and Herbert Simon, who were trying to explain why many people did not seem to optimize in the way that neoclassical economics assumed they would. Their work was meant to explain by means of dynamic models what Simon called "satisfactory" behavior, that is, why firms' behavior did not correspond to microeconomic models.[17] John Muth turned that work on its head, writing,

> It is sometimes argued that the assumption of rationality in eco-
> nomics leads to theories inconsistent with, or inadequate to explain,
> observed phenomena, especially changes over time....Our hypothesis
> is based on exactly the opposite point of view: that dynamic eco-
> nomic models do not assume enough rationality.[18]

Muth held that in modeling it is reasonable to assume that expectations, since they are informed predictors of future events, are essentially those that would be consistent with the relevant economic theory. As Simon wrote, "[Muth] would cut the Gordian knot. Instead of dealing with uncertainty by elaborating the model of the decision process, he would once and for all — if his hypothesis were correct — make process irrelevant."[19]

With his assumption of a "dynamic rationality," Muth turned disequilibrium into equilibrium. Just as neoclassical writers used rationality to ensure static individual optimality, or to assure that the individual moves to a tangency of his budget line and his indifference curve, Muth used it to express "dynamic" individual optimality — to set the individual on his intertemporal indifference curve. As long as the private actors in the economy are optimally adjusting to the available information (and there is no good reason to assume the contrary), then they will always be on the optimal adjustment path.

17. Simon later received a Nobel Prize in economics for his work.
18. John Muth. "Rational Expectations and the Theory of Price Movements," *Econometrica*, 29 (July 1961), p. 316.
19. Herbert Simon, "Rational Decision Making in Business Organizations," *American Economic Review*, 69 (March 1979), p. 505.

Although Muth wrote his article in 1961, the rational expectations assumption did not play an important role in economics until it was adopted by macroeconomics and combined with the work being done in microfoundations of macroeconomics. The rational expectations hypothesis struck at the heart of the compromise between micro-foundations economists and Keynesians, because it held that people did not adjust their expectations toward equilibrium in stages. They can discover the underlying economic model and adjust immediately, and it would be beneficial for them to do so. Assuming people have rational expectations, anything that will happen in the long run will happen in the short run. Since in the microfoundations-Keynesian compromise the effectiveness of monetary and fiscal policy depended on incorrect expectations, the rational expectations hypothesis was devastating. In the new view, if Keynesian policy is ineffective in the long run it is ineffective in the short run.

In the mid-1970s rational expectations caught on in macroeconomics, and there were significant discussions of policy ineffectiveness and the unworkability of Keynesian-type monetary and fiscal policy. This developing work in rational expectations soon came to be known as New Classical, because its policy conclusions were similar to earlier classical views. By the late 1970s it seemed to many that the future of macroeconomics lay in New Classical thinking and that Keynesian economics was dead.

Macroeconomic Models and the Lucas Critique

One of the lasting influences of the New Classicals on macroeconomics was their contribution to the theory of macroeconomic modeling. Keynesians had developed macroeconomic models to a high level of sophistication in the work of economists such as Jan Tinbergen and Lawrence Klein. Klein describes the purposes of these models as follows:

> The purpose of building econometric models is to describe the way in which the system actually operates....If we know the quantitative characteristics of the economic system, we shall be able to forecast with a specified level of probability the course of certain economic magnitudes such as employment, output, or income; and we shall also be able to forecast with a specified level of probability the effect upon the system of various economic policies.[20]

20. Lawrence R. Klein, *Economic Fluctuations in the United States, 1921–1941* (New York: Wiley, 1950), Cowles Commission Monograph No. 11, p. 1.

In the 1960s and 1970s many of these models were not good predictors of future movements in the economy, and many economists were beginning to lose faith in them. Robert Lucas, a leader of the New Classicals, specified why these models were necessarily poor predictors in an argument that became known as the Lucas critique of econometric models. He argued that individuals' actions depend upon expected policies; therefore, the structure of the model will change as a policy is used. But if the underlying structure of the model changes, the appropriate policy will change and the model will no longer be the appropriate one. Thus it is inappropriate to use econometric models to predict effects of future policy.

The Neo-Keynesian and the New Keynesian Responses

The spread of the rational expectations hypothesis to macroeconomics led to two Keynesian responses. The neo-Keynesians, who accept *IS-LM* analysis, argued that the rational expectations hypothesis hardly deserved a response — it was simply ludicrous to think that everyone had rational expectations. Robert Solow wittily expressed this attitude when he said

> Suppose someone sits down where we are sitting right now and announces to me that he is Napolean Bonaparte. The last thing I want to do with him is to get involved in a technical discussion of cavalry tactics at the Battle of Austerlitz. If I do that, I'm getting tacitly drawn into the game that he *is* Napolean.[21]

The neo-Keynesians considered the modified *IS-LM* analysis to be sufficient to capture the essence of Keynesian thought and thus saw no need for the contributions of the rational expectations proponents.

A second group, the New Keynesians, were quite willing to accept the rational expectations criticism of the neo-Keynesians model; many of these economists had never believed that the *IS-LM* model adequately captured Keynesian thinking. But the New Keynesians argued that there is nothing inherently contradictory between Keynesian economics and the rational expectations hypothesis. They contended, moreover, that the assumption of rational expectations did not lead to policy ineffectiveness. Even if people had rational expectations, monetary and fiscal policy could still be effective. They reasoned that individual rationality can be quite different from collective rationality.

---

21. Arjo Klamer, *Conversations with Economists* (New Jersey: Rowman and Allanheld, 1984), p. 146.

Hence a society of rational individuals can find itself in an expectational conundrum in which all individuals are making rational decisions but the net result of those individually rational decisions is socially irrational. According to the New Keynesians, the rational expectations assumption leads to the New Classical conclusion that monetary and fiscal policy are ineffective only if it is combined with an assumption that all markets clear. It is this assumption, not the rational expectations assumption, that New Keynesians object to. They argue that the market-clearing assumption rules out both institutional constraints and slowly adaptive expectations, both of which New Keynesians believe exist. Moreover, they argue that both of these assumptions are consistent with individual rationality. For example, if demand for your product increases, should you immediately raise your price, in which case markets will clear? Or should you hold your price constant, maintaining good relations with your steady customers and rationing the product to nonsteady customers? Keynesians argue that the second strategy is often preferred, which means that markets will not clear.

The New Keynesian theoretical arguments against the strong New Classical policy conclusions were quickly accepted by the profession. But that does not mean that Keynesian economics regained its former status. In the 1970s there was growing concern about whether monetary and fiscal policy were politically effective tools, even if they were theoretically effective. Many Keynesians felt that monetary and fiscal policy were politically impossible to utilize and that politics, not sound economic principles, was determining the size of the deficit and the growth of the money supply.

The arguments between New Keynesians and New Classicals quickly become complicated. A history-of-thought course is not the place to go into them. What is important to point out is that most modern macroeconomic research and most graduate training in macroeconomics consists of acquiring the technical background necessary to understand the modern debate.

MODERN MACROECONOMICS — A SUMMARY

Although economists from the mercantilist era to the present have been interested in macroeconomic theory, there was a long period from roughly 1830 to 1930, when orthodox economic theory concentrated almost exclusively on analyzing the micro aspects of the economy. From 1870 to the 1930s, the major macro concern of orthodox theory was to explain the forces determining the general level of prices, while the macro issues of the forces determining the level of economic activity and the rate of growth were largely ignored. Although many of the mercantilists had emphasized the quantity of money as an important determinant of the level of activity, the rate of growth, and the general level of prices, from the time of Adam Smith until the 1930s one of the strong threads running through orthodox economic theory was that real forces determined the level of economic activity and the rate of growth of that activity. At that time orthodox theory held that the quantity of money had almost no effect on the level of output and the rate of growth of that output, its influence being wholly directed toward the general level of prices. Coupled with this lack of concern with the macro issue of stability and growth was the prevailing preconception of orthodox theory that market forces automatically led to desirable micro and macro results. Orthodox theory held that an unregulated market economy with the government following a policy of laissez faire would automatically result in full utilization of resources and optimum rates of economic growth.

J. M. Keynes was reared in the orthodox tradition with its acceptance of Say's Law, its view that the quantity of money influenced only the general level of prices, and its predisposition toward laissez faire. Under the force of many influences, he and some of his contemporaries began to move away from this orthodox tradition, and in the middle of the 1930s, Keynes offered a new analytical framework to explain the forces determining the level of economic activity. Keynes not only found capitalism inherently unstable, but concluded that the usual outcome of the automatic working of the market was to produce equilibrium at less than full employment. Following the leads of Marx, Tugan-Baranowsky, Wicksell, and others, he focused on the role of investment spending in determining the level of economic activity.

Keynes's *General Theory* became the immediate starting point for modern macroeconomic theory and policy. A great deal of literature followed which not only extended and improved the original Keynesian formulation, but also threw into sharper perspective the contrasts and similarities between the Keynesian and pre-Keynesian models. The Keynesian concepts were in a form which invited mathematical model building and empirical testing. The theoretical revolution was followed shortly by a policy revolution as the major industrialized economies began programs and constructed agencies designed to foster full employment.

The Keynesianization of macroeconomics developed in a rather curious manner: it took the form of consumption function models advanced by leading Keynesians such as Alvin Hansen and Paul Samuelson. The close association of the development of Keynesian macro theory with the use of fiscal policy as a compensatory action available by government to promote full employment probably accounts for this focus on the consumption function model. In response to internal inconsistencies in the pure Keynesian formulation and to issues raised by monetarists concerning the role of money, the *IS-LM* model became the dominant macro model by 1960. By around 1975, however, this model was found to be unsatisfactory for economic research. Inflation, as well as unemployment, seemed an important economic topic, and a new literature appeared which, in trying to uncover the microfoundations of macroeconomics, blurred the one aspect of Keynesianism which had divided economics into micro and macro spheres. With the rise of the microfoundations literature, the debates and theoretical developments returned closer to the framework of the early 1930s. The only exception was that general equilibrium analysis was increasingly replacing partial equilibrium analysis. Initially, macroeconomics was closely associated with econometrics and the development of large-scale models of the economy. While numerous such models exist, their early promise has not been realized. Thus, in the 1980s, there has been a movement away from such models and a focus on purely theoretical issues.

Modern macroeconomics is in a period of transition with scholars carrying on a wide range of research programs asking many different questions. The resulting confusion and diversity of approaches are not necessarily undesirable; the previously accepted Keynesian theory had a number of unresolved theoretical questions that economists swept under the rug. Uncovering them was bound to create confusion, but if doing so helps to provide better answers, the confusion will have been worthwhile.

SUGGESTED READINGS

Clower, Robert. "The Keynesian Counter-Revolution: A Theoretical Appraisal" in *The Theory of Interest Rates*. Eds. F. H. Hahn and F. Brechling. London: Macmillan, 1965.

Colander, David. *Macroeconomic Theory and Policy*. Glenview, Illinois: Scott Foresman and Co., 1986.

Fisher, Franklin M. *Disequilibrium Foundations of Equilibrium Economics*. New York: Cambridge University Press, 1983.

Harrod, R. F. *The Life of John Maynard Keynes*. New York: Harcourt Brace Jovanovich, 1952.

Hicks, John R. "Mr. Keynes and The 'Classics': A Suggested Interpretation" in *Readings in the Theory of Income Distribution*. Philadelphia: Blakeston, 1949.

——. *The Crisis in Economic Theory*. New York: Basic Books Inc., 1974.

Hsieh, Ching-Yao and Stephen L. Mangum. *A Search for a Synthesis in Economic Theory*. Armonk, New York: Sharpe, 1986.

Keynes, John Maynard. *The General Theory of Employment, Interest, and Money*. London: Macmillan and Co. Ltd., 1936.

Klamer, Arjo. *Conversations with Economists*. New Jersey: Rowman and Allanheld, 1984.

Leijonhufvud, Axel. *On Keynesian Economics and the Economics of Keynes*. New York: Oxford University Press, 1968.

Lucas, Robert. *Studies in Business Cycle Theory*. Cambridge: Cambridge University Press, 1981.

Skidelsky, Robert. *John Maynard Keynes*. London: Macmillan, 1983.

Weintraub, Roy. *Microfoundations: The Compatibility of Microeconomics and Macroeconomics*. New York: Cambridge University Press, 1979.

Chapter 12

The Development of Modern Nonmainstream Economics

Our survey of recent economics has concentrated thus far on the mainstream. But there are many dissident, or heterodox, economists within the economics profession today, as there were in the past. Finding a single economist who adheres to all the mainstream views would probably be impossible: all hold some dissident views. An important reason to study the history of economic thought is to keep sight of potentially useful dissident thought. In this chapter, therefore, we consider the history and ideas of some of the more interesting modern heterodox economists whose views have coalesced sufficiently to be grouped into schools of thought and summarized.

Since dissenters are often original and iconoclastic individuals, they tend to disagree with other dissenters as much as with the mainstream. Any organization of such writers into schools of thought thus does them some injustice, but not to present their views would be an even greater injustice. Hence this chapter should be seen as a guide to further reading rather than as a definitive interpretation.

After considering the role of the heterodox economist in the development of theory, we will discuss six dissident groups: radicals, institutionalists, post-Keynesians, public choice advocates, neo-Austrians, and experimental economists. We will also examine two important iconoclasts whose work fits into no school of thought. The first five schools represent the traditional heterodoxy, differing with the mainstream on policy issues, assumptions, and often methodology. The sixth group, experimental economists, do not differ from orthodox economists on policy issues but are heterodox in a perhaps more fundamental way.

THE ROLE OF HETERODOX ECONOMISTS

In Lakatos's "competing research program" approach to methodology, various groups compete for students to further their research program. The group most successful in competing becomes the mainstream, and groups that are less successful but do attract some researchers become nonmainstream. Some economists who use the Lakatosian approach tend to see mainstream theory as the "best" theory — whatever "best" might mean — but there is, in fact, no guarantee that mainstream theory constitutes "truth." It simply has yet to be falsified. Since there are many areas in economics where empirical testing is difficult, if not impossible, it is hard to devise tests that will lead to the discarding of any group's view. Rhetorical and sociological approaches to methodology offer even less assurance that the best theory will win out; they suggest that criteria irrelevant to the appropriateness of a theory play an important role in whether a theory is or is not studied.

Defining Heterodoxy

Before we can discuss heterodox economics, we must establish a criterion for heterodoxy. Since empirical testing is difficult, the mainstream of economics itself includes divergent approaches. For example, in our discussion of mainstream microeconomics we included two types of economics, one taught at the University of Chicago and one taught at the Massachusetts Institute of Technology. These are classified as mainstream because most mainstream economists see both approaches as legitimate, and graduate schools often try to have some representation from both groups to maintain a "balanced" program. Conversely, one defining characteristic of a heterodox school is "revealed illegitimacy." If the mainstream sees little or no need to consider a group's views, we define that group as heterodox. This doesn't mean a heterodox economist cannot teach at a mainstream school, but most who do have done mainstream work and have later been converted to heterodoxy, or have a foot in both camps.

Our criterion is not unambiguous. Mainstream graduate schools tend to take a narrower view of allowable mainstream thought than do undergraduate liberal arts schools, which are more likely to value diversity of thought. Nonetheless, the criterion of revealed illegitimacy provides some guidance in identifying modern heterodox schools.

How Dissenting Economists Change the Profession

One of the best ways to appreciate the role of the dissenting economist is to consider the history of the profession. It is a history of change, and what is heterodox in one time period can find a place in the mainstream in another. For example, the heterodox views of Malthus, Tugan-Baranowsky, and Marx were partially reflected in the Keynesian revolution. These shifts occurred because some economists were willing to take a heterodox stance and then to convince others of its correctness. As they did so, their views became integrated into the mainstream.

Alfred Marshall was able to found neoclassical economics by wrestling with the competing claims of historically oriented economists and abstract theorists. But since Marshallian economics was too formal and abstract for most American economists when the American Economics Association was formed in 1885, it was largely in the control of economists sympathetic to the German historical school and what has become known as institutional economics. There was open hostility between those who advocated historical-institutional methodological approaches and those who felt the future of economics lay in abstract-mathematical modes of analysis. From 1900 through the 1930s the importance of the institutional approach in American universities decreased, and neoclassical economics emerged as the American mainstream. From the perspective of 1900, though, it would have been difficult to predict what has historically transpired.

Nonmainstream schools play important roles in the evolution of a discipline: they pollinate the mainstream view and keep it honest by pointing out its ambiguities; they keep the history of thought alive by maintaining a connection with earlier ideas; they constitute "the back of the profession's mind." That pollination continues today. The focus on transactions costs that was a key element of J. R. Commons's thought is finally coming to the fore, as mainstream economists begin to heed the cries of institutionalists that institutions matter.

Nonmainstream economists can respond to the profession in two ways: they can operate on its fringes, reading mainstream literature and trying to improve the existing paradigm; or they can proceed independently of the mainstream, developing their own literature and paradigm and having little contact with mainstream thought. When a heterodox school is successful in operating on the fringe, its views can evolve into the mainstream. With the awarding of the Nobel Prize to James Buchanan in 1986, for example, the public choice school moved closer to being incorporated into the mainstream. On the other hand, the independent route will not succeed by evolution; *revolution* is the only way an independent school's views will take hold. The institutionalists are an example of a group that has chosen this separate route. They rarely interact with mainstream economists, focusing instead on their own journals and schools. A few bastions of institutionalist thought exist — Colorado State University, Nebraska, and Michigan State University, for example — and there are a number of outposts where their students can find jobs. But, by choice, they seldom interact with the profession as a whole.

Problems of Heterodox Economists

It is not easy being a heterodox economist. The profession does little to encourage heterodoxy and continually questions the legitimacy of heterodox views. Because of this, heterodox economists generally tend to focus on methodology, since it is through methodology that they can question the legitimacy of the assumptions, scope, and methods that mainstream economists take as given. A problem faced by almost all heterodox groups is moving beyond methodology to establish their own analysis and provide a viable competing research program. There is truth in the saying that a theory can be replaced only by another theory.

A second problem faced by heterodox groups is that people attracted to heterodox theory are often individualistic; they are as little prone to compromise with their heterodox colleagues as they are with mainstream economists. The result is almost inevitably a heterodoxy characterized by dissension. Often their most vituperative invective is saved for their fellow heterodox economists.

Heterodox economists also tend to have "a chip on their shoulder"; contending that the mainstream has been unfair to them, they lose their ability or desire to communicate with the rest of the profession. That chip may well be warranted. Mainstream economists often do unfairly reject heterodox arguments, but without communication there can be no hope that mainstream economics will ever seriously consider heterodox thought.

Modern Heterodox Groups

The following discussion of six groups of nonorthodox economists is intended to evince the diversity of modern American heterodox thought and to provide a brief introduction to some interesting reading. Five of these groups are organized according to political points of view, ranging from liberal to conservative. Their views are summarized in Table 12.1. We do not list experimental economists in this group because their heterodoxy is of a different, nonpolitical sort.

RADICALS

Bongo: Human beings should not eat each other.
Wowsy: Good Gooey Gow! You can't dictate to people what they're going to eat and what they're not going to eat. Men have always eaten each other and always will. It's natural. You can't change human nature.
Bongo: I love my fellow men.
Wowsy: So do I — with gravy on them.

The conservative economists, like Wowsy, argue that people are born with certain ideas — such as eating people, or holding slaves, or being a competitive capitalist — and that there is no way to change those ideas....

By contrast with conservatives, radical economists believe that all ideas and preferences — such as our desire for Cadillacs — are shaped by the society in which we live....Since our ideology is determined by our social environment, radical economists contend that a change in our socioeconomic structure will eventually change the dominant ideology....There is thus hope of a completely new and better society with new and better views by most people.[1]

The above was quoted from the beginning of Hunt and Sherman's radical introductory economics textbook. It demonstrates an important aspect of the way radicals view the economy. They believe orthodoxy accepts too much of the status quo; radicals want to change it, not accept it.

The radical school has its origins in Marx's analysis. Marx had few followers among Western economists, in part because of his inherent anti-market views. Societies and their institutions will not support analysis that advocates the destruction of those institutions. Marx's analysis did attract followers among noneconomists, however, and a few Marxian economists have succeeded in the economics profession. A number of important works in Marxian economics were published in the 1930s and 1940s, including Maurice Dobb's *Political Economy and Capitalism*, Joan Robinson's *Essay on Marxian Economics*, and Paul Sweezy's *The Theory of Capitalist Development*. Active discussion of Marxian issues has been kept alive in the *Monthly Review*, and the Monthly Review Press has been an outlet for book-length Marxian analysis.

Radical economics, based in part on Marx, bloomed and evolved into a school of thought in its own right in the late 1960s and 1970s, possibly in response to the social strains of the Vietnam War. In 1968 a group of young economists formed the Union of Radical Political Economy. This organization publishes *The Journal of The Union of Radical Political Economy*, which remains a central journal of radical economic thought, although it is supplemented by the *Monthly Review* and *Social Research*. Although radicals' views are diverse, certain ideas

1. E. K. Hunt and Howard Sherman, *Economics*, 4th ed. (New York: Harper and Row, 1981), p. xxiv.

Table 12.1 Heterodox Economists

	Radicals	Institutionalists
Views on individual rationality	Individuals follow class beliefs; self-expression is extremely difficult in a capitalist society.	Individualist psychology is incorrect; people learn tastes through culture.
Policy view	Government reflects ruling class; major changes in form of government are necessary for serious reform.	Favor more government intervention.
Theory of production	Some hold labor theory of value; some reject labor theory of value; capitalists extract surplus from workers.	Firms use rules of thumb to determine prices; focus on institutional constraints on pricing.
Theory of distribution	Class theory of distribution based on power of ruling groups.	Distribution determined by institutions and legal structure; market is less important.
Some leading living advocates	David Gordon, Anwar Shaik, Samuel Bowles, Herbert Gintis.	Mark Tool, John Adams, Wallace Peterson, Warren Samuels.
Primary journal	*Journal of the Union of Radical Political Economists (URPE).*	*Journal of Economic Issues.*
Main graduate schools emphasizing their view	University of Massachusetts, New School for Social Research, University of Utah.	Colorado State University, University of Nebraska, Michigan State University.
Macroeconomic views	Economy tends toward crisis and unemployment without massive state intervention.	Oppose neoclassical models; relevant models must have more institutional structure. Generally support Keynesian policies.

Post-Keynesians	Public Choice Advocates	Neo-Austrians
Uncertainty makes individual rationality difficult.	Individuals are rational in all aspects of life, including politics; rent-seeking is important.	Radical individualism; close association with libertarian philosophy.
Tend to favor government intervention.	Government is a reflection of individuals' political interest. The less government involvement, the better. Strongly oppose government intervention as a form of rent-seeking.	Strongly oppose government intervention on moral grounds; it violates individuals' rights.
Firms use cost-plus pricing; margin determined by need for reinvestment.	Profit maximization on individual level. Generally accept mainstream views, although rent-seeking can lead to monopolization.	Profit-maximizing firms.
Macroeconomic distribution theory determined by profit-wage mix.	Marginal productivity theory of distribution modified by rent-seeking.	Marginal productivity theory; focus on property rights.
Paul Davidson, Jan Kregal.	Gordon Tullock, James Buchanan, Robert Tollison.	Murray Rothbard, Don Lavoie, Ludwig Lachman, Israel Kirzner.
Journal of Post-Keynesian Economics.	*Public Choice.*	*Cato Papers.*
University of Tennessee.	George Mason University.	New York University, George Mason University.
Oppose *IS-LM*. Uncertainty makes modeling difficult. Believe in multiple equilibria.	Take an essentially microeconomic view; a separate macro-economics does not exist.	The market process is important; mainstream models lose the required focus on markets.

about what is wrong with neoclassical economics and market-oriented economics bind them together. The radical position is summed up in the following three points:[2]

1. Radical economists think that "major socioeconomic problems can be solved only through a radical restructuring of our society." They argue that poverty, racism, sex discrimination, destruction of the environment, alienation of workers, and imperialism "are not pathological abnormalities of the system, but rather are derived directly from the normal functioning of capitalism."
2. Radicals argue that there are major inconsistencies between neo-classical theory and real-world experience. Where mainstream economists see social harmony, radicals see conflict.
3. Following their Marxist heritage, radicals view society as an "integrated social system existing in concrete historical circumstance." They believe that mainstream economics simply accepts existing institutions, such as the market, as given and does not consider a wide variety of proposals to change those institutions. They see the incremental changes advocated by mainstream economics as hardly worth considering. As Eileen Applebaum states, radicals "are interested in ending — not salvaging or stabilizing — monopoly capitalism" and replacing it with "a socialist society based on participatory planning, public ownership of the means of production, the elimination of private appropriation of profit, and a genuinely egalitarian redistribution of income and wealth."

Given these views, radical analysis of the economy is necessarily significantly different from mainstream analysis. The radical premise, as Applebaum says, is that the problems of Western society "are inevitable consequences of the capitalist institutional structure." Radicals emphasize in their analysis that technology embodies the social relations between individuals and that any analysis must study why capitalism exists rather than take it as given. Radicals explain the existence of capitalism with class analysis, contending that any useful economics must incorporate class analysis. Most radicals also believe that capitalism embodies internal contradictions that inevitably will bring the

---

2. This section relies heavily on Eileen Applebaum, "Radical Economics," in *Modern Economic Thought*, ed. Sidney Weintraub (Oxford: Basil Blackwell, 1977), p. 560.

system down, although this process is slowed by the repressive state, which exists to serve the interests of the capitalist class, and by institutions such as schools, which are arms of the state.

Since the mid-1970s radicals have played a smaller role in mainstream economic debate. The reasons for this are varied. Some radicals have turned inward to debate doctrinal Marxian issues, such as the transformation problem (the problem of how one can move from a labor theory of value to a set of values or prices of goods in a multi-industry model). But other radical work of the 1970s has influenced mainstream analysis. An example is Steven Marglin's "What Do Bosses Do?"[3] Marglin argued that technology is not given but is chosen by a particular group of individuals within the society. In capitalism this group is the managers, or "bosses," who choose the technology that provides them with the strongest role. In stating his argument Marglin reconsiders Adam Smith's example of the pin factory, which Smith used to demonstrate the advantages of the division of labor. Alternatively, Marglin argued that by bringing all the workers under one roof, the bosses (organizers) gained control over the workers, securing their own role in the production process and allowing them to extract a larger surplus from the workers. Although this analysis is not found in introductory textbooks, it is known to most economic organizational specialists.

A second radical argument to gain some recognition within mainstream economics concerns the economics of education. One mainstream analysis of schooling holds that individuals invest in schooling and receive a return in the form of increased future earnings. The investment makes them and society better off. Significant empirical research has gone into showing what that return is, and neoclassical economics has concluded on the basis of this research that we have underinvested in schooling. Samuel Bowles and Herbert Gintis disagree, arguing that schooling does not necessarily enhance the well-being of society. Their hypothesis is that the higher earnings of educated persons are sometimes simply a return to being allowed into a monopoly. Schooling, they contend, does not necessarily increase the true value of workers it may merely provide a union card allowing individuals into a set of professions they could not enter without it. Bowles and Gintis assert that, since econometric work cannot separate these two hypotheses, the question of education's contribution to society remains open.

Another inroad of radical thought into mainstream economics came from a "more acceptable" radical (so acceptable that he might not even be considered radical). That inroad is Michael Piori's dual-labor-market

---

3. Stephen Marglin, "What Do Bosses Do?", *Review of Radical Political Economics*, 7 (Summer) 1974, pp. 60-112.

analysis. Piori argues that it is wrong to view the labor market as a single market, since major structural and social constraints limit the mobility of labor. For example, a worker hired as a shipping clerk will find it almost impossible to be promoted to a managerial position, no matter how capable he or she is. It follows that the relative desirability of various jobs cannot necessarily be ranked by pay, since a position with possibilities of upward mobility may initially pay less than a position without such possibilities. Since each job is done by a separate class within labor, Piori says, neoclassical analysis of the labor market as competitive does not fit the reality. One should instead analyze the labor market as a structurally constrained market, which he calls a dual labor market. Although this analysis conforms to Marxian analysis in that it incorporates a type of class distinction, the dual labor market has become part of mainstream Keynesian analysis.

INSTITUTIONALISTS

Institutionalists from the turn of the century to the 1930s played a more significant role in economics than do contemporary institutionalists, since they were involved in implementing significant policy changes in the United States economy. Except for Marxists, the institutionalists have the longest history as a nonmainstream heterodox American school of economic thinking. The three central figures that represent the institutionalists of the early twentieth century are Thorstein Veblen, Wesley Clair Mitchell, and John R. Commons. Two other notable economists who have been called institutionalists, Gunnar Myrdal and John Kenneth Galbraith, are more iconoclastic than a typical member of this school. Although there have been a number of leaders of institutionalist thought in recent years, such as Allen Gruchy, Wallace Peterson, and Clarence Ayres, none has achieved the preeminence of these earlier figures; hence we will discuss modern institutional thought generally rather than in reference to a particular writer.

Thorstein Veblen

Thorstein Veblen (1857-1929) is the intellectual father of the institutionalists. His scientific and ethical dissent from mainstream theory significantly influenced the development of nonmainstream thinking in the United States. His views are partly explained by his background. The son of a Norwegian immigrant, Veblen grew up in rural Wisconsin and Minnesota. By the time he entered college, he still had not mastered the English language; he would never, in fact, be fully integrated into the American mainstream. He was like a man from Mars observing with satiric wit the absurdities of our economic and social order.

J. B. Clark, who was teaching at Carleton College, recognized Veblen's brilliance and encouraged him to pursue graduate education. After earning a Ph.D. in philosophy from Yale University, Veblen was unable to find a job in teaching. He returned to the farm, married his college sweetheart, and spent seven years reading and thinking. When he was thirty-five, still unable to get an academic appointment, he was given a fellowship at the University of Chicago. There Veblen was eventually appointed instructor of economics and assigned the editorship of *The Journal of Political Economy*. But throughout his academic career he moved rather frequently, encouraged by administrators to seek employment elsewhere. His personal life, moreover, was complicated by affairs and marital difficulties. Nonetheless, in the mid-1920s the American Economic Association offered Veblen its presidency, on the condition that he would join the association and deliver an address. He refused the offer, feeling it had not come at the time when he most needed it.

Thorstein Bunde Veblen

Veblen was a wonderful phrase-maker, and he used his wit to make his readers uncomfortable. He created the term "conspicuous consumption" to describe the purchases of the emerging affluent society and said that we are all members of the "kept class" or "the underlying population." He described university presidents as "captains of erudition" and businessmen as "captains of sabotage." The church was "an accredited vent for the exudation of effete matter from the cultural organism." W. C. Mitchell suggested that one needs a sense of humor to appreciate Veblen and that perhaps this is why he is so little appreciated by economists.

Veblen was not interested in making small changes in the theoretical structure. His attacks went to the heart of neoclassical theory, whose basic assumptions he held to be unscientific. He wanted to tear down the entire structure in order to rebuild a unified social science integrating economics, anthropology, sociology, psychology, and history. He argued that the neoclassical use of equilibrium was normative, since it implied, without proof, that the results of equilibrium are socially beneficial.

In his analysis Veblen borrowed concepts from philosophy and biology to argue that orthodox economic theory was teleological and therefore pre-Darwinian. By "teleological" he meant that it depicted an economy as moving toward an end — namely, long-run equilibrium — that had not been arrived at empirically but had been determined before the analysis began. Veblen argued that evolution was a process by which things developed over time in response to environmental circumstances. In evolution, he said, there was no purpose or design and hence no long-run equilibrium. Because classical thought refused to admit that the economy was constantly changing and evolving, and instead focused only on the static aspects of the theory, Veblen argued that it should be replaced by a dynamic Darwinian analysis of the evolution of the economy and society. This became a central tenet of the institutionalists; their chief organization is called the Association for Evolutionary Economists.

Veblen attacked the invisible hand theory, arguing that self-interest would not necessarily promote the best interest of society. Producing goods and making profits, he pointed out, were two quite different things. The business community's striving for profits, in fact, had deleterious effects on the economy and society. Although there may have been a relatively close connection between making profits and producing serviceable goods for the society in Adam Smith's time, Veblen said, this had changed as society evolved. He clearly distinguished between those who produced goods (the production managers, foremen, and workers) and those who managed firms. The aim of business, he argued, is pecuniary gain, which is not necessarily beneficial to society. Corporations, he said, were attempting to acquire monopoly power, and competition was not sufficient to prevent them from doing so.

Veblen also attacked the neoclassical view of the individual as independent of society. He argued that a complex set of relationships exists between human nature and culture and that as individuals develop within a culture, they find themselves acting within the selfish patterns of behavior that are a legacy of past interactions between individuals and culture. He said that relatively fixed underlying traits of human behavior, or "instincts" significantly influenced human behavior. The principal human instincts, according to Veblen, are the instincts toward parenthood, workmanship, idle curiosity, and acquisitiveness. Veblen argued that these basic human drives create tensions that lead individuals to work for their fellow human beings. But capitalist society and its institutions, such as absentee ownership, corporations, and money lending, blunt these instincts and make the economy worse, not better, off. Businessmen, he said, bring "illfare" not welfare to society, and far from being its benefactors, are its saboteurs.

Veblen's most widely read book is *The Theory of the Leisure Class* (1898). In it he describes a basic dichotomy between ceremonial and industrial behavior. Veblen calls activities that follow from the instincts of parenthood, workmanship, and idle curiosity "industrial employments." He contrasts this with "ceremonial behavior," which is static and past-binding and which manifests itself in totems and taboos and appeals to authority and emotion. Much consumption, Veblen says, is based on such ceremonial behavior, with its "conspicuous consumption," "conspicuous leisure," "conspicuous waste," and "pecuniary emulation." Veblen applied his distinction between pecuniary and industrial employment to a wide variety of areas, including the development of the business cycle and the tendencies of capitalism in the very long run, also pointing out, however, that the future of capitalism and private property is uncertain. To have thought otherwise would have violated his evolutionary views.

Wesley Clair Mitchell

The second giant of the institutionalists was Wesley Clair Mitchell (1874–1948). Although Mitchell never fully accepted many of Veblen's ideas, he developed his own approach to economics, which became a second building block of institutionalism. Following Veblen's prescription, however, Mitchell carefully researched all his theoretical work and grounded it in empirical information. Mitchell was impressed with Veblen, but he recognized that Veblen's system had the same methodological weakness as orthodox theory. Both failed to test either their assumptions or their conclusions. Mitchell wrote, "But if anything were to convince me that the standard procedure of orthodox economics could meet no scientific test, it was that Veblen got nothing more certain by his dazzling performances with another set of premises."[4]

In his analysis of fluctuations in the aggregate economy, Mitchell did not attempt to build another abstract model of the business cycle; he tried instead to explain what happens during the business cycle and gave what he called a descriptive analysis of the cycle. Mitchell's descriptive analysis, reflecting a scholar's judicious blend of theory, description, and history, and devoid of mathematics, is somewhat like Marshall's. But the hard theoretical core that underpins Marshall's microanalysis is missing in Mitchell's work; and it is missing to such an extent that some have called his work measurement without theory.

When Mitchell was forty-five he founded the National Bureau of Economic Research, which has been extremely important in financing

Wesley Clair Mitchell

4. W. C. Mitchell in a letter to J. M. Clark. See J. M. Clark, *Preface to Social Economics* (New York: Farrar and Rinehart, 1936), p. 412.

economic research in the United States. Control of it, however, has long since passed from the institutionalists to mainstream economists.

John R. Commons

The third founder of institutionalist thought is John R. Commons (1862–1945). A graduate of Oberlin College, Commons went to graduate school at Johns Hopkins University, which he left after two years to go to the University of Wisconsin. Wisconsin became the center of institutionalist thought and remained so until the mid-1960s.

Unlike most economists, Commons was extremely involved in political and policy issues and contributed significantly to social legislation. Much of his work underlay the beginnings of Franklin Roosevelt's New Deal. In designing this legislation, he would thoroughly study a problem, often with the help of his graduate students. He would then discuss the issues with those in the economy who would be affected by

John R. Commons

any new legislation and solicit the support of the more progressive business and labor leaders. If he succeeded in getting legislation passed in Wisconsin, he would travel to other states and try his best to spread the legislation he believed in to other parts of the country. Over the years, he played a significant role in influencing social legislation in the following areas: regulation of public utilities, industrial safety laws, workman's compensation, child-labor laws, minimum-wage laws for women, and unemployment compensation laws. Commons also contributed to labor economics and wrote a four-volume history of labor in the United States.

Commons's criticism of orthodox theory parallels that of Veblen and Mitchell. In his approach to social problems, he rejected the narrow static and deductive approach of neoclassical theory and tried to bring all of the social sciences, as well as history and law, into the analysis. He saw society and the economy as evolving and changing, and he sharply objected to the almost exclusively deductive orthodox approach with its assumptions of hedonistic agents and competitive markets. He found this assumed market harmony, and the laissez faire policy following from it, contrary to his empirical observation.

Commons argued that there were three types of transactions in the economy: bargaining transactions (transfer of ownership of wealth by voluntary agreement between legal equals); managerial transactions (commands by legal and economic superiors to inferiors); and rationing transactions (negotiations in reaching an agreement among several participants who have authority to apportion the benefits and burdens to members of a joint enterprise). Commons argued that these three types of transactions are brought together in a larger unit of economic investigation he described as "a going concern." These "going concerns, with the working rules that work to keep them going," he called "institutions."[5] Such a going concern, ranging in size from the family to the state itself, is fundamentally distinct from the individuals who compose it; it has a unique history and an entire set of sensibilities that neoclassical economics set aside. Commons's elaboration of the complex nature of institutions gave institutionalists their focus.

Modern Institutionalists

American institutionalism was at its peak in the late 1920s and early 1930s, but by the late 1930s it was waning. In his *Theory of Economic Progress* (1944), the well-known institutionalist Clarence Ayres described the victory of the neoclassical over the institutionalist approach

5. John R. Commons, *Institutional Economics* (New York: Macmillan, 1934), p. 69.

as complete. Since that time institutionalists have been outside the discipline; they are simply given credit for having called attention to important matters that economists should not overlook but that lie outside the scope of economic analysis.

Institutionalism maintained a stronghold through the 1960s at the University of Wisconsin, one of the top twenty graduate schools in economics, but by the 1970s Wisconsin's program had become another mainstream curriculum whose only vestige of institutionalism was its strong focus on empirical research. Modern institutionalists draw chiefly on Veblen, Mitchell, and Commons and maintain their own publication, *The Journal of Economic Issues*. They continue to oppose mainstream economics but, for the most part, have been little heeded by the mainstream.

A "new institutionalism" has recently developed, as part of the widening scope of neoclassical economics, but it is quite different from its older namesake. New institutionalists are so called chiefly because they include more institutional detail in their theoretical models than is usual for neoclassical economists, but they have retained the conventional individual maximization procedures of the neoclassical model. Transactions costs play a central role in their analysis. Robert Coase's 1937 article on the theory of the firm is a seminal article for the new institutionalists. It argues that firms develop because the transactions costs of the market are too high for interfirm transactions.

New institutionalism is sometimes also called rent-seeking analysis or neoclassical political economy. Its proponents contend that rational individuals try to improve their well-being not only within a given institutional structure but also by *changing* that structure. Economic analysis, they contend, must include a consideration of the forces determining that institutional structure. An "equilibrium institutional structure" is one in which it is not worthwhile for individuals to expend further effort in changing the institutions. Only on the basis of an equilibrium institutional framework, they say, can one produce relevant analysis. Accordingly, neoclassical economics is irrelevant, not because of its maximizing assumption, but because its assumed institutional structure is not an equilibrium institutional structure. These ideas, unlike those of the few remaining followers of the original institutionalists, have provoked mild interest within the profession.

POST-KEYNESIANS

In our consideration of macroeconomics, we saw that mainstream macroeconomics followed only one of the many threads found in Keynes's writings. Post-Keynesians claim that they are the true keepers of the Keynesian faith and call mainstream macroeconomics "bastard

Keynesianism." Post-Keynesian economics formed a separate school in the mid-1970s. Economists have always debated about what Keynes really meant, but in the 1970s, led initially by Sidney Weintraub and Paul Davidson on this side of the Atlantic and Joan Robinson and John Eatwell in England, post-Keynesians joined forces in a criticism of the neo-Keynesian model specific enough to be called a school. They held an organizational meeting in 1974 at which they founded their publication, *The Journal of Post Keynesian Economics (JPKE)*. In the inaugural issue of that journal, the various founders and supporters stated what post-Keynesian economics meant.[6] Joan Robinson called it a "method of analysis which takes account of the difference between the future and the past"; J. K. Galbraith said it considers that "an industrial society is in a process of continuous and organic change, that public policy must accommodate to such change, and that by such public action performance can, in fact, be improved." Other writers focused on different issues, but all agreed that neoclassical and neo-Keynesian economics are inappropriate.

British Post-Keynesians

The general statements above embody the ideas behind most post-Keynesian analysis, but the specifics are more controversial. The British post-Keynesians (sometimes called neo-Ricardians) believe the correct approach is to go back to the Ricardian theory of production and supplement it with a Kalecki class theory of business cycles. Following the work of Piero Sraffa in *Production of Commodities by Means of Commodities: Prelude to a Criticism of Economic Theory* (1960), they argue that the distribution of income between wages and profits is indeterminant and independent of total output. Hence the distribution of income is determined not by marginal productivity but by other forces, which are macroeconomic in nature. In this view they follow a model similar to one presented by Michael Kalecki in 1933, which Kalecki summed up in the statement that workers spend what they get; capitalists get what they spend.[7]

Kalecki makes three central assumptions in his model. First he assumes that firms use a cost-plus method of pricing. Capitalists determine the profit rate and the wage rate but not the total profit or the total level of wages. That is determined by the total level of output. Second, no saving is translated into spending, so the total level of out-

6. *Journal of Post-Keynesian Economics*, Vol. 1, Fall 1978.
7. Michael Kalecki, 1933. "An Essay on the Theory of The Business Cycle," translated in *Studies in The Theory of Business Cycles 1933-1939* (Oxford: Basil Blackwell, 1969).

put is determined by the level of total demand in a type of Keynesian multiplier fashion. Third, workers spend 100 percent of their income, so their marginal propensity to consume is 100 percent.

Capitalists' spending on investment tends to be arbitrary and is not related to their level of profits (which constitute savings). If they spend all their profits, demand is sufficient to buy all the production; total output and profits will be high. If capitalists become pessimistic and do not spend their profits but save them instead, aggregate demand and total output will be low, profits will be low (though the profit rate will remain the same), and unemployment will follow. Thus the distribution of income between wages and profits is determined by macroeconomic forces, not marginal productivity. Most of the assumptions in this simple model can be modified, making the results somewhat more ambiguous, without invalidating the general insight that the macroeconomic level of activity is a determinant of the distribution of income.

American Post-Keynesians

The American branch of post-Keynesian theory is more diffuse than the British, but all its elements are variations on the theme that the economy is "in time." Alfred Eichner has extended the microeconomic analysis of the firm, which he calls the megacorp, arguing that it determines investment internally from retained profits. Hence to understand investment, and thereby total output, one must understand the modern corporation.

Paul Davidson, in *Money and the Real World*, contends that money's role is central to an understanding of how the macroeconomy works and that neoclassical economics has not adequately dealt with its role. In developing the post-Keynesian role for money, he emphasizes the existence of "irreversible time" and "true uncertainty," which cannot be reduced to a probability distribution and hence cannot be changed to risk and then to certainty equivalents. These two interrelated characteristics of the economy have "led man to develop certain institutions and rules of the game, such as (i) money, (ii) money-contracts and a legal system of enforcement, (iii) sticky money-wage rates, and (iv) spot and forward markets."[8] Thus institutions change the way in which the macroeconomy operates. Davidson's view is somewhat similar to that of Hyman Minsky, another well-known post-Keynesian, who argued that the financial system is like a house of cards in imminent danger of collapse.

---

8. Paul Davidson, *Money and the Real World* (Cambridge, England: Cambridge University Press, 1976), p. 360.

Post-Keynesian growth theory is partly methodological and hence a matter of focus. Post-Keynesians emphasize growth as an important aspect of the economic process, whereas mainstream economists emphasize static issues. For example, Roy Harrod's and Evsey Domar's analysis of growth, which in the 1950s was a fundamental part of mainstream macroeconomics, now hardly shows up in mainstream intermediate macroeconomics textbooks. This partially accounts for the post-Keynesian focus on instability, since the Harrod-Domar model suggested that equilibrium in the economy is always on a knife-edge bordering boom and bust.

In post-Keynesian work as a whole, one sees a consistency of conceptualization, if not of models. An enduring concept is that the economy is not stable; the invisible hand of the market does not work as well as neoclassical theory suggests. It follows that post-Keynesians see a much stronger role for government action in correcting the problems of capitalism than orthodox theory allows. Post-Keynesians are best known for their support of TIP (tax-based incomes policies).

The Mainstream Response to the Post-Keynesians

The mainstream's response to American post-Keynesians has been either complete disregard or the attitude "What else is new?" Robert Solow sums up the mainstream response to post-Keynesians as follows:

> I am very unsympathetic to the school that calls itself post-Keynesian. First of all, I have never been able to understand it as a school of thought. I don't see an intellectual connection between a Hyman Minsky, on the one hand, who happens to be one of the oldest friends I have, and someone like Alfred Eichner, on the other, except that they are all against the same thing, namely the mainstream, whatever that is.
>
> The other reason why I am not sympathetic is that I have never been able to piece together (I must confess that I have never tried very hard) a positive doctrine. It seems to be mostly a community which knows what it is against but doesn't offer anything very systematic that could be described as a positive theory. I have read many of Paul Davidson's articles and they often do not make sense to me. Some of Post Keynesian price theory comes forth from the belief that universal competition is a bad assumption. I have all my life known that. So I have found it an unrewarding approach and have not paid much attention to it.[9]

9. Arjo Klamer, *Conversations with Economists* (Totowa, N.J.: Rowman and Allanheld, 1984), pp. 137, 138.

Mainstream economists also argue that "there is no correct neo-Ricardian proposition which is not contained in the set of propositions which can be generated by orthodoxy."[10]

Although there are valid grounds for rejection of the post-Keynesians, orthodox economists often overstate their case when they refuse to see any value in post-Keynesian thought. Differences among economic theorists are more often matters of emphasis than of substance. And since post-Keynesians have chosen to emphasize areas in which mainstream economics is in fact weak, their criticisms do hold some truth. To date, however, they have not provided a satisfactory alternative to neoclassical thought.

TWO ICONOCLASTS

Every epoch has its economic iconoclasts whose rejections of the status quo often influence political, social, and intellectual affairs but have little effect on the economics profession and generate few followers. Hobson, for example, provided some of the ideas that the more practical thinkers of the New Deal modified and integrated into the welfare state. A few economists who fit into no school have played a significant role in modern intellectual thinking. Two of these are Gunnar Myrdal and John Kenneth Galbraith.

Gunnar Myrdal

Gunnar Myrdal began his career quite interested in questions of pure theory, but he soon developed a broader interest in more sociological issues. He made his reputation with the publication of *An American Dilemma: The Negro Problem and Modern Democracy in 1944*, a work that figured significantly in the legal battles for greater civil rights for blacks in the 1940s and 1950s. Although Myrdal was critical of orthodox theory, his criticism was not as strident as that of Veblen and Commons. His major criticism of orthodox economic theory centered around the value judgments implicit in that theory and the scope and methodology of theory. He held that attempts by orthodox theorists to develop a positive science free from normative judgments had failed. It was impossible, he argued, to separate completely normative from positive and to achieve an analysis devoid of "oughts."

Orthodox theory was to be condemned not because it made normative judgments but because those normative judgments were never made explicit. In his early work, *The Political Element in the Development of*

10. Frank Hahn, "The Neo-Ricardians," *Cambridge Journal of Economics*, 6 (1982), p. 353.

Economic Theory, Myrdal had argued that over time the normative and ideological elements would be more and more purged from theory. But by the time the English translation of this book came out, he had reversed his position, believing that there would always be normative implications to theory. The best one could do was to make one's normative judgments explicit.

Like the institutionalists, Myrdal felt that mainstream theory was too narrowly defined and wanted to integrate economics with the other social sciences. He attempted to discard static equilibrium analysis and to replace it with the concept of cumulative causation, a type of dynamic equilibrium framework in which sociological, cultural, and economic factors interacted.

John Kenneth Galbraith

John Kenneth Galbraith (1908-   ) was the first American economist since Veblen to be widely read by intellectuals among the general public. After finishing his graduate work at the University of California at Berkeley, Galbraith went to work in Washington, D.C. During World War II he served on the Price Control Board, and shortly thereafter he wrote a book on the theory of price control. He has said that he felt only six people read that book, even though he considered it his best work. He decided at that point to forgo the normal academic channels and to go directly to the public. He has been a professor of economics at both Princeton and Harvard universities.

Galbraith argued that competitive markets were not appropriate structures in which to analyze interactions in an economy. One needed a broader structure that allowed a wider range of interactions. The structure Galbraith proposed was countervailing power, an analysis of which could incorporate government, corporations, and unions. Unlike neoclassical economists, Galbraith argued that unions were not bad, they were a necessary countervailing power to the corporation. He argued that competition as the regulatory mechanism of the economy had been replaced by countervailing power. In this view, orthodox theory is incorrect in equating monopoly power with illfare. There is a certain optimistic quality to Galbraith's theory.

In *The Affluent Society* (1958), Galbraith extends Veblen's analysis of conspicuous consumption and argues that there is a social imbalance; we produce and consume large quantities of high-quality consumer goods but low quantities of inferior public goods. Neither Myrdal nor Galbraith have left significant marks on the economics profession, but their works remain classics within economic literature.

PUBLIC CHOICE ADVOCATES

Economists assume that individuals are rational in economic affairs; why not assume that they are rational in other affairs as well? This is the question James Buchanan and Gordon Tullock asked in the early 1950s and so began the public choice school. Tullock and Buchanan left the University of Virginia in the 1960s, partly because of their unorthodox policy positions, and founded the Public Choice Center at

John Kenneth Galbraith

the Virginia Polytechnic Institute. In 1983 the Public Choice Center moved to George Mason University.

The central idea of the public choice school is that individuals are as rational in their interactions with government as they are in their economic affairs. Government is not an agency for good or for bad; it is simply an agency by which individuals achieve their economic goals through politics. The public choice theorists have devised an economic theory of politics; using the same framework classical and neoclassical theory uses in modeling household and firm behavior, they analyze political, or public, choice.

Their analysis of rent-seeking activities has spread into the mainstream, and a number of introductory textbooks with a public choice flavor have been widely adopted. In 1986 James Buchanan won a Nobel Prize, which reflects some acceptance from the mainstream. For the most part, however, mainstream economists hesitate to accept public choice theory. Some mainstream economists still see public choice theory as a front for conservative ideology.

AUSTRIAN ECONOMICS

In Chapter 7 we examined the role Karl Menger played in the early development of marginal utility theory. An active group of dissenters in the field of economics is the neo-Austrians, the followers of Karl Menger. Austrian economists parted company from the mainstream for much the same reason post-Keynesians did — the formalization of economics, which, they argue, lost many of the insights of the earlier writers. Up until 1960 Austrian economics was considered part of the mainstream, but as neoclassical economics became more formalized the Austrians reemerged as dissenters. Subsequent generations of what are now called neo-Austrian economists, especially Ludwig von Mises and Friedrich von Hayek and their students Murray Rothbart, Israel Kirzner, and Ludwig Lachman, contend that many of Menger's important insights have been lost.

The central Austrian economic view is that economic analysis is a process, not a static interaction of individuals, and that time is an essential consideration. It sees competition as a dynamic process through which high profits are eliminated over time. But those high profits play a very important role in driving the system. In Austrian economics, individuals are assumed to operate in a changing environment in which information is limited and the future unknown. The interesting analysis comes not from studying equilibrium but from studying the process through which individuals grope toward equilibrium. This process emphasizes the entrepreneur and what neoclassical economics calls disequilibrium.

Until recently there were strong political overtones in Austrian economics, and it is still difficult to find an Austrian who is not a conservative; most simply assume the market is desirable and necessary for achievement of individual freedom. Many Austrians would not characterize their political views as "conservative"; they would call them "radical libertarian" or "anti-statist."

Many Austrian economists formerly objected to econometric work and attempts to empirically prove economic theorems. Following von Mises's "praxology," their task was to deductively derive conclusions from the logic of human action. Because these were so derived, there was no need to test the theory, since the truth of those theories had already been established. Recently, however, they have taken a somewhat more conciliatory position and argue that it is the *type* of empirical work mainstream economics does — which does not include historical and heuristic elements — that is inappropriate.

A key seminal work in Austrian literature is von Hayek's *Economics and Knowledge*. Von Hayek argued that equilibrium is a situation in which all agents' plans are synchronized; knowledge, expectations, and beliefs are therefore central elements of any economic analysis. Because of uncertainty, coordination of individuals' plans is difficult and beyond a single individual's comprehension. Only through the spontaneous order that develops through the market does our system work. Hayek's policy position follows from his attitude toward knowledge and uncertainty, namely, that we do not know the ultimate effects of our actions. It follows from this that we should accept institutions that have developed spontaneously, particularly the market, which solves our economic problems much more efficiently and effectively than do political processes. Some Austrians accept this view, whereas others believe an active policy of reducing government's role in the economy is preferable.

Most mainstream economists understand that an Austrian perspective involves an acceptance of existing institutions and a belief that uncertainty is important, which makes formal modeling and empirical work difficult. But they argue that the Austrians (1) overemphasize the difficulties, (2) have not developed an acceptable alternative, and (3) have allowed value judgments to creep into their heuristic analysis.

EXPERIMENTAL ECONOMISTS

The claim that economics is a science has long been treated skeptically. One of the reasons for this is the inability of economics to perform controlled experiments to test theories. Recently, though, a group of economists have begun to undertake what might be called controlled experiments. They use animals or people to act as buyers and sellers of an unnamed commodity, and knowing the underlying supply and demand conditions, they see if the theory correctly predicts the results that occur in the experiment. Some people call this group "rat economists," because experimenters sometimes use rats to test propositions, but their more common name is experimental economists. Experimental economists claim they have proven through their experiments that the invisible hand theory actually holds.

Let us consider a test they did using a procedure called a "double oral auction market," in which buyers and sellers publicly announce bid and offering prices. Vernon Smith, a leader and developer of much of this work, conducted a laboratory experiment in 1956 to test whether equilibrium would be achieved in a double oral auction market. Students took roles as suppliers and demanders and called out their price, and within fifteen minutes, with a market of fourteen students on each side, the price approached very close to the equilibrium price; and once it arrived there, it tended to stay there. When demand shifted (when students were given sheets of paper telling them different cost and demand conditions), the price adjusted relatively quickly to the new equilibrium price. This experiment was duplicated by a number of other economists.

This approach has several possible uses. By using the experimental method, economists can see how markets react under different institutional conditions. In a recent experiment, researchers tested a posted-price market and compared it to a double oral auction market. In a posted-price market, firms and buyers post a price for a period of time and stick to it. Researchers found that prices tended to be higher in posted-price markets than in double oral auction markets, a finding that led the U.S. Department of Transportation to ask the help of experimental economists in solving a problem concerning the pricing of railroads and barges. The railroads had asked the Department of Transportation to switch from privately negotiated freight rates to publicly posted rates. The railroads argued that public posting would protect both themselves and small barge owners from unannounced price-cutting by large barge owners. Experimenters simulated the two types of markets and found the opposite to be the case. Price posting tended to yield higher prices than private negotiation and hurt small barge operators. The railroads dropped their request.

Another test done by experimental economists was of the Coase theorem, which states that parties who are capable of harming one another but who can negotiate will bargain to an efficient outcome, regardless of which side has the legal right to inflict damage. The experimental results confirmed this prediction. However, the experiment found that when individuals were endowed with the legal right by means of a coin flip, they almost inevitably did not extract the full individual rational share of the bargaining surplus that is predicted by game theory. Instead the bargainers almost inevitably shared the surplus equally, suggesting that a fairness ethic, not pure rational individual maximization, governs distribution. This suggests that individuals do not perceive asymmetric property rights as legitimate if they are awarded randomly. When, however, property rights were awarded to the individual who won a game of skill before the experiment, the experimenters noted that two-thirds of the individuals with the property right obtained most of the joint surplus, whereas under the random assignment treatment none did.

Given the problems of mainstream economists in empirically testing their theories, it is not surprising that they generally welcome this new work, though somewhat skeptically. But most have not thought through its wide-ranging implications. To adopt such procedures would require significant changes not only in the training of economists but also in their role in society and their whole approach to economic problems. In view of the upheaval in the profession that such changes would entail, we suspect that experimental economics will gain adherents only in the face of considerable mainstream resistance.

NONMAINSTREAM ECONOMICS — SUMMARY

Heterodox economists have little in common besides an objection to orthodoxy. Various authors manifest their objections in various ways but, generally speaking, they constitute a dissent from the scope, method, and content of orthodox theory. Radicals, institutionalists, and post-Keynesians reject the orthodox view that harmony prevails in a market economy and that laissez faire is therefore the proper governmental policy. Public choice advocates and neo-Austrians, who tend to be to the political right of mainstream economics, are uneasy with the degree of governmental intervention in markets which orthodox theory finds acceptable. The dissent of nonmainstream economists, whether to the left or to the right of the mainstream, is often ethical as well as scientific.

Interesting contrasts and comparisons exist among the heterodox groups. First, even though they often differ among themselves concerning the shortcomings of mainstream economics, they nearly always concur on the necessity of extending the scope of mainstream analysis. For example, even though public choice theorists and radicals fall on opposite sides of the political spectrum, they agree that politics and economics cannot be separated. Second, even though heterodox economists are often ignored by the mainstream, they nonetheless influence it. As they do, and as their ideas are incorporated into the mainstream, their role as heterodox economists is reduced. Thus longevity is not necessarily a positive attribute of heterodox thought. Third, heterodox economists have a tendency to turn inward and separate themselves from the profession — in which case their analysis becomes a separate field of study that either totally replaces mainstream economics or continues its existence independently of the mainstream. Fourth, nearly all heterodox schools are partisan, and for a group to have a significant impact it must be non-partisan, associated with neither the left nor the right.

In the 1980s public choice seems to be close to being absorbed by the mainstream. With the development of rent-seeking analysis more liberal economists, and its use of neoclassical tools, it offers the highest potential of having its views integrated into the profession. Neo-Austrians are less likely to be absorbed. They will probably be able to continue their struggle, however, partly because significant funding is available to them that provides publishing outlets and other means by which they can influence economic thought. Radicals find themselves in a more difficult position; they receive less outside funding and thus have fewer publishing outlets, and some of their best ideas have been incorporated into "widely construed" mainstream theory. Without an outside political force radicalizing the population, they are unlikely to significantly affect mainstream economics. Institutionalists have followed the inner-directed route. They have little contact with the profession and desire little. The same is true to a great extent of the post-Keynesians, although they are a much more diverse group, some of whom do play a more active role in the mainstream profession.

Experimental economics is still a very small part of economic research, but its potential for changing the direction of mainstream economics is considerable. It offers enormous numbers of workable dissertation topics and, at a time when faith in the empirical content of present economics is at a low point, it provides a method of empirically testing economic propositions. Because of economists' perceived need for a more empirical method, the growth of the new behavioral economics may be the most important heterodox phenomenon in the late 1980s.

Some commentators have concluded that since particular versions of heterodox theory have failed to replace orthodox theory, heterodox theory has been a failure. For this reason heterodox theory is often omitted from histories of economic theory. Our view is different. An examination of heterodox thinking reveals that, although it has not replaced the accepted stream of economic thought, it often forces orthodox theory into new channels, and sometimes offers seminal ideas which become part of the accepted theoretical structure. These contributions to the direction and content of the flow of ideas cannot be ignored. They may well be the ideas twenty-first-century historians look back on as forerunners of mainstream thought.

SUGGESTED READINGS

Blaug, Mark. "A Methodological Appraisal of Radical Economics" in *Methodological Controversies in Economics: Historical Essays in Honor of T. W. Hutchison*, ed. A. W. Coats. Greenwich, CT: JAI Press, 1938.

Bowles, Samuel, and Herbert Gintis. *Schooling in Capitalist America: Educational Reform and Contradictions of Economic Life*. New York: Basic Books, 1976.

Coase, Ronald. "The Problem of Social Costs." *The Journal of Law and Economics*, 3 (October 1960).

Edwards, R. C., Michael Reich, and T. E. Weisskopf. *The Capitalist System*, 2nd ed. Englewood Cliffs, NJ: Prentice-Hall, 1978.

Eichner, Alfred S. *Toward a New Economics: Essays in Post-Keynesian and Institutionalist Theory*. Armonk, NY: M. E. Sharpe, Inc, 1985.

Galbraith, John Kenneth. *A Life in Our Times*. Boston: Houghton Mifflin Co, 1981.

Gordon, David M., Richard Edwards, and Michael Reich. *Segmented Work, Divided Workers: The Historical Transformation of Labor in the United States*. New York: Cambridge University Press, 1982.

Hicks, John R. *Value and Capital*. Oxford: Clarendon Press, 1946.

Klamer, Arjo. *Conversations with Economists*. Totowa, NJ: Rowman and Allanheld, 1984.

Lindbeck, Assar. *The Political Economy of the New Left*, foreword by Paul Samuelson. New York: Harper and Row, 1971.

Mermelstein, David, ed. *Economics: Mainstream Readings and Radical Critiques*. New York: Random House, 1970.

Myrdal, Gunnar. *The Political Element in the Development of Economic Theory*. Cambridge: Harvard University Press, 1955.

Weintraub, Sidney, ed. *Modern Economic Thought*. Oxford: Basil Blackwell, 1977.

Wolff, Richard and Stephen Resnick. *Economics: Marxian versus Neoclassical*. Baltimore, Maryland: Johns Hopkins University Press, 1987.

Index